Myra Inman

A Diary of the Civil War in East Tennessee

Myra Inman

A Diary of the Civil War in East Tennessee

William R. Snell, Editor

Mercer University Press
Macon, Georgia
2000

ISBN 0-86554-590-1
MUP/H443

© 2000 Mercer University Press
6316 Peake Road
Macon, Georgia 31210-3960
All rights reserved

First Edition.

∞The paper used in this publication meets the mini-
mum requirements of American National Standard
for Information Sciences—Permanence of Paper for
Printed Library Materials, ANSI Z39.48-1984.

Library of Congress Cataloging-in-Publication Data

CIP data are available from the Library of Congress

Table of Contents

Acknowledgments

John Allen Carter, a friend, and grandson of Myra has my unending gratitude for making this publication possible. While no longer with us, he shared information on the Inman and Carter families that expanded our knowledge on the history of Cleveland and Bradley County.

There are a number of others who have helped. Barbara Fagen, Director of the History Branch of the Cleveland Public Library, helped locate photographs, Inman family papers, and court records. I appreciate not only her talents but also her friendship.

In order to get the diary ready for publication, in 1990, Lee College students in History of the South were assigned a year of the diary to type and put into computer format so it could be edited. Their contribution was priceless. I wish to thank Sheri Carpenter, Cindy Lee, John Coppler, Kent Lumm, Jay Peoples, and Bryan Reed. Others who helped were Daphne Landers who retyped a year; Kathy Willard and Leon Shehan, who did the final typing, and footnote arrangement; and Stephanie Gibson, who prepared the final disc for the publisher.

Tom Crye designed a map of Cleveland during the1840s that locates the main streets, homes and buildings mentioned in the diary. Tim Hooker read several sections and made comments.

A grateful thanks is extended to my good friend and local history enthusiast, Robert L. George, who read the manuscript and made suggestions. More importantly, he offered encouragement and advice when needed.

Lee University provided a grant and allowed me time to complete the research and editing of the diary. I would like to thank the administration of Lee University and the Behavioral and Social Sciences Department for their support and assistance.

A great deal of appreciation is extended to my wife, Jan, who is always my best editor, advisor, and when it is all over, still my friend, my best friend; and our sons Michael and Jeffrey who gave me a new computer and taught me how to use it.

Family Members Living in Inman Home
Cast of Characters

Mother	Ann Jarnagin Inman
Aunt Eliza Adeline	Ann Inman's sister
Rhoda	Rhoda Ann Inman
Diarist	Myra Adelaide Inman
Mary E. or "Lizzie"	Mary Elizabeth Inman
Sister	Darthula Inman Carter
Mr. Carter	John Goodly Carter
Annie	Anna Elizabeth Carter
Jimmie	James Inman Carter
Johnnie	John Bowie Carter
Baby Rhoda	Rhoda Inman Carter

For everything its season, and for every activity under heaven its time:
  a time to be born and a time to die;
  a time to plant and a time to uproot;
  a time to kill and a time to heal;
  a time to pull down and a time to build up;
  a time to weep and a time to laugh;
  a time for mourning and a time for dancing;
  a time to scatter stones and a time to gather them;
  a time to embrace and a time to refrain from embracing;
  a time to seek and a time to lose;
  a time to keep and a time to throw away;
  a time to tear and a time to mend;
  a time for silence and a time for speech;
  a time to love and a time to hate;
  a time for war and a time for peace.

Ecclesiastes 3:1-8
The *New English Bible*

Myra Inman

Myra Inman

John G. Carter, Myra Inman Carter, and family. L-R: August Carter, Myra Inman Carter holding Darthula (Della), Peyton Carter on ground, John G. Carter; Mae Carter(daughter of Darthula Inman Carter, first wife of John), Serena Carter Shadden (in chair), John's sister. The house was located at Charleston. Photograph courtesy of Larry Holcomb and Cleveland Bradley Regional Museum.

Cumberland Presbyterian Church (built 1856), Cleveland, Tennessee, where Myra and her family attended.

Surgeon J. T. Woods, 99th Ohio Regiment, USA, a serious suitor, called on Myra when his unit was in Cleveland and wrote to her when conditions permitted. He gave Myra a picture made when he was 31 years old.

Lieutenant A. Simmons, USA, was in love with Myra. He called on her when possible and they corresponded while he was on duty. While she was "more pleased with him than other Yankees," she refused his proposal of marriage.

Mrs. Delany was the wife of Edwin Stanton Delany, a real estate broker who boarded with the Inman family when he came to Cleveland. Mrs. Delany, a friend of Myra's mother, was a teacher at the Cleveland Masonic Female Institute.

Jackson J. Kennedy, carpenter and cabinetmaker from North Carolina, pastored the Baptist Church during the difficult period from 1863-1867. The Kennedy family members were frequently in the Inman's home. Reverend Kennedy pastored churches until his death in 1898. He was buried in Fort Hill Cemetery.

The Cleveland Masonic Female Institute (opened 1856) was frequently mentioned by Myra. While a student there, she studied Latin, botany, history and music. She also wrote compositions and made speeches. Coming much later, in 1886, the horse-drawn streetcar lasted until 1899. The Masonic building is presently (2000) the Houston Apartments.

Myra's husband, John G. Carter at their Charleston, Tennessee farm long after the war.

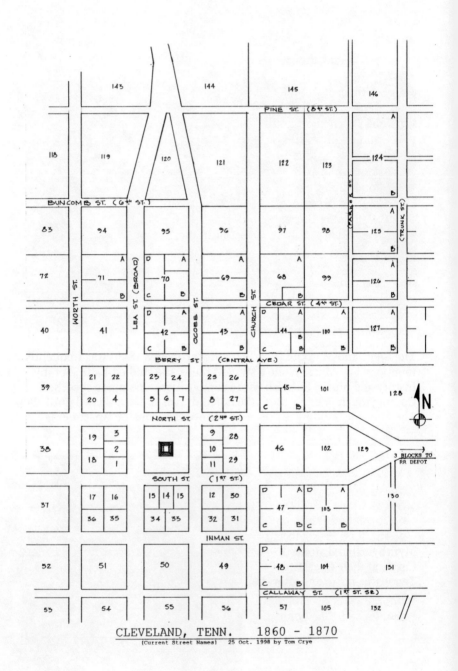

CLEVELAND, TENN. 1860 - 1870

(Current Street Names)   25 Oct. 1998 by Tom Crye

Map of Cleveland, 1860-1870
Legend

Courthouse located between North and South Streets

Lot Number

1. John D. Traynor, home
4. Grant and Russell's Store
5. Brashears' Saloon
7. Ark Building
8. Banner Building
11. Carson's Drugstore
12. C. J. Shields' Store
13. Berry House (hotel), James Berry; later: Railroad House; then, Ocoee House
14. Middlecoff and Mills' Store
15. C. H. Mills' Saddlery and Harness Shop
16. Jesse Poe's Tavern
23. Paschal Carter's Blacksmith Shop
26. Robert McNelley, Home
27. Dr. J. B. Pepper, office
29. Sam Y. Brown's Store, (tools)
31. Mrs. Ann Inman, garden spot; later: Baldwin Harle's General Store
32. John C. Gaut's Store
42 (b). Dr. Gideon B. Thompson, office
43 (b). Dr. G. A. Long, office
45 (c). Cumberland Presbyterian Church
47 (a). Livery Stable
47 (b). Cleveland Baptist Church
48 (d). Jockey Lot
69 (a). Gideon B. Thompson, home
69 (b). James Berry, home
70 (b). First Presbyterian Church
71 (b). Mrs. James W. Inman (Ann) home, after the war
102. Mrs. James W. Inman (Ann) home, during the war
120. Cleveland Masonic Female Institute (opened 1856)
143. Pleasant M. Craigmiles, home
144. Caswell Lea, home

Introduction

Petite and pretty, Myra Adeline Inman was thirteen when she began her diary in 1859. She kept the diary religiously until 24 January 1866. Born 13 March 1845, she was a member of a family of diary-keepers, a tradition established by her sister, Darthula, who was Myra's senior by eleven years. Darthula kept a diary which included the year 1851. Some entries from her diary were included in Myra's diary which gave it a sense of continuity. According to Charles F. Bryan, Jr., former director of East Tennessee Historical Society, "Viewing the Civil War through the eyes of Myra Inman proved to be one of my most interesting research experiences and her account was an invaluable source for my study of the Civil War in East Tennessee. For that matter, the Inman diary is one of the most interesting documents concerning the war years in Tennessee."[1]

The original diary, written in ink in small feminine script, filled seven ledger books each measuring 7 3/4 inches by 12 1/2 inches. Each one recounted about one year of her life. Volume I: January 1, 1859 to February 16, 1860; Volume II: February 17, 1860 to August 31, 1861; Volume III: September 1, 1861 to August 21, 1863; Volume IV: August 22, 1863 to August 24, 1863; Volume V: August 25, 1863 to January 30, 1864; Volume VI: January 31, 1864 to December 5, 1864; Volume VII: December 7, 1864 to January 24, 1866.

The original manuscripts are in the Southern Historical Collection of the University of North Carolina at Chapel Hill. In 1984 I compared the typed manuscript with the original. Permission to publish this diary was granted by Myra Inman's grandchildren: John Allen Carter, Peyton Rowell Carter, and Mrs. Earl (Marjorie Carter) Clemens. In 1997, Myra Inman's descendants Gloria Brantly and Catherine Carter Brantly Ivy, also granted permission for

---

[1]*Cleveland Daily Banner*, 18 November 1984

publication. They also graciously donated a collection of Myra Inman memorabilia to the History Branch of the Cleveland Public Library. John Allen Carter supported this project from its inception until 1984 when the diary was printed in the *Cleveland Daily Banner*. Unfortunately, he did not live to see the diary published in book form.

Brief excerpts from the diary appeared in the *Chattanooga Times* in 1938 and in the *Bradley County Journal*, a weekly, in 1939 and 1940. The diary was published in the *Cleveland Daily Banner*, in weekly installments, from 18 November 1984 to 17 April 1988. Fortunately, in addition to donating the diary for preservation, other family members made earlier contributions. In 1940 Adelia Inman Morgan, Myra's niece, transcribed the original documents. Earlier, in 1935 Myra's sister, Mrs. E. Inman Hayes, the "Mary Elizabeth" in the diary, gave Adelia Inman Morgan information which helped explain some of the entries. Adelia inserted information throughout the diary usually in parentheses. The ledgers were transcribed for the years 1859 to 1865, but did not include the entries from 1 January to 24 January 1866, which the editor transcribed.

Myra Inman's Relatives

In order to understand Myra Inman, we need to look at her genealogy. A family tradition maintains that the three Inman brothers, Shadrack, Meshack, and Abednego, left North Carolina because of their stepmother. Meshack was killed by Indians; however, he left descendants. Shadrack and Abednego settled in upper East Tennessee where both served as elders in the Presbyterian Church. Myra's line developed from Abednego Inman II, who was born 1 July 1752, and was a participant in the Revolutionary War. He married Mary Richie (Ritchy) and settled near Dandridge, Tennessee. Their oldest son, William Hardin Inman, born 28 September 1779, married Eleanor Wilson. Their fourth child was James Wilson Inman, Myra's father, born 1 March 1808, who came to Cleveland, Tennessee in 1844.

On 1 April 1833 James Inman married Anna (Ann) Jarnagin Lea the "Mother" in the diary. Ann was born 16 April 1809. The couple had eight children, five daughters and three sons. Only four of their daughters lived to maturity. Two sons and a daughter died in infancy, and one son died as a young child. All the children were born in Tennessee. Those listed in the 1850 federal census were: Darthula Inman, age sixteen, born 17 February 1834; Rhoda Ann Inman, age seven, born 30 January 1842; Myra Adelaide Inman, age five, born 13 March 1845; and Mary Elizabeth, age two, born 1 April 1848. Their son Houston was born in September 1850 after the census was taken; sadly, he died in 1857. Other family members listed in the household included Mrs. Inman's mother, Rhoda Lea, age seventy-three, and her sister, Eliza Adeline Lea, age thirty-three.

James Inman was in failing health and Darthula recorded the progressive nature of his illness. In June 1850 she stated that he "kept to his bed all day." In September, she wrote: "Father has commenced taking salt baths, a last remedy." The summary review of Darthula's diary as transcribed by Myra, did not report the death of their father, James Wilson Inman on 25 March 1851.

John Goodly Carter, who came to Cleveland before the Inmans, became an important member of their family. John Carter was born 14 April 1823, about seven miles from Danville, Pittsylvania County, Virginia. While young, his family moved to Dandridge, Jefferson County, Tennessee. The trip in a one-horse-wagon took a month and his sister walked the entire distance. In 1838 when John was fifteen years old, he migrated with Caswell Lea, Myra's uncle, by horseback, and traveled through Wetmore and Benton in Polk County, where Caswell Lea owned property. Polk County was a part of Bradley from 1836 to 1839 when it became a separate county.[2]

Caswell Lea moved into the Ocoee District when it was opened for settlement. About 1858 he moved to Bradley County, had a log cabin and farm, and later, he moved into Cleveland.[3] Myra spoke of Uncle Caswell more than any other relative. He was one of Cleveland's outstanding citizens. John Carter arrived in Cleveland on 10 November 1838 and became a clerk in Dr. P. J. G. Lea's— Myra's uncle—store at four dollars per week. The youngsters—the city of Cleveland and John G.—grew up together.

---

[2] *Cleveland Journal and Banner*, 15 April 1912.

[3] Caswell Lea's homestead is on the present day (2000) site of the home of Robert Card III (deceased), at the corner of Church and 15th Street.

The village of Cleveland had a population of 250 people at that time. The Presbyterians were the first denomination to build a church edifice in town. At that early stage of development, the five dry good stores included: Dr. P. J. G. Lea's store, White, Staley & Smith; Boggle and Greene; Lowry and Wasson; and John D. Traynor. Pleasant (P.J.G.), younger than Caswell, was the first merchant, among the first city commissioners, and was the person for whom Lea Street was named. While Cleveland did not have a drugstore at the time, it had its share of saloons. Medicine was often sold by the shopkeepers.4

Nine years after coming to Cleveland John Carter was called to Charleston, S. C. to become a traveling salesman. His territory included East Tennessee, North Georgia, and North Alabama. After fifteen years of superior sales he was made a member of the firm.

On 13 March 1853, Darthula Inman married John Goodly Carter, in a Presbyterian ceremony conducted by the Reverend Edward Caldwell. The wedding took place in a building located on the original site of the Railroad Hotel, owned by Darthula's parents. Upon occasion Darthula traveled with him, sometimes spending as much as five months of the year in Charleston, South Carolina. Politically, Carter was a Whig and supported Henry Clay in the 1844 election.5

After twenty years of marriage, Darthula died in 1874. John G. Carter chose Myra, her younger sister, for his wife and they were married two years later on 25 October 1876. Myra preceded him in death on 7 December 1914, and was survived by John Carter until his death on 14 February 1915. They were buried in the family plot in the Fort Hill Cemetery.

Myra's maternal line, the Leas, were descendants of James Lea of Cheshire, England. In about 1740 he migrated to the United States and settled in Caswell County, North Carolina. They were undoubtably pleased with what they found there since Caswell was a common name among the males of the family. Anna Jarnagin Lea was the daughter of Major and Rhoda Jarnagin Lea, Myra's grandparents. The home of Anna (Ann) Inman was a perfect

---

4*Cleveland Journal and Banner*, ca. 1900.
5*Cleveland Journal and Banner*, ca. 1910.

example of Southern hospitaltiy. They received family, friends, even Union soldiers for tea, meals, overnight, or for longer periods of time. As Myra recorded these events, her family, friends, and strangers came to life on the pages of the diary. Much time was spent visiting the sick and sitting up with the dead and dying. (An abbreviated genealogy of the Lea-Jarnagin-Inman-Carter families is included in the appendix so the reader can refer to it for clarity.)

Inman Family Slaves

The Inmans owned a few slaves, received through the mother's family estate. As the results of some legal action, Ned and his wife Phoebe were inherited by Ann J. Inman. Ned was born about 1800 in South Carolina where he was bought. The Inmans treated their slaves well and considered them like members of their family. Much time was spent sewing for the slaves and caring for them when they were sick. This is evident as the thread of slavery is woven through the fabric of Myra's diary. The family considered Ned and Phoebe as the only slaves they could trust completely. Upon their deaths they were buried in the Inman family plot. Money that the couple saved paid for an iron fence to protect their graves. The iron fence is no longer standing and the original tombstones are not decipher-able. New gravestones were added by Inman family members to remember this couple who had been faithful in life and were remembered in death. Other slaves mentioned include: Frank, Susan, Emeline, Sues, yellow George, Stepheny, and Black George, and will be identified when they first appear in the diary. (See appendix for more information on Ned and Phoebe.)

Bradley County and the Village of Cleveland

Bradley County was the "frontier" where land-hungry Americans met the proud Cherokee people. Before 1835 the lands of the county were included within the boundaries of the Cherokee Nation which spread into North Carolina, Georgia, and Alabama. In anticipation of the removal, whites began to move rapidly into the area. A sizeable white population lived in the area by 1836 awaiting the organization of a county government. In the winter of 1838-1839 the Cherokee Indians were collected into camps and forts and sent on the Trail of Tears. These humble but proud Native Americans were transported across the Mississippi River to their ultimate destination in Oklahoma. The noble Cherokee left their farms, homes, and undisturbed whitened bones of their ancestors. But they carried much with them—Euro-American names, the Christian religion, an agricultural economy, and a lingering culture of the Old South. Many Cherokees were prosperous. In the first quarter of the nineteenth century the tribe fashioned a democratic government patterned after that of the United States. Their success was the envy of land-lovers and gold-seekers near Dahlonega, Georgia.

The legislative act of 10 February 1836 created Bradley County, which was named for Edward Bradley of Shelby County. The county seat was to be designated as Cleveland for Benjamin Cleveland, a participant in the Battle of King's Mountain. The site of Cleveland was chosen because of a number of free flowing springs at the southern terminus of Spring Street. Bradley County was carved from the former Ocoee District of the Cherokee Nation in the limits of Tennessee. The white pioneers that arrived in the soon-to-be-created county came mostly from the nearby counties of McMinn, Monroe, Rhea, and some more distant counties: Jefferson, Greene, and Roane. The 1850 Federal census revealed that others came from the eastern states of North Carolina (40%), Virginia (23%), South Carolina (15%) and Georgia (7%).

The 1837 report listed 646 adult male taxpayers in the new county, which until 1839 included all of Polk County. Population figures jumped twenty-seven percent in 1838, but increased only by 23 persons in 1839 to 846. The first federal census for the county listed 7,385 persons, an impressive gain over four years. These newcomers, from different backgrounds, knew they would have to make adjustments and get along with their neighbors. New traditions emerged as they cooperated in house raisings, corn shuckings, and worshiping together.

The village of Cleveland was settled like a New England town. The state of Tennessee made two half sections of land available, which were surveyed, divided into streets and numbered lots, and sold to the public. In August 1836, John C. Kennedy received $5.00 for surveying the town using Lea Street as the baseline. Nine commissioners collected the money, paid the state, and volunteers constructed a log courthouse on the southwest corner of the courtyard. Cleveland was formally designated as the county seat on 20 January 1838.

Dr. P. J. R. Lea, register of the land office in Cleveland, was assisted by entry taker Luke Lea. While the young community was taking shape with a few log cabins, much of the surrounding land consisted of woods and swamps, inhabited with a variety of wild life. As the streets began to emerge, townspeople learned that some were named for early settlers. The court square was the site of government for the community.[6] The log courthouse was replaced in 1840 when Thomas Crutchfield, from Chattanooga, built a brick courthouse and jail. R. M. Edwards reported that Cleveland was "well-enough off," and had "grown into about as pretty shape as any town in the state."[7]

Meanwhile, the legislature allowed Cleveland to incorporate with a mayor-alderman form of government. The first election was scheduled for 4 April 1842, with subsequent elections announced for the first Saturday of January. An array of leaders served the fledgling community. Merchants opened shops, and artisans offered their services. Among these were blacksmiths, tailors, cobblers, tanners, saddlers, and harness makers. Professional townspeople included bankers, ministers, doctors and lawyers.[8]

Several taverns emerged including that of Jesse Poe and his wife. It was built on the lot where the Fillauer House is presently located (2000). When court was scheduled, clients, lawyers, judges and citizens came. Located within earshot of the courthouse, Mrs. Poe shouted the readiness of lunch. Judge Edward Scott received the news and addressed court with: "That is a summons we must all obey; adjourn court Mr. Sheriff".[9]

---

[6] *Cleveland Weekly Herald*, 11 January 1883.

[7] William R. Snell, *Cleveland, the Beautiful* (Cleveland: Cleveland National Bank, 1986) 6.

[8] Ibid., 11.

[9] Ibid., 12.

A gazetteer described Cleveland as the county seat of Bradley County located near the Georgia line, and serviced by the East Tennessee and Georgia Railroad. "It is an active business place, and contains the county building, four churches, one Masonic Female Institute, one Masonic Lodge, one weekly newspaper...one bank... [and] about twenty stores of various kinds, one steam flouring and one saw mill, with diversified trades and professions."[10]

The first quarter century was a time of growth and accomplishment. The newcomers grew up together and were seemingly well-grounded in business, religion, and government. Strong bonds developed between churches and the county government functioned smoothly. By 1850 the two-party system worked well. The railroad came in 1851 connecting them with the outside world of commerce and trade. The Ocoee Bank was chartered in 1854 and capitalized at over $100,000; and of newspapers there were two. The *Cleveland Dispatch*, a Whig newspaper, appeared two weeks before the *Cleveland Banner*, a Democratic sheet, published by Robert McNelley (pronounced Mac Anelley). Editors of the *Dispatch* were complimentary of the Democratic sheet, and wished them well. The Whig party disintegrated in 1857 and *Cleveland Dispatch* met the same fate.

Education

Education was important to the community in 1837. The Tennessee Legislature granted a charter for Oak Grove Academy, a boy's school, to seven trustees in 1837. They paid $1 for a portion of city lot no. 88 in 1840. Tradition holds that Henry Walker—the first teacher—worked in temporary facilities. A brick building was completed by Henry Crutchfield in 1839. James Tedford was the next teacher. In 1842 he was followed by Henry W. von Aldehoff.

Born in Prussia, Aldehoff migrated to the United States in the 1830s and settled in Kentucky. He traveled westward in 1836, but

---

[10]John L. Mitchell, *Tennessee State Gazetteer and Business Directory 1860-1861*, 42.

returned and settled in Athens, Tennessee, where he taught at Forest Hill Academy. He moved to Cleveland after being named principal of Oak Grove Academy. Henry W. von Aldehoff became a naturalized American citizen 7 May 1846. After a few years at Oak Grove he relocated in Chattanooga where he took charge of Rittenhouse Academy.

Citizens of Cleveland pushed for a girl's school to round out the educational system. The project fell short of completion and the promoters asked the Masons for financial help, which they provided. Ultimately, the school was named the Cleveland Masonic Female Institute and opened its doors in 1856. Since this was the school Myra attended, a brief history is included.

Cleveland Masonic Female Institute

The citizens of Cleveland had a school to educate their sons, but were concerned about their daughters. They wanted a school to help educate their daughters, but were unable to complete the building. They called upon the Masons who helped complete the building for an opening of school in September 1856. The supporters made arrangements to hire Henry W. von Aldehoff, who earlier served as professor of Oak Grove Academy for boys. Fifty local citizens agreed to fund his services for five years, however, he served until 1859 when A. E. Blunt, Jr. came to lead. Born to missionary parents at the Brainerd Mission, he was reared in a devout and well-educated home. Graduating from Dartmouth College in 1859, he came immediately to town to assume leadership. Blunt served until 1861 when he resigned to serve in the Union army.

In the fall of 1861 the school opened under the leadership of the Reverend Mister J. N. Bradshaw, former pastor of the First Presbyterian Church, Chattanooga. Additional furnishings were installed in the school. A Mrs. Jarnagin, formerly of Athens, opened a boarding house to care for students needing that service. When Bradshaw assumed leadership the school was at a low point. In an advertisement in *The Rebel*, the principal urged fathers to educate their daughters. The school had many positive features. Cleveland was a healthful location. The principal satisfied the trustees, he was aided by capable assistants, and money was plentiful because of price increases, while tuition remained at low levels. The decision was to be made by the public. Robert McNelley, editor of the *Cleveland Banner*, was generous in his praise and spoke from experience. He wrote, "We have been sending two little girls to it, and we were really astonished at their rapid progress."[11] Bradshaw continued as principal fifteen months and enrollment reached 125 students. Bradshaw, however, was forced to close the school when Federal troops occupied the city in 1864. In 1871 Bradshaw was elected president of Southern Masonic Female College at Covington, Georgia.

Professor Henry von Aldehoff returned to Cleveland as the professor of the girls' school. He was headmaster until September 1859, when A. E. Blunt took charge until the school was closed because of the war. After serving as an officer in the military, Blunt returned in 1865 to resume leadership of the institute. Myra Inman frequently referred to von Aldehoff and Blunt.

What can be learned from Myra Inman about education, religion, society, and other events? Myra was intelligent and mature for her years, and while a student at the Institute she wrote and presented compositions. At her young age Myra was encouraged and challenged by the awarding of "praise points" rather than "black marks," which was a means of grading. Examinations were scheduled over several days in order to feature the individual accomplishments in composition, declamation, and making speeches. An examining board was sometimes responsible for evaluating the students' work and abilities. Educators from neighboring areas were present at school examinations, trying to discover educational techniques that contributed to the development of outstanding students.

---

[11]*Chattanooga The Rebel*, 9 August 1862, reprint; *Athens Post*, 18 October 1861; *Chattanooga Gazette and Advertiser*, 4 January 1862; 13 February 1862; *Cleveland Banner*, 25 April 1862.

Church Attendance

Worship was vital to the members of the developing community as well as the Inmans. By 1837, Methodist, Presbyterian, and Cumberland Presbyterians had established congregations. Some were organized in the log courthouse. The church people cooperated by allowing others temporary use of their building. The construction of the Presbyterian Church was a community project of about thirty volunteers. Myra frequently mentioned worship services, Sunday School, prayer meetings, and revivals. She reported her family's attendance at church and Sunday School. She often named the ministers. Since most churches did not have services every Sunday, it was customary for Christians to visit other congregations' services. Myra was pianist and organist at Cleveland Baptist Church and was a member of the choir. At first she was skeptical of the Baptist denomination, but she and her mother joined the church on Inman Street. During the summer revival season, she attended the camp meetings that seemed to be the preference of most Methodists. Baptists tended to favor the protracted meeting whose beginning date and location was revealed. The services continued as long as results warranted the recognition. The conclusion of the meeting was noted as the "breaking." Upon occasion Myra attended the annual meeting of the Ocoee Baptist Association.

Social Life and Customs

Myra included everyday social life as well as more formal occasions in here diary. Social activity in the small village in 1859 centered around several balls and parties in the three hotels: Ocoee House, Johnston's Hotel, and Cleveland Hotel. The Ocoee House, built on the south side of the court square, contained fifty rooms and was of brick construction. Johnston's Hotel and Cleveland Hotel were small but adequate. The attendance of the young ladies was usually requested by personally delivered notes and sometimes by tickets. Myra was a member of a circle that encouraged reading and discussing books. She attended concerts, balls, participated in tableaux, enjoyed masquerades, and took piano lessons. Tea, that sometimes included fruit and cake, was served in the afternoon.

This tradition seemed more popular in 1865 than earlier. Many references were made to weaving material, needlework, and making clothes.

One quaint custom of that period was giving New Year's Day gifts. On 1 January Myra lamented that she had received no presents. On 13 January Uncle William Lea presented her with gifts of "one lead pencil" and "two apples." Other social activities included the visit of a fortuneteller, an animal show, and a circus. While the summer months were traditional times for religious meetings, the annual fairs were well attended. She often mentioned walks to springs and staying at watering places during the hot weather.

Myra occasionally referred to a scrapbook. Her daily journal became increasingly important to her. She noted the discipline of recording her activities and thoughts. While on most days she shared the details of her daily life, sometimes, she would mention some incident or event but did not make full disclosure. Ultimately, her journal became her trustworthy confidant, her "friend," in whom she faithfully wrote and came to trust more and more. A haunting fear she experienced was the loss of her diary by theft or fire.

Myra's use of descriptive language and the quality of writing declined after the war started. The days of casual shopping and doing needlework were filled with making clothes for soldiers and caring for them. As Federal troops camped in and moved through Cleveland, they left destruction in their path. Many friends were either injured or killed and destruction was everywhere. Small wonder then that Myra would lament being in her hometown. In July she wrote, "Cleveland has no charms for me." In August, she and others explored places more to their liking. Some mentioned New York, South America, or "anywhere to get away from here." Myra traveled only as far as Ooltewah, in Hamilton County.

In later years Myra and John Carter lived out their days in Chattanooga. They became the parents of three children, two sons and a daughter: August Jarnagin Carter, born 11 August 1878; Peyton Lea Carter, born January 8, 1884; and Darthula Inman Carter, born 1 May 1887, when Myra was forty-two and Mr. Carter was sixty-four.

Early Taverns and Inman Inn

George W. Featherstonehaugh was perhaps the individual who gave the first description of early Cleveland including its hotels, or taverns as they were called. This information describes what hotels were like in the years before the Inmans purchased their establishment. On 28 July 1837, he wrote:

> I proceeded on, and my horse being in a tolerable willing humor, we at length reached an American settlement called Cleveland, newly made on the road from Calhoun on the Hiwassee, in Tennessee, to Gainesville in Georgia. Being now on a stage road, and no longer being embargoed, I inquired for the best tavern, and was directed to a clean house kept by a person named [Major James] Berry....Twelve months ago there was not a building of any sort here; but such is the activity of these people that already they have got a street and a square, and a tavern, and stores upon the plan of the older settlements.[12]

Because Major Berry, a veteran of the War of 1812, was a strong supporter of the Whig party, his hotel was called the Whig Corner. John Glass another hotel-keeper was a Democrat whose hotel appealed to adherents of that party's beliefs. Colonel Richard M. Edwards explained that politics were so intense in those days that the traveling public would inquire of the political persuasion of the hotel keepers in the next town."[13]

In March 1846, James and Ann bought Major Berry's hotel and renamed it "The Railroad Inn," sometimes called the Railroad Eating House or the Railroad Hotel. The Inman family moved into the "Inn" on 18 March 1846.[14]

---

[12]George W. Featherstonehaugh, *A Canoe Voyage up the Minnay Sotor*, 2 vols. (Saint Paul: Minnesota Historical Society, 1970) 220-221.

[13] Eugenia Rodgers, *Cleveland Daily Banner*, 4 November 1984.

[14]Ibid.

While Myra Inman did not start her journal when the family lived in the Inman hotel, it probably had a great influence on her. From an early age she met many people, encountering many different ideas as well. These factors broadened her horizons and helped her be more outgoing, observant and expressive. Since her family's livelihood, the hotel, contributed to who she became, its story is valuable to her history.

At the time the inn was bought it was located on the northeast corner of South and Ocoee Streets. Inman Street was probably named for Mr. Inman. Just when their move to Cleveland was completed and the hotel purchased, a double tragedy struck; her husband died in 1851 and Houston died in 1857. Ann J. Inman, determined and resourceful, continued to operate the hotel, which prospered because of its good reputation.

Sam P. Ivins, editor and proprietor of the *Athens Post*, spoke well of the Railroad Hotel in Cleveland. He declared the inn to be "one of the best houses in the whole country." He continued his praise, "The table is always amply supplied with the best eatables, and everything connected with the house is conducted in admirable order. We commend everyone traveling in that direction to call at Mrs. Inman's hotel."[15]

Before the railroad reached Cleveland the mail and some passengers were carried by hacks or stagecoaches between communities. The Inmans and their slaves, Ned and Phoebe, had a plan to attract these tourists. In the middle of the hotel dinning room stood a large table lined with candles dipped in turpentine. When the hack from the South reached the gap at Fort Hill Cemetery, a watchful slave speedily lit the candles that gave a quick surge of light. The food was ready and placed on the table family style. The passengers ate as the hack's horses were exchanged for the next leg of the journey.

In 1852 Rosine Parmienter of New York traveled by train to Cleveland and stayed in the Railroad Hotel. She wrote: "Cleveland is about 300 yards from the depot. The courthouse stands in the middle of the village and the houses and the streets are built all

---

[15]*Athens Post*, 7 May 1852.

around the square." She described Cleveland as the "county town of Bradley County."[16]

Not only had Ann Jarnagin Inman lost a husband, a son, and was left with a family to support while operating a hotel, she learned some shocking news. When forty-three year-old James died, he had not prepared a will, or was intestate. His youthful widow served as oratrix on behalf of her minor children. This matter, supervised by the Chancery Court, shows how deed transversals and sales were carried out in this era. Acting in the best interest of her children, she sold the hotel to Lorenzo DeLano for $3,000. The property consisted of three lots, a small one, no. 13, upon which the hotel stood, a garden plot, no. 31, and an acre stable lot, no. 47. The wooden buildings were decaying and liable to fire.[17]

In February 1853, Mrs. Inman advertised the Railroad Hotel for sale. She preferred an individual buyer. The buildings were "all in good order and the stand is an excellent one." The choice property would be sold at "reasonable terms." The advertisement was dated 25 February 1853.[18]

On 3 October 1854, Lorenzo DeLano sold the property to John Dunwoody and William R. Davis, who signed a note for $1,000 and interest due. Later that day, Dunwoody and Davis executed two bills for $1,000 due on 3 October 1854, and another note due 22 May 1856, in lieu of notes Mrs. Inman held on DeLano. In 1855 Mr. Davis and his wife conveyed their interest in the lots to Dunwoody, who, in turn, sold the property to John N. Cowan and William H. Tibbs. The newest owners signed two notes for the balance payable on 22 March 1855, and the other a year later in 1856.[19] The Railroad Hotel was dismantled and the material used in the building of Wiggins' Wagon Lot on the corner of Church and Inman Streets.[20]

---

[16] Ben H. McClary, and LeRoy P. Graf "'Vineland' in Tennessee, 1852: 'The Journal of Rosine Parmienter,'" *East Tennessee Historical Society Publications*, 31 (1959): 102-110.

[17] Chancery Court, Bradley County, Tennessee, #479.

[18] *Athens Post*, 6 May 1853.

[19] Chancery Court, Bradley County, Tennessee, #479.

[20] *The Cleveland Journal*, 22 December 1900; *Cleveland Daily Banner*, Eugenia Rodgers, 4 November 1984. The R. J. Farroe Callaway house was

Homes of the Inman Family

After the sale of the hotel and property, Mrs. Inman moved the family to a house on North Street. Situated on an acre lot no. 102, the house was a brown wooden frame structure, which served as home until she purchased the Callaway house on Lea (now Broad) Street in October 1865 after the war. The Callaway house was located on a half-acre plot designated as lot no. 71. Mrs. Inman paid $3,300 and they called it home for a number of years. Mrs. Inman later sold the brown house to A. C. and Henry Joseph in December 1869.[21] This was Myra's home when she began her diary in 1859. Located three blocks from the courthouse and a like distance from the train depot, it was still standing in 1935. After John G. Carter married Darthula, they lived with Mrs. Ann J. Inman until 1867, when they moved to a farm on the Hiwassee River at Charleston, Tennessee.

The move from the hotel was completed over a period of time, as family members moved furniture, planted shrubs, flowers, and grapes. Some speculated that Mrs. Inman might not be able to support her family with boarders, but she was successful. After the war, a number of Northern and Southern soldiers as well as other boarders stayed with the Inmans. Seemingly, they were well-received as was their money.[22]

A Divided Nation and County

At mid-century Bradley County was well-populated, economically sound, prosperous, and reasonably tolerant. Change was inevitable. However, the national problem became evident in the 1860 presidential election. The Whig party was shattered and the

---

located on the site of the original Church of Christ building which is still standing. It is now the Cornerstone Church.

[21] *The Cleveland Journal*, 22 December 1900; *Cleveland Daily Banner*, Eugenia Rodgers, 4 November 1984.

[22] Eugenia Rodgers, *Cleveland Daily Banner*, 4 November 1984.

Democratic party was divided. There were four candidates and something akin to two elections, one in the South among Democrats and another in the North between the Republicans as a sectional party and the Northern Democrats. The election of Abraham Lincoln as president ultimately resulted in the secession of South Carolina in 1860, which was quickly followed by the secession of six additional deep Southern states. They soon fashioned the Confederate States of America in Montgomery, Alabama.

The issue of secession became a lively subject in Cleveland and Bradley County since there were supporters for both sides. Bradley Countians faced hard choices. These actions polarized the population in East Tennessee; some favored the Union, while others supported the Southern Confederacy. As many as 50,000 East Tennesseans left their mountainous homeland to serve in Union units. A similar number joined Confederate units.[23] From reading Myra's diary, it is obvious that Bradley County's citizens were divided in their loyalty to the Union.

After Georgia seceded, Tennessee was pressured to act quickly. How would a decision be made? In a February election, an overwhelming number in East Tennessee voted against calling a convention. Abraham Lincoln was inaugurated on 4 March 1861. One month later, Confederate guns fired on Fort Sumter. President Lincoln issued a call for 75,000 troops to put down the rebellion. Governor Isham Harris of Tennessee vowed not to "furnish a single man." In a special session, the legislature decided to secede, and preparations were made to mobilize.

On 25 April 1861, the loyal Unionists erected a pole on the courtyard in Cleveland and raise a flag. In June, a soldier in a Mississippi regiment spotted the flag and began shooting. The flag was hastily lowered and hidden by Unionists. When they needed inspiration, "Old Glory" was deployed in secret.[24]

---

[23] A compilation of the names of men who served from Bradley County is included in J. S. Hurlburt's, *History of the Rebellion in Bradley County, East Tennessee* (Indianapolis: Downey and Brouse, 1866) Appendix 16-24; for further details see *Tennessee in the Civil War*, 2 vols. (Nashville: Civil War Centennial Commission, 1965) 418.

[24] Roy G. Lillard, ed. *The History of Bradley County* (Cleveland: Bradley County Historical Society, 1976) 323.

On 8 June 1861, Bradley Countians voted 1,382 to remain in the Union while 507 voted for separation. But on 6 May the Tennessee Legislature had already adopted an ordinance for secession and the state had ratified it. The people of Bradley County had to choose sides.

During the war, John G. Carter's business and home were destroyed, forcing him to join the Confederate army, seeing action in a single battle at Chickasaw Bayou. After becoming ill he returned to Bradley County. Later he hired a Mr. McGuire for $2,000 as a substitute for him. The use of substitutes was a common practice for both sides. After federal troops controlled much of Tennessee, John rejoined the military.

Bridge Burners and Federal Occupation

Myra mentioned that some men from Bradley County were involved in a plan to stop federal troops from entering East Tennessee by rail. William Carter of Carter County, Tennessee, contacted Union authorities about a proposed plan to burn railroad bridges from Bridgeport, Alabama, to Bristol, Tennessee-Virginia. Approved by President Abraham Lincoln, William H. Seward (Secretary of State), General George B. McClellan, and General George Thomas were to move federal troops into East Tennessee in October 1861. Confederates, under General Felix Zollicoffer, advanced toward Kentucky causing General [William T.] Sherman to remain in Kentucky. The bridge burners started five fires, among them, one at Charleston, Tennessee, between Bradley and McMinn counties. The episode did not seriously damage the rail system, but it did intensify the suspicion, distrust, and treatment of local Unionists. A reign of terror followed which disarmed Union supporters. Of the six men accused of bridge burning, five were hanged and one was acquitted. All but one from Bradley County died before their names were made public in 1898.[25]

---

[25]Melba Lee Murray, *Bradley Divided: Bradley County, Tennessee During the Civil War* (Collegedale: College Press, 1992) 54-58.

Southern forces maintained control of Cleveland and Bradley County with the help of Confederate troops. Among these was Joseph Espey who was stationed in Cleveland in April 1863. His company of fifty men lived in five tents and a house. Espey wrote: "This is a fair looking country here and the town of Cleveland is a very handsome one and is nearly as large as Rome."[26] Federal troops arrived in force in September 1863 and occupied Cleveland. A few days later, Robert McNelley was arrested and his *Cleveland Banner*, one of the casualties of the war, was suspended for two years. On 17 September 1863 Myra reported McNelley's arrest.[27]

Most of the military action in and around Cleveland was brief skirmishes rather than large protracted battles. However, the military importance of the town was appreciated by President Abraham Lincoln, when he sent a telegram to General Henry W. Halleck on 30 June 1862 stating, "To take and hold the railroad at or east of Cleveland, Tennessee, I think is as fully important as the taking and holding of Richmond."[28]

Yankee soldiers described Cleveland and the surrounding areas in letters to their families. F. M. Griswold, a private in Company C, 93rd Ohio Volunteer Infantry passed through Harrison, "a little village," before reaching Georgetown. On 30 November 1864, "we passed through a forlorn little hamlet, called 'Georgetown,' twelve miles from Cleveland. As we passed this town we were surprised to see the old 'Stars and Stripes' spread to the breeze. The boys gave them 'three times three' hearty cheers. As we passed out of town, we were saluted by singing. One poor old woman had a little babe in [her arms] and was shedding tears of joy at seeing the old flag and its defenders. We, it seems, were the first Yankee Infantry that had passed through this part of Tennessee since the war began and these loyal people were overjoyed at seeing us. It was a sight that did my heart good for there had been so few females in the South so far that had not been Rebels of the deepest dye."[29] It is obvious when

---

[26] Letter of Joseph Espey to parents, Cleveland, Tennessee, 22 April 1863, Wilson Library, University of North Carolina, Chapel Hill.

[27] Snell, *Cleveland the Beautiful*, 51.

[28]Lillard, 318.

[29]Charles S. Harris, *Regimental History of 93rd Ohio Volunteer Infantry*, manuscript, 100.

reading Myra's diary that she would be described as being of the "deepest dye," because of her loyalty to the Confederacy.

Captain Edward Dale, U. S. Army, in Chattanooga, Tennessee, was ordered to proceed toward Knoxville to purchase food for the Union forces. On 9 November 1864, he wrote his wife: "I went to Cleveland, a place about thirty miles from here, and I think it was, at one time, until visited by the ravages of war, a very pretty place"[30].

Conclusion

Amid a changing family situation and the horrors of the war, the diary entries stopped when Myra was twenty years old. Changes were evidently the law of life, many of which had been recorded during the seven years Myra kept her journal. Myra's diary was kept with caution as was revealed when she wrote on Tuesday, 21 June 1864: "I wish I could tell you, my old friend Journal, the source of my troubles, but for fear some truant eye might peer between these leaves, I will desist." She was aware that her private thoughts and comments might someday be read by others but could never have dreamed of the historical significance the diary would have.

We, the readers, who cherish history, owe this young Clevelander a debt of gratitude. Her dedication to her writing allowed us to get to know her family, her friends, and her Cleveland as we experience the daily events with her. More importantly, the reader is able to follow Myra's maturing process. She was a teenager when she began the diary with thoughts of algebra and gentleman callers. Before the diary closed she was coping with hardships and the death of friends and family members. The Civil War affected the community, county, and all she held dear. War takes a toll, and the division in Bradley County caused immeasurable pain for Myra Inman.

---

[30]Letter of Edward Dale to wife, 9 November 1864, transcript of letter in the personal collection of Charles S. Harris, Ooltewah, Tennessee.

Chapter 1

1859

January 1859

Saturday 1. New Year's day. Cousin John Lea was here this morning. Mother, Sister, Jimmie and Annie spent the day at Dr. Brown's. I went to Dr. Brown's this evening. Sister and I went to the hotel to call on Mrs. Hoyl, but called on Miss Mary only and went around shopping. A beautiful day but very muddy. I did not get any New Year's presents. Mr. Carter came home tonight from Manchester, Tenn. Bettie Jarrett and Rhoda went up to Mrs. Carter's this evening and went shopping.

Sunday 2. A very pleasant day, it [is] not so muddy as yesterday. I did not go to Sunday School this morning nor to church. Mr. Carter, Sister, and Annie went to church today. I did not go. I went to the Bible class this evening at 3 o'clock. I went to church tonight. Cousin John Lea came here this evening and went to church with us. Mr. Slocard preached an eloquent sermon. Mr. Carter and Annie went up to the Carter's this evening. Uncle William Lea was also here. Eliza Keebler came from home this evening.

Monday 3. I went to school this morning as usual. I stopped by Mr. McCroskey's this evening and got *Major Jones' Courtship.* Jimmie has been sick today. Mother bought a horse today. A very pleasant day, a little muddy. Elvira Lea and I went to Mr. McCroskey's and to Mr. [G. W.] Cook's store this evening; we saw an eagle. Mary Elizabeth and Elvira Lea also went to Mr. McCroskey's store.

Tuesday 4. A very pleasant day, but muddy. I went to school as usual. Mr. William Davis took dinner here today. Mr. Carter went to Georgia this evening. Mrs. Onie Campbell and Mrs. Serena "Aunt Renie" Shadden were here this evening. Elvira Lea and Mary Elizabeth went to Mr. Collins' shop after her ring, also went to Mr. McCroskey's and Mr. Hardwick's store. Jimmie is a little better today.

Wednesday 5. It is a very pleasant day, but a little muddy. Jimmie is a little better today. Mr. Aldehoff taught school[1] in the forepart of the day, but not in the last. Miss Mary Lea, Mr. Aldehoff and Sidney Bell ran off today. Elvira Lea and Mary Elizabeth went up to Mr. Collins' shop after her ring also went up to the academy after their books. Eliza Keebler and I went to Mr. Aldehoff's, Mr. Middlecoff's, Mr. Carter's and Mr. Hoyl's this evening. We also went to the post office; got a letter for Mr. Carter. Bettie went up to Mr. Gourdon's after her sash, it was not done. Mother went down to Mr. McNutt's[2] and Mr. Hassle's. Bettie, Rhoda and I went to prayer meeting tonight. Mr. Slocard and Mr. Caldwell carried it on.

Thursday 6. A little colder today, it rained a little in the afternoon. Jimmie is a little better today. I went to school. Mr. Keebler has been here today. Mr. Carter came home from Georgia tonight, brought some large hickory nuts.

Friday 7. It is very cold this evening, the wind is very high. Jimmie is better today. Mr. Carter has gone to Georgia on the two o'clock train, and will be back tonight on the 7 o'clock train. I went to school, had to stay in at dinner for prompting Francis Tucker, Mary Davis and Mary Mee. Tonight is very cold.

Saturday 8. Today is as cold as last night. I have been reading *Woman's Friendship* nearly all day. Uncle William Lea took supper here tonight. Eliza went to Mr. Russell's today.

Sunday 9. Not as cold as yesterday. I went to Sunday School this morning. I wrote my composition this morning. Rhoda and I went to Baptist Church this evening. Mr. McNutt preached on the doctrine

---

[1] Cleveland Masonic Female Institute.
[2] William McNutt, Pastor of Cleveland Baptist Church.

of baptism by immersion. Sister and Annie went to Mr. Grant's this evening. Uncle William and Cousin John Lea was here tonight. Uncle William ate supper. Mr. Caldwell preached on baptism by sprinkling this morning. Eliza Keebler came home from Mr. Russell's this morning.

Monday 10. Tolerable cold. Mr. Carter went to Pikeville, Bledsoe County, Tennessee this morning. I went to school. Mother went to Mrs. Cook's this evening.

Tuesday 11. Colder than yesterday. Jimmie is one year old today. I went to school. Mother went out to Uncle Caswell Lea's this evening. I came home before school was out to tend to Jimmie while Mother and Sister went around shopping. I got through synonyms today. Bettie told me a great secret this evening.

Wednesday 12. A very pleasant day, like a spring day. Mother, Sister, Annie and Jimmie spent the evening at Mr. William Craigmiles'. I went to Mr. Craigmiles' this evening to take a bonnet. Mrs. Alexander was here this evening but Mother and Sister were gone. Rhoda and Mary Davis went out to Mr. Robert Swan's to see Virginia Harris, she was at Col. Mills'. Cousin John Lea was at the gate this evening; he did not come in. Mother, Eliza and I went to prayer meeting tonight. Mr. Slocard carried it on, he got very happy. Mary Elizabeth had to stay in at dinner. I went to school as usual. Elvira Lea got 6 black marks for prompting Mary Elizabeth.

Thursday 13. It rained this evening. I went to school; nothing occurred interesting. Mother and Sister intended to spend the evening at Mr. Carter's but it rained. This day 6 years ago Mr. Carter and Sister Darthula were married. Uncle William Lea was here tonight; he brought us our New Year's presents, they were one lead pencil, 2 apples. I was too late for school this morning, that is Bettie, Rhoda, Mary Elizabeth. Mattie Weir was 13 years old today.

Friday 14. This day 6 years ago Mr. and Mrs. Gamble and John left our house. It has been a very pleasant day, but muddy. Mother, Sister, Annie and Jimmie spent the evening at Mrs. Onie Campbell's. Elvira had to stay in for prompting Mary Elizabeth at school. Eliza Keebler went home this morning. Bettie did not go to school today; she had the headache. Mrs. Shadden stayed all night here tonight. Uncle William Lea was here this evening. Mary Elizabeth and Elvira went to Mr. Aldehoff's this evening after my shoe and then went over to Academy to get my other shoe, but could not get in. They also went up to the stores. I had 21 praise marks and 1 black mark.

Saturday 15. I went to Mr. Aldehoff's today and then went over to the Academy. Sue Aldehoff came home with me and stayed until after dinner. Rhoda, Bettie and Cousin John Lea went over to Limestone³ this morning. Sister and Annie went over to Cousin Mary Harle's today; she is sick. Cousin Mary Lea was here this evening. Uncle William was here tonight. This day 4 years ago Aunt Lucinda Callaway Lea, Uncle Pleasant's wife, died. It looked like it would rain all day but it didn't.

Sunday 16. A very pleasant day. Mr. Carter came home this evening. I went to Sunday School, Elvira also. Sister, Elvira and I went to the Bible class at three o'clock. Mrs. Ervin's child was entered this evening. Dick Grant and Charlie Grant were 32 years old today.

Monday 17. A very pleasant day. I went to school today. I had to get my composition lesson over. Mrs. William Grant and Bell were over here this evening. Cousin John Lea took tea here tonight. Mr. Carter went to Benton⁴ this morning. Bettie and I were at Mr. Hardwick's this evening. Elvira Lea and Mary Elizabeth went to Mr. Collins' to get Bettie's pin, also to Mr. Cook's, Guthman's and Hardwick's. Uncle Caswell Lea took dinner here. Tonight I wrote a letter to Alfred Lea.

Tuesday 18. A very pleasant day. I went to school. Mrs. Kate Rogers was here this evening. Mother and Sister went up town shopping. Mary Harle and I spoke today. Mr. Carter came home from Benton sick.

Wednesday 19. A very pleasant day. I went to school. Emma Lea is 12 years old today. Mr. Carter went to Concord tonight. Elvira went to the drugstore after a sponge for her; also some envelopes for Bettie; did not get any. Also went to Mr. Hardwick's. Elvira, Rhoda, Mother and I went to prayer meeting. Mr. Slocard carried it on. Mr. Paschal Carter [father of John G. Carter] was there.

---

3 Washington County, Tennessee.
4 Polk County, Tennessee.

Thursday 20. I went to school. It looked like it would rain; sprinkled a little this evening, not so hard though. I did not come home for dinner. Sister went around shopping got Annie a worsted dress. Mother had the tombstones hauled upon the graveyard; she went to see them.

Friday 21. It rained nearly all day. Went to school; I had 19 praise marks and 5 black marks. Eliza Keebler went home this evening. We had a candy stew this evening. There is going to be a ball at Mr. Johnston's Hotel. Rhoda Ann, Eliza and Bettie were ticketed[5]. I was not ticketed. The omnibus [bus] stopped to see if Bettie and I were going to the ball.

Saturday 22. A very cold day. Emma Lea and Ella DeLano were here this evening, also George Cook. Bettie and I went to Uncle Caswell Lea's this evening.

Sunday 23. A very cold day; colder than any this winter. I did not go to Sunday School, church, or Bible class. Mr. Pascal Carter was here this evening. Eliza Keebler came from home this evening. There was a woman at the door to see if we would let her stay all night, on her way to Kentucky. Did not stay.

Monday 24. Was not as cold as yesterday. I went to school. Mrs. McNutt was here this evening, also Virginia Harris and Callie Swan. Bettie and I went to Mr. Cook's, Rogers', Simmon's after envelopes and fancy paper. Got it at Mr. Cook's.

Tuesday 25. Not as cold as yesterday. Went to school. Mrs. Rogers spent the day here. Frances Tucker stayed all night. Bettie went to Mr. Cook's [and] got some envelopes. Sallie Shields, Frances Tucker, Rhoda and I went to Mr. Simmon's store after white kid shoes; did not get any. Cynthia, Mary Hardwick and Lucretia Tibbs were here tonight.

Wednesday 26. A very pleasant day. I went to school. Mother, Sister, Annie, Jimmie and Mr. Carter spent the day at Uncle Caswell's. Mrs. Pickens was here this morning; did not see Mother. They came by Mr. Carter's this evening. Little Mary Lea was at the schoolhouse, also here. Elvira Lea went to Mr. McNutt's with her.

---

[5] Ticketed in this case means received a written invitation from a gentleman to attend a particular social function (*American Heritage Dictionary of the English Language* [Boston: Houghton-Mifflin, 1970], henceforth *AHD*).

Eliza went to her uncle's this evening. Rhoda and Bettie went to the stores. Mrs. Guthman was here this evening; did not see Sister and Mother. Capt. Guthman was here this evening after Bettie to go home. Grandmother Lea, if she had lived, would be 78 years old today. Mr. Jessie Gaut's youngest child died tonight. If Grandmother Inman was alive she would be 81 today.

Thursday 27. A rainy day. I went to school this morning. Mr. Callaway took dinner here today. Bettie went to school, said her dictionary lesson and went home before school was out. Eliza went home from school with the toothache. Capt. Jarrett ate dinner here today. Mrs. Cook's examination commenced today ends tomorrow forenoon. Bettie is packing up to go home. Mr. Carter went down to Dalton[6] on the two o'clock train. Mr. Callaway was here this evening. Capt. Jarrett is going to stay here all night. A very rainy and dark night. Eliza, Bettie, Rhoda and I stayed home this evening from school. Bettie and Rhoda went around shopping, also up to Mrs. Cook's.

Friday 28. I went to school this morning, we said our dictionary lesson and went home. A very pleasant, but muddy day. The last day of school, the concert comes off tonight. Bettie started home this morning. I have been sewing this evening. Rhoda Ann, Mary Elizabeth and Eliza went out to Mr. Keebler's this evening. Elvira intended to go to the concert tonight but has not got any person to go with her. There was a man here that we thought was Mr. Grant, his name is Kelly. Sister went up to Mrs. Cook's, Grant's and Cousin Mary Harle's. Henry L. Jones came after Sister to go to the concert. We had a serenade[7] tonight; 11 praise and 2 black marks.

Saturday 29. A very pleasant but muddy day. I did not go up to the Academy after tickets; Emma Lea was here this morning and brought them. Elvira and I went out to Uncle Caswell's and stayed all morning. Cousin Joseph Lea sent Annie 2 pigeons. I made them a little house. Mr. Carter made another one, mine was too small. Rhoda and Mary Elizabeth came from Mr. Keebler's this evening. Mr. Carter came home this evening. Sister and Mother went shopping and down to Mr. Jessie Gaut's.

---

[6] Whitfield County, Georgia.
[7] A serenade is a musical performance given by sweetheart (*AHD*).

Sunday 30. A very pleasant day. Rhoda Ann's birthday, 16 today. I did not go to Sunday School, Elvira Lea and Mary Elizabeth went. Rhoda went to church, I did not go. Mr. Carter and Annie went over to the depot. There was a Bible class as usual, I did not go. Mother, Mr. Carter, Sister, Rhoda, Mary Elizabeth, Elvira Lea, Annie and I went up to the graveyard. Could not go the Bible class. Lizzie Campbell and Cleopatra Watkins were here this evening. Uncle William Lea was here tonight. We heard today that Jack Nat was killed on the [railroad] cars.

Monday 31. A very pleasant day. Elvira went down to her Uncle Tom Callaway's with her Aunt Rebecca. Uncle Frank, Carrie and Annie Lea here this morning. Mother, Sister and Annie went over to Mrs. Hardwick's, Mrs. Stuarts', Cousin Mary Harle's and Mrs. McNutt's. Mr. Carter went down to Georgia on the 2 o'clock train. Margaret Shadden is here. Mary Elizabeth went up to the stores after a spool of thread this morning. Stephney[8] is five years old today. Our cow has got a calf. Rhoda Ann, Elvira and I fixed up the little room, been sewing off and on all day. Mrs. Lea stopped here waiting for Mr. Lea to come. Cousin John Lea is here tonight.

February 1859

Tuesday 1. Not quite as pleasant as yesterday. Annie Tibbs is to be married tonight to Mr. Bryant from Virginia. Lizzie Campbell, Margaret Mee, Mr. Patent and Mr. Gideons, bridesmaids and groomsmen. We're baking cake today. I have been sewing nearly all day on my apron. Mother and Sister went to Mrs. Pickens', Mrs. Judge Gaut's, Mrs. Mill's, Mrs. Guthman's, and Mrs. Shield's, she was not at home. They went to Mrs. DeLano's, also went to Mr. Simmons' and Mr. Campbell's; got some domestic[9] for Mary Elizabeth and I a dress. Mary Elizabeth went to Mr. Montgomery's shop after some raisins, she got some. Rhoda Anne has gone out to

---

[8] A slave.

[9] Domestic is a cotton cloth as distinguished from linen (*AHD*).

Uncle Caswell Lea's to stay all night. There was a gentleman here this morning, wanted to know if Mr. Carter was at home, he did not come in, asked Uncle Ned [slave].

Wednesday 2. A rainy and muddy day, rained all night. I have been sewing all day on my apron. Rhoda has not come from Uncle Caswell's yet. Mr. Posey Roberts and Mr. Hambright were here this evening to pay Mr. Carter some money. Thundered and lightninged last night and this morning some. Dwight Tibbs brought Rhoda's ring to her sent by Mary Mee. Rhoda came back this evening. Mr. Wm. Davis was here this night; came from Limestone this evening late.

Thursday 3. A tolerable cold day. I have been sewing all day. Sister is packing up some of her clothes to go to Charleston, S.C. It had snowed a little when we got up. Mrs. Cook spent the evening here. Mr. Cook took supper here, [and] came back after Mrs. Cook at bedtime. Mr. Carter came home on the 7 o'clock train from Georgia. He brought home a paper printed in Atlanta, Ga. telling us a very distressing tale about a man committing suicide. Elvira and Carrie were here this evening, going on down home.

Friday 4. A tolerable pleasant day. Uncle William Lea took dinner here today [and] fixed Mother's door. Mrs. Shadden and Mrs. Onie Campbell were here this evening. Mrs. Shadden stayed all night. I have been sewing all day. Mother bought some land today from Mr. Joseph Middlecoff. Gave Mr. Henry 30 feet to build a stable on. Mrs. William Craigmiles has a boy.

Saturday 5. As pleasant a day as yesterday. I sewed all the first part of the day and some this evening. Mrs. Grant and Bell were here this evening.

Sunday 6. It snowed this morning. We did not go to Sunday School this morning, it was too wet. I read all day, did not go anywhere.

Monday 7. A very pleasant day, but muddy. Mr. Carter, Sister, Annie, Jimmie, and Emeline [slave] started to Charleston, S.C. Uncle Caswell, Mother, Mary Elizabeth and I went over to the depot; rode in the omnibus. Uncle Caswell, Aunt Elizabeth, Bettie Bell, Mrs. E. Cook, Mrs. K. Rogers, Mrs. E. Carter, Mrs. S. Gaut and Alice Pickens were all here today. Mother and Aunt Elizabeth went over to Cousin Mary Harle's this evening. They all took dinner but Mrs.

Cook, Mrs. Rogers, and Mrs. Gaut. We went over to the depot and saw the telegraph[10] and the men communicating with one another[11]. I went to Mrs. Shields' this evening. Cousin John Lea stayed all night.

Tuesday 8. A rainy day. I have been sewing all day on Sister's basket [pattern] quilt.

Wednesday 9. A rainy day, snowed a little this evening. Pieced on Sister's quilt in the forenoon, a little in the afternoon. Went for some of Elvira's things this evening. I have had a crick[12] in my neck all day; do not feel very well. Cousin John Lea is here to stay all night.

Thursday 10. A cold day in the morning, tolerable pleasant in the evening. Cleaned up the house in the forenoon. Sewed on George's [slave] shirt in the afternoon. He was here tonight after a pair of shoes. Joseph Lea was here after John this morning, did not come in. Mr. Wm. I. Campbell was here this morning, also this evening for Mother to pay.

Friday 11. A very pleasant day. Sewed on George's shirt all day. Mother went down to Mrs. William McNutt's this morning after her book, *Spurgeon's Gems*. Aunt Adeline is sick today. Mary Elizabeth went to Mr. William McNutt's this evening. Cousin John stayed all night. Amanda McCroskey was here this evening. I finished *Women's Friendships* tonight; a most excellent book.

Saturday 12. A very pleasant but muddy day. Mr. Cowan was here this evening and paid mother $250.[13] Mr. Henry was here this evening and concluded to take all of that ground.[14] Rhoda wrote Sister this evening. Eliza Shields was here this evening. We went up and called on Mary Ann Smith. I have been sewing on my dress this morning.

Sunday 13. A beautiful day. We went to Sunday School today. Mr. Slocard carried it on. Mother, Mary Elizabeth, Rhoda and I went to church this morning. Mr. McNutt preached on baptism by

---

[10]The telegraph was invented by Samuel F. B. Morse in 1844.

[11] By Morse code.

[12]A crick is a painful muscle spasm(*AHD*).

[13] To hire her slave George.

[14]See 4 February 1859 entry for details.

immersion. Martha Reynolds came home with me from Sunday School and went to church.

Monday 14. A cloudy day, Valentine's Day. Sent Bettie one. Been sewing all day. Mrs. Henry and Naomi here this evening. Uncle William Lea here this evening. Mary Elizabeth and Sues [slave] went up to Mr. Carter's after kittens.

Tuesday 15. A rainy and cloudy day. I went to Mr. McNutt's this morning. Mr. Keebler stopped at the fence and paid Mother five dollars for Eliza's board, also got Eliza's slate[15]. Been sewing today some and reading the rest of *Nelly Bracken*. Mother and I fixed to go up in town to the stores and Mrs. Craigmiles' but it commenced raining. Rhoda received a Valentine this evening.

Wednesday 16. A rainy day, a hard storm the night before. Been mending [repairing] my clothes all day. Cousin John [Lea] stayed here tonight. Finished reading *Nelly Bracken*. Rhoda received a letter from Frank Lea and Anna Gaut; also a Valentine; answered Frank's letter.

Thursday 17. A muddy and cloudy day. Mother and I went up to Mr. A. A. Campbell's store. Got Aunt Eliza (Adeline) 2 dresses. Mother went to Mr. Aldehoff's also to Mr. William Craigmiles' and Mr. George Cook's. Sister is 25 years old today.

Friday 18. A windy and muddy day. Mother mashed her finger today, cannot sew. Mary Elizabeth went up to the store after some domestic for Aunt Eliza Adeline. Been ripping and tucking my dress today. Rhoda and I got ticketed [invited, received an invitation to] to the ball to be held at the Cleveland Hotel the fourth of March.

Saturday 19. A very pleasant but windy and muddy day. Been piecing quilts; finished one and commenced another. Sallie and Cass Shields were here tonight, also Mrs. Serena Shadden and Margaret[16] Shadden. They stayed all night. I stayed all night with Martha Reynolds tonight.

Sunday 20. Like yesterday. Went to Sunday School. Rhoda and Mary Elizabeth did not go. We did not go to church. Got a letter from Sister; all well. We went to the Bible class at three o'clock. Cousin John Lea stayed all night.

---

[15]A slate is a writing tablet of slate material which could be written on and erased (*AHD*).

[16] Or "Mag."

Monday 21. Got a letter from Alfred Lea, answered it and wrote one to Sister. Uncle William Lea was here this evening, took dinner, brought a book with flowers. Rhoda went up to Mr. Aldehoff's this evening. Tucked my dress today. Lavena Seavey and Callie Grant were here this evening. Mother and Mrs. Cook called on Mrs. Garrison this evening. Mrs. Cook came after her.

Tuesday 22. A beautiful day. Cousin Maria is 25 today if she had lived. (She was Cousin Mary Harle's daughter.) I went up to Mr. Cook's, Mr. McCroskey's and Campbell's store after lining and slate, also Mr. Guthman's after Rhoda's dress; did not get any. Rhoda went up to Mr. Hardwick's, Kenner's, Conn's and Jack Tibbs's store; got a dress at Tibbs's. Been making me a hoop skirt[17]. Rhoda and I fixed to go [to] the choir but were disappointed. Went up to Mr. Campbell's for a hoop skirt for Aunt Eliza Adeline; did not get any.

Wednesday 23. A pleasant day. Mr. Walker was here this evening after roses. We all went to prayer meeting; stopped in at Mrs. Cook's. Cousin John came home with us from the meeting, did not stay all night. Aunt Elizabeth was here this evening. Mother and I cleaned up the yard today.

Thursday 24. A cloudy day, sprinkled a little today. Thinned out some of the rose bushes. Went down to Mrs. Shields' after 4. Uncle Caswell Lea took dinner here today, we all went up to the graveyard except Aunt Eliza and Rhoda, to put up Houston's and Caswell's tombstones.[18] Mary Sevier and Emma Aldehoff were here while we were gone up to the graveyard. Rhoda and I went up to Mr. Aldehoff's this evening after some magazines.

Friday 25. A rainy day. Mr. Coffman's oldest daughter was buried this evening. Needleworked[19]on my band[20] all day. Nothing of importance occurred today. Cousin John Lea was here tonight, stayed all night. Received a letter from Sister tonight; all were well.

---

[17]A hoop skirt is a large full skirt worn over lightweight circular support (*AHD*).

[18] Houston, the brother, died at seven years old, and Caswell died in infancy.

[19]Needlework is hand stitches like embroidery.

[20]A band is a narrow strip of fabric used to trim or decorate sleeves or waist bands (*AHD*).

Saturday 26. A beautiful day. Went to Mr. McCroskey's this evening. Mother went over to Mrs. Grant's and Cousin Mary Harle's this evening. Mrs. Cook was here this evening. Uncle William took tea here tonight. I went up to Mr. A.A. Campbell's store after Aunt Eliza Adeline some hose, got 3 pair. Needleworked on my band all day.

Sunday 27. A beautiful day. We went to Sabbath School. Did not go to church. Went to the Bible class at 2 o'clock this evening, as usual Mr. Caldwell carried it on.

Monday 28. A pleasant day. We started to school today, had 64 scholars. Did not teach in the afternoon. Rhoda came home before school was out with the toothache; commenced taking music lessons. Mother went up to Mr. Parker's after our tickets also out to Uncle Caswell's. Miss Fry was here after rose slips, also Mary Davis came for Rhoda to go to Mrs. Pickens to ice some cake for the supper; did not go; had the toothache. Needleworked all evening on my band. Rhoda and I went to Dr. H. E. Dodson's (dentist), he was not there. Mrs. Dodson found some creosol[21] in it. Mother went to Mrs. Ryan's and Henry Davis'. Mrs. Mill's had a boy. Mother and Mary Elizabeth went to Mrs. Black's for some medicine.

March 1859

Tuesday 1. A pleasant day, went to school the night of the supper. Lillie Davis stayed all night here tonight. Sue Kenner's 16th birthday. Wrote a letter to Sister tonight. Mr. Callaway was here this evening. I went to Mr. Simmon's, Conn's, Hardwick's, Cook's and Craigmiles' store after writing paper and books. Went to Mr. Davis' to get Lillie to stay all night. Father would have been 51 if he had lived.

Wednesday 2. A cloudy day, rained a little tonight. Went to school as usual. Rhoda Ann went to Dr. Henry E. Dodson's this evening and got Mrs. Dodson to put something in her tooth. Mother

---

[21] Creosol is a colorless to yellow aromatic liquid (*AHD*).

went to Aunt Elizabeth Lea's, Caldwell's, Mr. Black's, and Mr. Gains'. Finished my letter to Sister.[22]

Thursday 3. Rained this morning, sun shone this evening, very windy. Cousin Milton Jarnagin and his wife took supper here. Went to school. Rhoda wrote to Anna Gaut, Bettie Jarrett and Adelia Thompson, did not go to school this morning, afraid of taking the toothache.

Friday 4. A windy day. No school in the evening. Sue Kenner and Ada Donohoo were here this evening, Mother and Aunt Elizabeth went over to Mrs. Ross'. Cousin Emily Jarnagin was here; didn't come in. Mother was gone. Mary Davis was here after shrubbery.

Saturday 5. A beautiful day. Miss Lizzie Phillips and Sue Gatewood were here this morning. Went up to Mrs. Cook's this evening. Rhoda and Mother went over to the graveyard and set out some grass on Houston's grave. Mr. Robinson was here after shrubbery also Mrs. Dodson. Rhoda went up to Mrs. Shield's. Uncle Caswell Lea took dinner here.

Sunday 6. A windy and cloudy day. We went to Sunday School, also to church, but Rhoda. Mr. Slocard preached. We all went to the Methodist Church tonight. Mr. McNutt preached.

Monday 7. A windy day. Went to school as usual. Mother went to Dr. Brown's, Mrs. E. Cook's and Mr. Carter's this evening. Lilly Davis was here this evening after a keg of moss. Elvira Lea was here this evening.

Tuesday 8. A beautiful day. Eliza and Mr. Keebler took dinner here. There was a fortuneteller here today; did not tell any of our fortunes. Mrs. ____ was here after shrubbery. Sallie Reeder and Naomi Henry were here this evening. Went to school.

Wednesday 9. Another beautiful day. Mother went to see Mrs. Cook and Mrs. Mitchell Edwards. Rhoda and Mother went over to

---

[22]Henry E. Dodson, born in 1828, was a graduate of Baltimore College of Dental Surgery. He arrived in October 1856 and began his practice in Cleveland as possibly the town's second resident dentist. He was an officer in the newly formed Odd Fellows lodge. In 1857, his office was at the corner of Ocoee and Meadow Street. He was listed as a dental surgeon in the 1860 federal census. In 1866 Robert McNelley, editor of the *Cleveland Banner* endorsed him as having "the character of being a most skillful workman." In July 1880 Dr. Dodson relocated in an upstairs room in the Banner building.

see a sick lady at Mrs. Davidson's, also at Mrs. Campbell's. Went to prayer meeting tonight, Mother and I. Eliza Shields, Sallie Reeder and Naomi Henry were here. Went to school.

Thursday 10. Another beautiful day. Mother went to Mr. Cook's, Col. Mills', Mr. B. Grant's and Cousin Mary Harle's. Went to school. Elvira Lea was here this evening. Rhoda Ann received a letter from Sister this morning. All were well, also wrote one and sent it by Mr. John Rogers. Miss Candy Bell started to school.

Friday 11. A very windy day. I went out to Uncle Caswell's this evening was caught in a storm, stayed all night. Rhoda Ann went out to Mr. Joseph Swan's; got back before the storm. Cousin John stayed all night. Rhoda received a letter from Anna Gaut.

Saturday 12. A beautiful but muddy day. Bettie Jarrett is 17 years old today. Eliza Shields and Ann Stuart were here this evening, also Mrs. Thompson and Walker. Rhoda and Mother went to Mrs. Thompson's, Traynor's, Mrs. Carter's and the stores, got Susan[23] a dress and an apron. Rhoda received a letter from Adelia Thompson, answered it and wrote one to Anna Gaut. George[24] got a hat tonight, cost one dollar. Mother went to Mrs. James Craigmiles'.

Sunday 13. A cloudy day. We did not go to Sunday School. I am fourteen today. We all went up to Mrs. Cook's and went from there to see Lizzie Harrison baptized, went from there to the Cumberland Church. Mr. McNutt preached; also went tonight. Uncle William stayed all night here. Rhoda and Mary Elizabeth went out to Uncle Caswell's this evening. Gov. Aaron V. Brown died on the 8th; was taken down on the cars this evening at 2 o'clock.

Monday 14. A rainy and windy day. Went to school as usual. Mrs. Cook was here this evening. Did not come home for dinner; Mother sent it to us.

Tuesday 15. A pleasant day. Went to school. Mother went to Mrs. Walker's and got a great many flower seed. Rhoda and I went over to Mrs. Hardwick's and stayed a while after supper. Uncle William Lea was here tonight; did not stay all night. Naomi Henry is 14 today.

Wednesday 16. A beautiful day. Mother went to Uncle Caswell's, Mr. J. Middlecoff's, Mr. Carter's, Mr. Joseph Swan's, Mr. Garrison's

---

[23] A slave.
[24] A slave.

and Mr. Leonard Ross'. Aunt Elizabeth and Mrs. Caldwell went with her. Went to school today. Mrs. Grant and Bell were here, Mother was not here.

Thursday 17. A very rainy day. I went to school. Nothing of importance occurred today. Review night.

Friday 18. Rained, snowed, and hailed today. Went to school; had 31 praise marks and 4 black marks. Mr. Frank Baker and a gentleman were up to the schoolhouse. Took a song [piano music] today. Cousin John Lea stayed all night here tonight. Received a letter from Cousin Alfred Lea.

Saturday 19. Pieced on my quilt all day. Rhoda commenced one. We got Jimmie's daguerreotype[25]from Charleston, S.C. Rhoda received a letter from Frank Lea. This evening Mag Shadden was here. Very pleasant day.

Sunday 20. A beautiful day. We went to Sunday School, also to the Bible class, did not go to church today. Rhoda wrote to Frank Lea.

Monday 21. A windy and cloudy day. Went to school; Mother went to Mrs. Mitchell Edwards', Mr. Bill Grant's, Cousin Mary Harle's, Mrs. Carter's, Mrs. Traynor's. Mrs. Shadden was here this morning. Mary Hardwick, Mary Tibbs, and Lucretia Tibbs were here a little while tonight. Florence Johnston and Frances Tucker stayed all night here.

Tuesday 22. Tolerable hard storm this evening. Mother and I wrote Sister this evening. Mary Elizabeth stopped in at Mr. P. Craigmiles'. Rhoda and I in at Mrs. Davis' until the storm was over. Went to school.

Wednesday 23. A pleasant day. We went to school. Bettie Bell Lea stayed here. Mother went up to the graveyard, and up to Mr. Cook's and Davis'. Cousin Jane Ann Lea died at 1 o'clock last night. (She and Cousin Martha were Uncle Caswell's daughters by a former marriage.) Wrote to Alfred Lea tonight.

Thursday 24. It rained very hard about noon. Went to school this morning from there to the graveyard to see Cousin Jane Ann buried. Rhoda and I did not go to school this evening, had the headache.

---

[25]Daguerreotyping was an early photographic process (*AHD*).

Went to Mr. Davis' this evening. Sister Myra would have been twenty-four today.[26]

Friday 25. Went to school; had 29 praise marks. Mother went out to Uncle Caswell's this morning. This day eight years ago Father died. A beautiful day. Mr. and Mrs. Cook sat until bedtime with us.

Saturday 26. A beautiful day. Pieced on my quilt all day. Sallie Shields, Sou Hunt, Lavenia Seavey and Callie Grant were here last night. Mother went to the Presbyterian Church this morning. Cousin John Lea was here tonight to see if any person wanted to go to church; did not go.

Sunday 27. A rainy day. We did not go to Sunday School or church too rainy and muddy. I read nearly all day. Elvira Lea was here also Cousin John Lea; went to church with Rhoda tonight.

Monday 28. A cloudy and very windy day. Went to school. Uncle Caswell Lea took supper here tonight. Emma Lea was whipped at school this morning. Took a new piece [of piano music] this morning.

Tuesday 29. A pleasant day. Mrs. Cook, Mrs. Traynor, Kate Rogers, Margaret Shadden and Harriet Chestnutt were all here. Mary Elizabeth went after our bonnets got them at Mr. Miller's.

Wednesday 30. A pleasant day. Went to school. Mother and Mrs. Cook went to Mr. McNutt's, and Mr. [James A.] Hassle's. Mother also went to Mrs. Cook's and to church. We all went to church tonight; stopped by for Mrs. Cook.

Thursday 31. A pleasant day. Went to school. Frances Tucker stayed all night here, went up to Mrs. Cook's and stayed awhile. Rhoda and Frances went around shopping this evening.

April 1859

Friday 1. A pleasant day. We went to church tonight. Mr. and Mrs. Hassell were here this evening. Mary Elizabeth is 11 years old

---

[26]A daughter named Myra was born and died in infancy.

today. I went up to Mr. Hardwick's store and got a pair of shoes at dinner. Had 42 praise marks.

Saturday 2. A rainy day. Got my lessons and pieced on my quilt. Wrote a composition on "Alfred the Great". I received an April Fools' letter. Cousin Martha Lea stayed all night here.

Sunday 3. A pleasant but muddy day. We all went to Sunday School, but there was not any. Mother and Mary Elizabeth went to church at the Cumberland.[27]

Monday 4. A pleasant day. Went to school. Cousin Martha went home today. Mother went with her and spent the day.

Tuesday 5. A pleasant day. Went to school. Stayed all night with Frances Tucker.

Wednesday 6. A tolerable cold day, heavy frost last night. Went to school. Mother went to Mrs. Cook's this evening. Rhoda received a letter from Sister today.

Thursday 7. A pleasant day. Went to school. Mother went to Mrs. Grant's this evening.

Friday 8. It rained this evening a little. I went to school; had 57 praise marks. Mother spent the day at Mr. Carter's. Mrs. Gallagher was here this evening.

Saturday 9. A pleasant day. Rhoda Ann stayed all night at Mr. Tucker's; came back this morning. Mother went to church today. Rhoda, Cynthia Hardwick and Mother went out to Uncle Caswell's this evening. Cynthia came by after them. Martha Reynolds came down here and stayed awhile this evening. We all went to church tonight. Mr. McNutt preached.

Sunday 10. We all went to Sunday School, also to church. Mr. McNutt preached. George [slave] took down sick at Mr. Cowan's this morning. Went to church tonight; could not get any seat, came back home. A pleasant day.

Monday 11. We went to school. It rained today a little in the forenoon. Mother went to prayer meeting this morning at 10 o'clock, Rhoda and I went up to Mrs. Cook's after supper and stayed an hour. Got rank 39; Rhoda, 7; Mary Elizabeth, 38.[28]

---

[27] Presbyterian Church.
[28] Ranking of students ability at the academy.

Tuesday 12. A tolerable hard rain this evening. Went to school; nothing of importance occurred today. Rhoda wrote to Sister.

Wednesday 13. A pleasant day. Went to school. Mrs. Pickens and Mrs. Cook were here today.

Thursday 14. A pleasant day. Mrs. McNutt and Lou Gatewood spent the day here today. Aunt Elizabeth was here today. Rhoda did not go to school this evening. Mr. Carter was here this evening.

Friday 15. A pleasant day. Mother went up to Mr. Carter's this morning. Rhoda stayed all night with Lou Gatewood. Sallie Shields, Cleo Watkins and I went out to hunt wild flowers this evening. Had 51 praise marks. Went to school.

Saturday 16. A pleasant day. Uncle Caswell took supper here tonight. Rhoda Ann and I went to the Methodist Church with him, Rev. Slocard preached. Cousin John brought his blanket to him; did not come in. I went to Martha Reynolds' this evening. This day 26 years ago Mother was married.

Sunday 17. A tolerable cold and windy day. We went to Sunday School; did not go to church. Rhoda, Mary Elizabeth and I went to the Methodist Church tonight. Reading all day.

Monday 18. A tolerable cold day. Went to school. Nothing of importance happened today.

Tuesday 19. A pleasant day. Went to school. Rhoda got a letter from Sister today. Rhoda, Mary Elizabeth and I went to church tonight. Aunt Hannah House died today.

Wednesday 20. I went to school. A pleasant day. Mrs. Cook was here today; she and mother went down to Mr. McNutt's this evening. Rhoda and I went to church. Mr. Caldwell preached.

Thursday 21. A pleasant day. I went to school. Uncle Caswell took supper here tonight. Mother went out to [his] house today; she also went to Mrs. Carter's and Mrs. Berry's. We stopped in at Mr. A.A. Campbell's store to hear from Sister. Lizzie Campbell and Bill Woods were married tonight. Review tonight, did not go to church.

Friday 22. A rainy day, very cold tonight. Had 35 praise marks. Nothing of importance occurred today. Mrs. Bradford and Lucinda Lane took dinner here. Rhoda Ann and I went to church tonight. Rev. Bates preached.

Saturday 23. A very cold day, wind blowing very hard and cold. Nothing of interest occurred today. I pieced on my quilt and got my lessons.

Sunday 24. A pleasant day. We went to Sunday School. Harris Keebler was here this morning. Uncle William Lea and Joseph were here tonight, went to church with Rhoda. Meeting ended tonight. I have had a sick headache all this evening; went to sleep one hour. Aunt Adeline had the neuralgia[29].

Monday 25. Another pleasant day. Mother went over to Cousin Mary Harle's this morning. Mrs. Shadden spent the evening with mother. Mr. and Mrs. Cook stayed until bed time with us tonight.

Tuesday 26. It has been raining off and on all day. Went to school.

Wednesday 27. A pleasant day, rained a little this morning. Mother and Rhoda went up to Mrs. Cook's tonight. Cousin John Lea is here tonight. Rhoda got a letter from Bettie Jarrett. Went to school.

Thursday 28. Another pleasant day. Mother went up to Mr. Carter's today. Review tonight. Took a walk with Mary Hardwick this evening.

Friday 29. A rainy day. Went to school; had 32 praise marks. Wrote to Alfred Lea tonight. Annie is four years old today.

Saturday 30. A rainy day. Pieced on my quilt. Elvira Lea was here this evening.

May 1859

Sunday 1. A pleasant day. We went to church and Sunday School. Rhoda and I went to church at night. Mr. Davis and Cousin John took dinner here. Joseph Lea was here this evening.

Monday 2. A pleasant day. Rhoda has been sick all day. Mr. Cowan's black woman [slave], Darthula, died last night at 12 o'clock. Mr. Keebler, Mrs. Lizzie Harris, Cousin Martha, Nannie Browder

---

[29]Neuralgia is a sharp pain that runs along the path of the nerve (*AHD*).

and Lillie Davis were here. Mother went to Cousin Mary's, Dr. Long's, Mrs. Cook's, Mr. Carter's, Col. Lea's, and Mrs. Garrison's. Took a new piece, "Commencement March."

Tuesday 3. A pleasant day. Went to school. Mother went up to Mr. Carter's. [She also visited] Aunt Elizabeth, Uncle Caswell, Sissy, Mat Martin, Mary Davis, Rosa Bell, Polly Witt and Mrs. Grant. Rhoda did not go. Robert Sloan was here today.

Wednesday 4. Another pleasant day. Mrs. Col. Lea was here today. Mother has been up to Mrs. Onie Campbell's, Judge Gaut's, Mrs. Bell Hardwick's, Dr. Brown's. Rhoda received a letter from Sister this evening. Rhoda and I went up to see Harriet Chestnutt this evening.

Thursday 5. Another pleasant day. Mrs. Cook, Margaret Shadden, Lavena Seavey, Callie Grant were here this evening. I came home from school sick with the headache this evening. Looked for Sister this evening. Review night.

Friday 6. A pleasant day. There is an animal show today. We went to the show. Sister, Annie, and others came from Charleston, S.C. this evening. Taught school first half of today.

Saturday 7. Nannie stayed all night here. Mrs. Cook, Cousin Mary, Mrs. Harris, and Mag Shadden were here. Went to the depot with Eliza Keebler. A pleasant day.

Sunday 8. A pleasant day. Mr. Paschal Carter was here this morning. Did not go to Sunday School or church. Mr. Carter, Sister, Annie, Jimmie, and Mary Elizabeth all went up to old Mr. Carter's this morning.

Monday 9. A rainy day. Mrs. Campbell and Lizzie were here this morning. Went to school.

Tuesday 10. A pleasant day. Mrs. Campbell and Mrs. Shadden were here. Uncle Caswell and Aunt Elizabeth Lea took supper here. I went up to Mr. Campbell's and got Aunt Adeline a hoop skirt and shoes. Went to school.

Wednesday 11. A pleasant day. Mrs. Jessie Gaut, Mag Shadden, Mrs. Bates, Mrs. Thompson and Mrs. Jonas Hoyl were here today. Mother, Sister, Mary Elizabeth and Annie all went over to Cousin Mary Harle's this evening. Mrs. Grant and Bell were here tonight.

Thursday 12. A pleasant day. Went to school. Cousin Martha stayed all night here tonight. Uncle William Lea took supper. Mr.

Carter came home from Blair's Ferry today, went yesterday. Uncle Caswell Lea was here this evening. Our old mare has a colt.

Friday 13. A pleasant day. I had to stay in at dinner. Had 54 praise marks. Mr. Carter went up the road, came back on the 7 o'clock train. Mary Hardwick was here this evening. Our colt died tonight.

Saturday 14. Pleasant day. Went down to see Elvira Lea. Uncle William Lea took supper and dinner here.

Sunday 15. It rained this evening. Mother, Mary Elizabeth and I went to the Baptist meeting. Annie, Mary Elizabeth and I went to Sunday School.

Monday 16. A rainy day. Mrs. Cook and Kate Rogers were here today. Mother, Sister and Annie went up to Mrs. Cook's tonight. Went to school.

Tuesday 17. A cloudy day. Went to school. Mother and Sister went up to Mr. Carter's this evening, also Mrs. Onie Campbell's.

Wednesday 18. A rainy day. Mother, Sister, and Rhoda went up to see Harriet Chestnutt this evening.

Thursday 19. A rainy day. Mother went up to see Harriet Chestnutt. Took a new piece today, "The Gipsy Girl."

Friday 20. A pleasant day. Had 47 praise marks and 1 black mark. Stayed all night with Lillie Davis tonight.

Saturday 21. Another pleasant day. Mr. William Davis was here. Mother and Sister went up to Mr. Carter's today. Rhoda stayed all night at Mrs. Cook's. Martha Reynolds and Mrs. Cook were here today. Mother set up at Mr. Carter's tonight, came home at 2 o'clock in the night. Rhoda went up to see Sallie Shields, Virginia Harris, Mag. Martin, and Ada Anderson. Mr. Carter went up to Mr. Howard's today but came back this evening.

Sunday 22. Another beautiful day. Mr. Carter, Sister, Rhoda and Annie went to the Methodist Church. Mary E., Annie and I went to Sunday School. Mr. Carter went to his father's and stayed awhile this morning after church. Cousin Joe Lea was here this evening. We all went to the graveyard.

Monday 23. A pleasant day. Mr. Carter, Sister, Rhoda, Aunt Phoebe [slave], Mary E., Annie and Jimmie all started to Aunt Charity Lea's today. Mrs. Jane Hall and Martha Hall spent the day here today. Mrs. Cook was here, also Uncle Caswell and Aunt

Elizabeth Lea. Mother and I went up to Mrs. Cook's this evening and stayed awhile. We all went to the depot this evening. Cousin Joe Lea stayed all night here. Mrs. Stuart and Mrs. Morris were also here this morning.

Tuesday 24. Pleasant day. Elvira Lea stayed awhile here this evening. We went to see Naomi Henry, Sallie Reeder, and Mary Hardwick. Mother went in to see Mrs. Harris and Cousin Mary Harle.

Wednesday 25. A pleasant day. Mother, Aunt Eliza and Mrs. Jane Hall spent the day at Uncle Caswell's today. Cousin Martha Lea and Frances Tucker stayed all night here tonight. Mother went up to Mrs. Cook's and Carter's.

Thursday 26. Another pleasant day. Mr. and Mrs. Cook and Davie Jones were here tonight. I went up to see how Harriet Chestnutt was. Mother and I went to see Cousin Mary Harle, and Dr. Brown about Frank.[30]

Friday 27. A tolerable cold evening. Wrote to Sister. Mother went up to see Harriet Chestnutt. Had 29 praise marks. Cousin John Lea stayed all night with us tonight.

Saturday 28. A pleasant day. Cleaned up the parlor. Mother and Mrs. Cook went down to see Mrs. Garrison this morning. Mrs. Cook, Mrs. Pickens, Tresse Torbit, Mrs. Thompson, Mary and Mrs. Hardwick, Mrs. Reynolds and Mrs. Dodson were all here today.

Sunday 29. A pleasant day. I went to Sabbath School this morning. I went to the Bible class, did not stay until it was over.

Monday 30. A pleasant day. There was not any school today. Two girls[31] joined together were exhibited today, did not go. Uncles Caswell and William Lea, Aunt Elizabeth and Sissy took tea here this evening. Mr. and Mrs. Cook were here tonight. Mother went over to Cousin Mary's, Mrs. Cook's and Mrs. Carter's today. Old Aunt Becky Outin buried today.

Tuesday 31. A rainy morning. Went to school as usual. Mrs. Gallaher has a boy. Mrs. Grant was here today. Mother got a letter from Sister this morning.

---

[30] A slave.
[31] Siamese or conjoined twins

June 1859

Wednesday 1. A shower soon this morning, pleasant ever since. Went to school as usual. Mother spent the day at Mr. Carter's.

Thursday 2. A pleasant day. Mother went up to see Harriet Chestnutt today; also to see Aunt Fannie (Cousin Mary Harle's mother). I went over to see Mary Hardwick this evening. Mrs. Cook was here today.

Friday 3. A pleasant day. Mother spent the day at Mrs. Carter's . Went to see Mrs. Mitchell Edwards, Mrs. Capt. Gaut and Mrs. DeLano. Mrs. Walker here today. Sister and the others came from Alabama today. Had 25 praise and 3 black marks

Saturday 4. A pleasant day. Mrs. Carter and Mag Shadden were here today, also Uncle Caswell and William Lea. Mother and Sister went up to Mrs. Carter's this morning. I went up to Mrs. Shadden's to see Harriet this evening.

Sunday 5. A pleasant day. Annie and I sat up with Harriet tonight. Cousin Joseph Lea took dinner and supper here this evening. Sister and Mother went over to Mrs. Grant's and Cousin Mary's.

Monday 6. A beautiful day. Harriet Chestnutt died at a quarter past 6 o'clock this morning. Mother is sick today, sent for Dr. Brown. I wrote to Rhoda this evening. We all marched down to the creek with the corpse. Mr. Carter went on down. Annie and I went over to Mrs. Hardwick's and Cousin Mary's. There was not any school in the evening. Mrs. Thompson, Cook, Walker, Aunt E. and Uncle Caswell Lea, Mrs. Dr. Brown and Mr. Carter were all here today. Mrs. Shadden stayed all night. Mary Tibbs was here this evening.

Tuesday 7. A pleasant day. Mrs. Cook, Mrs. Grant and Bell, Aunt Elizabeth Lea, Cousin Martha Lea, Mrs. James Craigmiles, Mrs. Henry and Mrs. Carter were all here today. Went to school. Sister went over to see Aunt Fannie Lea. Mother is a little better today and sat up a little.

Wednesday 8. A pleasant day. Rained tonight. Mrs. Cook, also Dr. Brown were here today. Went to school as usual today. Second

Caswell died, 1842.[32] Mrs. Keebler was here today. Sister went shopping with her.

Thursday 9. Pleasant day. Mrs. Shadden and Mrs. Campbell were here today. Mr. Carter started to Alabama today.

Friday 10. A pleasant day. Sister went to Cousin Mary's today. Mrs. Smith was here today. Uncle William took dinner and supper here today.

Saturday 11. A pleasant day. Emma Aldehoff and I went over to see Sallie McMillin and Callie Grant this evening. Uncle William Lea took breakfast here this morning. Sister went over to Mrs. Traynor's and Mrs. Carter's. Sister and I to the Baptist meeting.

Sunday 12. A pleasant day. I [went] to the Methodist Sunday School this morning and the Cumberland in the evening. I went to church this morning. Mr. McNutt preached. Emma Aldehoff and Mary Sevier were here this morning and went to church. Cousin Joseph and Uncle William took supper here. Uncle William took dinner and breakfast here. Received a letter from Rhoda.

Monday 13. A pleasant day. Uncle William Lea was here today. Went to school. Jimmie was sick this evening, a little.

Tuesday 14. A pleasant day. Went to school. Sister commenced papering her room at noon. Uncle William took supper here this evening. I went up to Mr. Reynold's store at noon to get some wallpaper. Sister went to Mr. Reynold's, Hardwick's, Campbell's, Craigmiles' stores after some wallpaper for her room. Kate Rogers was here today.

Wednesday 15. A pleasant day. Went to school. Was sick this evening. Uncle William Lea put up Sister's window blinds this evening.

Thursday 16. A rainy day. We finished history this evening. Uncle William Lea took dinner and supper here today.

Friday 17. A pleasant day. Mrs. Cook, Aunt Elizabeth and Sissy Lea were here this evening.

Saturday 18. A pleasant day. Sister, Annie and I went up to Mr. Carter's this evening. Uncles Caswell and William Lea took supper

---

[32]James W. and Ann Inman had two sons born two years apart with identical names, who died in infancy, thus the term second. The first Caswell died in 1839, several years before Myra was born. The second son is designated as "Second Caswell."

here tonight. I went to a circus show tonight with Uncle William. He took me in two shows. He stayed all night here.

Sunday 19. It rained this morning a little. We went to both Sunday Schools. Annie went to the morning one. Sister and I went to the Methodist Church. Mr. Bates preached.

Monday 20. Pleasant day. Got rank 14. Went over to Mrs. Hardwick's this evening. Went to practice for the anniversary, tonight at the Cumberland Church. Stopped in at Mrs. Cook's at dinner to give two books. Sister, Mother, Annie and Jimmie went up there this evening. Mother took supper. Mr. Carter came from Alabama today.

Tuesday 21. A pleasant day. Uncle William took supper at our house. Went up to see Anna Gaut this evening. Received a letter this evening from Rhoda. Mr. Carter went to Ringgold, Ga. this evening. Cousin Mary and Aunt Fannie were here this evening.

Wednesday 22. A pleasant day. Mother went over to Mrs. Grant's today.

Thursday 23. Mrs. Cook was here twice today. Mother made some blackberry jelly today. Mrs. Shadden took supper here. Mr. Carter went to Loudon[33] this evening.

Friday 24. A pleasant day. School half of the day, Mr. Aldehoff went to Chattanooga to a Masonic celebration. I went out to Uncle Caswell's this evening, stopped in to get Lillie Davis; did not go. Uncle William took supper here tonight. Cousin Joe was here. I went to singing tonight.

Saturday 25. A pleasant day. Went to the anniversary at the fairground. Mrs. Cook, Anna Gaut and Sissy Lea were all here this evening. Mother went to the celebration. Commenced a letter to Rhoda Ann this evening.

Sunday 26. Went to both Sunday Schools. Cousin Joe Lea was here this evening. All of us went to the Presbyterian Church. Mr. Caldwell preached. A pleasant day.

Monday 27. Mother and Sister went to Cousin Mary Harle's. A pleasant day.

Tuesday 28. A pleasant day. Mother and Sister went over to Cousin Mary's, Mrs. Cook's and prayer meeting. Mr. Prichard took

---

[33]Loudon is the County Seat of Loudon County, Tennessee.

dinner with us today. Mrs. Carter and Mrs. Rickman spent the day here today.

Wednesday 29. A very rainy day. Rained a little this evening. Sister went up to Mrs. Pickens', Carter's, and Edward's. Speaking in town today. School only half the day. Uncle William Lea took dinner here today. Mr. Carter went to Ringgold this evening.

Thursday 30. There was a storm this morning. Annie has been sick all day. I went to Mrs. Carter's this evening. Lillie Davis and I went to school as usual. Mr. Maples took supper here.

July 1859

Friday 1. A shower of rain this evening. Mrs. Cook, Mrs. William and Mrs. Pleasant Craigmiles, Mary Hardwick, Margaret Shadden and Cleo Watkins were all here today. Went up to Mrs. Davis', this evening, after a Sunday School book.

Saturday 2. A pleasant day. Sister and I went to Mrs. Stuarts', Traynor's, Carter's, Thompson's and Lizzie Wood's, also to Mr. Cook's store, Rogers', Guthman's, Simmon's, Middlecoff's, Craigmiles' and Campbell's. I went to see Mary Hardwick. Got me a palm leaf fan. Sister and Annie went to church.

Sunday 3. A pleasant day. Cousin Joseph Lea was here this evening. I went to both Sunday schools. Sister and Annie went to church today. Mother and I went over to Cousin Mary Harle's and Mrs. Carter's this evening.

Monday 4. A windy day. Adelia Thompson and Margaret Shadden were here today. Aunt Elizabeth, Uncle Caswell and Bettie "Sissy" took supper here this evening. Sister and Aunt went over to Cousin Mary's this evening. We all went up to the speaking in the courthouse yard. Dick Harris and Mr. Goldsmith spoke. Old Mr. Pickens died this evening.

Tuesday 5. A tolerable cool night, a pleasant day. Wrote to Rhoda tonight. Mother and Sister went up to Mrs. Carter's, Cook's, Sister went up to Mr. Carter's. Annie went over to Mrs. Grant's. Mr. Carter went off tonight.

Wednesday 6. A pleasant day. Mrs. Alexander was here this evening. I wrote a letter to Bettie Jarrett today.

Thursday 7. A pleasant day. Mr. McNutt, Mrs. Middlecoff, Mrs. Seavey and Mrs. Garrison were here this morning. I went to school as usual. Review night.

Friday 8. Rained all night last night. It was cold enough to have a fire this evening. Mr. Cook was here today. Sister and Mother were up there this evening. Had 27 praise marks, no black ones.

Saturday 9. A pleasant day. Martha Reynolds and Sallie McMillin were here this evening. Mother and Sister went up to Mrs. Berry's, Mrs. Guthman's, Mrs. Carter's and Mrs. McNutt's this evening. Cousin John Lea brought us some honey this morning.

Sunday 10. A pleasant day. Annie and I went to church. Mr. McNutt preached. I was sick, did not stay for church, came home. Sister and Mother went over to Mrs. Grant's and Mrs. Cook's.

Monday 11. Mrs. Cook and Mrs. Henry were here, also Henry Jones. Mother and Sister were up at Mrs. Cook's this evening. A warm day.

Tuesday 12. Very warm day. Lillie Davis stayed all night here tonight. we went up to Mrs. Gaut's a little while. I was up at Mrs. Davis' this evening.

Wednesday 13. Very warm day. Mrs. Hickman, Mrs. Gaut, Mary and Elvira Lea were here this evening. Mother and Sister were at Mrs. Carter's, Shields', Jessie Gaut's, Reynolds' and Dodson's this evening. Mrs. Joe Shields has a boy. Uncle William took dinner here. Mr. Carter went to Campbell Station[34] this evening.

Thursday 14. A very warm day. Mr. and Mrs. Hickman were here today. They went home today. Received a letter from Rhoda Ann today. Cousin Mary Fulton and Cousin Martha Lea spent the day here and stayed all night. Mother and Annie went out to Uncle Caswell's this morning. Cousin Martha, Cousin Mary, Sister and I went up to the graveyard after supper this evening.

Friday 15. A warm day. Cousins Mary Fulton and Martha Lea spent nearly all day here. Cousin Mary and Sister went around shopping before noon. I had 31 praise marks. Mr. G. R. Knabe was here this morning.

---

[34] Near Knoxville, Tennessee.

Saturday 16. A very warm day. Had a thunder storm about noon. Uncle William took dinner here. Mr. Knabe tuned our pianoforte [piano] today. Sister went to the Cumberland Church. Mr. Templeton preached. Mother and I went to the Cumberland Church tonight. Mr. Templeton preached.

Sunday 17. The warmest day we have had. Received a letter from Bettie Jarrett. Annie and I went to Sunday School. We all went to church this morning. Our sow has pigs. Mr. Carter came from Campbell Station this evening. Mother and I went to church tonight. Cousins Martha Lea and Mary Fulton all night here tonight.

Monday 18. A very warm day. Uncles William and Caswell Lea, Cousins Mary, Martha and Sissy were here today. Cousin Mary went off today. Mrs. Lea and Mrs. and Dr. Long were here today. Mother went over to the depot. Wrote Bettie Jarrett tonight.

Tuesday 19. A warm day. Mother and Sister went up to Mrs. Carter's, Traynor's, Mills', Uncle Caswell's, Judge Gaut's, Berry's and the stores.

Wednesday 20. A warm day. Anna Gaut, Adelia Thompson, Mag Shadden, Mrs. Cook and Uncle Caswell took supper, also Elvira Lea and Anna Gaut. Rhoda Ann and Mary Elizabeth came home today from Alabama. Mother and Sister went over to meet them off the cars.[35]

Thursday 21. A warm day. Cynthia Hardwick, Frances Tucker and John Campbell were here. Mother and Sister went up to the stores, also awhile at Mrs. Carter's. Sister spent the day there today. Mrs. Carter is very sick.

Friday 22. A warm day today. The last day of school. Margaret Martin, Sid Bell, Rose Bell and Mary Davis were here today. Mother and Sister went to the stores today. Cousin Mary Harrison came down with Mrs. Carter from New Market today, at 12 o'clock. Cousin John Lea was here this evening. Uncle William Lea took supper.

Saturday 23. Rained this morning, warm this evening. Cousins Martha and John Lea were here tonight. I went up after my ticket this morning, had rank 11. Sister and Annie went up to Mr. Carter's this evening; she went to Mrs. William I. Campbell's; she is sick.

---

[35] Train cars.

Sunday 24. It rained this morning, windy this evening. We did not go to church or Sunday School today, it rained. Mother, Sister, Cousin Mary Harrison, Rhoda Ann, Annie and I all went up to the graveyard this evening. Sister, Annie and Mr. Carter went to Mr. Paschal Carter's this evening. Cousin John and Uncle William Lea were here this evening. Rhoda and Cousin Mary Harrison went to the Methodist Church tonight.

Monday 25. Rained this morning, pleasant this evening. Rhoda and Cousin Mary went to Uncle Caswell's this evening, also to the stores. Sister and I went up to Mrs. Carter's, Campbell's and Thompson's. Mr. and Mrs. Cook were here tonight. Mr. Carter went over to Harrison, Hamilton County, Tennessee, this morning. Sewed on my underskirt.[36] I went over to the institute this morning.

Tuesday 26. A pleasant day. Rhoda and Cousin Mary Harrison came back this evening. Margaret Shadden was here today. Mr. Carter came back tonight. I sewed on my underskirt nearly all day; finished it, commenced making points to put around the bottom of it. Mother and Sister went around shopping this morning, went to Mrs. Cook's tonight. Mary E. took Mary Edward's bonnet patterns home this evening.

Wednesday 27. Rained nearly all day; very cool, had a fire. Been making points to go around my underskirt. Uncle William took supper here tonight.

Thursday 28. Tolerable cool in the forenoon. Mary and Anna Gaut, Florence Johnston and Emma Lea were here today. Been making points all day. Rhoda and Cousin Mary Harrison went out to Uncle Caswell's to stay all night. Uncle William was here this morning, took dinner here also. I went to Mr. Guthman's [for] garter tape and Florence silk. Rhoda went to Dr. Thompson's, Mr. H. Davis' and Mrs. Cook's.

Friday 29. A pleasant day. Rhoda and Cousin Mary Harrison went form Uncle Caswell's to Mr. Caldwell's; spent the day there. Mrs. Caldwell, Callie Grant and Florence Johnston were here today. Sister Myra died in 1837.[37] Been making points part of the day; read

---

[36]An underskirt is a skirt worn under another all day, i.e., a petticoat (*AHD*).

[37]See entry for 24 March 1859.

The Old Stone Mansion, the other part. A soiree[38] at the Ocoee House tonight, no person from here went.

Saturday 30. A pleasant day. Cousin Martha Lea and Callie Swan took supper here. Uncle William took dinner here today. Uncle Caswell Lea was here this evening. Sister and Annie went up to the stores this evening. Aunt Fannie Lea was here this morning.

Sunday 31. A pleasant day. Rhoda, Mary Elizabeth and I went to Sabbath School. Sister, Mr. Carter and Annie went to the Methodist Church. Mother, Cousin Mary Ann Harrison, Rhoda and I went to the Cumberland Church. Mr. Slocard preached. Cousin Mary, Annie and I went to the Methodist Church tonight. Mr. Brooks preached.

August 1859

Monday 1. Rained this morning, pleasant this evening. Mrs. White, Sallie Shields and Mag Shadden were here this evening. Cousin Mary and Rhoda Ann went up to Mrs. Judge Gaut's. Uncle William took supper here tonight. I made tape points all day.

Tuesday 2. Pleasant day. Mr. and Mrs. Cook set until bedtime. Sister, Annie and Jimmie spent the evening at Mrs. Cook's, took tea. Made tape points, reeled and twisted yarn today. Mr. Carter went up to Charleston (Bradley County, Tenn.) and back today.

Wednesday 3. A pleasant day, very warm tonight. Mrs. Hassle[39] and Florence Johnston were here today. Mr. Carter, Sister, Annie and Jimmie spent the day at Mrs. Carter's. Mary Elizabeth is sick this evening. Been making points and reeling today.

Thursday 4. Rained this evening. The day of the election. Mr. Bradford took supper here tonight. Uncle William took dinner. Finished my skirt this evening. Mary Elizabeth is better today.

Friday 5. A storm at dinner time. It rained very hard all night. Uncle William took supper here. Mary Elizabeth had a chill today. I did not do anything particular today.

---

[38]A soiree is an evening party or reception (*AHD*).
[39] Formerly Mrs. Bower.

Saturday 6. A pleasant day. I needleworked all day. Ann and Ada Stuart and Mary Smith were here this evening. First Caswell died in 1839. [Myra's parents first son who died in infancy.] Cousin Mary, Rhoda and I went to the new Baptist Church to preaching tonight. Mr. McNutt preached.

Sunday 7. Rained all night, nearly, last night, rained just before dinner and after also. I read all day. Uncle William took dinner here today. Mr. Carter, Sister, Cousin Mary (Harrison), Rhoda, and Annie all went to the Methodist [Church], Mother to the Baptist [Church]. Mary Elizabeth had a chill today. I stayed at home with her. Cousin Mary and Rhoda went to the Methodist Church tonight.

Monday 8. A pleasant day, a little shower this evening. Mrs. Cook, Mrs. McNutt and Anna Gaut were here today. Cousin Mary (Harrison) and Rhoda went out to Mr. Robert Swan's, Aunt Elizabeth (Lea's) and up to Mr. Guthman's store. Mr. Carter went to Athens [McMinn County, Tennessee], today. Sister went over to Cousin Mary Harles's, Mrs. Gaut, and Mrs. Davis'.

Tuesday 9. A little shower this evening. Mrs. White and Eliza Shields were here this evening. Sister went over to Cousin Mary's Harle's this morning. Sister, Mother, and Annie spent the evening at Uncle Caswell's. I read the *Out-Cast* today.

Wednesday 10. A very rainy day. I have been reading *King Philip's Daughter* and knitting on my stocking. Rhoda and Cousin Mary (Harrison) came back this evening. Mr. Carter went up to Charleston, [Bradley County, Tennessee] and back today.

Thursday 11. It rained all morning. Mrs. Shadden was here today. We had a watermelon and muskmelon, also grapes. Cousin Mary (Harrison), Rhoda and I went up to Mrs. Cook's tonight. Sister and Annie came up there as "beggars" (masquerading). Mr. Carter went up to Athens [McMinn County, Tennessee], today.

Friday 12. Rainy morning. Mr. Carter came back today. Cousin Mary and Rhoda went up to Florence Johnston's and Mag Shadden's. Been knitting on my stocking all day.

Saturday 13. A pleasant day. Mother, Cousin Mary (Harrison) and Mr. Carter went up to New Market [Jefferson County, Tennessee] this morning. Mrs. Cook, Mag Shadden and Martha Reynolds were here this morning. Mrs. Dr. Campbell (of Georgetown) [Hamilton County, Tennessee], Cousin Martha Lea, and Luther Campbell took supper here. Knitted all day. Anna Gaut stayed all night here tonight. Mary Elizabeth and Annie went over to Mrs. Grant's. Sister and Rhoda Ann went over to Mrs. Stuart's this evening.

Sunday 14. A pleasant day. Rhoda, Mary Elizabeth and I went to Sabbath School, also to the Presbyterian Church. Mr. Harvey Alexander preached. Cousin Joseph and Uncle William took supper here. Mary Elizabeth, Annie and I went to Mr. Hunter's lecture at 3 o'clock. Rhoda, Mary and I [went] at night also.

Monday 15. A pleasant day. Uncle William took dinner here today. Knitting all day. Mr. Carter went to Calhoun, Georgia.

Tuesday 16. Mrs. Carter, Sue Kenner, Ada Anderson, and Lillie Davis were here today. Cousin John Lea's 19th birthday. Rhoda Ann and Annie went to Mrs. Carter's and Lizzie Woods' (not at home), this evening. Rhoda went to see Cynthia Hardwick (not at home) this evening, and Anna Gaut. Rhoda and Sister went up to Mrs. Henry Davis' tonight. Mr. Carter came home from Calhoun, Georgia today. Been sewing on my dress today. Uncle William took dinner here today.

Wednesday 17. Pleasant day. Virginia Harris and Uncle William were here today. Mr. Carter went to Ooltewah today, came back tonight. Sister went to Squire Davis', Berry's Guthman's. Sewed on my dress all day. Rhoda and Sister went to Judge Gaut's, Shield's, Henry's this evening.

Thursday 18. Rained a little this evening. Uncle Caswell took dinner here. Margaret Shadden, Pryor Lea and George Lea were here. Finished the skirt of my dress today, knitted the rest of the day on my stockings.

Friday 19. Two hard storms this evening, the first rained harder than I ever saw it, hailed a little. Cooked a meal of victuals today for dinner. Cleaned up a little. Sister, Rhoda and Annie went over to Dr. Long's, Mrs. Col. Lea's and Mrs. DeLano's.

Saturday 20. A pleasant day. Mrs. Keebler took dinner here. I went home with her. Mrs. Wilson and her children were here today.

Sunday 21. A pleasant day. Mr. Glaze and Mollie spent the day here today. Mr. Keebler went off today. Mr. Wilson was here also. Old Mr. and Mrs. Keebler were here today, stayed all night. Uncle Caswell Lea is 57 today.

Monday 22. A pleasant day. Mrs. Keebler was here again for Eliza to make a dress. I read *Alonzo and Malissa* all day. Hawes Keebler came this evening.

Tuesday 23. A pleasant day. Eliza and I went over to Mrs. Wilson's after supper. Mr. Keebler came home tonight. Mr. Finley stayed all night here.

Wednesday 24. A rainy day. Nothing of importance occurred today. Mr. Gum Keebler stayed all night here.

Thursday 25. A pleasant day. Went to Mrs. Garrett's and Mrs. Cass Tipton's this evening.

Friday 26. A pleasant day. Came home on the cars. Anna Gaut and Adelia Thompson were here this evening. Rhoda and I went to Mrs. Grant's this evening; Rhoda and I went to Mr. Knabe's, Sister went over to Mrs. Grant's this evening.

Saturday 27. Pleasant day. Mag Shadden was here today. I went down to Mr. Reynolds' this evening.

Sunday 28. Mrs. Shadden was here this evening. We all went to preaching. Mr. Bates preached. Rhoda and Mother went to Sunday School.

Monday 29. Martha Reynolds was here this evening. Rained a little today. Cooked today. Martha Morrison and Tom Knox were married at Hayes Campground[40] this evening.

Tuesday 30. A cool day. Had a fire this morning. Sister and Rhoda went shopping this morning. Rhoda and Sister went up to Mrs. Cook's this evening and took tea. Henry Jones and Mrs. Cook were here tonight. Mrs. Cook would have stayed all night but Mr. Cook came after her.

Wednesday 31. A pleasant day. Rhoda received a letter from Cousin Mary Harrison, Sister, and two from Mother. Mrs. Charles Gallaher's baby died this evening with croup. Sister, Rhoda, Annie and Jimmie went up to Mr. A.A. Campbell's and Mr. Reynolds' store, got Rhoda a dress, Annie two. They went to Mr. Carter's and Mrs. William Craigmiles'. Rhoda Ann sat up there tonight. Been reading *The Hidden Hand*; finished all the numbers I have. Been knitting also.

---

40 Bradley County, Tennessee.

September 1859

Thursday 1. A pleasant day. Mrs. Henry and Naomi were here this evening. Mag Shadden and Mrs. Shadden stayed all night. Sister went to Mrs. William Craigmiles' and Mrs. Shadden's. Knitted and needleworked all day.

Friday 2. A pleasant day. Needleworked all night on my chemise band. Sister and Rhoda went over to Mrs. Grant's tonight. Uncle Caswell and Cousin Martha Lea were here this morning.

Saturday 3. A pleasant day. Rained tonight a little. Ada Anderson [eventually marries Perry Gaut] was here this morning. I hemmed two dresses today. Dug up the grass in the walk.

Sunday 4. A rainy day. Nothing of importance occurred today. Received a letter from Mother.

Monday 5. A pleasant day. The first day of school. Mrs. A. A. Campbell's baby died this evening with croup. Sister and Mother went up to Mrs. Carter's, Mrs. Henry Davis', Mrs. Cook's and shopping. Lillie Ann Davis was here tonight.

Tuesday 6. A pleasant day. Went to school. Sister went to Mrs. Mitchell Edward's, Traynor's and Mrs. Carter's. Mrs. Walker was here today.

Wednesday 7. A pleasant day. Sister went up to Mrs. Rogers' and Mrs. Carter's. Mag and Mrs. Shadden stayed all night here tonight.

Thursday 8. Pleasant day. Sister and Rhoda went up to Mrs. Cook's tonight. Mrs. Judge Gaut was here today, also Lucretia and Mary Tibbs, Mary Hardwick and Ada Anderson. Rhoda went up to Mr. Hardwick's store after books this evening.

Friday 9. Pleasant day. Mr. Ramsey Swan was here this evening. School only half day. Sister went.

Saturday 10. Mother and Cousin Martha came home this day. Pleasant day. They all went to the depot but me. Mr. and Mrs. Cook, Old Mrs. Carter, Emma Middlecoff, Mary Kelly, Mrs. Caldwell, Uncles William and Caswell Lea, Aunt Elizabeth and Sissy were here today. Sister and Rhoda went to Mrs. Tom Campbell's, Pleasant Craigmiles', and Dr. Bate's this evening. I went up to Mr. Guthman's and got me some skeleton hoops. This morning Sister went to Mrs. Traynor's.

Sunday 11. A pleasant day. All went to Sunday School, Rhoda and Cousin Martha went to the Presbyterian Church; all the rest of us went to the Baptist, Mr. McNutt preached. Cousin John Lea was here this evening. Rhoda and Mother took a walk out to Uncle Caswell's.

Monday 12. Pleasant day. Uncle William and Cousin Jimmie were here. Mother and Sister went all around town shopping. Rhoda and Cousin Mary went out to Uncle Caswell's for supper.

Tuesday 13. Pleasant day. Cousin Mary Fulton came up today. Mother went down to Mr. Frank Lea's, stayed until the next day. Sister, Cousin Mary and Martha went out to Uncle Caswell's and stayed until after supper. Uncle Caswell was here today.

Wednesday 14. A pleasant day. Mrs. G. R. Knabe was here, gave Cousin Mary a lesson. Uncle William was here to tea.

Thursday 15. A pleasant day. Mrs. Shadden was here today. Uncle Caswell also. Uncle William was here this morning.

Friday 16. Very rainy day, rained all day. Went to school, came back before dinner; did not go back. Cousin John and Uncle Caswell were here tonight.

Saturday 17. Cool day in the morning. Uncle Caswell came this morning and took Cousin Mary Fulton up to Mr. Tom Campbell's. Mr. Dodson and Uncle William were here. Sister went up to Mrs. Traynor's and Cam Johnson's this evening. Mary E. went up to the store after hose for Cousin Martha. Got "Believe Me If All Those Endearing Young Charms" today.

Sunday 18. Pleasant day. Went to Sunday School. No church in town. Meeting at Eldridge's Campground[41] today. Uncle William Lea was here this morning and this evening. Lizzie Bell stayed all day here. Cousin Martha Lea and Rhoda went out to Uncle Caswell's tonight to stay all night. Cousin Martha, Rhoda and Mary E. went up to the graveyard this morning.

Monday 19. A rainy day. Nothing of importance occurred today. Mr. Wills died tonight at 6 o'clock. Brother Caswell's 18th birthday.

---

[41] Bradley County.

Tuesday 20. Pleasant day. Cousin Martha Lea, (Uncle Preston's daughter), Cousin Mary Fulton, Uncle William, Mrs. Thompson and Adelia were all here. Mother and Sister went shopping; got me a pair of shoes, to Mr. Carter's, Traynor's, Berry's, Guthman's, Cook's and James Craigmiles'. Mary E. went up and brought them down.

Wednesday 21. Rained this morning. I went up to the stores this evening. Mother and Sister went up to the stores. Mother and Sister went to Mrs. Harris' and DeLano's also.

Thursday 22. A pleasant day. Mother and Sister spent the day at Aunt Elizabeth's. Cousin John Lea and Uncle William were here today. Mother and Sister were at Mrs. Cook's. I went up to the stores after shoes. Mary E. went up and brought them down.

Friday 23. Pleasant day. Cousin Ellen Jarnagin, Cousin Mary Fulton, Mr. Caldwell, Aunt Elizabeth, Cousin Martha (Preston) and Lizzie Lea were here this evening, the last three stayed for tea. This day two years ago, Houston died in the evening at 6 o'clock.[42]

Saturday 24. Pleasant day. I went down to Mrs. Reynolds' this evening. Martha Reynolds and I went up to the drugstore. Rhoda Ann and Cousin Martha went up to Mrs. Carter's and Mrs. Cook's. Sister and Annie went over to Mrs. Grant's tonight. Mrs. Cook was here this evening. Henry Jones tonight. We baked cakes and cleaned up all day for Synod. Mary E. went out to Uncle Caswell's for eggs. Cousin Mary came in with her.

Sunday 25. A pleasant day. We all went to Sunday School. Sister, Annie, Mary Elizabeth, Rhoda Ann and Cousin Martha went to the Presbyterian Church.

Monday 26. A pleasant day. Martha Reynolds stayed here all night. I went down tonight after her. Uncle Caswell took dinner here. Sissy was here this morning.

Tuesday 27. A pleasant day. Went up to the music room and took my lesson. No school the rest of this week. Martha Reynolds and I went up to Mr. Tom Campbell's, Mr. Aldehoff's and Mr. McMillin's. Rhoda Ann went over from the music room to see Emma Aldehoff. Rhoda and Cousin Martha (Preston) went out to Uncle Caswell's

---

[42]Houston Lea, son of James Inman, died 23 September 1857, age 7 years 2 months, Ernest L. Ross, *Historical Cemetery Records of Bradley County, Tennessee*, Two Volumes (Cleveland: Author, 1973) II:184.

and stayed all night. Cousin John was here this evening. Sister put down her carpet today.

Wednesday 28. Pleasant day. A very hard rain this evening. All but Mother and Jimmie went out to the fair. Elvira Lea and Mary stayed all night here tonight. Adriance Osment was buried this evening.⁴³ Uncle Caswell was here today.

Thursday 29. Pleasant day. All of us went to the fair today. Cousin Betsy Harrison, Mr. Harrison, Meek, White, Armstrong, Martin and Uncle Caswell stayed and all took dinner here. Cousin Betsy, and Mr. Weir Armstrong stayed all night. Cousin Martha and Rhoda went to church with them tonight.

Friday 30. Pleasant day. All went to church but Rhoda and I. Last day of the fair, did not go.

October 1859

Saturday 1. Rained all day. Cousin Betsy Harrison came in from Uncle Caswell's. None of us went to church.

Sunday 2. A pleasant day. We all went to Sunday School and heard Mr. Ray talk. Went to the Presbyterian Church and heard him preach. Mr. and Mrs. Minnis took dinner here, and others. Cousins Betsy and Martha, Rhoda and I went to communion this evening. Mother, Cousin Betsy, Martha, Rhoda and I went to night meeting. Mr. Minnis preached.

Monday 3. Pleasant day. Nothing occurred today. Cousin Betsy went home today. Cousin Martha and Sister went to Mrs. Caldwell's this evening.

Tuesday 4. Pleasant day. Cousin Mary Fulton stayed all night here. Cousin Martha (Preston) went out home with Martha (Caswell). [Both Uncle Preston and Uncle Caswell had daughters named Martha.] She spent the day. Sister and Mother went to see Mrs. Cook, and out to see Sarah Israel.

---

⁴³John Adriance Osment, son of John and Mary Osment, died 28 September 1859, at 11 years 11 months. He is buried in Fort Hill Cemetery. Ross, *Cemetery Records*, II:221.

Wednesday 5. Mother and Sister spent the day at Mrs. Caldwell's today. Mrs. Carter was here this morning. Pleasant day. Mary has a baby girl.

Thursday 6. Pleasant day. Nothing occurred today. Mrs. Alexander was here this evening, also Lillie Davis.

Friday 7. Pleasant day. School only half day. Mr. Aldehoff went to Chattanooga. Mrs. Craigmiles, Mrs. Caldwell, Cousin Martha, Aunt Elizabeth Lea and Mary Jane Howell spent the day here. Uncle Caswell and Mr. William Craigmiles took dinner here. Mary Mee, Sallie Weir, Callie Grant and Cousin Mary Fulton were here today. Sister went over to Mrs. Grant's awhile this evening. Sister, Mother and I went to prayer meeting to the Baptist Church tonight. Cousin Martha (Preston) went up home today, 4 miles from McMillin's Station. Mrs. Parker has a girl.

Saturday 8. Rained very hard this evening. Wrote to Sid Bell this morning. All of them went to the Baptist Church but Annie. Rhoda and Sister went to the Baptist Church to prayer meeting tonight.

Sunday 9. A cold day. We went to Sunday School. Mother and Mary E. went to the Baptist Church. Sister, Rhoda and Annie went to the Presbyterian Church. Sister and I went to prayer meeting, tonight, at the Baptist Church. Mrs. Shadden was here this evening.

Monday 10. A cold day. Mother went out to Uncle Caswell's and over to Cousin Mary Harle's. Mrs. Dodson and Mrs. Cook were here. Sister, Mrs. Cook, and Annie went over to see Sarah Israel. Rhoda got a letter from Mrs. Collins.

Tuesday 11. A pleasant day. Cousin Mary Harle's mother, Aunt Fannie was here today. Uncle William took dinner and supper here, also went with Sister to the Baptist Church.

Wednesday 12. A pleasant day. Rhoda Ann and Sister went to the Baptist Church tonight.

Thursday 13. A pleasant day. Mrs. Cook and Cousin Mary Fulton were here this evening. Cousin Mary took supper. Mother and I went to church tonight, also this morning.

Friday 14. A pleasant day. Mother and Sister went to church this evening, also out to Mr. Robert and Joe Swan's. Rhoda, Sister and I went to the Baptist Church tonight.

Saturday 15. A tolerable cold day. Mother and Sister went to the Baptist Church this morning. Mr. Cook was here this morning.

Rhoda, Sallie, Eliza Shields and I went out to see Nep Swan. Sister, Mother, Rhoda and I went to church tonight. Adelia Thompson and Rhoda went to see Ada Anderson, Puss Foute, Martha Coulter and Carrie Bell. Adelia came down here.

Sunday 16. A pleasant day. Mother, Sister, Rhoda, Mary E. and I all went to church. Mother , Sister, Rhoda and I all went to church at night. Rhoda, Mother and I went to Sabbath School. Mrs. Cook, Sister, Mother and I went out to see Sarah Israel this evening. Mrs. Sneed took dinner here today.

Monday 17. Rained all this evening. Cousin John Lea was here. He is going to start up to Uncle Preston's tomorrow.

Tuesday 18. A pleasant day. Nothing occurred today.

Wednesday 19. A pleasant day. Aunt Fannie Lea stayed all day here today, and all night. Sister, Annie and Jimmie spent the day at Mr. Robert Swan's, went to Mr. Carter's also. I received a letter from Bettie Jarrett this morning.

Thursday 20. A pleasant day. Review night. Mr. McSpadden was buried this evening, he died yesterday at 7 p.m. Mother and Sister went to the burying also to the house. Mother went to see Dr. Ford's son.

Friday 21. Pleasant day. Mrs. Shadden and Mrs. Cook were here this evening.

Saturday 22. A pleasant day. Sister and Rhoda went shopping, also to Mrs. Cook's and Dr. Edward's. Callie Grant and Henry Jones were here tonight. Uncle William took dinner here today. Aunt Fannie and Uncle Pleasant Lea were married today in Ohio.

Sunday 23. A pleasant day. Rhoda, Sister and Annie went to church this morning. Rhoda, Mary E. and I went to Sabbath School. Mr. McNutt was here this evening. Rhoda and I went over to Cousin Mary Harle's.

Monday 24. A pleasant day. Nothing of importance occurred today.

Tuesday 25. A pleasant day. Mother and Sister went around shopping and to Dr. Ford's. Got me a blue dress. Mrs. Gallaher here today.

Wednesday 26. A pleasant day. Nothing of importance occurred today. Mother and Sister went to Dr. Ford's.

Thursday 27. A pleasant day. Mother and Sister spent the day at Mrs. William Craigmiles'. Sister went to Mrs. Bates' and Mrs. Carter's. Mother went to Mrs. Berry's. Rhoda and I went over to Cousin Mary Harle's.

Friday 28. A pleasant day. Mother and Sister spent the day at Mrs. Carter's. I stayed all night at Mrs. Reynolds' tonight. Nannie Browder stayed all night here last night. Sister, Rhoda and Nannie went up to Mr. Cook's store.

Saturday 29. Last night was the coldest night and day yet. Mrs. Gallaher, Puss Foute, Julia Tucker, Mrs. Billie Shadden and Sister went to church, also to Mrs. Cook's and around calling. Sister and Rhoda went over to Cousin Mary Harle's.

Sunday 30. A cold day. Mr. Alex Sharpe and Cousin Martha Lea took dinner here. Martha Reynolds was here this morning. Sister and I went to preaching. Mr. Slocard preached. We all went to Sabbath School. Mr. Haywood was here this evening.

Monday 31. A cold day. Mother and Sister went to see Nep Swan, Mrs. Aldehoff and Aunt Elizabeth. Mrs. Shadden and Cousin Martha here today.

November 1859

Tuesday 1. A pleasant day. Cousin John Lea, Mother and Sister went over to the depot to meet Uncle Pleasant and Aunt Fannie Lea.

Wednesday 2. A pleasant day. Uncle Pleasant and Aunt Fannie came today. Nep Swan died today at 12 o'clock.[44]Aunt Elizabeth and Uncle Caswell took dinner here. Rhoda went out to Mr. Swan's today. Frances Tucker stayed all night here.

Thursday 3. A pleasant day. Mother and Sister went out to Mr. Swan's this morning. Rhoda did not go to school today. Mr. Aldehoff did not teach this evening, we all went to the funeral. Mr. Carter came home tonight.

---

[44]Penelope M. Swan, b. 10 October 1842, d. 2 November 1859, Ross, *Cemetery Records*, II:270.

Friday 4. A pleasant day. Mother, Sister, and Mr. Carter spent the day at Aunt Elizabeth's. Annie spent the day at her grandfather's[45]. Sister went to the stores this evening. Mrs. Cook was here tonight. Adelia Thompson stayed with Rhoda tonight.

Saturday 5. A pleasant day. Uncle Pleasant and Aunt Fannie Lea were here this morning. Augusta Craigmiles and Sue Aldehoff were here this evening. Aunt Fannie dressed Annie's doll today. Mary E. and Annie took it up to Mrs. Cook's after it was dressed.

Sunday 6. A pleasant day. We all went to Sunday School. Uncle Pleasant and Aunt Fannie came back from Mr. Callaway's today. Mr. Callaway, Cousin John and Uncle Caswell were here tonight. Uncle Caswell took supper here tonight. Aunt Fannie played some on the piano.

Monday 7. A pleasant day. Uncle Pleasant and family started for Missouri today. Mr. Carter went to Cassville. Mother and Sister went over to Cousin Mary Harle's after we came from the depot.

Tuesday 8. A pleasant day. Mr. and Mrs. Rogers were here today. Sister and Mother went to Cousin Mary's and the stores and to see Sarah Israel. Mother sat up with Lizzie Callaway tonight.

Wednesday 9. A pleasant day. Eliza Keebler, Sis McMillin, Aunt Fannie [Mary Harle's mother] and Julia Tucker were here today. Sister went to Cousin Mary Harle's this evening.

Thursday 10. A pleasant day. Callie Knox was married this evening. Rhoda, Annie and I had our daguerreotypes taken this evening. Mr. Carter come home today.

Friday 11. A pleasant day. No school today. Rhoda and I sewed all day on our worsted dresses. Mrs. Cook was here this evening. Mary E. went up to Mrs. Cook's. I went to the stores today.

Saturday 12. It blew very hard tonight, rained some. Sewed all day today. I went around shopping. Sister's magazine came today. Mother and Rhoda went to [the Baptist] Church. Dr. Hunt was here tonight.

Sunday 13. It snowed some this morning, very cold tonight, the coldest night we have had. Mr. Carter and sister went to the Methodist Church. Rhoda and Mother went to the Baptist. I was so cold I walked home. Mr. Hunter and Rachel Young were married

---

[45] Paschal Carter.

today. Rhoda and I went over to Cousin Mary Harle's this afternoon. Tresse Torbit and Posey Roberts were married this morning at Dr. Thompson's.

Monday 14. A pleasant day. Nothing occurred today.

Tuesday 15. Pleasant day. Mother and Sister went to Uncle Caswell's.

Wednesday 16. A pleasant day. Ann McNelley was here today.

Thursday 17. A pleasant day. I had the headache, did not go to school this evening. Mrs. Shadden, Margaret and Mrs. Harris were here this evening. Mr. Carter came home tonight. Sister spent the day at Mrs. Traynor's today. Ann E. Bryant has a baby.

Friday 18. Rainy day. Night of the concert, Martha Reynolds is 15 today.

Saturday 19. A tolerable pleasant day. Nothing occurred today.

Sunday 20. A pleasant day. Sister, Annie, Rhoda and Mr. Carter went to the Methodist Church. We all went to Sunday School. Callie Swan was here this evening. Mother and Sister went over to Cousin Mary Harle's. Rhoda and Mother went to the Methodist Church.

Monday 21. A muddy and rainy day. Rhoda went to a party down at Mr. Tibbs' tonight.

Tuesday 22. A pleasant day. Mrs. Cook was here this morning. Rhoda come back this morning. She went around visiting. Mother and Sister went up to the stores, to see Sarah Israel and Mrs. Guthman.

Wednesday 23. Pleasant day. Mother, Sister, Rhoda, Jimmie and I all went up to Mrs. Cook's. She was down this evening. Cousin Mary Fulton, Mrs. Onie Campbell and Bell took supper here this evening. Cousin Martha and Bettie took dinner here.

Thursday 24. A beautiful day. Mother and Sister went over to Mrs. Reynold's, Mrs. McMillin's and Mrs. Frank Hardwick's this evening. They sat until bedtime at Mrs. Berry's. Thanksgiving Day. Mother and Sister went to church this morning. I went down to see Martha Reynolds this evening.

Friday 25. A windy day. We cleaned house today. Rhoda and Sister went out to Judge Rowle's today to spend the day. Capt. Jarrett was here this evening. Hettie Shields, Lettie and Lizzie Swan. Joe Kerns is 16 today, Uncle Houston 54 today.

Saturday 26. A very rainy day. Nothing of importance occurred today. Mr. Carter came home today.

Sunday 27. Rained all day. Got a letter from Elvira Lea today.

Monday 28. A warm, cloudy day. Betsey Grant and Mary Edwards were here today. I have been sick today. I answered Elvira's Letter today. Mother went to Mrs. Cook's, Mr. Alderhoff's and Sarah Israel's this morning.

Tuesday 29. A very pleasant day. Rhoda, Ann, and I went up to Mr. Aldehoff's and worked on our bookkeeping. We have been quilting today. Uncle Caswell to supper here.

Wednesday 30. A pleasant day. Mr. Carter came home today. Quilted part of the day. Aunt Adeline has been very sick today. Sister, Mr. Carter, Annie and Jimmie went up to Mr. Carter's. Sister went to see Sarah Israel. Old Mrs. Gallaher and Mrs. David Gallaher were here.

December 1859

Thursday 1. A pleasant day. Mr. Carter went off today. Sister, Rhoda, Annie, and Jimmie spent the day at uncle Caswell's. He was here this morning. Cousin Miranda Lea was married yesterday to a Mr. McCampbell. Teresa McCarty died last night. First day of winter. I worked on scales today.

Friday 2. A pleasant day. Mother and Sister went to see Sarah Israel, she died this morning. Rhoda and Sister went to Teresa's burying. I sewed all day on Jimmie's drawers. Old [John] Brown was hung today [in Charleston, West Virginia]. Mother, Sister and I went to Sarah Israel's burying at 3 o'clock. Callie Grant was here this morning. Rhoda and I went over to Mrs. Hardwick's after supper. Mr. and Mrs. Cook were here tonight. It rained tonight.[46]

---

[46]John Brown, a strange and demented person, had an amazing appeal to men of culture and education. Establishing himself in Canada, Brown collected a small band of followers. His scheme was to liberate the Southern slaves by taking up arms, resisting any militia, educating, and forming some type of government. By taking slave holders hostage, they hoped to force

Saturday 3. A rainy day. Mr. Carter came home today. Mother and Rhoda went to the Baptist meeting.

Sunday 4. A rainy day. Mary and I went to Sunday School. Mother, Rhoda went to church. Mother went to Mrs. Cook's. Rhoda, Ann, and Sister went to Cousin Mary Harle's. Mr. Carter went to see his father.

Monday 5. A rainy day. Mr. Carter went partridge hunting. I stopped by Mr. Aldehoff's. I went to take my music lesson. We parched[47] some meal tonight.

Tuesday 6. A muddy day. Mr. Joseph Shields' little son died today. Sister and I went up there in the evening. Uncle William took dinner and supper here. Rhoda, Uncle William and I went to the Baptist prayer meeting.

Wednesday 7. A very cold day. Mother killed hogs today. Rhoda ironed today. I got nearly all of the dinner. It spit snow a little today.

Thursday 8. Colder than yesterday. Uncle Pryor and his family come today. Uncles Caswell and William and Cousin John were here today.

Friday 9. No change in the weather. Cousin John was here this morning. Rhoda, Ann and I went to Uncle Caswell's to a party.

Saturday 10. Cold as yesterday. Uncle Pryor, Sister and family went out to Uncle Caswell's. Rhoda and Sister went over to Cousin Mary Harle's this evening. Mary Hardwick was here this evening. Cousin John and Uncle William stayed all night here.

---

southern states to free the slaves. On 16 October 1859, Brown led 18 followers in an assault on Harpers Ferry. They seized some hostages, but there was no response made by the Virginia slaves. The group was in an engine house where they were routed by United States Marines under Col. Robert E. Lee. There was shock and consternation throughout the South. In October 1859, a jury found John Brown guilty of treason against Virginia and inciting a slave rebellion. He was sentenced to death and on 2 December 1859, he was hanged until dead in Charleston, West Virginia. In death John Brown became larger than life in a cause to abolish slavery. J. G. Randall and David Donald, *The Civil War and Reconstruction* (Boston: D.C. Heath, 1965, end ed.) 124-126.

[47]To parch something was to dry or roast by exposing to heat (*AHD*).

Sunday 11. Not quite so cold as yesterday. We went to Sunday School. Martha Reynolds came home with us and we went to the Presbyterian Church. Cousin John stayed all night here.

Monday 12. A pleasant day. Mr. Carter started to Alabama this morning. Uncle Pryor [Lea] took dinner here. Uncle William was here today. All but Mr. Carter starting to Al [abama] this morning, he went up to Athens.[48] Mother and Sister went over to Cousin Mary's this evening. Uncle Pryor's family came in from Uncle Caswell's this evening. Rhoda Ann and Cousin Martha Lea sat up with Lizzie Callaway, she died at 15 minutes after 12 o'clock.

Tuesday 13. Pleasant day. Uncle Pryor, Aunt Lizzie, May, Lizzie, Lila, and Emma all started to West Tennessee, near Trenton. Uncle Caswell and Uncle William took dinner here. Cousin John was here this morning. Cousin Martha went home soon. Emma Aldehoff was here for me to go to Mr. Tuckers'. Mr.Carter came home today.

Been working on Jimmie's petticoat all day. Mother went over to the depot.

Wednesday 14. A pleasant day. Mrs. Brown and Martha Coulter [were here]. Mr. Carter started to Alabama today. Rhoda Ann went out to Rev. Caldwell's tonight. Mother to Mrs. Cook's, McNutt's, and the stores. Sister went up the stores and Mrs. DeLano's. I went up to Mr. Aldehoff's and down to Mr. Reynolds'. Mrs. Hawkins was married tonight. Lizzie Harris has a girl.

Thursday 15. A pleasant day. Sou Hunt and Mr. Carter Rowan were married this morning. Mary Snead was married today to a gentleman from Winchester. Mr. Ore was buried today. Rhoda Ann went up to Mrs. Cook's this morning.

Friday 16. Pleasant day. Mother went to Mrs. R. Swan's, Aunt Elizabeth's and Mrs. Carter's. Cook, Coppie, Stevens, Lewis, etc., were hanged today. It rained all night. Finished Jimmie's needleworked underskirt today.

Saturday 17. It spit off an on all day. A wet, muddy and disagreeable day. I finished my undersleeves today. Read aloud tonight.

---

[48] McMinn County, Tennessee.

Sunday 18. Pleasant day. We all went to Sunday School. Sister went to preaching at the Cumberland Church. Joe Osment was here to go to church tonight with Rhoda, did not go.

Monday 19. A pleasant day. Rhoda Ann and Sister went to the stores after Rhoda a worsted dress. We received five tickets today, a party out at Mr. Kenner's tonight. A rainy night and evening. Henry Jones was here this morning, brought us tickets to a party at Col. Mills'.

Tuesday 20. Spit snow a little today. Mary Davis and Mag Shadden were here today. Made Jimmie three shirts today.

Wednesday 21. Spit snow today, colder than yesterday. Dick Johnson was here today. Mother got me a worsted dress yesterday. Mr. Bates was here to pay Mr. Carter some money. Grandmother died this day 7 years ago, about 9 o'clock p.m. Made Jimmie a shirt, knit [knitted] on my stockings the rest of the day. Mr. Shaler Smith and Henry Jones called on Rhoda and I .

Thursday 22. Mother is 50 years old today. Colder than yesterday. Rhoda Ann and Sister went up to the store this evening and got Rhoda a sash. I knit [knitted] on my stocking all day. Received an invitation to a party out at Mr. Tucker's this evening. I am not going.

Friday 23. Pleasant day. I went down to see Martha Reynolds this morning, she has a toothache. Rhoda and I went to a party this evening at Col. Mills'. Mother spent the day at Cousin Mary Harle's. Mother had her calf killed today.

Saturday 24. A pleasant day. Mr. Carter came home from Alabama this morning. Sister and Rhoda Ann went and called on Cousin Ellen Jarnagin, Cousin Mary Fulton, Mrs. Caldwell, and spent the day at Aunt Elizabeth's. Rhoda Ann and I received a note from Mr. R. Swan to join the choir, did not go, had no one to go with us. Mr. Carter came home today [from Alabama].

Sunday 25. Pleasant day. Christmas day. Mr. Carter, Sister, Mary E., Annie, Jimmie, and Sues[49] all went up to Mr. Carter's this morning. Rhoda Ann has been sick all day in bed. Mr. and Mrs. Rogers and John were here this morning. I did not go anywhere today.

---

[49] Sues was a slave.

Monday 26. Pleasant day. Lucretia Tibbs took dinner here. Sou and Cherokee Parks were here this evening, also Alice Pickens. She wanted Mary E. and I got to go to a party at their house Wednesday night, cannot go. Sister and Rhoda Ann went out to Mrs. Robert Swan's this evening. Sam Hunt and Cousin John Lea were here this morning after Rhoda to go partridge hunting, did not go. I took dinner over to Cousin Mary Harle's today.

Tuesday 27. Ball at Johnston's Hotel [Ocoee House]. Rained all evening, cleared off in the night. Mr. Carter, Sister, and Annie went up to Mr.Carter's and stayed all night. Sister commenced weaning Jimmie today. This day three years ago, Annie was weaned. Uncle Caswell was here after an umbrella this evening. Sister went down to Cedar Bluff to see Mr. Carter, he is sick.

Wednesday 28. Muddy day. Party at Mr. Parks' tonight, did not go. Cousin Mary Fulton, her little son and Uncle William took supper here. Mr. and Mrs. Cook were here tonight. Anna Gaut was here this evening. I altered my brown worsted dress. Worked on my chemise sleeve the rest of the day.

Thursday 29. Rained hard all day, did not stop two minutes. The darkies have a ball up at Mr. Johnston's old hotel. Emeline[50] went at 8 o'clock. I knitted on my stocking and finished my chemise sleeve.

Friday 30. Muddy day. I was sick today. Received and wrote a letter to Elvira Lea. Sister and Mr. Carter sat till bedtime with Mrs. Traynor. Rhoda went up to Mrs. Jessie Gaut's this evening, stayed all night. If brother Caswell had lived he would have been 22 today.

Saturday 31. Snowed this morning very hard, covered the ground an inch. Sister and Rhoda went up to Mrs. Cook's this evening. We made some candy tonight. I worked on Emeline's collar all day.

---

[50] A slave.

1860

January 1860

Sunday 1. New Year's Day. Colder than it has been this winter. Cousin John Lea took dinner here. We ate twice today. Did not go anywhere. I finished Guilliott's *Biographies* today.

Monday 2. Colder than yesterday. I was sick today in bed. Uncle William was here tonight. Practiced nearly all day.

Tuesday 3. Like yesterday. Took a music lesson today. Knitted and hemmed Sister's chemise[1] today.

Wednesday 4. Warmer than yesterday. Received a ticket to a party tomorrow evening at Mr. Cam Johnston's, also one at Col. Lea's Friday night. Sister and Mother were at Mr. Carter's, also around shopping. Mr. Leon was here this evening to settle his wood account. Mrs. Jane Hall's oldest child is 3 years old today.

Thursday 5. Colder than yesterday. Uncle William Lea took dinner here today. Rhoda has been sick all day, and yesterday also. Received and answered a letter to Sid Bell. Finished my stocking and commenced another. One year ago Hugh Hardwick was married to Miss Dean.

Friday 6. Pleasant day. Mr. Lauderdale and Dr. Carson called in to see if we would attend the party at Col. Lea's; cannot go. Been knitting on my stocking all day. Uncle William was here this evening.

Saturday 7. Pleasant, but muddy, and rained all night last night. Mr. John Sharp and Uncle William took dinner and supper here. Tucked[2] two petticoats for Annie, knitted the rest of the day. Mrs. Hoyl has twins, one dead.

---

[1]A chemise was a loose shirt like undergarment for ladies (*AHD*).
[2]To tuck, one makes small folds and stitches them down (*AHD*).

Sunday 8. Pleasant but very muddy, and disagreeable. Cousin John Lea took dinner here. Uncle William was here this evening. Read all day. Did not go anywhere today. Mrs. Davis, Mrs. Cook, and Rhoda and I went over to the graveyard this evening.

Monday 9. Beautiful day. Mr. and Mrs. [G.W.] Cook sat until bedtime. Mag and Mrs. Shadden stayed all night here. We had a candy stew. John Campbell came down after us to go to a ball at the Ocoee [hotel], did not go. Rev. McCallie was here, also Uncle William. Miss Coulter and Miss McMahan spent the day here. I went up to Mr. [George W.] Middlecoff's and Mr. Cooks' after some paper cambric[3]. Rhoda and I went over to Mrs. Hardwick's.

Tuesday 10. Beautiful day. Rhoda and I went over to Mrs. Hardwick's, also up at Mr. [C.J.] Shields' and over to the depot to see Mr. [Henry von] Aldehoff's family go to Chattanooga. Sister and Rhoda went up to Mrs. Cook's. Rhoda went over to see Virginia Harris; was not at home. Uncle William fixed our bed today. Sister went over to Cousin Mary Harle's this evening. Aunt Fannie Lea was here, spent the day.

Wednesday 11. A cloudy day. Adelia Thompson [later Craigmiles] spent the day here. Rhoda stayed all night there. They went over to the depot to see Sue Rowan off. I went up to the stores after some velvet to trim my dress. Cousin James Carson took dinner. Mr. Carter came from Campbell Station [Knoxville] today. Jimmie is 2 years old today.

Thursday 12. Rained all last night. Cousin James and Uncle William were here today. Mr. Carter went up the road; be back tomorrow. Been sewing on my dress all day.

Friday 13. Rainy day. Seven years ago Sister was married. Been practicing today. Uncle William took dinner, supper, and stayed all night. Rhoda and I went up to Mr. Tom Campbell's to the choir, did not meet.

Saturday 14. Rained some today. Uncle William took dinner here. Made me a pair of undersleeves. Jimmie and Annie are both sick, sent for Dr. [Gideon B.] Thompson. Mr. Carter went off today. Martha Reynolds and Callie McConnell were here.

---

[3]A Cambric is a finely woven white linen or cotton fabric that is paper thin and flimsy (*AHD*).

Sunday 15. A beautiful day, but muddy. Mrs. Shadden stayed all day with us. The children are better. Old Mr. [Paschal] Carter was here today. Mary E. [short for Mary Elizabeth] and I went to Sunday School.

Monday 16. A beautiful day. Sister took Jimmie and went up to Mrs. Cook's. Mother and Mary E. and Annie went out to Uncle Caswell's this evening. Mr. Carter went to Benton today. Cousin John sat until bedtime with us. The frogs hollered tonight.

Tuesday 17. Snowed, rained, sleeted and wind blew last night. A beautiful day. Mr. Carter came home this evening. Rhoda Ann stayed all night with Mag Shadden tonight. Fixed my scrapbook today.

Wednesday 18. Beautiful day. Mother went to Mrs. Berry's and Mrs. Bates' to see Mrs. Hoyl. Sister and Mother went to Mrs. Traynor's. Kate has a boy. Sister and Rhoda went up to Mrs. Cook's and sat until bedtime.

Thursday 19. A beautiful day. Annie went over to Mrs. Traynor's. Mary took Jimmie up to Mrs. Cooks'. Virginia Harris stayed here tonight. Rhoda was there to see Martha Coulter. Mr. Reynolds was here this evening.

Friday 20. Beautiful day. Uncle William was here today. We went to the choir at Mr. Tom Campbell's tonight. Ramsey Swan was here this evening. Callie Swan stayed all night. Sister spent the day at Mrs. Carter's.

Saturday 21. Beautiful day. Ada Anderson was here this evening. Mother, Annie, Rhoda, and I took a walk this evening. Annie fell off the fence. Sister went to Mrs. Traynor's and Mrs. Hardwick's. Mr. Carter came home today.

Sunday 22. Beautiful day. Mother, Rhoda, and I went to Sunday School. Mother, Sister, Rhoda, and I all went to the Presbyterian Church today. Sister, Rhoda, Mary E. and I all went at night with Uncle William. Mother, Mary E., Annie, Jimmie, Rhoda and I went to the graveyard.

Monday 23. Beautiful day. Mother, Annie, Sister and Mary E. went out to Aunt Elizabeth's and Mrs. Berry's. Concert in town. Received an invitation from R. P. Johnston. Rhoda and I went up to the academy to sing this evening. Mrs. Cook was here this evening.

Tuesday 24. A beautiful day. Old Mrs. Harris, Mrs. Lizzie Harris, Cousin Martha Lea, Mrs. William Craigmiles, Mr. Craigmiles and Mr. Gallagher took dinner here. Mrs. Bell Hardwick and old Mrs. Tucker were here this morning. Mrs. Garrison, Virginia Harris, Mrs. Pickens, Mrs. Nannie Johnston were here this evening. Mr. and Mrs. Cook stayed until bedtime. Mother and Sister went to Baptist prayer meeting.

Wednesday 25. Beautiful day. Mrs. Adda and Caroline Craigmiles were here this morning. Martha Reynolds was here this evening, Mrs. Cook this morning. Rhoda went with John Traynor to a musical soiree [evening party or reception] at Dr. Thompson's this evening. Mother and Sister went out to Mr. Hughes' this evening, sat at Mrs. Cook's until bedtime.

Thursday 26. Beautiful day. Martha, Nep Smith and I went out to Mrs. Tucker's. Frances stayed all night here. Mother and Sister went out calling[4].

Friday 27. Beautiful day. We went to the choir at Mr. Pleasant Craigmiles'. Mrs. Shadden and Mag stayed all night here. Mrs. Campbell and Cousin Ellen Jarnagin (McCallie) were here this evening. Cousin Mary Fulton was here yesterday evening.

Saturday 28. Beautiful day. A rehearsal at the academy [school] this morning, we went. Mother and Sister went to Mr. Cook's, Lizzie Wood's and Mrs. Bates'. Mary E. went to see Bell Campbell this evening. Cousin Mary Fulton was here this evening. Sallie McCroskey also. Mr. Carter came home today. Uncle Caswell took dinner here, Uncle William was here this morning.

Sunday 29. Beautiful day. Mr. Carter, Sister and Rhoda went to church at the Methodist [church]. We all went to Sunday School. Cousin John was here this evening, Uncle William also.

Monday 30. Sister, Mother, Annie, Mr. Carter and Jimmie spent the day at [old] Mr. Carter's. Mary E. and the rest to tea at Mrs. Onie Campbell's. Cousin John was here tonight. Rhoda's 17th birthday. Mrs. Grant, Bell and Mary Edwards were here this morning.

Tuesday 31. Rainy day. Stephney's [slave] 6th birthday.

---

[4]A call is a short social visit (*AHD*).

February 1860

Wednesday 1. Cold day. Uncle Caswell Lea here today. Sister went over to Cousin Mary's. Nannie Browder was married tonight.

Thursday 2. Beautiful day. Sister and Mr. Carter went to Charleston, (S.C.). Cousin Mary Fulton, Aunt Fannie, Cousin Martha, Sissy and Alice Pickens took dinner here. Uncle Caswell, Cousin John, Martha, Rhoda and I went up to Col. Campbell's and sat till bedtime. Aunt Elizabeth has a boy.[5]

Friday 3. Cold. Concert tonight. Went down to Mrs. Reynolds' this evening.

Saturday 4. Pleasant day. Mother and Rhoda went out to Uncle Caswell's, Rhoda also at Mr. James Craigmiles'. Cousin John and Mary Fulton stayed all night here, spent Sunday here. Cousin Mary is going home Monday. I went to Mrs. Shield's and Carrie Bell's.

Sunday 5. Rained all last night. I was sick part of today. Did not go any place.

Monday 6. Pleasant day. Rhoda and I washed today. Mrs. Jarrett and Ida came here today. Ida stayed all night. Rhoda and Ida went up to the stores this evening. She and Mother went to Mrs. Berry's.

Tuesday 7. A very windy [day]. Carrie Bell and I went out collecting, got $1.50. Ironed this evening. Callie Swan was here this evening, also Uncle Caswell. Sprinkled a little this evening. Party at Sam Brown's. Rhoda had an invitation from John Gaut, did not go.

Wednesday 8. Beautiful day. Pieced on my quilt all day. Mother went up to Mrs. Cook's. Uncle Caswell was here this evening. Messrs. J. Giddings and Shaler Smith called on Rhoda and I.

Thursday 9. Beautiful day. Mother and Rhoda spent the day at Mrs. Cook's. Rhoda went to Mrs. Jessie Gaut's and Dr. and Mrs. John G. Brown's. Received a note from James Harris, Rhoda one from J. Surguine to attend a party at Mrs. S. Y. Brown's tonight; we are not going. Piecing on my quilt today. Mrs. DeLano was at the fence today on importance.

---

5 Caswell M. Lea weighed thirteen pounds; see 14 June 1860 for death.

Friday 10. A beautiful day. Mr. J. T. Middlecoff died this morning at one o'clock with typhoid fever.[6] Lizzie Campbell, Mrs. G. Middlecoff, and Mrs. Guthman all have babies. Went down to Mrs. Reynolds' this evening. Mother and Mary E. went to Mrs. Shadden's, Middlecoff's and Mrs. Cook's. They went out to Uncle Caswell's this evening.

Saturday 11. Tolerable cold. Mr. McClatchey and Ida Jarrett came in today, took dinner here.

Sunday 12. A beautiful day. We all went to Sunday School and church, at night also. Cousin John took supper here. He and Cousin Joe went to church with us. Cousin Joe took dinner here.

Monday 13. Beautiful day. Started school to Mr. [A. E.] Blunt's, [Cleveland Masonic Female Institute.] Mother went up to Mrs. Traynor's, Carter's, Lizzie Wood's, and Cousin Mary [Harle's]. Rhoda Ann went to see Virginia Harris, Ann Waterhouse and Mrs. Shadden.

Tuesday 14. Rainy day, dark night. Rhoda and I received an invitation from Mr. Smith to attend a Valentine drawing, too rainy and muddy. I received two Valentines, Rhoda only one, Mother also one. Went to school as usual.

Wednesday 15. A beautiful day. Mrs. Bates and Mrs. Cook spent the evening here. Went to school. Received a new magazine this morning.

Thursday 16. A beautiful day. Mother, Rhoda and Mary went out to Uncle Caswell's this evening. Received 4 Valentines. Mag Shadden was here this evening.

Friday 17. Beautiful morning, rained this evening and all night. Answered Elvira Lea's letter. Had 119 praise marks today. Sister's 26th birthday.

Saturday 18. Pretty day. Tucked my dress, practiced, copied off *Isabella Polka* and wrote to Sister. Mrs. Cook was here, brought her magazines. Cousin John stayed all night here.

Sunday 19. Beautiful and cool day. We all went to Sunday School. Mother, Mary E. and Rhoda went to the Baptist Church. Cousin John Lea took dinner here, stayed all evening, and went to

---

[6] J. T. Middlecoff, b. 12 April 1824, d. 10 February 1860, interred in Fort Hill Cemetery. Ross, *Cemetery Records*, II:200.

the Methodist Church with Rhoda and Mary. Mother and Mary went down to Mr. McNutt's this evening. Mrs. Sam Brown has a baby. Cousin John stayed all night.

Monday 20. Cold this morning. Went to school. Mother, Rhoda Ann and Mary E. went up to Mrs. Cook's and sat until bedtime.

Tuesday 21. Rained all evening. Mother went to Mrs. Berry's and Uncle Caswell's today. Went to school.

Wednesday 22. Pleasant day. I went to school.

Thursday 23. Beautiful day. Adelia Thompson took supper here. Sou Coulter called on Rhoda today.

Friday 24. Beautiful day. Rhoda and Adelia Thompson went out calling. The choir met at Mr. Tom Campbell's. Jim and Virginia Harris went with us. Uncle William took supper here.

Saturday 25. Beautiful day. Mother went out to Uncle Caswell's and Mrs. Shadden's. Rhoda went over to Cousin Mary Harle's.

Sunday 26. Beautiful day. Rhoda and I went to the Presbyterian Church in the morning, we all went at night. Cousin John Lea came home with us. We all went to Sunday School.

Monday 27. Beautiful day. Rhoda got Aunt Adeline a calico dress, and went up to Mrs. Shadden's. Mr. and Mrs. Cook, and Davis were here tonight.

Tuesday 28. Beautiful but windy day. Mrs. Garrison was here today. Mother went up to the store to get Susan [slave] a dress.

Wednesday 29. A rainy day. Mrs. Shadden stayed all night here[7].

March 1860

Thursday 1. Mother and Rhoda went up to Mrs. Cook's tonight. Mr. Jack Henderson's black girl was buried today.

Friday 2. Beautiful day. Mary Davis and Cousin John Lea were here, Mary stayed all night here. Rhoda went with Virginia [Harris], Jim Harris, Messrs. Hardwick, Mills and Tom Hoyl were at the academy.

---

[7]The year 1860 was a leap year.

Saturday 3. Rained a little tonight. Mary Smith was here this evening. Cousin John stayed here all night. Took up sister's carpet this morning. Mother went to Aunt Elizabeth's as did Mary E.

Sunday 4. Beautiful day. Mother and I went to Sunday School. Mother went to church at the Baptist [church] today. Rhoda and John Lea to the Methodist Church tonight.

Monday 5. Beautiful day. Nothing occurred. Rhoda and I went over to Mrs. Hardwick's after tea.

Tuesday 6. Pretty day. Mother put down her bacon in ashes[8] today.

Wednesday 7. Beautiful day. Mrs. Wheeler and Mrs. Cook were here this evening. We went to Mrs. Cook's to see three dwarfs.

Thursday 8. Beautiful day. Rained and blew very hard this evening. Nearly all got very wet coming from school.

Friday 9. Beautiful day. Choir met here tonight, a night long to be remembered. No school today. Mr. Blunt had the academy repaired.

Saturday 10. A very pleasant but windy day. Sister, Rhoda and I went to see Lavena Seavey. Cousin John stayed all night here.

Sunday 11. A beautiful day. Cousins John and Joe Lea took supper here. Cousin John stayed all night. Sister, Rhoda, and I went to the Presbyterian Church at night and morning. Mr. Bradshaw preached. All went to Sunday School. Lavena Seavey came by after us.

Monday 12. Windy. Bettie Jarrett's 18th birthday.

Tuesday 13. Tolerable windy day. My 15th birthday. Received a letter and bandbox from Sister by Mrs. McNutt. Mrs. Tresse Roberts was here this morning. Rhoda and I went up to Mr. [James E.] Surguine's store to inquire about Sallie Weir. Mary Smith stayed all night with me tonight.

Wednesday 14. Beautiful but windy day. Uncle Pryor Lea's 42nd birthday. Mr. Tom Campbell and Mrs. Pleasant Craigmiles were here today. Mother was gone from home. She got me two aprons today. Mother, Rhoda and Sister went down to Mrs. McNutt's tonight. Mother went up to see Mrs. Dr. Brown today. Mrs. Hunt,

---

[8]Meat was preserved or cured in a variety of ways, this is one example.

Mrs. Thompson, Mrs. Roberts, Adelia Thompson and Rhoda went to spend the day at Mrs. Swan's today.

Thursday 15. Beautiful day. Naomi Henry's 15th birthday. Mrs. Cook and Davie Jones took supper here. Mrs. Garrison and Lavena Seavey were here this evening.

Friday 16. Rained a little tonight. Could not go to the choir tonight. Davie Jones came after us. Mother and Sister Rhoda spent the day at Mrs. Cook's. Mrs. Cook gave me a knife. Read my composition today on "Twilight."

Saturday 17. Beautiful day. Mrs. P_____ and Saphira were here this evening. Sewed on my calico apron all day. Mrs. Frank Hardwick, Cynthia and Mary were here tonight. Rhoda went to see Adelia Thompson, also at Tresse Roberts' this morning.

Sunday 18. A beautiful day. Mary Smith, Mary E. and I took a walk out to Mrs. Caldwell's this evening. Mother, Mrs. Cook and Rhoda went up to graveyard, came by Mrs. McNutt's. We went to Sunday School.

Monday 19. Rainy day. Nothing of importance occurred today.

Tuesday 20. Beautiful but windy day. Lavena Seavey came over this evening; we took a walk. Rhoda went up to Dr. Thompson's and stayed all night. Mary Smith came over this evening. Mother and Mary E. went to the Baptist prayer meeting.

Wednesday 21. A beautiful day. All of the botany class went botanying this evening over by Dr. [G.W.] Ford's. Lavena Seavey and Sallie Shields were here this evening.

Thursday 22. Beautiful day. Adelia Thompson stayed here tonight. Wrote to Mary Sevier this evening.

Friday 23. Rained this evening. Did not go to the choir, too muddy.

Saturday 24. Beautiful day. Cousin Ellen Jarnagin took tea here. We went up to Col. Campbell's and then went to the choir. Adelia Thompson came down here this evening and she and Rhoda went around calling. Sewed on my apron all day. Mrs. Shadden was here this evening.

Sunday 25. Mary E., Rhoda and I all went to the Presbyterian Church and Sabbath School. Cousin Martha and John Lea came home with us from Sunday School and then went to church. Cousin

John stayed all night here last night and tonight. Rhoda and I went to church this evening.

Monday 26. Cold and windy day. Rhoda and Mary E. are sick, she [Mary E.] has chills.

Tuesday 27. Cold as yesterday. Sallie Weir and Mr. (James E.) Surguine were married this evening at 2 o'clock. (Sallie and James Surguine were parents of several children, one of whom was Marie. She later married August Jarnagin Carter.) Adelia Thompson and Mag Shadden were here this evening.

Wednesday 28. A very pretty day. Mother and Rhoda spent the day at Mrs. Garrison's. Rhoda took tea. Cousin John was here tonight. Mrs. Alexander and Mrs. McMillin were [here] this evening.

Thursday 29. A pretty day. Mother spent the day out at Uncle Caswell's.

Friday 30. Like yesterday. Did not go to the choir; there was not any. Mr. and Mrs. Cook and Davie Jones sat until bedtime with us. Lavena was over this evening. We had a serenade from the string band tonight. We had some company at the institute this evening -- Messrs. Parks, Davis, Ellison, L. Hardwick, Traynor, Reeder and Jim Johnston. Mrs. Thompson and Tresse Roberts were here this evening.

Saturday 31. Very windy. Rhoda went up to Dr. Thompson's this evening. Miss Coulter and Miss McMahan, Alice Brown and Carrie Bell were here today. Made my underskirt longer.

April 1860

Sunday 1. Very windy, rained very hard, thundered and lightened. Tolerable cold this evening. We did not go anywhere today. Mary E. went to Sunday School. John Lea took tea here.

Friday 6. The choir met tonight at Dr. Thompson's. Dr. Carson went with Rhoda Ann.

Sunday 8. Beautiful day. Went to church tonight and today. Cousin John Lea stayed all night here tonight and last night.

Friday 13. Beautiful day. Mrs. McNutt here this evening. Quilted awhile on Rhoda's quilt. Rhoda and Adelia Thompson after flowers this evening; did not get any. Nat and John sent them. Dick Johnson's and Joe's party is to be given tonight at the hotel. John Gaut, Rhoda's escort.

Saturday 14. Beautiful day. Martha Reynolds, Ada Anderson, Lavena Seavey and Kate Britton were here this evening. Mother and Mary E. went out to Uncle Caswell's this evening. We went to the choir tonight at Mr. Craigmiles. Rhoda, Adelia and Mrs. Thompson, John Craigmiles, Nat Carson, Augusta and Ellen Jarnagin went after flowers today.

Sunday 15. Beautiful day. Went down to the graveyard this evening. I went down to Ada Anderson's and S. Hoyl's. Ada and I went over to the graveyard. Cousin John stayed here tonight and last night. Rhoda, Lavena and I all went to church today and tonight. Turn one leaf and you will see the next.

[Entries missing for 16, 17, 18, 19]

Friday 20. Pretty day. Went to the choir tonight.

Saturday 21. Beautiful day. Lavena here this evening. Mr. Tom Campbell and Mrs. Pleasant Craigmiles came here this evening and asked us if we would perform at the concert [in] about two weeks hence; we are going to. Been making me a dark calico dress all day. Finished it.

Sunday 22. Pretty day. Did not go to church at all today. Cousin John here this evening. Rhoda over at Mrs. Garrison's.

Monday 23. Beautiful day. We went to the rehearsal. Lavena Seavey was here. Mother put Sister's quilt up Saturday.

Tuesday 24. We went to the rehearsal tonight. We felt the shock of an earthquake about twilight. Pretty day.

Wednesday 25. We went to the rehearsal tonight.

Thursday 26. Pretty day, cold enough to have fire. We went to the rehearsal tonight.

Friday 27. A pretty day. Rhoda and I went to the Presbyterian Church tonight. Cousin John and Lavena Seavey went with us, Davie Jones also.

Saturday 28. Beautiful day. Mother and Mary E. went [to the] Presbyterian Church. Mother went to Uncle Caswell's, it rained and had to stay all night, Mary and Cousin John came in and stayed with us.

Sunday 29. Beautiful day. Tonight Rhoda and Mary E. went to the Presbyterian Church. Beautiful moonlight night. Went to church tonight with Jim Campbell. Lavena Seavey over here this evening. Mr. and Mrs. Cook, Mrs. McNutt, Mother and Mary Elizabeth took a walk this evening out to Mr. Caldwell's.

Monday 30. No rehearsal tonight on account of the meeting.

May 1860

Tuesday 1. A beautiful day. No school today. We has a picnic out at Candy's Creek. Mr. Carson came home with me. I never enjoyed myself as well in my life. We came home that evening and went to rehearsal. Dr. Carson came home that night with Rhoda. Maria Kirk here this morning.

Wednesday 2. Beautiful day. Went to the choir tonight. Adelia and Ann did not go. They were both sick.

Thursday 3. Beautiful day. We have concluded to meet in the evening. Adelia Thompson and Anna Gaut were not there.

Friday 4. Beautiful day. We met this evening also. Adelia and Anna were there.

Saturday 5. Beautiful day. Sister and Mr. Carter came home this evening. We went to the rehearsal tonight. Dr. Carson came home with Rhoda. Mrs. and Mag Shadden, Kate and Mr. Rogers were here this evening. Wesley, Uncle Caswell's black man, died today with disease of the heart.

Sunday 6. Beautiful day. Old Mr. and Mrs. Carter were here this evening. Did not go anywhere today.

Monday 7. Beautiful day. We went to the rehearsal tonight. Cousin John Lea was here awhile tonight. John Traynor came after me, Dr. Carson after Rhoda.

Tuesday 8. Beautiful day. We went to our concert tonight at the Presbyterian Church. Mr. Hunt with Rhoda, Mr. Traynor with me. Uncle William Lea is here sick.

Wednesday 9. Rained all this morning, damp and cold this evening. I did not go to school today. Felt too bad. Rhoda stayed all night with Lavena Seavey.

Thursday 10. Hailed a little this evening. Went to school.

Friday 11. Cloudy day. The choir met here tonight, only 9 of us. Dr. and Mrs. Thompson came down and stayed until it was over.

Saturday 12. Rained all day. Sewed on my dress all day. Nothing of importance occurred today. Lavena stayed all night here.

Sunday 13. Beautiful day. Sister, Mr. Carter, Rhoda and I went to the Presbyterian Church. Rhoda, Mother and Mary E. went to the Baptist [church]. Mother, Mary E., Mr. Carter, Sister, and Annie took a walk out to Mr. Caldwell's. Rhoda, Cousin John Lea and Sister went to the Presbyterian Church tonight. I ate a piece of pickle and it made me sick, (could not go). Went to Sunday School as usual. Mr. Carter went up to Madisonville, Tenn. this evening.

Monday 14. Nothing of importance.

Tuesday 15. A tolerable hard storm occurred this morning. Dr. Carson, Mr. Giddings called on us tonight.

Wednesday 16. Beautiful day. A hard storm tonight. Mother and Sister went up to Mrs. Traynor's, had to come back.

Thursday 17. Rhoda has been sick all day. I was sick tonight. Mrs. Rogers came down and stayed awhile tonight. They found a man dead out by Mr. Tucker's this evening. Mr. Freedman is his name.

Friday 18. Pretty day. Rhoda and I are both sick, cannot go to the choir. Lavena Seavey over here this evening, also Jim Harris.

Saturday 19. Pleasant day. Ada Anderson and I went out calling this evening. Aunt Fannie took dinner here, Cousin John also. Mrs. Carter was here today. Mother, Sister, and Mrs. Carter went out to Uncle Caswell's.

Sunday 20. Beautiful. Mrs. Garrison's family and ours went up to the graveyard this evening. We went to Sunday School. All went to church except Mother and I; we were sick. Dr. Carson, Fred Montgomery and Henry Jones called on us; I did not go in.

Monday 21. Pretty day. Old Mr. Jake Brown died yesterday, the Masons buried him today. We had a serenade [musical performance given by sweetheart] tonight.

Tuesday 22. Mother is very sick, sent for Dr. Brown. Cousins Martha and John Lea took supper here.

Wednesday 23. Pretty day. Mother is better. Mrs. Cook, Mrs. Campbell and Cousin Ellen Jarnagin were here this evening.

Thursday 24. A storm this morning. We had the cats killed today. The blinds put up also. Martha Coulter and Ada Anderson were here this evening. Uncle Caswell has taken tea here 3 evenings.

Friday 25. Rainy day. I am sick, did not go to school. Sister, Annie, Mr. Carter went down to Mrs. Bradford's, be back tomorrow. Mother is improving. Dr. Carson took Lavena, Rhoda and I up to the choir up to Mr. Campbell's.

Saturday 26. Rained this morning. Lavena Seavey, Rhoda and I went up to Mouse Creek, Bradley County, Tennessee, today to a celebration with Fred Montgomery. Came back Sunday.

Sunday 27. Beautiful day. Slept all this morning. We all stayed at home today. Joe Lea took tea here.

Monday 28. Beautiful day. Mrs. Gambol and John came today, will go off tomorrow. Eliza Keebler came in today.

Tuesday 29. Beautiful day. Mrs. Thompson and Adelia spent the day here. Mrs. Pleasant Craigmiles and Mrs. Tom Campbell called on Mrs. Gambol today. Mrs. Gambol took tea at Mrs. Pleasant Craigmiles'.

Wednesday 30. Nothing of importance occurred today.

Thursday 31. Beautiful day. Eliza Keebler went home today.

June 1860

Friday 1. Pretty day. Lavena Seavey, Rhoda Johnson, Jo Johnson, Cleo Watkins and Mrs. Guthman have all been here. Mrs. R. P. Johnson, John Johnson, Florence Woods, Mrs. Daily, Lavena Seavey, Rhoda, Sue Parker, Lucius Osment, Sam Hunt, Capt. Grant, Walker McSpadden, George Swan and Green Craigmiles were up to the academy today.

Saturday 2. Beautiful day. The celebration today, we did not go. Rhoda took a fondue on cherries yesterday evening. Mrs. Cook, Mrs. Middlecoff, Lou Parker[9] and Mag Shadden here this evening.

Sunday 3. Rained this evening. Not one of us went to church or Sunday School today, it looked so much like rain. Sister, Mother, Mr. Carter and the children took a walk over to the field after the rain.

[Entries missing for 4, 5, 6, 7, 8, 9].

Sunday 10. Pretty day. We all went to church today.

[Entries missing for 11,12,13].

Thursday 14. Rained all morning. Aunt Elizabeth's baby died last night at 12:30 o'clock; buried at 4 o'clock this evening. I have been out there all day.[10]

Friday 15. Pretty day. Went to school.

Saturday 16. Pretty day. Lavena, Rhoda and I went out to Mrs. Peters' this evening and got some June apples. Mary Mee and Mag Shadden were here this evening. Mr. and Mrs. Cook here tonight.

Sunday 17. Pretty day. We all went to Sunday School. Lizzie (a new name for Mary E.), Rhoda and I went to the Presbyterian Church. Mr. Bradshaw preached. Had a serenade tonight from the harpist. Jimmie took sick.

[Entries missing for 18 through the remainder of June]

July 1860

Sunday 1. Pretty day. Went to Sunday School.

Monday 2. Pretty day. First day of Mr. Blunt's examination.

Tuesday 3. Pretty day. Exhibition last night. Concert tonight. Did not go. Stayed all night with Lavena. Cousin Ellen Jarnagin took supper here. Dr. Carson went with her to the concert, Fred Montgomery went with Rhoda.

---

9 Cleo's Aunt.

10Lea, Caswell M., son of Caswell and Elizabeth Lea, b. 3 February 1860; d. 14 June 1860, buried at Fort Hill Cemetery (Ross, *Cemetery Records,* II:184).

Wednesday 4. Pretty day. A Fourth of July celebration. I went to a party at Mr. Tom Campbell's tonight with Dr. Carson. Rhoda and Lavena Seavey stayed all night to Uncle Caswell's. A party at old Mrs. Hardwick's and one at the hotel. Mrs. Bradford and Rebecca Wise spent the day here.

Thursday 5. Pretty day. Practiced awhile. Rhoda stayed all night with Lavena.

Friday 6. Pretty day. Lavena, Rhoda and I stayed all night with Mrs. Cook.

Saturday 7. Pretty day. We stayed again tonight with Mrs. Cook. Sister ground coffee to take up to the springs[11], all day. Went over to Mrs. Garrison's a little while this evening. Dr. Carson and Adelia Thompson were here tonight.

Sunday 8. A tolerable cool day. Went to the Presbyterian Church this morning. Dr. Carson and Fred Montgomery called on us this evening. Dr. Carson and Rhoda went to the Methodist Church tonight. I stayed with Mrs. Cook tonight.

Monday 9. Pretty day. Sister and Mr. Carter went to Laddville.[12] to see about getting a camp. Mrs. Traynor, Kate Rogers, Mag and Mrs. Shadden and Uncle Caswell were here tonight.

Tuesday 10. Pretty day. Sister ironed all day. Lavena here this evening.

Wednesday 11. Pretty day. We went to Ladd's Springs [at Laddville] today.

Thursday 12. Cleaned up some today.

Friday 13. Sewed a little. Been sick a little.

Saturday 14. Sick again today.

Sunday 15. A large crowd today. Very lonesome.

Monday 16. Nothing of importance occurred today.

[Entries missing for 17, 18, 19]

Friday 20. Rhoda came today. Mr. Carter went down for her yesterday.

Saturday 21. Martha Shields, later Howell, was here today.

---

[11]East Tennessee had a number of mineral springs which were used for medicinal and recreational activities; they were popularly called watering places.

[12]Laddville, which had a number of springs, was located fifteen miles southeast of Cleveland in Polk County; it was a popular local watering place.

Sunday 22. Cass Shields here today.

[Entries missing for 23, 24, 25]

Thursday 26. Pretty day. Lavena Seavey and Cousin John came up today.

Friday 27. Pretty day. Cousin John, Mel Osment, Walker McSpadden, Lavena Seavey, Mary Davis, Rhoda and myself took a canoe ride this morning.

Saturday 28. Pretty day. They all went deer driving.[13]

Sunday 29. Cousin John Lea, Sam Hunt, Mel Osment, Lavena, Rhoda and myself went down to Mr. Cass to get some peaches.

Monday 30. Nothing occurred to disturb the quiet of this little watering place called Laddville. John Lea, Sister and Mr. Carter went to Cleveland this morning.

Tuesday 31. Pretty day. Aunt Elizabeth's folks came today. Sister also.

August 1860

Wednesday 1. Pretty day. Cousin John, Lavena and myself went down and sat on Mailad Island this morning. We went down and took a canoe ride, I poled it by myself. Mr. Perry Gaut, John and Anna Gaut and Rhoda took a canoe ride before us. Anna Gaut, Rhoda, John Lea, Sam Hunt, Mel Osment and myself went down to Mr. Mantooth's to get some apples.

Thursday 2. Pretty day. All went deer driving.

Friday 3. Pretty day. Nothing of importance occurred.

Saturday 4. Pretty day. Cousin John and Lavena went to Cleveland this morning.

Sunday 5. Pretty day. Very lonesome. Read newspapers all day.

Monday 6. Nothing of importance occurred today.

Tuesday 7. Nothing of importance. John Traynor and Jim Johnston came today.

---

[13]In deer driving a person was sent into the woods to frighten the deer out of their habitat, so they could be observed. This was also done with partridge.

Wednesday 8. A very hard storm this evening. George went home this evening. Dr. Long's folks went also. Will Seavey's 19th birthday.

Thursday 9. Sam Hunt and Jim Johnston went home this evening. All went deer driving. A pleasant day.

Friday 10. An awful gloomy day, rained all day hard. Mel Osment and Anna Gaut went home this evening. Mary and Lillie Davis went this morning. I am very lonesome; want to go home.

Saturday 11. A cloudy, dull day. Mary and Helen Pharis, Mr. Callaway and Joe Robinson spent the day here. Went deer driving, caught a deer for the first time.

Sunday 12. A very rainy and very dark and gloomy day. Read all day.

Monday 13. We all went to the springs to see the creek. The river is up so they cannot pass with a buggy. Mr. Hunt's and Mr. Davis' families left today.

Tuesday 14. Pretty but cool day. Mr. Earnest's family left today. John Traynor also. Mrs. Lizzie Grant and a Dr. Maury were married this evening.

Wednesday 15. Pretty day. Mrs. Craigmiles, Mrs. McSpadden and our family left the springs today. Mrs. Cook and Lavena were here this evening. Nancy Cradock was married to Dr. Thompson this evening.

Thursday 16. Pretty day. We went out to Uncle Caswell's this evening. Sam Hunt and Mel Osment were there. We stayed until 10 o'clock at night.

Friday 17. Pretty day. Lavena Seavey and Sam Hunt, Mel Osment and took a ride this evening, went way out to Mrs. Traynor's big spring.

Saturday 18. Pretty day. Lavena Seavey went to Atlanta today. I went over to Mrs. Hardwick's this evening, over to Mrs. Garrison's this morning. Rhoda and Sister up to Mrs. Cook's this evening. Mother spent the day at Uncle Caswell's then came home from the spring. This evening, Frank Tucker took tea here. Dr. Carson called on us this evening. Had a serenade last night. Lavena stayed with us. Old Mrs. Garrison and Mrs. Seavey over here this morning. Lavena and Rhoda went up to the gallery to have her likeness taken for Rhoda.

Sunday 19. Pretty day. All went to Sunday School; all but myself to church. Mother went out to Uncle Caswell's this morning. Georgie Lea is sick. Mr. and Mrs. Earnest took dinner here. Went to church tonight. Sam Hunt came home with me; Cousin John with Rhoda.

Monday 20. Pretty day. I washed today. Mel Osment to Lebanon, [Tenn.] this evening. Mr. Carter started to Charleston, S.C. this evening.

Tuesday 21. Beautiful day. Sam Hunt and Cousin John Lea took dinner here today. Sam started to Emory and Henry College [Virginia] today. I wrote to Elvira Lea and Maria Kirk, did not send them. Sister and myself called on Cousin Ellen Jarnagin, Mrs. Swartz and Sallie McMillin.

Wednesday 22. Like yesterday. Went over to Mrs. Garrison's this evening. Sister and Cousin John Lea went out to the farm and got some peaches today. Mrs. Shadden stayed all night here. A balloon ascended tonight.

Thursday 23. Rained this evening. Cut peaches to dry. Cut out my dress today.

Friday 24. Beautiful day. Dr. Carson came home with Rhoda from the choir, Davie Jones with me, from Mr. Pleasant Craigmiles'.

Saturday 25. Beautiful day. Made me two collars this evening. Gov. Isham G. Harris spoke here today. Sent up a balloon with John Bell's name on it, also one with Breckinridge and Lane. Rhoda went up to Mr. Thompson's, Mother to Mrs. Garrison's and the Baptist Church to clean it out. Mrs. Cook here this eve.

Sunday 26. Beautiful day. Sister, Mother, Annie and Lizzie went to the Baptist Church, Rhoda and myself to the Presbyterian. We went to Sunday School this morning. They organized a Sunday School at the Baptist Church this morning. Mother, Sister and Mary E. went to the Baptist at night. Cousin John took tea here tonight. Rhoda and I went to the Presbyterian Church.

Monday 27. Pretty day. I helped wash today. This evening, Rhoda went up to Dr. G. Garrison's. Sister to see Nancy Johnson. Mother went down to Mr. McNutt's and over to Mrs. Garrison's.

Tuesday 28. Pretty day. Rhoda stayed all night with Adelia Thompson. Mrs. Garrison senior and Mrs. Garrison junior were here this evening. All of them went to hear Mr. Graves preach, he did not come. Mr. Snead preached. Mrs. McGriff, her two daughters,

Cousin Mournin Moore, Cousin Merill Witt and Mr. Miller took dinner here. Rhoda went over to see Sallie Surguine and Virginia Harris this evening. Mother and Sister went to prayer meeting tonight.

Wednesday 29. Nothing occurred as usual. Rhoda stayed with Anna Gaut.

Thursday 30. Pleasant day. Went over to Mrs. Garrison's this evening. Finished my dress today.

Friday 31. Pretty day. We went to the choir at Mr. Tom Campbell's tonight. Dr. Carson and Davie Jones came in and stayed awhile. Mrs. Garrison senior and Mrs. Garrison junior were here this evening.

September 1860

Saturday 1. Pretty day. Mended my clothes today.

Sunday 2. Went to Sunday School, did not go to church, none in town. Camp Meeting at Eldridge's.

Monday 3. Pretty day. First day of school. Went up in town after my books today. Mary E. and myself started.

Tuesday 4. Pretty day. Went to school. Lillie Davis and I went out to Uncle Caswell's.

Wednesday 5. Like yesterday. Lillie Davis stayed with me tonight.

Thursday 6. Like yesterday. Nothing occurred today. This evening Mrs. Garrison and Mrs. Hughes were here.

Friday 7. Pretty day. The choir met here today. The house is full.

Saturday 8. Pretty day. Old Mrs. Garrison went home today.

Sunday 9. Pretty day. Sister, Mother, Annie, Mary E., and Jimmie went to the Baptist Church. We went to Sunday School as usual. Rhoda and I went to the Presbyterian Church. Joe Lea here.

Monday 10. Like yesterday. Went to school.

Tuesday 11. Like yesterday.

Wednesday 12. Like yesterday. Went to school. Rhoda went with John Traynor to see the rehearsal. Mrs. Garrison over here tonight.

Thursday 13. Like yesterday. Went to school. Sister went over to Mary's this evening. Mrs. Cook here this evening. Lucretia Tibbs stayed here tonight.

Friday 14. Pretty day. Aunt Fannie Lea (Cousin Mary's mother) and Aunt Polly Lea took dinner here. Mrs. Shadden, Mrs. Cook and Aunt Elizabeth Lea here this evening. Mr. Carter sent for Sister to come down to Charleston, S.C. this evening. She and Uncle Caswell started this evening. Mrs. Hughes invited us to go out and eat some watermelons this evening; did not go. I went over to Mrs. Garrison's this evening. Mr. and Mrs. Cook sat till bedtime tonight.

Saturday 15. Pretty day. Virginia Harris and Cynthia Hardwick here this evening. I went with Mrs. Garrison up to the stores and over to the mill[14] this evening. Had the headache all day. Aunt Polly stayed all night here. Mrs. Cook sat till bedtime.

Sunday 16. Cloudy this morning, rained all evening, gloomy day. Did not go to Sunday School. Mother and Mary went to the Methodist; Rhoda, Annie and myself to the Presbyterian Church; did not go at night. Cousin Joe took supper and stayed all night.

Monday 17. A wet, disagreeable day. Went to school as usual. Cousin James Carson stayed all night here. Mrs. Cook sat until bedtime with us.

Tuesday 18. Pretty day. Rhoda went to rehearsal with Dr. Carson at Dr. Thompson's. Mrs. Rogers, Henry Davis and Ramsey Swan here about Mr. Carter. Mr. Bradford took supper here.

Wednesday 19. Pretty day. Uncle Caswell came home from Charleston, S.C. this evening. I went over to Mrs. Garrison's this evening. Mrs. Dodson took tea here. Mr. Rogers, Jonas Hoyl and Charlie Tibbs were here. Rhoda went over to Mrs. Garrison's today, also up to Judge Gaut's.

Thursday 20. Tolerable cool tonight, for the first time. Rhoda went over to Mrs. Gaut's and up to Mrs. Garrison's. Adelia Thompson was here this evening. Aunt Polly Lea stayed all night here this evening. Went to school as usual.

Friday 21. Pretty day. Mrs. Daily and Eliza Wood were at the academy this evening. Rhoda went to the rehearsal with Dr. Carson

---

[14]A mill was powered by water and was used to grind corn (meal) and wheat (flour) (*AHD*).

this evening. I stayed with Mrs. Garrison this evening until Mr. Garrison went to the lodge. Rhoda commenced her concert dress today.

Saturday 22. Pretty day. Went up to Mrs. Neilen's and the stores after some black ribbon. Been over to Mrs. Garrison's all day sewing on Rhoda's dress. Over there tonight. Aunt Polly stayed all night here. Mag and her cousin Billy Shadden were here tonight. Rhoda went up to the academy and rehearsed pieces tonight.

Sunday 23. Pretty day. None of us went to church today. This day three years ago, Brother Houston died. Mary E. and myself commenced going to Sabbath School this morning at the Baptist Church. I got a little tipsy [unsteady] this evening. Dr. Carson called on Rhoda and I tonight.

Monday 24. Pretty day. Mrs. Garrison's 27th birthday, her seventh marriage day. I went to school; went over to Mrs. Garrison's. I fell down in the street this evening. Mag Shadden, Mrs. Shadden and Mrs. Billy Shadden were here tonight.

Tuesday 25. Pretty day. Aunt Polly Lea stayed all night here. Rhoda and I went over to Mrs. Garrison's after supper. Rhoda went up to Mrs. Thompson's this evening.

Wednesday 26. Pretty day. Aunt Polly went home today. Rhoda went up to Mrs. Thompson's this evening. The assistant teacher came this evening, Miss Boyd.

Thursday 27. Pretty day. Rhoda went to the rehearsal tonight.

Friday 28. Pretty day. I went out to Uncle Caswell's this evening, took supper. Cousin John Lea sat until bedtime with us.

Saturday 29. Pretty day. Cousin Mattie Gentry, Sister, and Mr. Carter came this evening. Rhoda went up to the Presbyterian Church this morning and evening. Dr. Carson came for her tonight, she had gone with Sallie McMillin.

Sunday 30. Pretty day. Rhoda and Cousin Mattie Gentry went to church today. I went to Sunday School. We went to the graveyard this evening. Cousin Joe Lea here tonight awhile.

October 1860

[*Monday 1*. Entry missing]

Tuesday 2. Pretty day. Dr. Carson went with Rhoda to the rehearsal.

Wednesday 3. No school the rest of this week. Rained all this morning. Over to Mrs. Garrison's this evening. Went to the concert tonight with Cousin Joe Lea. Dr. Carson went with Rhoda. First day of the fair.¹⁵ Adelia Thompson here twice, once with Augusta Craigmiles and once for Sister to curl her hair.

Thursday 4. Pretty day. Went to the fair this evening, marched. Cousin Mattie Gentry, Sister, Annie and Mr. Carter went also. Sister, Mattie and myself went with Cousin Joe to the tableaux¹⁶ tonight. Dr. Carson went with Rhoda. Adelia here twice, once with her mother and once for Sister to curl her hair. I went to Mr. Stuart's after grapes this eve.

Friday 5. Sprinkled rain a little today. Mrs. Keebler and Eliza here today. Cousin Ellen Jarnagin here this morning. The fair over today. Augusta Craigmiles and Pauline Hereford here this morning. Mr. Howell took tea here last night. Mr. Earnest was here this evening.

Saturday 6. Rained this morning a little. Nothing of importance occurred this evening. Mr. Earnest brought me two very large watermelons today.

Sunday 7. Rained this morning and evening about four hours. Cousin John Lea took dinner here. I went to Sunday School. Sister, Mary E., Rhoda and Cousin Mattie Gentry went to the Methodist Church.

Monday 8. Nothing of importance as usual.

Tuesday 9. A tolerable cold day. I went out to Uncle Caswell Lea's this evening. Rhoda, Sister and Mr. Carter went out and spent the day. Cousin Mattie stayed all night. I commenced reading

---

¹⁵The fair featured inventions and agriculture, they displayed plants and animals in a field south of town.

¹⁶A tableau was an interlude during a scene when all of the actors on stage freeze in position and then resume action as before (*AHD*).

Milton's *Paradise Lost*. Dr. Carson and Fred Montgomery were here tonight, also Mr. Carter's Aunt Jane and her children.

Wednesday 10. A tolerable cool day. Mother and Sister went up in town and got Rhoda and myself a dress. Rhoda and Sister went up in town and to Mr. William Craigmiles' this evening.

Thursday 11. Pretty day. Rhoda went up to the stores. Nothing of importance occurred today.

Friday 12. Pretty day. Drs. Long and Grant were at the academy today. I wrote to Mary Sevier and Cleo Watkins today. The Presbyterian meeting commenced tonight.

Saturday 13. Cold night; frost for the first time. Mary Hardwick was over here this evening. Mother and Sister went up to Mrs. Cook's this evening and out to Aunt Elizabeth Lea's. Rhoda went to see Adelia Thompson this evening.

Sunday 14. Cold day, white frost tonight. Went to Sunday School and church today and night. Cousin John took supper here this evening.

Monday 15. Pleasant day. Went to prayer meeting this morning. I came home from school, was sick.

Tuesday 16. Pleasant day. I did not go to school today. Cousin John went with Rhoda and Mattie Gentry to church.

Wednesday 17. Pretty day. I went to church tonight. Cousin John Lea went with Rhoda and Mattie. Dr. Carson and Fred Montgomery called here this evening.

Thursday 18. Pretty day. Went to prayer meeting and church, considerable excitement tonight. Mrs. Solomon stayed all night here.

Friday 19. A rainy day. Did not go to church nor prayer meeting. I did not go home for dinner. Cousin Joe Lea took supper here.

Saturday 20. Pretty day. Nothing of importance occurred today. Went to church tonight.

Sunday 21. Pretty day. Went to church today and also tonight. Mother and Cousin Mattie Gentry went up to Mrs. Cook's this evening to see Mr. Southerly.

Monday 22. Pretty day. Went to prayer meeting and church. Mr. Southerly took dinner here.

Tuesday 23. Pretty day. Went to prayer meeting and church also. Rhoda took a ride this evening. Mr. Caldwell and Mr. McCallie here this evening.

Wednesday 24. Pretty day. Went to prayer meeting and church.

Thursday 25. Pretty day. Went to prayer meeting and church. Mr. Caldwell and Mr. McCallie here this evening.

Friday 26. Pretty day. Went down to see Ada Anderson this evening. Mr. Bradshaw took tea here. Went to church tonight.

Saturday 27. Pretty day. Went out to Dr. Grant's and stayed all day.

Sunday 28. Rained all day, very dark. Stayed at home and read *Children of the Abbey.*

Monday 29. Pretty day. Went to school. Meeting broke [church revival ended] yesterday.

Tuesday 30. Pretty day. Mr. Ewing will give a free concert tonight. None of us went.

Wednesday 31. Pretty day. Dr. Carson took Rhoda to the concert, all went but me. Mr. Levi O. Shugart died today.[17] Mary Hardwick's 16th birthday.

November 1860

Thursday 1. Rained very hard all evening, very dark. Mr. Shugart was buried.

Friday 2. Pretty day. Mag Shadden, Misses Narritt and Johnson, and Jim were at the academy, Mr. Ewing's free concert tonight. All went but Mother and myself. Stayed home and wrote my composition, subject "Pleasures of Memory."

Saturday 3. Tolerable windy. I went to see Cousin Ellen Jarnagin this evening. Rhoda and Cousin Mattie Gentry went out calling. Cousin Mattie Lea took tea here. Dr. Carson went with Rhoda to the singing.

---

[17] Levi Shugart, b. 14 September 1808; d. 31 October 1860, Fort Hill Cemetery. Ross, *Cemetery Records*, II:253.

Sunday 4. Tolerable cool day. I went to Sunday School. Sister, Mrs. Carter, Rhoda and Cousin Mattie Gentry went to the Methodist Church. Dr. Carson and Fred Montgomery called on us this evening. Mattie, Rhoda, Mary E., and I went up to the graveyard.

Monday 5. Tolerable pretty day. Nothing occurred. Jimmie is sick tonight. Cousin Mattie Gentry, Sister and Rhoda went over to Mrs. Garrison's and sat till bedtime. Rhoda and Sister went up to the drugstore today. Dr. Carson sent Rhoda a bouquet.

Tuesday 6. Cool day. Election day. Bob Sloan stayed here tonight. Sent for the doctor today for Jimmie. Dr. Carson took Rhoda to the singing.

Wednesday 7. Rained tonight; tolerable cold all day. Frank Ragsdale went with Rhoda to the singing. Could not get my examples in Algebra. Quit History tomorrow.

Thursday 8. Very rainy and cold all day. Dr. Carson came back with Rhoda from the singing. Sister gave Rhoda a music book yesterday. A cold, wet night. Wrote to Mary Sevier and Ida Jarrett. Quit History of England today.

Friday 9. Cold and rainy day. Was sick and did not go to school today. Stayed home and read *Children of the Abbey* today. Rhoda went with Dr. Carson tonight.

Saturday 10. A very pleasant but muddy day. Dr. Carson went with Rhoda to the singing school tonight. I finished *Children of the Abbey;* a most excellent book. Mother went up to Mrs. Cook's and over to Mrs. Garrison's. Sister also went over to Mrs. Garrison's. Cousin Mattie Gentry stayed all night with Mag Shadden. She and Rhoda went up there this evening.

Sunday 11. Tolerable pretty day. All went to the Baptist Church but me. Mr. Miller took dinner here. Mr. and Mrs. Cook came down this evening.

Monday 12. Pleasant day. Nothing of importance occurred today.

Tuesday 13. Pleasant day. Rhoda and Cousin Mattie went out to Uncle Caswell's before dinner. Mr. Ragsdale went to the singing tonight. Cousin Joe here tonight. Mr. Joel K. Brown and Mrs. Childs were married tonight.

Wednesday 14. Pretty day. Cousin Mattie Gentry went home this morning on the three o'clock train. Cried over my Algebra.

Thursday 15. Pretty day. Mattie Lea took supper here. Mr. Carter and Sister went to church with her. Mr. Ragsdale went with Rhoda, Sister came home from Mrs. Bradford's this evening. Julia Grant here this evening.

Friday 16. Rained this evening and until one o'clock this morning. Julia Grant stayed all night with me; we talked until 1:08 o'clock; a night long to be remembered. Mr. M.H.B. Burkett's school[18] came up this evening, that is a part of it. Mother went up to Mrs. Cook's this evening, she and Sister over to Mrs. Garrison's.

Saturday 17. Tolerable muddy. I went part of the way home with Julia Grant this morning. Mrs. Grant here this evening. All went to the singing but me. Mr. Ragsdale went with Rhoda.

Sunday 18. Pleasant day. Went to Sunday School. Went to the Presbyterian Church tonight; Mr. Aiken preached. Sister, Mother and Rhoda went to the Presbyterian Church this evening. Rhoda and Mother went to the Methodist this morning. Mr. Carter is sick today. I wrote a letter this morning to Maggie [probably Margaret] Barrett.

Monday 19. Cloudy day. Received an invitation out to Col. Lea's. Mrs. Garrison took Rhoda to the singing last night. Wrote in Rose Bell's album.

Tuesday 20. Pretty day. Rhoda went with Mr. Ragsdale to a party at William Craigmiles'.

Wednesday 21. Snowed a little this morning for the first time. Lucius Montgomery and Miss Aloia Henderson[19] were married tonight. Rhoda sat with Mrs. Garrison tonight. Adelia Thompson tuned our piano today. Mother and Sister spent the day at Mrs. McNutt's.

Thursday 22. Sleeted this evening, a dark, gloomy and rainy night. Rhoda went to the fair with John Traynor. I did not go.

Friday 23. A dark gloomy day. Will Keener and Charlie Tibbs were up at the academy this evening.

Saturday 24. A cold day.

Sunday 25. So cold we did not go to preaching; no prayer meeting.

Monday 26. Not so cold as yesterday. We killed hogs today.

---

[18] An academy called Student's Home.
[19] From Benton, Polk County, Tennessee.

Tuesday 27. A rainy day. Mollie Grant stayed all night with me.

Wednesday 28. Charlie Swan and Sid Bell were married tonight in Harrison [Hamilton County, Tenn.].

Thursday 29. Tolerable muddy. Mary Tucker's 12th birthday, she stayed all night with Mary E. tonight. Rhoda and Sister went up to Mrs. Mills' and over to Mrs. Garrison's this evening. Rhoda went and sat till bedtime with Mrs. Cook. Mrs. Garrison, Sister and Mr. Carter went and sat till bedtime with Mrs. Craigmiles. Wrote to Mary Sevier tonight.

Friday 30. Pretty day. I read a composition today. Mr. Blunt delivered an address to the young men; a great many there. The reading circle met as usual. Mother and Sister went to Mrs. William Craigmiles' this evening. Rhoda and Sister went out to Uncle Caswell's, also Cousin Joe here tonight; also out to Mrs. Rob Swan's. Mr. Carter started to Charleston, S.C. I feel so sad tonight about my composition for examination yesterday evening. And something else [private thoughts]. Chris Seavey's 21st birthday.

December 1860

Saturday 1. A very windy day. Did not go anywhere today, learned my lessons. Callie Swan, Mollie Howell and Cousin Mat.[20] Lea were here this morning, also Mrs. Shadden, Mrs. Cook this evening. Sister and Mrs. Cook went over to Mrs. Garrison's. Rhoda went at night.

Sunday 2. Rhoda went to church this morning and at night. Mrs. Cook here this morning. Cousin John Lea here tonight. Tolerable cold.

Monday 3. Tolerable cold. Went to school as usual. Snowed a good deal last night, ground covered this morning, sleeted and rained also.

---

[20] Possibly an abbreviation for Matilda.

Tuesday 4. Too cold to snow. Went and got my ticket from Mr. Parks, Miss Ellen sick, went home. Sister and Rhoda went to singing tonight.

Wednesday 5. A very cold day, snowed a little today, ground covered last night. Rhoda went over to Mr. Garrison's tonight. Mrs. Garrison going to Atlanta tomorrow. Mrs. Shadden and Mag here this evening.

Thursday 6. A tolerable pleasant day. I wrote to Mag Barrett tonight. Cousin John stayed all night here. Mrs. Cook and Mrs. Alexander here this evening. Sister, Rhoda and Mother went over to Mrs. Garrison's to see her off.

Friday 7. A pleasant day. The reading circle met this evening. We laughed so much we could scarcely proceed. Dr. Carson went with Rhoda to the choir at the church tonight. Fred Montgomery stayed with me.

Saturday 8. A very pleasant day. I learned my lessons as usual.

Sunday 9. A pretty day. I went to Sunday School, Mary E. did not go. Rhoda, Mr. Carter, Sister and I went to the Presbyterian Church. John Lea and Mr. Garrison took tea here. Cousin John went with Rhoda and me tonight.

Monday 10. A pleasant day. Rhoda stayed all night with Adelia Thompson. She came down after her.

Tuesday 11. A pleasant day. Cousin Ellen Jarnagin, Adelia Thompson, Dr. Carson, Frank Ragsdale and Mr. Thomas here tonight.

Wednesday 12. A rainy morning. Went to school.

Thursday 13. A pleasant day. I wrote my composition for examination subject, "I thought so myself." Mr. Thomas here tonight. Maria Kirk told me something today.

Friday 14. A rainy evening. Aunt Elizabeth Lea and Mrs. Lizzie Harris spent the day here. Mr. Thomas here this evening. Cousin Ellen Jarnagin, myself and a great many school girls went over to Mr. Burkett's examination. Mrs. Garrison sat until bedtime tonight. Cousin John Lea took tea here, also stayed all night.

Saturday 15. A cloudy day. Copied off my composition and sent it up to Cousin Ellen to correct. A surprise party at Mr. Johnson's. Rhoda is invited, is going with Frank Ragsdale.

Sunday 16. A pleasant day. I went to Sunday School as usual. Sister and Rhoda went to the Methodist Church. Mr. Thomas called on Rhoda tonight.

Monday 17. A pleasant day. Adelia Thompson took tea here. Mr. Thomas went with Rhoda up to Dr. Thompson's after tea. She stayed all night. I did not go to school this morning, was sick. Sister went up to Mrs. Traynor's this morning.

Tuesday 18. A pleasant day. Sister and Mother went out to Uncle Caswell's this evening. Cousin John took tea here. Mr. Thomas here this morning. I have had the "blues" [state of depression or meloncholy] all day very bad. Sister and Mother went to prayer meeting at the Baptist Church tonight. Anna Waterhouse here this evening, at three o'clock. Rhoda went to the wedding. Mary and Lillie Davis, Ada Anderson, Chuckie Stuart and myself went up on top of the hotel to view the constellations. South Carolina seceded today![21]

Wednesday 19. A rainy, muddy evening. Sister went over to Cousin Mary Harle's this evening. I copied off my examination tonight.

Thursday 20. A pleasant day. The last day of school. After school was out some of us stayed at the academy, acted the dialogues and read our compositions.

Friday 21. A cold day. Examination day; the exhibition tonight. Cousin John Lea took tea here. Cousin John, Mr. Carter, Sister, Rhoda, Mary E. and I all went to the exhibition. A very windy day. Rained this evening, thundered and lightninged tonight, and muddy coming home from the exhibition.

Saturday 22. A pleasant day. Rhoda and I went to see Cousin Ellen. I went to see Martha Reynolds, Sallie Shields (they were not at home) and Ada Anderson. Rhoda went to see Anna Gaut and Anna Waterhouse.

---

[21] South Carolina was the state that precipitated the Nullification Controversy when the state tried to overturn the Tariff of 1832 by not collecting the tariff in South Carolina. It was resolved by the Compromise Tariff of 1833 that solved the immediate issue. South Carolina was the first state to secede from the Union in 1860.

Sunday 23. Rhoda and I went to the Methodist Church. I went to the Baptist Sunday School in the evening. Ada Anderson here this evening.

Monday 24. Pleasant day. Mary Parker and Ada Anderson here this evening. I stayed all night with Ada tonight. It rained tonight.

Tuesday 25. A pleasant day. Christmas Day. Ada Anderson and I went to the Ocoee House this morning. Mother spent the day at Mrs. Cook's. All except Mother went up to see the masquerade.[22] Mr. Carter, Sister and Rhoda dined at Mrs. Alexander's today. I was invited but did not go. Mr. Fred Montgomery took me to a party at C. H. Mills', Frank Ragsdale with Rhoda. Anna Waterhouse down here this evening, Dr. Carson also. I went down to see Sallie Shields this evening. Ada Stuart here this evening.

Wednesday 26. A cold and windy day. I went to a party at Mr. Pleasant Craigmiles' with J. H. Johnson. Rhoda with John Traynor.

Thursday 27. A pleasant day. Mary E. and I went to see Sue Aldehoff this morning. Sallie Shields and I went to see Julia and Mollie Grant today. Rhoda took tea at Judge Gaut's. I did not get in from Mrs. Grant's in time to go. Rhoda and Sister spent the day at Uncle Caswell's today.

Friday 28. It rained a little tonight. I received a note from Lil Snead to attend a party at Mr. Fate [Lafayette] Hardwick's. I did not go. Rhoda went with Frank Ragsdale. Sue Aldehoff and Augusta Craigmiles were here this evening.

Saturday 29. A rainy day. Read *Life of Josephine* nearly all day.

Sunday 30. This morning the ground was covered with snow, snowed all day without ceasing a moment. Made some snow cream today. Cousin John ate dinner here, stayed all evening and night.

Monday 31. The snow is between 8 and 9 inches in depth. I read *Life of Josephine* nearly all day. Mr. Alex Sharpe to dinner here. Cousin John also. Mother thinned out my hair this morning.

---

[22] Masquerade is a costume ball or party where masks are worn (*AHD*).

1861

January 1861

Tuesday 1. Tolerable cold day. Nat Carson and John Traynor sent their cards down for us to go to a party at Col. Campbells'. We went in a sleigh, had a merry ride, enjoyed myself finely. Cousin John Lea at the fence[1] to tell us about the party. I knitted on my stocking all day. New Year's Day.

Wednesday 2. Been raining nearly all day. Knitted on my stocking all day. Cousin John Lea here after Uncle Caswell's letters, brought us some kraut.

Thursday 3. A very pleasant day but very muddy. Rhoda received a note from Bob Grant, myself one from Fred Montgomery; declined both. We are going to the party at Mr. Henry Tibbs, I finished knitting my stocking this morning. I made me a nightgown the rest of the day. Mr. Carter went down to Mr. Mitchell's, came back today also. Sallie McMillin's 15th birthday. We felt an earthquake this evening.

Friday 4. A tolerable cold day. Sallie Shields here this evening. Sister, Rhoda, Annie and Jimmie spent the day at Mr. Carter's. Aunt Elizabeth Lea and Lizzie Bell were here this morning. Rhoda went to Mr. Cook's this evening. I patched my breeches and made pockets for my dresses. Awful muddy. Fast day appointed by the President.[2]

Saturday 5. A very muddy day. Julia and Lou Grant took dinner here. Mattie Reynolds and Anna Waterhouse here also. Mother and Sister went to Mr. Dr. Brown's, and Mr. Reynolds' store, got me a set of hoops and two dresses, Rhoda a dress also. A party at the Ocoee

---

[1]Family and friends often stopped at the fence gate to talk without coming into the house.

[2]Fasting was abstaining from eating or drinking for religious discipline. Presidents of both sides encouraged their citizens to observe fast days.

House; we were not invited. Mr. Carter went away and came back
this evening. I was very lonesome and had the "blues" very bad.

Sunday 6. A beautiful but very muddy day. Rhoda went to the
Methodist Church this morning. Mary E. and I went to Sunday
School this evening, was not any. Mother and Rhoda went up to
Mrs. Cook's this evening. Rhoda stayed all night.

Monday 7. Very muddy, rained last night and this morning very
hard. The first day of school. Cousin John Lea took dinner here. I
went up to Mr. Fate [Lafayette] Hardwick's store after a Latin
grammar and reader. Mary E. went after a United States history.
Received a letter from Mary Sevier. Have to go six months and then
I will get to see Maria no more.

Tuesday 8. A very muddy day, very foggy this morning. Received
a letter from Cleo Watkins. Mother went up to Mrs. Cook's this
evening. Rhoda stayed all night with her. Answered Mary's and
Cleo's letters. Mrs. Carol Tibbs has a baby. I cut out some of my hair
today.

Wednesday 9. A very rainy evening; muddy. Rhoda stayed with
Mrs. Cook. Had our lamps made to burn kerosene oil.[3] Julia Grant
told me something today. What was it? Shan't tell you.

Thursday 10. A tolerable muddy day. Mrs. Cook was here today.
Cousin John Lea and Joe Alexander sat till bedtime with us tonight.
Uncle Caswell took dinner here. I read a letter to Julia Grant that
was written about ____.[4]

Friday 11. A tolerable cold day. Sister and Mother went to see
Mrs. Carol Tibbs (she had a baby). Also up to Mrs. Cook's . Julia
Grant here this evening, wanted me to stay all night with her. Have a
very bad cold and cough, could not go. Jimmie's 3rd birthday. This
time five years [from now] I wonder where I will be, also my friends,
Sallie Shields, Julia Grant, Lucretia Tibbs, Sallie McMillin, Mattie
Reynolds, Lillie Davis, Maria Kirk, Ada Anderson. We learned today
that a battle was fought lately in South Carolina.[5]

---

[3] Whale oil was the basic oil for lamps. Kerosene was often called "coal
oil."

[4] Myra would leave a space in her diary to indicate private thoughts or
people whose name was not provided.

[5] Fort Sumter in Charleston harbor was one the few Federal forts under
Union control. President Abraham Lincoln decided to provide provisions

Saturday 12. A very pleasant day. Mrs. Rogers was here this evening. Sister and Mother went up to Mrs. Berry's. Cousin Milton Jarnagin here this evening. Uncle Caswell dined here. Got my lessons and darned my stockings today.

Sunday 13. A beautiful day, sleeted a little tonight. Sister, Mr. Carter, Rhoda and Annie went to the Presbyterian Church. Cousin John went with Rhoda tonight. Mother and Mary E. went to the Baptist Church today. Sister, Mother, Mr. Carter and Jimmie went up to Mrs. Cook's this evening. Nat Carson and Fred Montgomery called on Rhoda and I this morning. Wrote my composition today, subject: "The close of day."

Monday 14. A rainy day. Went to school as usual. Joe Alexander here tonight.

Tuesday 15. A very rainy day. Went to school as usual.

Wednesday 16. A beautiful but windy day. I stayed all night with Julia Grant. She told me something_____the best. Sister and Jimmie spent the day at Mrs. Carter's. Mother, Rhoda, and Annie spent the day at Uncle Caswell's. Rhoda and Sister and Mother want to hear Dr. Crane lecture. I cried about my Algebra lesson. Mrs. Garrison came home today (from Atlanta). Rhoda went over to see her.

Thursday 17. A pretty day. Went over to Mrs. Garrison's this evening. Misses Matilda McMahan and Martha Coulter spent the day here. Cousin John Lea here this evening for Rhoda's head to be phrenologized by Dr. Crane; she would not go.[6]

Friday 18. It rained last night; muddy today. After school was out I went down to see Sallie Shields; got a book from her: *The House of Death.*

---

for the troops, but not reinforce its manpower. South Carolina refused and demanded the surrender of the fort. A compromise was not possible.

Southern batteries opened fire early the morning of 13 April. The bombardment lasted 34 hours and the fort was surrendered. No one was hurt in the action. By firing the first shot, the Union's cause was strengthened. Several days later Lincoln declared an "insurrection" in the South and called for 75,000 volunteers. This was the first significant action in the war. See entry for 12 April 1861.

[6] Phrenologize is a verbal form of phrenology, the practice of studying character and mental capacity from the configuration of the skull (*AHD*).

Saturday 19. A beautiful day. Eliza Shields here this evening, also Mrs. Garrison. Rhoda went out to Mr. Peters' with her to see a sick black girl. Mother and Sister went to see Mrs. Cook, also to Mr. Reynold's store. Mother went to see Mrs. Shadden. I learned my lessons, practiced today. Read *The House of Death*.

Sunday 20. A most lovely day. Rhoda went to the Methodist Church. Joe Lea dined here, spent the evening and took tea here also. Mother and Sister went up to see Mrs. Shadden. Mr. Carter went to Benton this morning. Jim Johnston went to Cincinnati, Ohio today.

Monday 21. Another lovely day. Aunt Elizabeth and Lizzie Bell here this evening. Rhoda went over to Mrs. Garrison's this evening. Sister went to Mrs. Garrison's also. Julia Grant told me something the best ____ this morning.

Tuesday 22. A tolerable cold day, ice in the milk this morning. Mr. Carter came back from Benton this evening. Mrs. Henderson here this morning. Sister went up to Mrs. Carter's this evening. She and Mother went out to Uncle Caswell's this evening.

Wednesday 23. A rainy day. I cried [a second time; see January 16] about my Algebra lesson today. I wrote to Callie McConnell and Cleo Watkins last night. Got a scolding from my sister about my dress; have the blues tonight. Mr. Carter went to Harrison (Hamilton County, Tenn.) today.

Thursday 24. Another rainy day. Nothing occurred today.

Friday 25. A muddy day. Messrs. Montgomery, Snead, Hardwick, Brandon, Hardwick & Tibbs, Cynthia Hardwick, Nannie Knox, and Kate Rogers were at the Institute. Lizzie Lea was here today. Uncle Caswell took tea here tonight.

Saturday 26. It snowed all night last night and has been snowing some today; it is five or six inches deep. Got my lessons today. Read and sewed some. Cousin Joe Lea took dinner here. Cousin John Lea took tea here. I baked some cake today.

Sunday 27. It is so muddy we could not go to church. I went tonight. Cousin John Lea took tea here. Mrs. Peters' black girl, Scrap, died tonight.

Monday 28. Very muddy. Went up to the store, got me a pasteboard box of hairpins and some paper. Mag Shadden here this evening. Cousin John Lea took tea here. Mr. Carter started to Alabama today. Mr. and Mrs. Cook sat until bedtime with us.

Tuesday 29. A beautiful day. Mother and sister went to prayer meeting tonight. Rhoda and Sister spent the day at Dr. Brown's. Went up to Mrs. Campbell's and Carter's. Mother went down to see Mrs. Joel R. Peters.

Wednesday 30. A pleasant day. Fred [Montgomery] and Nat [Carson] here tonight. Cousin Sam Gentry and Cousin Sam Inman came from Texas today.

Thursday 31. Cousin Sam's still here. Cousin John Lea here tonight.

February 1861

Friday 1. A rainy day [causing a train wreck], rained very hard, did not go to school this evening. Uncle William Lea stayed all night here.

Saturday 2. Rained nearly all morning, very muddy. Uncle William stayed all night here. Cousin John Lea took dinner here. I got my lessons. The cars ran off the track below here.

Sunday 3. Sister and Cousin Sam Gentry went to the Methodist Church today. A beautiful but muddy day. Mrs. Earnest's (black girl) Fan died tonight.

Monday 4. Cousins Sam Gentry and Sam Inman went up to Dandridge this evening.[7] Julia Grant brought me a ring and something tonight.

Tuesday 5. A pretty day. Kate Britton to tea here. Mrs. Carter here a little while.

Wednesday 6. A beautiful day. Mag Shadden here, spent the day. Mrs. McGriff and Mrs. Garrison here today. Rhoda at Mrs. Garrison this evening.

Thursday 7. A beautiful day. Frank Ragsdale here tonight. Rhoda went to Mrs. Craigmiles' with Mrs. Garrison, and to several other

---

7 The Inmans lived in Dandridge before moving to Cleveland.

places. Mother and Sister spent the day at Uncle Caswell's today. Dr. Carson was [to] come.

Friday 8. A beautiful day. Aunt Elizabeth, Uncle Caswell and Lizzie took tea here. Mother went over to Cousin Mary Harle's and Mrs. Garrison's. I was there also. Sister and Rhoda called on Mrs. Guthman, Mrs. Smith, Mrs. Thornton, Mrs. Garrison, Cousin Ellen Jarnagin, Mrs. Berry, and James Craigmiles and Thompson. I read a composition this evening. Jim and Florence Johnston, Mrs. Hassle, Henderson, Smith, Daily, Eliza Wood, Bob Grant, Walker McSpadden, Mr. Thornton, etc. were at the Academy.

Saturday 9. A beautiful day. I spent the day at Uncle Caswell's, also Julia Grant. Cousin John Lea stayed all night here. Mrs. Haywood and Cousin Joe Lea were down here tonight. Election day.

Sunday 10. A very, very windy day. Cousin John here this evening. Mr. Carter got back from Alabama. I went over to Mrs. Garrison's this evening. Rhoda, Sister, Annie and I went to the Presbyterian Church this morning. Mother went to the Baptist.

Monday 11. It rained this morning.

Tuesday 12. A beautiful day. Mr. and Mrs. Craigmiles and Mr. and Mrs. Mills took tea here. Jimmie Tibbs and Mrs. Roberts here today. Cousin Martha came home with Mr. Carter. I have the "blues" so bad this evening. Received a letter from Cleo Watkins.

Wednesday 13. A beautiful day. Sister and Rhoda went up to Mrs. Keebler's today. Mr. Carter brought a black girl (Ann) home. A windy night. Mrs. Posey Roberts spent the day here. Old Mrs. [Paschal] Carter here today.

Thursday 14. St. Valentine's day. A pretty day. Received three Valentines, Rhoda also. Dr. Carson called on Rhoda tonight.

Friday 15. It rained this morning. Mr. and Mrs. William Grant took dinner here. Mother and Sister went up to Mrs. William Craigmiles' to a quilting this evening. Had company to the academy. Dr. Carson went with Rhoda to a party at Mr. Frank Hardwick's. Cousin John Lea here this evening. Mr. and Mrs. Jarrett and Ida were here today. Mr. and Mrs. Jarrett have [gone] home; left Ida to go to school.

Saturday 16. Rained this morning. Turned to snow. Snowed off and on all day. Went down to see Ida Jarrett this evening. Cousin John Lea took tea here. Rhoda and Sister went up to Mrs. Carter's and Thompson's, were weighed. Sister weight 109 [pounds], Rhoda 108. Mr. Carter went away this eve.

Sunday 17. It snowed pretty hard this morning. Cousin Joe Lea took dinner here. Dr. Carson and Mr. Montgomery called on us tonight.

Monday 18. Very cold day. Mrs. Traynor, Mrs. Rogers, and Mrs. J. Gaut were here this evening. Cousin John Lea here also. Rhoda and myself received an invitation to attend a military ball in Knoxville Friday. We are not going. Panorama in town tonight.[8]

Tuesday 19. It has been pouring down rain all day, like one of our cold, gloomy rains.

Wednesday 20. This is a delightful day. Mrs. Rogers spent the day here. Mrs. Hoyl and Stuart here this evening. Joe Alexander and Cousin John Lea here tonight, stayed until after one o'clock. We heard that Bettie Jarrett (Giles now) died yesterday a week ago. I feel very sad about hearing of her death.

Thursday 21. A beautiful day. Mr. and Mrs. Garrison here awhile tonight. Uncle William here also. Cousin Martha Lea stayed all night here. Aunt Elizabeth Lea and Mrs. William Craigmiles here this evening. Mrs. Henderson and Mrs. Davis here this evening.

Friday 22. A beautiful day. Mother and Aunt Elizabeth spent the day at Cousin Mary Harle's. Sallie Shields, Cousin Ellen Jarnagin and myself took a walk out past Mr. Joe Swan's after school was out, we had a very pleasant walk. Rhoda and Dr. Carson went to the choir. I went with Cousin John.

Saturday 23. It rained today. Learned my lessons, mended my clothes and washed today. Very lonesome, as Saturday evenings usually are.

Sunday 24. A very beautiful but cold day, Sister and Rhoda went to the Presbyterian Church. Cousin John took dinner and supper here.

Monday 25. A tolerable cold day. Mag Shadden and Rhoda went out to Uncle Caswell's and Mrs. Robert Swan's. Sister, Rhoda and Mrs. Garrison went down to the steam mill this evening.[9]

---

[8] A panorama is a picture or series of pictures representing a continuous scene.

[9] The steam mill was located on Mill Street near the depot.

Tuesday 26. A pleasant day. Mr. Carter came today. Rhoda stayed with Mrs. Garrison. A. S. Simmons' 15th birthday.

Wednesday 27. A pleasant day. Mr. Carter came today. Rhoda stayed with Mrs. Garrison.

Thursday 28. A beautiful day. Mrs. Garrison spent the day at Mrs. William Craigmiles'. Got 5 imperfect [marks] in arithmetic. Received a letter from Cousin Sam Inman. Mrs. T. Callaway here this evening.

March 1861

Friday 1. A most delightful day, very warm. Julia Grant and Aunt Elizabeth Lea here this evening. Julia and I went up to Mrs. McMillins' this evening. Received a composition this evening. Mrs. Carter, Uncle Caswell took dinner here. Mr. Carter started for Charleston, S.C. this evening. Mr. Carson went with Rhoda to the choir tonight. Mr. Montgomery with me. Mr. and Mrs. McNutt sat until bedtime with Mother. Received a letter from Mary Sevier.

Saturday 2. A delightful day. Learned my lessons and mended my clothes as usual. Answered Cousin Sam Inman's letter. Sister and Mother went over to Mrs. DeLano's to see two cannon go down the road.

Sunday 3. A pleasant day. Cousin John Lea dined here today. Cousins John and Joe both took supper. Cousin John stayed all night. Dr. Carson and Mr. Fred Montgomery called on Rhoda and myself tonight. Sister and Rhoda went to the Methodist Church.

Monday 4. A pretty day. Mr. Lincoln was inaugurated today.[10]

Tuesday 5. A frost and freeze tonight.

Wednesday 6. A tolerable cool day. Did not go to school today; was sick. Mrs. William Craigmiles, Mollie Gallagher, Mollie and Julia Grant and Sallie Shields were here this evening.

---

[10] President Lincoln hoped to preserve the Union and considered the Southern states to be in rebellion rather than a separate nation. He served from 1861 to 1865.

Thursday 7. A pleasant day. Mrs. Dr. Brown spent the day. Mrs. Stout here. Sister and Rhoda went shopping this evening. Cousin Ellen Jarnagin and myself walked out to Uncle Caswell's this evening; no person at home; went down to the spring and ate apples.

Friday 8. A very, very windy day. Came home from school today, was sick. Uncle William Lea took dinner here. Mrs. Shadden, Uncle Caswell, and William took tea her. Rainy night.

Saturday 9. A windy day. Mother and Sister went to church today [to the] Baptist [Church]. Mrs. Snead and Laura took dinner here. Joe Alexander and John Lea here this evening. Rhoda had the headache very badly. Sister and Rhoda went over to Mrs. Garrison's this evening. Pasted pieces in my scrapbook and learned my lessons.

Sunday 10. A pleasant day. Cousin Joe Lea here this morning. Cousin John took dinner here. Sister, Rhoda and myself went to the Presbyterian Church. I went over to the Garrison's this morning. Fred Montgomery went with me to the Presbyterian Church. Frank Ragsdale with Rhoda, Cousin John with Sister. Joe Alexander wrote Rhoda a note also, but her company had been engaged.

Monday 11. A cold day. Went down to see Sallie Shields this evening, she is sick. Rhoda stayed with Mrs. Garrison tonight, she is sick.

Tuesday 12. Dr. Carson and Rhoda called on Mary Gaut tonight. The Mother and Sister have gone to the Baptist prayer meeting. A very warm day. Sister spent the day at Uncle Caswell's. Rhoda stayed all night. Bettie Jarrett's 19th birthday. The Ducktown[11] hack just came, makes me have the blues.[12]

Wednesday 13. My 16th birthday. Wonder where I will be on my 18th. Mrs. Garrison, Aunt Elizabeth, Uncle Caswell, and Mrs. Grant spent the day here. Rhoda gave me a chemise, a birthday present. She stayed all night with Mrs. Garrison tonight. Sister and Rhoda went around shopping and up to Mrs. Carter's. A beautiful day.

Thursday 14. A windy and cold day. Mother, Sister, Annie, Jimmie and Rhoda spent the day at Mr. Carter's. I did not come

---

[11] Polk County, Tennessee.

[12] A hack was a horse drawn buggy or wagon which carried passengers to towns not serviced by the train.

home today for dinner; had the headache very bad. Uncle William [Lea] took tea here. Uncle Caswell here tonight.

Friday 15. A tolerable cold day. Nat Carson went with Rhoda to the choir. Cousin John Lea with me. I went down to see Sallie Shields this evening.

Saturday 16. It rained this evening and all night. Mr. Alex Sharpe and Uncle Caswell took supper here. Joe Alexander called on Rhoda tonight. Mr. George Middlecoff hurt a Mr. Owens very badly this evening.

Sunday 17. It rained all this morning nearly. None of us went to church. Joe [Lea] took dinner here, John took supper. Fred [Montgomery] and Dr. Carson here tonight.

Monday 18. It snowed nearly all day very hard, did lay, only on the houses scarcely on account of the dampness of the ground. Joe Alexander and John Lea here tonight.

Tuesday 1 9. A tolerable cold day. Had a very nice serenade tonight. A beautiful moonlight night.

Wednesday 20. Rained this evening. Wrote to Cousin Sam Inman tonight. Felt very sad about something Rhoda and I were talking about.

Thursday 21. Cold this evening. Aunt Elizabeth (Lea) and Cousin John here tonight, came home with Rhoda and Sister from prayer meeting.

Friday 22. A beautiful day. Cousin John and Rhoda went to the choir. A dance at the hotel tonight. I stayed all night with Lillie Davis. Sallie Shields and I went over to Mrs. McMillin's. Sallie went with us to get weighed. Sallie Shields weight 122 1/2 lbs., Sallie McMillin, 102 1/2, myself 104 lbs. I had to read in the reading circle. Sister spent the evening at Mrs. Hughes'.

Saturday 23. It rained nearly all morning. Got my lessons and mended my clothes. Mrs. Thompson here this evening.

Sunday 24. A beautiful day. Cousin John [Lea] took tea here. All went up to the graveyard except Rhoda and myself. Dr. Carson and [Fred] Montgomery came after Rhoda and I to go the church. I did not go. Sister, Rhoda and myself went to the Presbyterian Church today.

Monday 25. A pleasant day. Nothing occurred today. The serenaders here tonight.

Tuesday 26. A tolerable day, very windy. A great many of us school girls went after flowers, were caught in the rain.

Wednesday 27. A beautiful day. Aunt Elizabeth, Cousin Martha, Mrs. Carter, Mrs. Onie Campbell, Mrs. William Craigmiles, Mrs. Mollie Gallaher were here, also Mrs. Thornton.

Thursday 28. A pleasant day. Rhoda and I went out calling. Mother spent the evening at Uncle Caswell's.

Friday 29. A beautiful day. Went to choir tonight. Fred wrote Rhoda a note, went with her.

Saturday 30. A beautiful day. Cousin Ellen [Jarnagin] here this evening. Sister went up to Mrs. William Craigmiles', Rhoda over to Cousin Mary Harle's. I cleaned up at the parlor today.

Sunday 31. A beautiful day. Julia and Jeanette Grant here. Sister and Annie went to the Methodist Church. Joe Lea took tea here.

April 1861

Monday 1. A cloudy day. Mary Elizabeth's thirteenth birthday.

Tuesday 2. A rainy day. Uncle Caswell and Cousin John took dinner here. Mr. Blunt,[13] Joe Alexander and Cousin John here tonight. Mr. Dick Harris and Mr. Ramsey Swan here to take Mother's deposition.[14]

Wednesday 3. A beautiful day. Mother and Sister went to prayer meeting. We read our discussion this evening. Mrs. Garrison and Sister went up in town.

Thursday 4. A pleasant but cloudy day. Was sick, did not go to school this evening. Mrs. Pepper, Florence Johnston, Mag Shadden, Mrs. Joel K. Brown, Mrs. Frank Hardwick and Mrs. McGriff here this evening. Mother and Annie went out to Uncle Caswell's this evening. Mr. Carter came home today from Charleston, [S.C.]

---

[13] A.E. Blunt became principal of Cleveland Masonic Female Institute in 1859 and served until 1861 when the school temporarily closed.

[14] A deposition is a written statement by a witness for use in court in his absence.

Friday 5. A cloudy day. Sallie McMillin, Lillie Davis, Mary Hardwick and myself read our discussion today. Went down to see Ida Jarrett. Received a magazine. Got a shaker.

Saturday 6. A rainy day. Trimmed my shaker, got my lesson and read today. Wrote to Cousin Sam Carson.

Sunday 7. It rained all night. None of us went to church. Bettie [Jarrett] Siler's funeral is to be preached today. Slept nearly all evening.

Monday 8. A rainy day. Joe Alexander here tonight. Mr. Carter went up the road.

Tuesday 9. A muddy day. Mother and Sister went to the Baptist prayer meeting.

Wednesday 10. A pleasant day. Rhoda stayed all night with Cousin Martha Lea. Sallie Shields and myself took a walk this evening. Mr. Carter came back today. "Honor and shame from no condition rise, act well your part there all the honor lies."[15]

Thursday 11. A pleasant day. Ida Jarrett here for my dress pattern. Sister and Rhoda went over to Mrs. Garrett's this evening.

Friday 12. A rainy day. Discussion: "Does the Farmer have the greatest influence over society?" No choir tonight. Cousin John here this evening. I finished a novel: *While it was Morning*; a most excellent book. Mr. Douglas commenced fighting at 4 o'clock this morning at Charleston, continues until the thirteenth.[16]

Saturday 13. A pleasant day. Dr. Carson here tonight. Mr. McCallie took dinner here. I got my lessons some, and looked over my clothes to mend them.

Sunday 14. Rained tonight. Cousin Joe [Lea] took tea here. Mother and Mary E. went to the Baptist Church, Rhoda, Mr. Carter, Sister, Annie and I went to the Presbyterian Church. All went to the graveyard except Rhoda and myself. Mother and Mary E. went to the Baptist Church very much against my will for I do not like the Baptist denomination.[17]

---

[15]Myra did not identify the source of this quote.

[16] The opening shots of the war were fired at Fort Sumter in Charleston harbor. The fort surrendered after thirty-four hours of bombardment. See entry for 11 January 1861.

[17] See entry for 21 September 1861.

Monday 15. A very pleasant day. Sister and Rhoda went out to Dr. Grant's this evening, went to see Sallie Surguine, Mrs. McGriff, called on Mrs. Guthman. Rhoda, Sister and I over to Mrs. Garrison's after tea.

Tuesday 16. A rainy day. Cousin John took dinner here.

Wednesday 17. A pleasant day. Mrs. McNutt and Laura here this evening. Cried about my Algebra lesson today. Ada Anderson came home with me to get me to stay with her; Mrs. Gaut gone. Mother not willing for me to go.

Thursday 18. A pleasant day. Perry Gaut and Dr. Carson here this morning to get us to assist making a Union Flag. Mother would not let us. Sister and Rhoda went up to Mrs. O'Conner's and got me a bonnet. Rhoda and I went up over to Mrs. Garrison's after tea. We heard today that Virginia and they are fighting up there.[18]

Friday 19. A windy day. Went to the choir tonight. Heard today that the school at Lebanon[19] was broken up. The *Harper's Magazines* for the "Reading Circle" have come. Elvira Lea's fourteenth birthday.

Saturday 20. A beautiful day. Mr. Carter went out in the country this morning. Sister and Rhoda went up to Mrs. Dr. Brown's this evening. Cousin John Lea took tea here. Mrs. Frank Lea and Annie stopped here this morning on their way to the Cumberland Presbyterian. Learned my lessons and wrote a composition on "What is Life?" The two Mrs. Guthmans here today.

Sunday 21. A very pleasant but windy day. John and Adelia Craigmiles came this morning. We all went to the Cumberland Church to hear Mr. Templeton preach this morning and tonight also.

Monday 22. A warm day. Rhoda went up to see Adelia Craigmiles. Sister and Rhoda went over to Mrs. Garrison's also to Mrs. Traynor's. Mr. Robert Sloan here tonight. Rhoda and myself took a walk here this evening for the first time.

---

[18] Virginia separated after the firing on Fort Sumter and the call for troops. Being so close to Washington, D.C. would insure that fighting would erupt there.

[19] Warren County, Tennessee.

Tuesday 23. A warm day. Sallie Shields presented the Unionists with a flag today.[20] Received a letter from Cousin Sam Inman. Mother and Sister went to prayer meeting. Rhoda and Cousin John Lea went over to Mrs. Garrison's tonight, he took tea here. Uncle William here this evening. Mr. Carter went down the road.

Wednesday 24. A pleasant day. Mother went over to see Sallie Surguine this evening. Sister went down to Mrs. Stuart's this afternoon.

Thursday 25. A beautiful day. Mrs. Hughes here today. Spent the day.

Friday 26. A rainy evening. Cousins Sam Inman and Will Harris came this evening. We went to the choir. Dr. Carson went with Rhoda. Venie Seavey's 18th birthday.

Saturday 27. It has been raining a good deal today. Mr. Carter went up to Knoxville and back this evening.

Sunday 28. A beautiful day. All except Mother went to the Presbyterian Church today. Cousins Will Harris and Sam [Inman], Rhoda, Annie, Jimmie, Mother, Mary E. and I went up to the graveyard this evening. We all went to church tonight except Sister at the Presbyterian Church to hear Bradshaw preach.

Monday 29. A beautiful day. Cousins Sam [Inman], Will [Harris], and John Lea went out to Candy's Creek to fish. Cousin John took dinner here. Sam Hunt and Mr. Maston, from Athens, called on us tonight. Annie is six years old. Cousins Sam and Will fooled us tonight.

Tuesday 30. It rained this morning some. All spent the day out at Uncle Caswell's except Mother and Jimmie. Mrs. Dr. Brown, Misses Sallie Aiken and Mattie Coulter here tonight. Dr. Carson here tonight. Cousin John Lea also. Dr. Carson sent for his violin; Cousin Will played for us. Enjoyed myself very much.

---

[20] Most of the flags and banners for military units were handmade and presented to the units.

May 1861

Wednesday 1. A beautiful day. Had a picnic out at Candy's Creek. Rhoda, Sister and I went. Had a very nice time. Mr. Jim Johnson brought me home in his buggy. Sam Inman and Will Harris went home this morning. Very sorry to see them leave. Have the "blues" this evening. I fired a gun today; John Traynor held it. Rhoda and Dr. Carson called on Adelia Craigmiles. I attended a party at Mrs. Traynor's tonight. Lucius Osment went with me. Jim Johnston talked to me nearly all the time. Mrs. Garrison here this evening. Cousin John stayed all night with us. Heard today that Lincoln was coming down upon us, do not hardly believe it.[21]

Tuesday 2. A pleasant day. Went to school as usual. Mother and Sister went over to the depot to see the troops. Cousin John Lea and Rhoda went out to Candy's Creek to get our basket. Sister left it there. Mr. and Mrs. Aiken and Mattie Coulter spent the day here.

Friday 3. A beautiful day. Sister, Rhoda, Mother and I went over to the depot this evening, 1300 [troops] went up. Rhoda and Sister gave them bouquets, they are going to Richmond, Virginia. Mr. Blunt gave me a permission form to let me go. Cousin John and Rhoda went to the choir, I went to bed. Mr. and Mrs. Aiken and Mattie Coulter stopped in here from the depot. Mrs. William Craigmiles here this evening, also Mrs. Garrison. Cousin John stayed here all night. Callie Swan here today.

Saturday 4. A very pleasant day. Received a letter from Julia Grant. Got my lessons and mended my clothes. All of us walked out to Mrs. Grant's after tea. Great excitement here about war. Wrote a letter to Cousin Sam Gentry. Sister and Mother went to Dr. Brown's this evening.

Sunday 5. A rainy day. Cousin John stayed all night here. Mr. Carter and Sister went up to see Sallie Aiken this evening.

Monday 6. A rainy and dark day. Mary and Martha Montgomery stopped here this morning and told me that Mr. Blunt did not

---

[21] President Lincoln considered the South to be in rebellion. After the shelling of Fort Sumter he called for 75,000 volunteers to meet the challenge.

intend having any school, it was raining so bad. Wrote a letter to Cousin Sam Inman. Mr. Blunt here this evening.

Tuesday 7. A pleasant day.

Wednesday 8. A beautiful day. Lavena Seavey came this morning. We all went over to the depot and to Mrs. Stuart's. I gave a soldier a bouquet, got acquainted with several of them, gave a great many of them bouquets. Went to school this evening. Lavena, Mrs. Garrison and myself walked out to Mrs. Peters' after school was out. Sister and Rhoda called on Adelia Craigmiles, Mr. Craigmiles. Sister and Rhoda went to a party at Mr. William Craigmiles' in honor of the marriage of Mr. Trewhitt and Lizzie Narritt. "I stayed all night with Lavena (Venie); we threw out some bouquets. Rhoda also had a serenade but did not hear it.

Thursday 9. A pleasant day. Over at Mrs. Garrison's this evening, Rhoda and I. All of us took a walk, Dr. Carson left this evening, never to return; sent Rhoda a bouquet. Vena and I made some bouquets to give to the soldiers, but did not come. Rhoda stayed with Adelia tonight. Got through Algebra this evening.

Friday 10. Rained this evening. Mel Osment, Jim Johnston and others went to the academy this evening. Mr. Carson sent me a beautiful bouquet this evening. Cousin John [Lea] came down for us to go to the choir. Rhoda and Venie were at Mrs. Garrison's; I did not want to go.

Saturday 11. A pleasant day. Was sick today, went over to Mrs. Garrison's. Sister and Rhoda to Mrs. Stuart's, Mother to Uncle Caswell's. Wrote a composition on "Earthly Joys."

Sunday 12. A beautiful day. All went to church but me. Sister, Rhoda, Mr. Carter and Annie to the Methodist, rest to the Baptist. Maria Kirk and I went out to see Julia Grant this evening, took tea. Fred [Montgomery] and Nat [Carson] here tonight. Cousin Joe [Lea] took tea here. Aunt Elizabeth, Uncle Caswell, Sissy and Pryor here this morning.

Monday 13. A rainy and damp day. Cousin John [Lea] and Uncle William took tea here. Uncle William, dinner also. Mother and Rhoda went to church tonight. Mr. Carter got a pistol today. Annie's and Jimmie's chairs came today. Last night the Negroes were to have an insurrection (so it was reported).[22]

Tuesday 14. A beautiful day. Sister spent the day to Mrs. Traynor's. Cousin John [Lea] took tea here. Rhoda and Venie went to see Alice Brown today, going off tomorrow to Texas. Mother and Rhoda went over to the depot to see the troops this morning.

Wednesday 15. A pleasant day. Mother and Sister were out at Uncle Caswell's and Mrs. Berry's this morning. Mr. Carson sent Rhoda a bouquet after she had retired for the night.

Thursday 16. A pleasant day. Rhoda, Venie and I walked out to Mrs. Peters' place to get some green apples to eat. Mr. Callaway and Mr. McHaney were here this evening. Lavena spent the afternoon here.

Friday 17. A beautiful evening. Read a composition. Sallie [Shields] came to school this evening, has been sick. We all went to the choir. Mr. Carson came home with me, Fred Montgomery with Rhoda, and Cousin John with Venie. Cousin Ellen and Miss Lizzie Boyd [were] here this evening. Sallie McMillin went to see Maria Kirk, Mary Parker and Venie Seavey this evening. Venie and Rhoda also went to see Florence Johnston and Mag Shadden.

Saturday 18. A beautiful day. Cousins Ellen [Jarnagin] and John, Augusta Craigmiles, Roe, Willie and Davie Campbell, Venie, Rhoda and myself went fishing on Mouse Creek. I caught six fish. Mel Osment and Maria Kirk here this evening. Cousin Martha Lea here this evening. Sister, Mr. Carter and Cousin Martha went up to the courthouse to hear Mr. Foote and Mr. House speak. Had the sick headache very badly this evening. Venie got scared and stayed all night with Rhoda. Julia Grant here to see me, was not at home.

Sunday 19. A very rainy day, rained all day. Mother, Sister, Mrs. Carter, Annie, Mary E. went to the Methodist Church. It rained so Julia, Mollie and Jeanette Grant had to take dinner here. Mrs. Summers, Cousins John and Joe Lea also. Uncle William here but went home. Bob Grant came after dinner and stayed nearly all evening. George Summers and Joe Osment took the girls home in buggies.

---

[22] There was a persistent fear of slave uprisings in the South during the colonial era.

Monday 20. Rained a little this morning. A pleasant evening. Sallie Shields and myself went to see Cousin Ellen after school was out. The tea party over this evening. Made me feel very sad to think of so many having left since last year. I have not written any on my examination, and am in trouble about it. One month until the examination. A storm tonight.

Tuesday 21. A pleasant day. Venie here all day.

Wednesday 22. A beautiful day. Mrs. Walker here this morning. Mother and Sister went down to Mrs. Dodson's this afternoon. Mrs. McNutt here this evening. Venie and Rhoda went out to Mr. Peters'.

Thursday 23. A pleasant day. Mrs. Carter and Mrs. Jennie Davis here this afternoon. We went to the choir tonight. Meeting commences tomorrow night.

Friday 24. A beautiful day. Venie and I went out and took supper at Uncle Caswell's this evening, had a delightful swing. Sam Hunt was there a little while. We all went to church tonight. Mel Osment here this evening. Rhoda took up the parlor carpet.

Saturday 25. A beautiful day. Mother and sister went to the Presbyterian Church this morning. Sister, Mr. Carter, Annie and Mary E. went to hear Mr. Haynes speak. Frank Ragsdale went with Rhoda, Fred Montgomery with Venie. Sister and Mrs. Garrison sent Mrs. Haynes a bouquet. Mrs. Swan and Samantha, also Uncle Wood took dinner here. Cousin John and Venie here this evening; also Warren Rowles. He took tea here and went to church with Rhoda. Venie and I heard this morning that the Northern army had taken possession of Alexandria, Virginia. They pinioned 40 men of ours and took them prisoners.[23]

Sunday 26. A beautiful day. Venie, Rhoda and I took a walk out to Dr. Grant's this evening; did not get to the house. We went to the Presbyterian Church, morning and evening. Rev. Bradshaw preached. I went over and spent the evening with Venie. Mrs. Garrison went to church with us at night.

Monday 27. Adelia Craigmiles and Rhoda went around calling all day. Venie and Rhoda went out and took tea at Uncle Caswell's. Sam Hunt came home with Rhoda. Cousin John Lea stayed all night here. A beautiful day but windy.

---

[23]Pinioned means to restrain, to keep immobile in one place.

Tuesday 28. A beautiful day. Adelia Craigmiles tuned our piano this morning. Rhoda, Mother and Sister went to Frank Stout's burying. Cousin Martha and Lizzie Bell were here to dinner. Mr. Blunt dismissed school. Went over to Mrs. Garrison's this evening. Mr. Pleasant Craigmiles' Negro house was burned down this evening.[24]

Wednesday 29. A pretty day. Venie and Rhoda spent the day at Mr. Tucker's. Venie shot a pistol off eight times, Rhoda bursted a cap. Florence Johnston and Sallie McMillin here this evening. Cousin John Lea took tea here.

Thursday 30. A beautiful day. Over at Mrs. Garrison's this evening. Florence Johnston here this evening. Rhoda and Florence sent Mary E. down to Mrs. J. Gaut's after some rose buds. Venie, Rhoda and myself were invited to a party this evening at Col. Campbell's. Nat went with Rhoda, Cousin John with Venie. I did not know I was invited until it was too late to dress. Mrs. Rogers, Mollie Dardis here this evening. Thought the "Flying Artillery" were coming up, did not come until night, very beautiful. Mrs. Cook came today. I went to see her at noon on my way to school.

Friday 31. A beautiful day. Venie and Rhoda went to see Mrs. Cook this morning. They got ready to go to the choir and Cousin John did not come after them. Venie stayed all night here. I stayed all night with Sallie McMillin. Frank Ragsdale came up there, and we all went down to the spring[25] and learned how to shoot. Mr. Montgomery joined us there. I shot twelve times, loaded the gun three times and the pistol three. Enjoyed myself finely.

June 1861

Saturday 1. A very hard rain this evening. After the rain Venie, Rhoda, Sister, Mary E., Mrs. Garrison and I went down to Mrs. Stuart's to see the troops: they did not come, met with an accident

---

[24] The Negro house was most likely the slave quarters.

[25] Traynor's Spring was located about one block west of the courthouse on South Street.

down at Glass' Station, and did not get here till night. Wrote my composition "Every Sweet has its bitter" examination.

Sunday 2. A beautiful day. No preaching in town today. Some troops have just passed on their way to Virginia.

Monday 3. A beautiful day. Messrs. Thomas, A. R. Nelson, and Horace Maynard spoke here today. Did not go. Elvira Lea came from Missouri today. Did not go to school this evening. She and I went around shopping this evening. This evening about dusk we went over to the railroad to see the troops but were disappointed. Rhoda stayed all night with Venie.

Tuesday 4. A tolerable hard storm this evening. Elvira went down to Mrs. Lea's this evening. Uncle Caswell, Venie and Mrs. Rogers here this evening.

Wednesday 5. A beautiful evening. Sister and Rhoda spent the evening at Uncle Caswell's.

Thursday 6. A beautiful evening. Venie and I went out to Mr. Peters' and got some cherries and green June apples.

Friday 7. I did not go to school today. Mother, Mr. Carter, Sister, Rhoda, Lizzie and I went to hear Hon. John Bell and Col. Campbell deliver secession addresses this evening in the courthouse yard. Uncle Caswell took dinner here. Rhoda and Sister went to the Presbyterian Church to hear Dr. Styles preach. Rhoda went to church with Mr. Garrison and Venie tonight. Mr. Nat R. Carson and Mr. Fred Montgomery called on Rhoda and me tonight.

Saturday 8. An appearance of a storm this evening, but [it] passed off. I took Jimmie up to see cousin Ellen Jarnagin this evening. Sister and Rhoda went to church today. Rhoda and I went with Venie and Mr. Garrison tonight. Mrs. Cook here this evening, also Cousin John Lea, would scarcely speak to me. Mrs. Earnest also here. Mother sick today, Annie tonight. Sister, Rhoda and Annie went over to Mrs. Garrison's this evening. Annie ate too many cherries. The state of Tennessee voted out of the Union today.[26]

---

[26] Middle and West Tennessee voted to follow the actions of the governor and legislature. East Tennessee voted for "no separation." The legislature and governor had acted and pulled Tennessee from the nation's bosom. Tennessee was one of four additional states that seceded after the firing on Fort Sumter. There were eleven states in the Confederacy.

Sunday 9. A lovely day. Cousin Joe took tea here. Went to church with Rhoda, Mary E. and I tonight. Over to Mrs. Garrison's this evening. Venie went with Jim Johnston out to Tucker Springs[27] this evening. Mother and Mary went to the Baptist Church today, Rhoda and I to the Presbyterian. This evening I had the "blues" so bad before church, I could not cry. Wrote to Cousin Sam Inman. Mr. Garrison asked me a very singular question about our cow this evening.

Monday 10. A beautiful day. Sister and Rhoda went to church today. John Lea went with Rhoda tonight. I did not speak to him. took a good, long cry tonight. Venie and Rhoda up to Mrs. Cook's this evening. Read *Naomi's Vow.*

Tuesday 11. A beautiful day. Mr. and Mrs. Earnest and her two children spent the day here. Lavena's brother, Lt. Willard Seavey, came today on his way to the wars. Rhoda, Sister, Mother and the children went over to the depot to see the troops pass up. I went by Mrs. Garrison's and brought Venie and her brother home with Mrs. Garrison; came over and stayed awhile. Uncle Caswell Lea took tea here.

Wednesday 12. A beautiful day. Mother sent for Cousin Martha Lea and Aunt Elizabeth to come in and see the soldiers this morning. They took dinner here. Sister, Rhoda and I sent Will Seavey and his Capt. a bouquet this morning.

Thursday 13. Pleasant day. We went over to see some troops at the depot, took a walk over there after supper. An accident happened down below here, the engine bursted, three men were killed.[28]

Friday 14. Pretty day. Venie over here today. Rhoda and Venie went down to Mr. Stuart's to see the soldiers. Venie, Cousin John and Rhoda went to the choir tonight, very few persons there; met for the last time I expect.

Saturday 15. Lovely day. Rhoda and Venie went to see Sallie Surguine and Ada Anderson this afternoon. Mary E. and I went up to the academy to rehearse the dialogues for our examination.

---

[27] Tucker Springs is South of Cleveland near McDonald, Bradley County.

[28] Sometimes steam engines built up too much pressure causing the steel to crack or burst.

Caught cold this evening, was sick. The Arkansas troops went on down the road to protect their own borders from the Federal troops.

Sunday 16. Lovely day. Fred and Nat were here tonight. Venie over here this evening, stayed in the parlor all evening. Sister, Rhoda and Mrs. Carter went to the Methodist Church this morning. I had a sore throat, did not go.

Monday 17. A beautiful day. Rhoda cleaned up Aunt Adeline's room. I had [a] sore throat, did not go to school this evening. Rhoda altered my hat this evening.

Tuesday 18. A pretty day. Mother and Sister went out to Mrs. Lizzie Harris' this evening. The last day [of] school.

Wednesday 19. Pretty day. The first day of the examination. Had the headache so badly, had to come home before they were through. Was examined in Ancient Geography and Latin. Rhoda and Venie went up in the forenoon. Elvira Lea came in this evening.

Thursday 20. Pretty day. Elvira, Venie and Rhoda were at the Academy. I came home as soon as I recited my Arithmetic, and did not return until it was time to recite Dictionary. Walker McSpadden went with me to the exhibition, Nat with Rhoda, Jim Johnston with Sallie McMillin, Sam Hunt with Venie. Mr. Ragsdale sent Rhoda a card but her company was already engaged.

Friday 21. Pretty day. Cousin Sam Inman came from Dandridge this evening. Julia Grant, Mattie Reynolds and Virginia Grant took dinner here. Cousins Mary and Ellen Jarnagin took dinner here. Walker McSpadden wrote Venie a note, Sam Hunt one to Rhoda, Fred Montgomery one to me to go to a party at Col. Mills'. I went. Venie and Rhoda did not. Did not enjoy myself. We all read our compositions. Maria Kirk and Ada Anderson received their diplomas today.

Student	Subject
Mary Grant	"Thoughts at Twilight."
Mary Parker	"Beware."
Mary Hardwick	"Fast Men."
Sallie Shields	"Men are Rare."
Lucretia Tibbs	"Childhood Days--Poems."
Sallie McMillin	"Excelsior--Valedictory."
Maria Kirke	"Progression."
Ada Anderson	"Every Crisis Has its Hero."

Saturday 22. A pretty day. Cleaned up today. Sue Rowan and Mary Hunt here this morning.

Sunday 24. A pretty day. Mr. Carter and Miss Bowie came from Charleston, S.C. this morning. All but myself and Mother went to the Presbyterian Church. Mother went up to see Mrs. Cook. Fred and Nat here tonight to take us to church, but declined going as we had very bad colds. Cousin John here this evening.

Monday 24. Rained a little this morning. Anna Gaut here this morning. Started to help Emeline wash, but had the headache so bad had to decline.[29]Mr. Blunt took tea here. Cousin Sam Inman and I went out to Uncle Caswell's after supper. Venie and Rhoda came directly afterward. Cousin Ellen Jarnagin and her mother were out there.

Tuesday 25. A pretty day. Cousin Sam Inman and Rhoda went up to Mr. Howard's to have their daguerreotypes taken, but did not get them. Sallie McMillin, Tom McMillin and myself intended to have gone to see Mattie Reynolds, but she came in. I went over to Mrs. Garrison's.

Wednesday 26. A cloud came up, very dark, but it did not rain this evening. Venie and I started out to Dr. Grant's twice but were afraid it would rain, so went to see Sue Rowan. Went out to Mr. Peters' and got some June apples, came around by Dr. Grant's. Cousin Sam and Rhoda went out to Uncle Caswell's, came 'round by Dr. Grant's and stayed about an hour. Venie, Cousin Sam and I took a walk down to Mouse Creek. Cousin Sam and I went and got his daguerreotype.

Thursday 27. Cousin Sam Inman went home this morning. I have the headache this morning. Mrs. Garrison and Venie here this afternoon after tea.

Friday 28. A pretty day. Mel Osment was here this afternoon. Invited me to attend a picnic tomorrow down at Tucker Springs, did not go. Elvira Lea and Laura Callaway came down on the cars this evening, stayed all night here. Mr. Montgomery and Mr. Carson

---

[29]Myra began to help with some of the house chores. In June she began helping Emeline with washing. This assistance lasted through the year.

here tonight. Mother sick and in bed with a cold. Mrs. Henry Davis here this evening.

Saturday 29. Had a nice rain this evening. Rhoda went up to see Adelia Thompson this evening. Elvira and Lizzie went out to Uncle Caswell's this morning. Commenced reading *Twin Sister* this evening.

Sunday 30. Beautiful day. All except Mother went to Methodist Church this morning. A picnic out at Tucker Springs, did not go. Elvira Lea went down to her Aunt Rebecca's this morning. Bob Grant came inside of the gate and talked a long time about the war! Jim Harris here this evening. Cousin Joe Lea took tea here.

July 1861

Monday 1. Julia and Frances Tucker spent the day here. Rained nearly all evening. Mrs. Cook here this evening.

Tuesday 2. A beautiful day. Sallie McMillin and I went out to see Mattie Reynolds this evening, she was not at home. We then went out to Dr. Grant's. Venie and Rhoda went out to see Callie Swan and Mrs. Peters. Mother and Sister went out to see Uncle C[aswell] this morning. Sister and Rhoda went over to Mrs. Garrison's where she was this morning.

Wednesday 3. Lovely day. Rhoda and I went up to Dr. Thompson's after tea. Rhoda stayed all night [with] Anna Waterhouse.

Thursday 4. Sprinkled this evening. Venie, Anna Waterhouse and Mattie Reynolds were here this evening. Lavena and Rhoda went over to Mrs. McMillin's with Anna. Fred Montgomery and Mr. Robert Smith called on us tonight.

Friday 5. A pretty day. Venie here on her way out to spend the night with Mrs. Peters. Mrs. Garrison here after tea.

Saturday 6. Rained a little this morning. Mrs. Rogers, Mollie Dardis, Sister, Annie and I spent the day at Mrs. Hughes'. Ada Anderson and Mary Parker came out in the afternoon. Two secession speeches made up in town this evening. After tea Rhoda and I walked nearly out to Mrs. Peters' with Venie. Ramsey Swan came back with us. Received a letter and three pieces of music from cousin Sam Inman.

Sunday 7. A pleasant day. All but Mother and Mr Carter went to the Methodist Church. There were about five hundred "Union Men" collected together five miles from here to attack some troops they heard were going to Jimtown[30] or Cumberland Gap. Rhoda and I, after tea, went over to Mrs Garrison's, she had gone out to Mrs. Peters'. Mr. and Mrs. Garrison came over and stayed awhile after they came back.

Monday 8. Pretty day. Assisted Emeline wash this morning. Sister went over to Mrs. Garrison's this evening. Venie, Rhoda and I went out to Dr. Grant's this evening. I stayed all night. Venie stayed all night with Rhoda.

Tuesday 9. A storm this evening. Julia Grant came home with me this morning. Rained this evening. She and Cousin Martha Lea stayed all night. Aunt Elizabeth and Lizzie Bell here this evening. After tea Julia Grant and I went over to see Lavena Seavey. Mrs. Grant, Mrs. Stuart, Mrs. Hoyl, and Lizzie Burgis here this evening, hurried away by the rain.

Wednesday 10. Pleasant day. Julia Grant did not go home, was sick. Mr. Carter took her home in the buggy this evening. Frank Ragsdale and Fred Montgomery were here this evening.

Thursday 11. Pretty day. Sister and Mr. Carter and their children took a ride and got some blackberries. Rhoda stayed all night at Uncle Caswell's, tonight.

Friday 12. Pretty day. Mr. Blunt here this evening. Sister and Mrs. Garrison went up to see Mrs. William Craigmiles this evening. Mother went up to Mrs. Cook's. Lavenia and I went up in town to get some calico to make some flags. Mary, Lavenia and I went down to Mrs. Stuart's to see 8000 soldiers. Gave a Capt. a flag. Venie took supper here, we then took a walk. Rhoda came from Uncle Caswell's after supper.

Saturday 13. Pretty day. Venie, Lizzie, Sues (slave), Egbert and I went out after blackberries. We waded in the branch of Mrs.

---

[30] Jamestown, Fentress County, Tennessee. It was sometimes called Jimtown.

Traynor's Big Spring. In the evening I went over to a Mrs. Garrison's and Venie and I made some flags. Rhoda, sick. Eliza Shields here after tea, brought my hat home.

Sunday 14. Like yesterday. Mother and I went to the Baptist Church. Mr. Carter, Jimmie, Sister, and Annie went to the Methodist Church. Mother gave me a peach. Venie over here this evening. Rhoda no better.

Monday, 15. Sprinkled a little this evening. I helped wash today. Mrs. Carter, Tennie and Mrs. Hackman took tea here. Venie here this evening. Cousin John Lea at the door this morning.

Tuesday 16. Cloudy day. Uncle Caswell here this morning. Ramsey Swan, Manuel Guthman started to the war this morning. Mother and Sister went out to Uncle Caswell's to assist in baking for Cousin Martha's wedding. Rhoda and I twisted yarn all day. Wrote to Cousin Sam Inman this morning. Cousin John Lea, Mrs. Cook and Mrs. Dr. Edwards here this evening. Lizzie and I went with them to see a regiment go up.

Wednesday 17. Pretty day. Rhoda, Annie and I went out to see Cousin Martha this evening. Volunteers went up this evening.

Thursday 18. Cousin Martha C. Lea and Mr. Riggs were married this evening at three o'clock, started to Texas on five o'clock train. Rev. McCall married them. Our family went out. Rained very hard this evening and morning. Had a fight at Bull Run[31].

Friday 19. Mr. Brandon and Mag Shadden, Cousin John Lea and Venie, Sam Hunt, Jim Johnston and I, Bob and Mollie Grant, Will and Sue Kenner went up to Ladd's Springs to a picnic, at night had a dance in the Ladd House. Rained a little today.[32]

Saturday 20. Came back today from Laddville.

Sunday 21. Pretty day. Rhoda and Lizzie went to the Presbyterian Sunday School, to Church at the Cumberland. I had

---

[31] Or Manassas, see July 21 1861 entry.

[32] Adam Ladd, the original owner of the springs which bear his name, lived at the site of the springs in Polk County. The watering place was used for picnics and health retreats before and during the Civil War. The house on the grounds was known as Ladd House, while the community was known as Laddville. The springs were located seventeen miles southeast of Cleveland and were reached by following Ladd Springs Road.

three boils on my leg, could not go. Nat Carson here tonight. Had a large fight at Manassas Junction.³³

Monday 22. A rainy day. Venie stayed here tonight. Could not help wash today. Very cool tonight, had to have fire.

Tuesday 2 3. Pretty day. Mother and Sister went out to Aunt Elizabeth's this evening.

Wednesday 24. Pretty day. Mrs. Keebler died yesterday, and Mother and Sister went out to her burying. Adelia Craigmiles took dinner here. The secessionists illuminated in honor of the victory of

---

³³ Confederate General P. G. T. Beauregard was stationed at nearby Manassas where the Orange and Alexandria Railroad joined a line from the Shenandoah Valley. At this location Beauregard could defend Richmond and potentially threaten Washington, D.C.

Union General Irvin McDowell guarded Washington from a position twenty miles southwest of the city. Under pressure from speeches and newspaper accounts, McDowell decided to move toward the Confederate position. While his plans were well laid, he had a few regular troops and a sizeable group of inexperienced men. General Robert Patterson was to prevent the troops under Confederate Joseph E. Johnston from joining the main battle. Patterson was unable to accomplish his goal and Johnston slipped away and joined Beauregard on 20 July.

The next day McDowell's men attacked and dislodged the Confederate troops. Until mid-afternoon the Federals fought exceptionally well. Confederate reinforcements arrived and attacked the Federal positions in quick assaults, made more frightening by the fury of the "Rebel yell."

Confederate General T. J. Jackson did so well that he won his sobriquet "Stonewall." It took desperate fighting to dislodge the Unionist position on Henry Hill, but the Confederate assaults were successful. McDowell was forced to withdraw toward Washington which, at first, was in orderly fashion. When shot at on the road, jammed by spectators, panic resulted and men rushed to escape. While the ultimate result was indecisive, there were several important lessons developed by each side. This battle was important because it was the first significant battle and set the stage for the course of the war. It caused Southerners to believe they were superior to the Yankees and would need fewer men in the future. Confederate enlistments declined as men felt they would not be needed in the conflict.

The North realized that the struggle was going to be more costly and protracted than originally thought. They began to make long-range plans to successfully conclude the conflict. Randall and Donald, *The Civil War and Reconstruction*, 199.

Manassas, all went up in town except Mother and I. All except me went over to see the troops this evening. [34]

Thursday 25. Pretty day. Sister and Rhoda went up to Mrs. Traynor's and then went over to the depot to see troops. Mrs. Rogers came with her and stayed awhile. Rhoda came back very sick. I cannot walk a step on account of my boil.

Friday 26. Pretty day. Mother went down to Mrs Parker's and Mrs. McGriff's this evening. Sister [went] to see Mrs. Jessie Gaut. Ann Stuart here this evening. Rhoda and Venie went down to Mrs. Stuart's to see troops, two took tea here. Rhoda stayed all night with Venie.

Saturday 27. Pretty day. Uncle Caswell and Aunt Elizabeth came in, and all except me went over to the depot to see troops. I took tea at Mrs. Garrison's. Mary Jane Shugart here this evening, also Mrs. Garrison and Venie after tea. Uncle and Aunt took tea here. Mrs. McCall here this evening.

Sunday 28. Pretty day. Mary E. and Rhoda went to Sunday School. All except me went to church. Venie here after tea.

Monday 29. Pretty day. Sister went over to Mrs. Garrison's this evening. While there the sad intelligence reached them that Lt. Willard Seavey [Venie's brother] fell at the Battle of Bull Run on the 21st. Mrs. Edwards here this evening. Mother and Mrs. Cook went around to get the ladies to knit socks for the soldiers.

Tuesday 30. Pretty day. Ada Anderson, Mag Shadden and Mrs. Cook here this evening. Rhoda over to Mrs. Garrison's this evening, also Mrs. Cook and Sister. Governor Jackson of Missouri made a speech at the depot this evening.

Wednesday 31. A warm day. Mrs. Frank Lea, Miss Rebecca Weir, Annie Lea here this morning on their way down to Mr. Callaway's.

---

[34] With news of the so-called victory at Manassas, Cleveland's Confederates were so happy that they brilliantly illuminated the town area of Cleveland on 21 July 1861. Speeches were made by T. J. Campbell, S. A. Smith, G. W. Rowles, and W. H. Tibbs. Among the buildings lighted were the Ocoee Hotel kept by Thomas Johnston, 13 stores, and 6 dwellings. About 20 individuals participated in the event. J. S. Hurlburt, *History of the Rebellion in Bradley County, East Tennessee* (Indianapolis: Author, 1866) 144.

Sallie McMillin here this morning. Rhoda went up to Mrs. Cook's this evening. After tea Rhoda and I went over to Mrs. Garrison's.

August 1861

Thursday 1. The day of election for governor. A very warm day. Commenced knitting pair of socks for soldiers. Mrs. Peters and her children here this evening.

Friday 2. A very warm day. Mrs. Cook here this morning. Mother went over to Mrs. Garrison's and Mrs. Cook's. I also went to Mrs. Cook's.

Saturday 3. A very warm day. Mrs. Frank Lea's family stopped here on their way from Mr. Callaway's. Sister and children went up to Mr. William Campbell's. Sister and Rhoda after tea went over to Mrs. Garrison's.

Sunday 4. All went to church but Mary and I. Very warm day. Nat Carson came down to tell us good-bye, going North Thursday. Mrs. Hughes here this evening.

Monday 5. Warm day. Wrote in Sallie McMillin's album this morning. Florence Johnston and Mrs. Montgomery were here to get blankets for the wounded volunteers. Venie over here this evening. Mother cut out George's (slave) coat. I went over to Mrs. Garrison's in the evening.

Tuesday 6. Warm day. Venie's brother, Chris, went up this morning. Sallie, Julia and Jeanette Grant here this evening. We all went up to the Ocoee House and then over to the courtyard to see Miss McGriff present the Hamilton County Volunteers with a flag. Mollie Grant stayed all night with me, we did not go to sleep till four o'clock.

Wednesday 7. Warm day. Sister and Rhoda took Mrs. Garrison and Venie some grapes. Mrs. Cannon and Tresse Roberts spent the day here. Cried nearly all morning. I went over to see Lavena and Sallie McMillin. Mrs. Garrison and Venie came over after tea.

Thursday 8. Warm and cloudy day. Mrs. Cook and Ada Anderson here this evening. Been making two coats for our volunteers all day.

Friday 9. Sprinkled a little today. Cousin Merill Witt took dinner here. Rhoda and I spent the evening with Venie.

Saturday 10. Pretty day. Sister, Mother and Annie went to the Baptist Church. Anna Gaut here this morning. Sister and Annie went out to see Kate Britton (has a boy) and Aunt E., Rhoda went up to see Adelia Craigmiles, Mary E. down to see Mary Henderson and I over to see Anna Stuart. Our Company, Bradley Lancers, were mustered into service today.[35] Mr. Garrison, Venie, Rhoda, and I, also went to the Presbyterian prayer meeting. As we came back Venie stopped in and stayed all night.

Sunday 11. Rained and was very cloudy all day. Rhoda and Mary E. went to Sunday School. Rhoda and I went to the Presbyterian Church, practiced singing before church.

Monday 12. A drizzly, cloudy day, like autumn. Washed nearly all day. Old Mr. [Paschal] Carter came down this evening, brought Annie and Jimmie a muskmelon. Venie, Rhoda and I ate so many apples, peaches, grapes, muskmelons we could hardly live. We have concluded to live by ourselves and never marry, teach school. Uncle Caswell Lea here after school.

Tuesday 13. Cloudy day. Mrs. Guthman and Mrs. William Craigmiles have babies, also Jane Jordan. Adelia Craigmiles here this evening. Made me an underskirt[36] today. Sister went up to Mrs. Guthman's, Mrs. William Craigmiles' and Mrs. Garrison's. Uncle Caswell here after tea. Rhoda and Venie went up to Mrs. Cook's after tea. Mother has a boil on her leg.

Wednesday 14. A cool day, like autumn, had fire. Mr. R.W. Smith here tonight. Sister spent the evening at Mrs. Cook's. Mr. Carter

---

35 The Bradley Lancers was composed of men from Bradley and Polk counties under the leadership of Capt. S. W. Eldridge. In November the unit guarded the railroad bridge at Loudon. In May 1862 the unit was consolidated into 2nd (Ashby's) Cavalry Regiment. Murray, *Bradley Divided,* 289.

36An underskirt is worn under another skirt and could be called a petticoat

came home from Alabama this morning. I ironed some today. Had a watermelon and muskmelon off our lot.

Thursday 15. A pretty day. Venie and I went to see Sallie McMillin and Ada Anderson this morning. She and Rhoda went out to see Callie Swan and Virginia Harris. Rhoda and I went up to sing "Dixie" at Mrs. Rogers' tonight. Ada Stuart took tea here. Rhoda stayed all night with Venie.

Friday 16. A pretty day. Matilda McMahan and her two nieces took dinner here. Cousin John was here this morning. Rhoda and I went up to Mr. Campbell's and marched down with the rest of the girls to where Sallie Grant presented the flag to our company. All went up to the Courthouse except Mother. She has a boil on her and cannot walk. I went over to see Mag Henderson after we came back. Callie Swan took tea here. Venie stayed all night here. Cousin John and the rest of us sat on the doorstep until about ten o'clock. A beautiful, moonlight night. We took a walk and went out home with Callie.

Saturday 17. A rainy day and cloudy. Cousins John and Joe Lea and Mrs. Harris took dinner here. Aunt Elizabeth, Uncle Caswell and Lizzie Lea came in and we all went over to the depot to see the Company (Bradley Lancers) start. In the evening, Cousin John Lea, Rhoda and I went over to the depot to see Lavena Seavey start down to Atlanta. Davie Jones went with her. He came to tell us good-bye. Uncle Caswell took tea here. Rhoda and I went with Mr. and Mrs. Garrison to Presbyterian prayer meeting. Heard yesterday that Mr. Blunt was not coming back. My school days are past.

Sunday 18. Rained this morning before Sunday School, and the evening. All of us went to Sunday School. All went to church except Mother and I. Mother sent for Cousin Mary Harle to see her boil this morning. Cousin John came this evening. We did not have anything for tea except for peaches and cream. Bettie Haye was over this evening.

Monday 19. A warm day. Wasted today. Wrote to Cousin Sam Inman this evening. Mrs. Betsy Grant, Bell, Mrs. Cook and Cousin John Lea and muskmelons. Sister went up to the [Soldiers' Aid] Society that met at Mr. Kenner's old house for the benefit of the volunteers this evening. Mr. Rogers here to see Mr. Carter this evening.

Tuesday 20. Pretty day. Mr. Schreiner and Mrs. Cook here this morning. John Craigmiles came down for Rhoda to go up to Dr. Thompson's and sing some duets. Knitting all day.

Wednesday 21. Pretty day. Cousin Mary Harle and Aunt Fannie Lea here today. Sister and Rhoda made some grape wine for the soldiers. Mrs. Frank Lea sent her carriage up for Emma Lea, Ella DeLano and I went down there this evening. I was sick in bed this morning.

Thursday 22. Rained very hard this evening. Elvira, Emma and I took a walk down to the creek this evening. Sam Hunt left for Illinois this evening.

Friday 23. Wet and drizzly. Sewed some for Aunt Mary, and knitted some. All but I went over to the peach orchard. Mr. Bradford over this evening.

Saturday 24. Pretty day. Went over to Mrs. Bradford's, came home this morning. Went out to Uncle Caswell's to see Rhoda. She spent the day there, also Annie. We all took tea. Mr. McCallie was there. Mr. Garrison came by after us and we went to prayer meeting. Received a letter from Cousin Sam Inman. Brass Band played tonight.

Sunday 25. Pretty day. Went to Sunday School. All went to Presbyterian Church. Callie Swan came home with us to practice some pieces to sing at church. Mr. Garrison came after us to go to church at night. He came for us to go up to church at 4 o'clock to practice, did not go. Went with him to church at night.

Monday 26. A rainy and gloomy evening. Eliza Keebler and her father took dinner here. I helped wash today.

Tuesday 27. A very rainy and gloomy day. Made Annie a pair of drawers.

Wednesday 28. Like yesterday. Raining all day. Made Annie another pair of drawers.

Thursday 29. Rained some this morning. Bob Sloan, Mrs. Jessie Gaut, Mrs. Cook, Florence Johnston, Julia and Mollie Grant were here this afternoon. Made me a pair of drawers. Sister and Rhoda went to Methodist prayer meeting.

Friday 30. Pretty day. Sister and Rhoda spent the day at Uncle Caswell's. Mrs. Shadden here this morning. Mrs. Cook here in the evening. Mrs. Cook went with Rhoda to singing tonight.

Saturday 31. Pretty day. Went to the stores, and down to see Ada Anderson; she and I went to see Mary Parker. An earthquake this morning 4 o'clock. Rhoda and I went with Mr. Garrison to prayer meeting.

September 1861

Sunday 1. Pretty day. All went to Sunday School, also to Presbyterian Church. No church in town tonight. We all took a walk after tea. Sallie McMillin and Will caught up with us. Bob Sloan was here this evening.

Monday 2. Washed today. A pleasant day. Sister and Rhoda put some peaches up in cans this evening. Mother went up to Mrs. Cook's, the first time since her boil was well enough to go anywhere.

Tuesday 3. A pretty day. Cousin John Lea and Mrs. Cook here this evening. Sister and Mother went to Mrs. Edward's and Mrs. Dr. Brown's this evening. Rhoda and I went over to Mrs. Garrison's tonight. Bob Smith and Fred Montgomery called on us tonight.

Wednesday 4. A warm day. Ada Anderson and I spent the day at Mrs. Tucker's this evening, went over to Mr. Tibbs'. Lucretia Tibbs stayed all night with me tonight. Went up to see Mary and Lillie Davis after tea. Lucretia told me something about H_____.[37]

Thursday 5. Pretty day. Have two [boils] coming on my leg. Wrote to Cousin Sam Inman this morning.

Friday 6. Pretty day. Rhoda went with Mr. Garrison to the choir this evening. Sister, Mr. Garrison and Annie spent the evening at Mrs. Peters'.

Saturday 7. Pretty day. Mother and Sister went up to Mrs. Berry's and up to see Cousin Ellen Jarnagin, who came down yesterday evening, also Lizzie. Mrs. Stout here after dinner. Rhoda, Lizzie and I went with Mr. Garrison to prayer meeting. Mr. W. L. McSpadden came home with me.

---

[37] Indicates that Myra left out the full name in order to keep some information a secret in case someone read her diary.

Sunday 8. Pretty day. All of us went to Sunday School. All except Mother and I went to [the] Methodist Church. Mr. Carter came back home before preaching was out. Mr. Daily preached. Mrs. Cook was here this evening. Mother and I went to see Mrs. Henderson; she has a baby. Mrs. Cook stayed all night with us. Mr. Cook was gone.

Monday 9. Warm day. Cousin Ellen took tea here. Messrs. Fred Montgomery and Bob Smith called on Rhoda and me. Mrs. Cook here this evening. I made me two pairs of pantalettes. [38]

Tuesday 10. A pretty day. Fred Montgomery started for the war this morning. Mrs. D. Edwards was here this morning. Sallie McMillin here this afternoon. She and Rhoda went down to see Ada Anderson. Sister and Rhoda went over to Mrs. Garrison's after tea. Mother up to Mrs. Cook's. I made me an underskirt today. The Brass Band has been playing splendidly. Is now playing "Dixie." Lacks 5 minutes of 8 o'clock.

Wednesday 11. Pretty day. Mrs. Garrison over here this morning and evening. Altered one of my dark calico dresses. Mary E. went down to Mrs. Stuart's also to Mrs. Jessie Gaut's for some flowers to set out. Mother, Rhoda and I went to the Baptist prayer meeting.

Thursday 12. Pretty day. Mrs. Berry and Mrs. Stout started to Georgia today. They spent the day here. Mrs. Rogers, Mrs. Dr. Edwards, Mrs. Carter, and Mrs. Pepper were here this evening. Mother, Rhoda, Annie, Lizzie and I went out to see Cousin John. He is to start to Knoxville tomorrow.

Friday 13. Pretty day. Sister, Mother, Mrs. Rogers and the children spent the day at Uncle Caswell's. Rhoda over to Mrs. Garrison's this morning and evening. I went over a few minutes this evening. Mrs. G. W. Alexander and Mrs. Shadden here this morning. Mrs. Shadden and Mag down after tea. We all took a walk and as we came back stopped in at Mrs. Cook's. Heard today that Dr. McNabb and Naomi Henry were married last Tuesday night. Been making a pin cushion for soldiers. Cousin John started to Knoxville this morning to join Capt. Eldridge's Company.

Saturday 14. Pretty day. Mrs. Garrison started to Atlanta this evening. Sister went over and told her goodbye. Mr. Carter came

---

[38] Pantalets are long underdrawers, trimmed with ruffles extending below the skirt.

home this evening. Cousin Ellen Jarnagin came down this evening to assist Mr. Bradshaw [in the academy]. Mother and Sister went to meeting today. Rhoda and I went out to get Cousin John to take some cake to Cousin Sam Inman. He is sick with the fever. Mother went to Baptist Church tonight.

Sunday 15. Mother, Rhoda, Lizzie and I went to Baptist Church. Mr. Carter and family went to Methodist. Pretty and very warm day. All went to Sunday School. Mother, Sister, Rhoda, Lizzie and I went to the Baptist Church at night. Sister, Mother, Annie and Jimmie went to church this evening at 3 o'clock. Cousin John Lea, Mr. Caywood and Mr. Hawkins took dinner here. Cousin John, Rhoda, Lizzie and I went to the choir at 3 o'clock this evening.

Monday 16. Very warm I helped Aunt Phoebe wash. Emeline was sick. Rhoda and I went out to Mr. Robert Swan's; from there to Uncle Caswell's where Cousin Ellen [Jarnagin], Mrs. Edwards and we took tea. Cousin John came in with us and told all of us goodbye. Sister and Mother went to church today and tonight also. Mr. Carter went to Benton and back today. Rhoda, Mother and Sister, have been making drawers for soldiers all day.

Tuesday 17. Pretty day. Mother, sister and I went to church this morning. Mother, Rhoda and I went at night. Mr. Bradshaw was here with Mr. Haskins to get boarding for his two daughters. Did not board them. Mr. Carter and family took tea at old Mr. Carter's. Mother, Rhoda and I went up to Mrs. Cook's this evening. Nora Stuart here this evening, brought ten pairs of socks. Lizzie started to school to Mr. Bradshaw yesterday. Commenced knitting me a pair of stockings.

Wednesday 18. Pretty day. Mr. Carter went up the "road" today. Sister, Rhoda and Mother went to church this morning. Mrs. Hughes and Mattie Reynolds here this evening. I went out and stayed with Mattie. All but me went to the "Soldiers' Aid Society." Sallie McMillin came home with Rhoda. They both went over to see Sallie Surguine. Mr. Hawkins and Mr. Caywood took tea here.

Thursday 19. Warm day. Mother, Sister went to church this morning, and also tonight. Mrs. Hughes, Mattie and I stopped by to see Kate Britton as we came to town.

Friday 20. Day very warm. Mother took dinner at Mrs. Cook's, she joined the Baptist Church today. Prayer meeting at Mrs. Cook's this evening. Aunt Elizabeth and Uncle Caswell took tea here. Mother went to church tonight, and also today. Mr. Hawkins and Mr. Caywood stayed all night here.

Saturday 21. A fall day. Aunt Elizabeth Lea here this morning. She, Rhoda and I went over to see Lea Caywood. He is sick, has the flux[39] Mother, Sister, Rhoda and I went to church. Sister joined the Baptist Church today. At 3 o'clock, afternoon, she and mother were baptized by Dr. McNutt down by steam-mill. Mother, Rhoda, Lizzie and I were at church tonight.[40]

Sunday 22. Very cool day, had fire. All went to Sunday School. Rhoda and I went to Presbyterian Church. All but Lizzie went to Baptist church. Mr. Caywood and Mr. Hawkins took dinner here. They went home this evening, preaching broke. Joe Lea took tea here. Rhoda and I went to Cumberland [Church] tonight.

Monday 23. Cool day. Helped wash today. Mrs. Cook and Sallie McMillin here this evening. Sallie and Rhoda went around calling this evening. Mr. [Bob] Smith called on Rhoda tonight. Mother sat up with Lea tonight. Aunt Adeline [is] sick. Houston died this day four years ago.[41] Adelia Craigmiles here this morning.

Tuesday 24. Cool day. Uncle Caswell brought in some yarn for me to knit Cousin John a pair of socks. Old Mrs. Cook here to get some yarn to finish her son a pair of socks. Mother went up to Mrs. Cook's to get her to show her how to make a pair of pantaloons for soldiers. Sister went over to see Lea Caywood this evening. Received a letter from Cousin John Lea.

Wednesday 25. Autumn day, high and cool winds. Aunt Adeline is better. Knitting on Cousin John's socks all day. Mr. Carter, Sister and children went over to Mr. Bacon's to get some yarn dyed. Received a letter from Emma Aldehoff [this] morning.

Thursday 26. Pretty day. Mother and Sister went over to Cousin Mary Harle's to see Lea (Caywood), [he is] better. Finished Cousin John's socks.

Friday 27. Pretty day. Mother and Sister went over to see Lea.

---

[39] The flux was a disturbance of the intestinal tract.

[40] See entry for 14 April 1861 where Myra states how she strongly dislikes the Baptist denomination.

[41] 23 September 1857.

Saturday 28. Cool day. Aunt Elizabeth, Uncle Caswell and "Sissy" took supper here this evening. Got Cousin John's daguerreotype this evening. Julia Grant and Ann Stuart here this evening.

Sunday 29. Cool day. We all went over to see Cousin Lea Caywood die. He died at 4 o'clock. Rhoda sat up there all night. Cousin Joe Lea took tea here.

Monday 30. Pretty day. Washed today. Florence Johnston came down this evening to get Rhoda and me to assist in giving concert for "Soldiers." Aunt Adeline is better. All went to the burying this evening.

October 1861

Tuesday 1. Pretty day. Tacked a comfort this morning[42]

Wednesday 2. Rained some today. Mother and Sister went to the Sewing Society. Aunt Elizabeth and Mrs. Grant came home with them. Mrs. Grant and Julia took tea here. Rhoda and I went up to the Ocoee to see about the concert.

Thursday 3. Pretty day. All of the girls met at our house to select tableau this evening. Went over to Mrs. McMillin's to see if Sallie had a duet for us to play.

Friday 4. Pretty day. Sue Kenner, Lucretia Tibbs, Florence Johnston, Rhoda and I met at Mr. McMillin's this evening. Rhoda and I went with Mr. Garrison to the choir. Walker McSpadden came home with me.

Saturday 5. Met at Mrs. Rogers to practice this evening. Florence Johnston and Sallie McMillin here this morning to practice duets. Rhoda and I went up to Cousin Ellen Jarnagin's to get a duet for us to play.

Sunday 6. Rainy day. Mother, Uncle Ned and I went down to Baptist Association, 7 miles from here. Mrs. Cook and we took dinner at Mrs. Clingan's. Joe Lea took tea here.

---

[42]Tacked in this case means to fasten with a loose basting stitch.

Monday 7. Rainy day. Mother went down to the association, got as far as Candy's Creek. The creek was too high, came back. The girls met here to practice this evening. Mrs. Rogers here this evening. Julia and Mollie Grant took tea here. Mollie stayed all night. Sallie and Tom McMillin came by after us and we went up to the Ocoee House to practice the tableau. Fred Montgomery was there this evening, went to Loudon this morning.

Tuesday 8. Windy day. All met here to make the crowns [for the tableau] this morning. Met at Mr. McMillin's to practice. Mr. Knabe met with us. Mother went up to Mrs. Cook's.

Wednesday 9. Pretty day. Met at the hotel to practice the tableau tonight. Frank Ragsdale came home with us. Anna Gaut here this evening. Sallie McMillin and Rhoda went up to the Ocoee House to make the programme. Sallie and I went up in the evening to assist in arranging the stage.

Thursday 10. Cloudy day. Met at the Ocoee House to practice this evening. Concert tonight, all went, Tom McMillin went with me.

Friday 11. A dark, rainy and gloomy day, such a day as I love. Read and knitted some. Kate Rogers, Mary Edwards and Mary Shugart were here this morning.

Saturday 12. Cold day, heavy dew. Knitted on my stocking. Mrs. Lewis and Mrs. Manuel Guthman were here this [evening]. Made kraut this morning.

Sunday 13. Pretty day. All went to Sunday School except me. I had [a] cold. Rhoda, Lizzie and I went to Presbyterian Church. All the rest went to the Baptist. Mother and Sister went up to Mr. Cook's in the evening. Mr. Kimbro, a Baptist preacher, took tea here. Mother, Rhoda and I went to the Baptist Church. As we came home we went and [sat] till bedtime at Mr. Cook's. Rhoda, Sister and I took a walk this evening up to Dr. Grant's, had a pleasant time.

Monday 14. Pretty day. Washed today. Mrs. Cook stayed all night here. Mrs. Shadden and Mag sat with us until bedtime. Uncle House here awhile after tea. Cousin Mary Harle here this evening. Mother and I went shopping and got me a new gingham dress. Aunt Elizabeth here this morning also and Uncle Caswell.

Tuesday 15. Pretty day. Made my calico dress. Mother, Sister and Cousin Mary Harle went out and spent the day at Uncle Caswell's Lea to make Cousin John an overcoat. Rhoda and Mr. Cook went out to Mrs. Peters' to call on Miss Laura Williams. Rhoda took tea at Mrs. Cook's and stayed all night there. Mr. Cook is gone to Atlanta.

Wednesday 16. A very rainy night and evening. Finished my dress. Mother and Sister spent the day at Uncle Caswell's again. Mother, Sister, Rhoda and I went to the "Soldiers' Aid Society." Rhoda and I went down to see Cousin Ellen Jarnagin afterwards. Mrs. Cook stayed all night here. Mrs. Shadden here this evening.

Thursday 17. A very rainy day. Mrs. Cook spent the day here. Mother and I spent the day at Dr. Edwards' we went to sew on Walker McSpadden's shirt, and pack two boxes to Capt. Eldridge's Company.

Friday 18. Pretty day. Walker McSpadden came down this evening and told us good-bye, he is going to war, going to join Capt. Eldridge's Company. I stayed with Aunt Elizabeth tonight. Uncle Caswell and Joe have gone to Loudon to see John. Mother and I went to see Mrs. Lafayette Hardwick, she has a baby boy. Sallie Surguine came over this evening to get Rhoda or I to stay all night with her. Mr. Surguine [has] gone to Georgetown (Hamilton County, Tennessee). Rhoda stayed with her.

Saturday 19. Rained all morning. "Sissy" (Lea) and I came in from Uncle Caswell's this evening. Lizzie went down to see Emma Barton this evening. Sister went over to Cousin Mary Harle's.

Sunday 20. Pretty day. All went to Sunday School. All went to Methodist Church except Mother and I. Mr. Glenn preached. Mother went up to Mrs. Cook's this morning. Mrs. Cook down here this evening. Ate a peach today. Emeline gave it to me.

Monday 21. Washed today. Had the headache, did not wash but half a day. Pretty day. Mrs. Cook stayed all night here.

Tuesday 22. Pretty day. Knitted on my stocking. Mrs. Cook stayed all night here.

Wednesday 23. Pretty day. Mrs. Cook stayed all night. Commenced my gingham dress [which is a yarn-dyed cotton fabric woven in stripes, checks, or solid colors.] Mrs. Cook stayed all night here.

Thursday 24. Pretty day. Worked all day on my dress. Mrs. Cook stayed all night here. Rhoda went up with John Craigmiles (he came after her) to sit until bedtime with Adelia. Mr. Carter and Sister went up to old Mr. Carter's to see Peyton Carter. He is going to war tomorrow! Mother and Sister went to see Mrs. McNutt with Mrs. Cook. Mrs. Jessie Gaut and Miss Hannah Alexander were here this evening. Mother and Sister were gone.

Friday 25. Mother and Sister went over to see Mrs. Leonard Ross with Mrs. Jessie Gaut. Mrs. Pepper and Mrs. Craigmiles were here this evening. Finished my dress.

Saturday 26. Cousin John Lea came down this evening with Mr. Fancier, he was killed on the railroad, belonged to Capt. Eldridge's Company.

Sunday 27. Windy day. All went to Sunday School. All except Mother went to Presbyterian Church. Mrs. Garrison here this evening. Rhoda, Mr. Carter, Lizzie and I, together with Mr. Garrison, went up to Mr. Fancier's burying at 2 o'clock. Cousin John came home with us. Rhoda, Mr. Garrison, Cousin John and I went up to the church at 4 o'clock to practice. Cousin John took tea here. He went with Rhoda and [I] to Presbyterian Church at night. Cousin John stayed here all night.

Monday 28. Mother and Rhoda spent the day at Uncle Caswell's. I helped wash half-day. Helped make some hoar-hound for Cousin John's cough.[43] Rhoda took tea at Uncle Caswell's, came in with Cousin John and went down to see Cousin Ellen Jarnagin. Cousin John stayed all night here.

Tuesday 29. Cool day. Mother, Sister, Rhoda, Annie, Jimmie and I went out with Cousin John and spent the day at Uncle Caswell's. Cousin John came in and stayed awhile after tea. Sallie Surguine, Mrs. Williams and Lucretia Tibbs came over after me to stay all night with Lucretia at Sallie Surguine's. I went, had a nice time.

Wednesday 30. Cool day. Aunt Elizabeth, Uncle Caswell, Cousin John spent the day here. Mother, Sister and Aunt Elizabeth went up to the Sewing Circle at 2 o'clock. Mrs. Tibbs and Mrs. Thompson came while they were gone. Mr. Bradshaw came down at night to see if Mother would let us take painting lessons from Mr. Cameron. Mrs. Traynor and Mrs. Rogers sat until bedtime with us. Mr. and Mrs. Cook came and stayed a while after prayer meeting. Cousin John came and told us good-bye. He going to Loudon tomorrow.

---

[43] Horehound is a candy or preparation flavored by an aromatic plant.

Thursday 31. Uncle William and Cousin Merill Witt took dinner here. Knitted on my stocking all day. Mother and Sister went up to Mrs. Cook's this evening. Rhoda and I put some tomatoes in salt this evening to make sauce tomorrow. Julia Grant came by after me and I went out there and stayed all night.

November 1861

Friday 1. A very rainy, dark, gloomy day. Rained so hard I had to stay all day and night at Dr. Grant's.

Saturday 2. A cold, dark, gloomy day. Came home this morning. Julia came part of the way with me. Mr. Cook gone, Mrs. Cook stayed all night with us.

Sunday 3. All went to Sunday School. All of us went to Baptist Church to hear an Indian preach, except Mother. She had a boil on her leg, could not go. Rhoda took dinner with Mrs. Cook. After dinner they went down to Mr. McNutt's. Mr. and Mrs. Rogers and Fred here this evening, also old Mr. Carter. Cousin Joe Lea here, took tea. He brought me a ring that somebody sent by him when he was at Loudon. Rained about dark so we could not go to church.

Monday 4. Pretty day. Helped wash today. Cousin Mary Harle over here this evening. Rhoda went down to see Anna Gaut this eve.

Tuesday 5. Pretty day. Commenced cording[44]me a chemise bosom [dickey] today.[45] Mother and Mrs. Cook went over to see Mrs. Joel K. Brown this evening. Sister took supper at Mrs. Carter's, went to Mrs. Traynor's. Mr. Carter came down on the train and brought news that Seward, Scott, and McClellan had resigned.[46] It is false.

---

[44]Cording means to fasten, bind, or trim with a piece of small twisted fibers made into a cord.

[45]Dickey, or part of a garment worn over the front of an outfit.

[46] This information was based on an element of truth. Changes were being made in national leadership which involved these three persons. William H. Seward was Abraham Lincoln's Secretary of State who advocated a strong foreign policy for the nation. Gen. Winfield Scott,

Wednesday 6. Pretty day. Still working on my chemise bosom. Mother and Sister went up to the society and around to see some ladies this evening. Sister, Mother, Rhoda and I went to prayer meeting at Baptist Church. Mr. and Mrs. Cook came and sat awhile after prayer meeting. Mel Osment here this evening.

Thursday 7. Beautiful day. Aunt Fannie Lea here, took dinner. Sister went out to get Aunt Elizabeth Lea help her stitch her shirt bosoms on sewing machine. They came in this evening and made some calls, then Aunt Elizabeth and Mother made some. Mrs. Cook, Emeline Aunt Ball and I all went down and cleaned out the Baptist church. Rhoda received a letter from Cousin John Lea. She, Mother and Sister went out after dark to Uncle Caswell's to get him to send John's carpet bag up by Lt. Kuhn in the morning. I copied off "Norma's March" while they were gone.

Friday 8. Very windy day. Mary Edwards here this morning. Mother and Sister went up to Mrs. Cook's and Mrs. Worley's this evening. Made some hoar hound candy for Sister's cold. Mr. Carter went down the road this morning. Mason and Slidell were taken by the Federals today.[47]

---

commander of the army, failing health which caused him to retire 1 November 1861. George B. McClellan , a major general in the regular army, was named general in chief in November 1861 succeeding Winfield Scott. Richard B. Morris, ed. *Encyclopedia of American History* (New York: Harper & Row, 1976), 1092, 1148.

[47]In 1861 the Confederacy sought to establish diplomatic relations with England and France. They chose James Murray Mason of Virginia for London and John Slidell of Louisiana for Paris. On 8 November 1861, one day after leaving port, their vessel was stopped by a United States warship. The two commissioners and their secretaries were arrested and placed on board the warship. The captain of the American vessel had to use some force to conduct the search. The Confederate officials were political prisoners who were placed in Fort Warren, Boston Harbor. The incident had serious implications and almost caused a war between the United States and England. Lord Palmerston said he would not stand for such actions. After some consultation and deliberation, it was decided to settle the matter short of war. Later, the Confederate diplomats were "cheerfully liberated." See Randall and Donald, *The Civil War and Reconstruction*, 360-362.

Saturday 9. A rainy day. Mrs. Cook came and told us that there were five bridges burned last night by the union people. Aunt Elizabeth and Uncle Caswell Lea came in this evening. Rhoda, Lizzie and I went to the Cumberland Church to hear Florence Johnston present Billy Brown's Company with a flag. Mrs. John Tucker brought ten pairs of socks. Heard today that we had gained a glorious victory at Columbus, Ky., under Gen. Pillow.

Sunday 10. We all went to Sunday School and to the Baptist Church. Mr. Kefauver and Mr. McNutt took dinner here. Rhoda and Mr. Garrison went to the choir this evening. All the rest of us went to the Baptist meeting at three o'clock. At night all of us went.

Monday 11. Pretty day. Mrs. Lea came in this morning. I helped wash today. Elvira Lea came in also. Anna Gaut here this evening. Went to the Baptist Church tonight.

Tuesday 12. Pretty day. Went to church today and tonight also. Mr. Kefauver preached on "Experimental Religion." Mother sick today. I helped sew on Mr. Kefauver's drawers. Five volunteers took dinner here, one took supper.

Wednesday 13. Pretty day. Went to church this morning and at night. Went to see Lizzie Foster baptized. Mother and Sister went to the Sewing Society this evening. Rhoda stayed all night with Sallie Surguine. Ada Anderson, Mary Hardwick and Callie Swan here yesterday.

Thursday 14. Pretty day. Elvira Lea and I went to see Frances Tucker today. We came in and went to the baptizing. Three were baptized. Went to preaching tonight. Volunteers went out to look for Mr. [William] Clift's men did not find them, they had fled. Took the citizens' guns away from them today. Rhoda stayed all night with Mrs. Cook.[48]

Friday 15. Pretty day. Went to church today and tonight, fast day. I fasted. Aunt Elizabeth [Lea] here today. Aunt Elizabeth and Sister went over to see Cousin Mary Harle, she is sick.

---

[48] William Clift was a large landowner in Hamilton County, who encouraged local men to remain loyal to the Union. Governor Isham Harris gave orders to capture Clift and his men "dead or alive." His followers escaped into the mountains and later operated out of Scott County. Murray, *Bradley Divided*, 327-329.

Saturday 16. Pretty day. Went to church tonight. Mr. Kefauver preached on the subject of baptism. Miss Bradshaw, Cousins Mary and Ellen Jarnagin and Emma Barton were here this evening.

Sunday 17. Cold day. Went to church, and at night also. Did not go to Sunday School, stayed at home and went to prayer meeting. Went to Mrs. Cook's with Mother this evening. Elvira went home.

Monday 18. Cold day. Washed today. Went to see Ada Anderson baptized this evening. Went to church tonight. Took sacrament[49] tonight. Preaching broke tonight.[50]

Tuesday 19. Cold day. Mrs. Cook here this evening.

Wednesday 20. Rained some today. Mother went to the "Sewing Circle" this evening. Mother, Rhoda and I went to prayer meeting tonight. Mr. Kefauver, Mr. and Mrs. Cook came in and sat until bedtime.

Thursday 21. Mr. Cook has gone down to Atlanta, Mrs. Cook stayed all night here. Mrs. Shadden took tea here.

Friday 22. Mrs. Cook stayed all night here. Commenced making Mr. Kefauver's shirts.

Saturday 23. Killed a hog today. Tacked down sister's carpet today. Mr. Carter went up the road today, will be back tomorrow. Mother and Aunt Elizabeth went out to see George Swan. Rhoda went out to see Kate Britton. Mrs. Cook and Uncle Caswell here this evening. Pensacola was bombarded, 22nd and 23rd of Nov. 1861.[51]

Sunday 24. Cold day. All of us went to Sunday School. Cousin Joe Lea took dinner here. Old Mrs. Carter, Mrs. Garrison and Mrs. Cook here this evening. Mr. Garrison and Rhoda Ann went to the choir at 3 o'clock.

---

49 Communion or Lord's Supper.

50Baptists preferred a protracted meeting for their revivals. They announced a beginning time and continued services until results were not encouraging. When they reached this point the meeting "broke" which meant that the services which lasted on nine days ended. The services were over.

51Florida seceded on 10 January 1861, and attention was focused on Fort Pickens, near Pensacola, Florida, which remained under Union control. Confederates wanted this to change. The first major battle in Florida occurred in October 1861 when Southern troops unsuccessfully assaulted the fort. Later, it was shelled, but not captured.

Monday 25. Cold day. Washed today. Mrs. Traynor and Mrs. Stout spent the day here. Uncle William Lea took dinner here.

Tuesday 26. Cold day. Went up to Mrs. Cook's to get her to cut out Mr. Kefauver's shirt collar for me to make this morning. Mrs. Cook and Mother went out to see George Swan. Sister and I baked some cake this evening. Rhoda stayed all night with Adelia Craigmiles. I wrote to Cousin Sam Inman tonight.

Wednesday 27. Rainy day. Rhoda spent the day at Mrs. Cook's. Made Mr. Kefauver's shirt collar. Mrs. Cook stayed all night here. Mrs. Cook, Mother, Rhoda and I went to Baptist prayer meeting tonight. We are very much disheartened about the acknowledgment of the Southern Confederacy.

Thursday 28. Windy, rainy, cloudy and muddy day. Cleaned a lamp this morning. Worked on my chemise band in the afternoon. Mrs. Cook stayed all night here. Mother is not well today.

Friday 29. Warm, very windy, sultry and muddy day. Mother is sick today. Worked on my chemise band. Heard today that we have gained a glorious victory at Pensacola under Gen. [Braxton] Bragg.

Saturday 30. Cold day. Emma Barton and Sue Bower were here this evening. Mary E. and Emma Barton went up to see Gussie Craigmiles. Mrs. Cook stayed all night here. I mended my hoop, washed, finished my chemise band, today.

December 1861

Sunday 1. We all went to Sunday School. Rhoda, Lizzie and I went to the Methodist Church. Mr. Glenn preached. Mother and Rhoda went up and sat with Mrs. Cook awhile this evening. Rhoda and I went up to the choir this evening. Mrs. Rogers here this evening. Mrs. Cook stayed all night.

Monday 2. Cold day. I helped Emeline wash today. Sister has a baby, a boy, weighs 8 lbs., named John Bowie, borne Dec. 1st, 1861. Mrs. Shadden, Mrs. Cook, Mrs. Rogers, Mrs. Traynor, and Mrs. Stout were here today. Mrs. Cook and Mrs. Shadden stayed all night.

Tuesday 3. Very cold day. We killed hogs today--twelve weighed 3088 lbs. Old Mrs. Carter, Mrs. William Craigmiles, Mrs. Pepper and Mrs. Worley were here today. Mrs. Cook stayed all night. Aunt Elizabeth and Mrs. Lizzie Harris here.

Wednesday 4. Cold day. Rhoda and I have been helping in the kitchen about the hogs. Mr. Perry Gaut and Ada Anderson were married this morning before breakfast at Mrs. Jessie Gaut's, and went to Benton. Mrs. Stuart and Georgie Lea were here this evening. George brought the children a rabbit. Lizzie Lea took dinner here, came to see Bowie. All of us weighed today. Mother 113, Mr. Carter 175, Rhoda 104, Mary E. 75, Annie 45, Jimmie 35. The following were Negroes: Uncle Ned 120 1/2, Aunt Phoebe 169, Emeline 110, Sues 68, Frank 47 1/2. I weighed 109, and Lizzie Lea 54.

Thursday 5. Pretty day. Rhoda and I have been making bags[52] for sausage meat all day, and stuffing them between 11 and twelve o'clock at night. Aunt Elizabeth here this evening, also Mrs. Dr. Grant, Mrs. Pleasant Craigmiles and Mrs. Thornton here this morning. Mrs. Cook all night here.

Friday 6. Pretty day. Rhoda and I finished with the bags this morning. Ironed all the rest of the day. Mollie and Bell Grant here this forenoon, Mag Shadden and Mrs. William Craigmiles in the afternoon, also Mrs. Cook. She stayed all night here.

Saturday 7. Beautiful day. A great many ladies met at Mrs. Cook's at 10 o'clock and we all went over to Camp Cleveland (at the fairground) to see the Van Dorn's Rebels. There were thirty of us went. After we came back, Mary Pharis, Anna Stuart and I stopped in to see Sallie McMillin, Mrs. Cook stayed all night here.

Sunday 8. Pretty day. We all went to Sunday School. Rhoda, Lizzie and I went to the Presbyterian Church. Mr. Dunn came home with us. Rhoda and I went up to the choir to practice at 3 o'clock. Went up to Mrs. Cook's and brought her down to sit a while this evening. Dr. Brown was arrested this morning. Mrs. Cook stayed all night here.

Monday 9. Very warm day. I helped Emeline wash today. Mrs. Bradford, Cousin Mary Harle, Mrs. Shadden, Mrs. Onie Campbell, Julia and Lou Grant were all here this evening. Mrs. Cook stayed all

---

[52] Bags were prepared from animal intestine or some other casing.

night here, she received a letter from Mr. Cook, has been very uneasy about him. Mrs. Hoyl has a girl. Mrs. Cook and Mother went up to see it this evening. Messrs. Williams. Davis, Gus Bradford, Sam Hunt, Kirby, Gamble and Dr. Brown were taken down the road this evening; were arrested several days since. Uncle Caswell took tea here. Sister sat up tonight for first time.

Tuesday 10. Very warm day. Mrs. Cook stayed all night here.

Wednesday 11. Tolerable warm. Mrs. Cook stayed all night here.

Thursday 12. Very cold day. Mrs. Cook and Uncle Caswell killed hogs today. Mrs. Williams presented Mr. Camp's Company with a flag this morning. Mr. Caywood here this morning. Mr. Carter came home today.

Friday 13. Very, very cold day. Mr. Hawkins here this morning. Mother and I called on Mrs. Bradshaw and Mrs. Dr. Edwards this morning. I went over to see Mary Hardwick, was not at home. Went down to see Anna Stuart. Received news that Charleston, S.C., was on fire this evening. Mrs. Cook stayed all night here.

Saturday 14. Cold day. Rhoda and I went to church this morning at Baptist Church. Mrs. Hawkins took dinner here. Rhoda, Annie and I went out to Dr. Grant's this evening. George Swan died this evening between 2 and 3 o'clock. Rhoda, Sallie, Mollie Grant and I went out there (sent Annie home by Uncle Caswell's Isabelle). We sat up all night, also Joe Osment, Henry Cate, Tom Hartley, Joe Lea, Charlie Hardwick and John Dunn, part of the night. Mrs. Cook stayed all night here.

Sunday 15. Cold day. Lizzie went to Sunday School. Mother went to Baptist Church. Rhoda and I slept all morning. Joe Lea took dinner here. Mr. Bradshaw preached George Swan's funeral at Presbyterian Church. Rhoda, Lizzie, Mrs. Cook and I went, also to the burying. Mrs. Cook stayed all night here.

Monday 16. Pretty day. I helped wash all day. Am sick today. Had the toothache last night a little. Rhoda received a letter from John Lea and Venie. Mrs. Garrison has a boy, born 3rd of December. Mrs. Cook stayed here all night. Mrs. John Hoyl here this morning.

Tuesday 17. Pretty day. Mr. Cook came today from Albany. Mr. and Mrs. Cook sat until bedtime with us. Messrs. Jasper Lillard and Frank Ragsdale called on us tonight. Mrs. Bradshaw and Sallie

Surguine were here this evening. Made my chemise bosom today. Mother went to see Mrs. Cook this evening, this morning to Mrs. McGhee's and Mrs. Dr. Edward's.

Wednesday 18. Beautiful day. Was not well this morning. Mother went to "Soldiers' Aid Society" at 2 o'clock. Mother and I went to the Baptist prayer meeting tonight.

Thursday 19. Beautiful day. Heard glorious news today, if it is so, that England demands the release of Mason, Slidell, etc., of the "United States." Cousin Mary Harle over here this morning, this evening Mattie Reynolds and Mollie Grant. Rhoda went up to Mrs. Cook's this evening. Mother went to Mrs. Dr. Edwards', and Mrs. Bell Hardwick's, and to Mr. Kenner's store to get Lizzie a ticket. Finished my chemise bosom today. Pryor Lea came to the fence after tea and brought us a rabbit.

Friday 20. Worked on my chemise all day. Lucretia Tibbs here this evening. Mrs. Cook stayed all night here.

Saturday 21. Cold day. Went out to see Ada Gaut [formerly Ada Anderson]. Dr. Hughes came down this evening to see if Rhoda and I would assist in making Mr. Dunn's Company a flag. We went up to Judge Gaut's this evening to see about it. Rhoda and I went to see Cousin Ellen Jarnagin afterwards. Mary Elizabeth and I went to church at Presbyterian Church with Mr. Bradshaw's family. Rev. Brown preached. Mr. William Shields here this evening.

Sunday 22. A very rainy dark day. None of us went to church today.

Monday 23. A very cold day. Rhoda and I went down to Judge Gaut's and helped make the flag. Ada Gaut, Rhoda and I took dinner there. Received a letter from Cousin Sam Inman.

Tuesday 24. Cold day. Rhoda went back and helped Mary and Anna to make a flag. I went up to see Lillie and Mary Davis this evening. Rhoda and I made some cake today. Mel Osment took supper here, he came after Rhoda and I to go to a party at Mr. Grady's, did not go.

Wednesday 25. Pretty day. Christmas day. Mother, Rhoda, Lizzie and I went down to Judge Gaut's to see Mary Gaut present a flag to Capt. Dunn's Company. They left for Knoxville today. Mother and R. went to the depot. Their name is "Rough and Ready Rifles;" motto: "We come to share the victory." Mr. and Mrs. Cook, Aunt E., and

Lizzie and Callie Swan took dinner here. Mary E. went up to see Gussie Craigmiles and Cousin Ellen Jarnagin. Annie, Jimmie and Sues (slave) went up to old Mr. Carter's, Dr. Thompson. Mother went to the Sewing Circle. Mother and I went to Mrs. Cook's this evening.

Thursday 26. Very windy day. Rhoda, Callie Swan and I spent the day at Mr. William Hughes' today, went over to Mrs. Joe Swan's in the evening. Mary Gaut and Laura McNutt here today. Uncle Wood took dinner here today. Cousin Joe Lea brought Cousin John's daguerreotype down to us this evening. Uncle Caswell came down from Knoxville and brought it. Capt. Eldridge's Company left Knoxville for Bowling Green yesterday. Dance at the Ocoee tonight. Emeline [slave] went to Aunt Molly's wedding down at Mary Bate's tonight. Mrs. Nannie Ray was at Mrs. Hughes'. Rhoda wrote to Davie Jones tonight. Annie had her hair cut off and a tooth pulled today. Heard today that Mrs. J. S. Bowie was dead, died 31st of last October at Philadelphia, Pa. Sister went up to Mrs. Cook's this evening. Mother and Mrs. Dr. Edwards went around to get clothing for the soldiers.

Friday 27. Pretty day. Fixed my scrap book all day. Cousin Joe Lea here this evening, took tea, gave me a gold pen. Rhoda and Mother went to Mrs. Taylor Reynolds' and Mr. Traynor's to see Warren Rowles this morning.

Saturday 28. Pretty day. Mother went around to get people to make Capt. McClary's company some coats. Mrs. Cook and Sallie McMillin were here this morning.

Sunday 29. Pretty day. Frank's [slave] 7th birthday. All went to Sunday School. Rhoda and I went to church at Methodist Church. I came back before preaching commenced. Cousin Joe Lea took dinner here. Rhoda, Mother and I went up to Mrs. Cook's and sat a while after tea. Rhoda received a letter from Emma Aldehoff today.

Monday 30. Pretty day. Emeline went out to Uncle Caswell's to get some lard. John and William Craigmiles are killing hogs for the government. Aunt Phoebe, Mary E., Sues and I washed today. Julia Grant took dinner here today. Part of Gen. Floyd's division came down today on their way to Bowling Green, Ky. Sister went to see Mrs. Hoyl this morning to get her to show her how to make a soldier's coat. Mother spent the day at Cousin Mary Harle's.

Tuesday 31. Pretty day. Mother, Rhoda, Sister, Johnnie, Mr. Carter and I spent the day at Mrs. Cook's today. Mr. and Mrs. Cook sat until bed time with us tonight. Heard today that Alice Brown went up the road Sunday.

1862

January 1862

Wednesday 1. New Year's Day. Pretty day. Mary Elizabeth and I ironed this morning. Rhoda and Lizzie this evening. Sister went over to Cousin Mary Harle's this evening. Mother over all morning, took dinner there to get Cousin Mary to show her how to make a soldier's coat. Johnson's moving from hotel to Mr. Kenner's house today. Rhoda went up to see Adelia Craigmiles this morning. Sister, Annie and Mrs. Cook called on Mrs. Bradshaw this morning. Mary Edwards here this morning. Mrs. Rogers here this evening, also Aunt Elizabeth and Callie Swan. Sent some socks to Capt. Dunn's Company. Rhoda, Mother and I went to prayer meeting. Mother went to Sewing Society.

Thursday 2. Mason and Slidell were released and sailed for England today.[1] Our commissioners to England, had been imprisoned by Lincoln. Rhoda, Mary Edwards and I went to a basket dinner at the courthouse. Uncle William and Uncle Caswell Lea took dinner here. Uncle William took tea. Mr. Carter went to Knoxville, Tenn. today. Judge Gaut, Mr. John Hoyl and Sam Smith made speeches calling for volunteers for Capt. J. G. M. Montgomery. Mrs. Cook and Anna Gaut here this morning. I went up to Mrs. Montgomery's to see about basket dinner.

Friday 3. Pretty day. Mrs. Cook stayed all night here. Adelia Craigmiles and Rhoda took a ride this evening. Mr. Garrison here tonight. Uncle Caswell took tea here. Cousin Mary Harle spent the day here. Mother and Sister went up in town today. Got Rhoda a pair of shoes, also Mary Edwards. I got myself a pair of shoes from

---

[1]See entry for 8 November 1861. These Confederate commissioners were released on 26 December 1861. News reached Cleveland in early January 1862. Randall and Donald, *Civil War*, 360-362.

Mr. Trewhitt's. Uncle Ned [slave] got them for me. Sallie McMillin's 16th birthday.

Saturday 4. A disagreeable, sad and gloomy day. Mother went up to Mrs. Hartley's shop and to Mr. Kenner's store this morning. Mr. Carter got an old blind horse today.

Sunday 5. Rainy and gloomy day. Lizzie went to Sunday School and preaching at Methodist Church tonight. Mr. Daily preached. Mother, Lizzie, and I went up to Mrs. Cook's and ate walnuts this weekend. Old Mr. Carter here this evening.

Monday 6. A cold, windy day. I helped Aunt Phoebe [slave] wash today. Only ate twice today. Emeline [slave] went out to Uncle Caswell's where they are killing hogs to get lard. Uncle Caswell, Mary Edwards, and Mary Stuart here this evening. Lizzie started to school to Mr. Bradshaw (Cleveland Masonic Female Institute) today. A dance at the Ocoee tonight. Mother and Sister went around shopping today.

Tuesday 7. Pretty day. Sister and Rhoda went to Mr. Cook's store to get Rhoda a dress. Mr. Carter has some merinos[2] to come today. Rhoda got a lawn dress from Mr. Guthman and two dresses from Mr. Carter. Mrs. Cook came down to get Mother to show her how to make a soldier's coat. Mrs. Shadden and Adelia Craigmiles here this evening.

Wednesday 8. Tolerable cold day. Mrs. Cook here all day working on her coat. Uncle Caswell took tea here. Mrs. Judge Gaut here this morning. Mrs. Crawford and McGill here tonight. Rained nearly all evening, cloudy all day. Sewed on my chemise all day.

Thursday 9. Pretty. Mrs. Cook came back and stayed all day. Mother went up to Mrs. Kenner's store and Mrs. Dr. Edwards', her sister (Mrs. Ann Bryant) died[3], was buried here yesterday. Mother went up to see Mrs. Bradshaw here this evening. Mr. Henderson from Madisonville stayed here all night. A dark and rainy night.

Friday 10. Pretty but muddy day. Pryor Lea came to the fence this evening and asked Rhoda and I to go out and stay all night. We

---

[2]Breed of sheep usually from Spain which produces a fine wool called merino.

[3]Ira Ann Bryant, wife of W.P. Bryant, b. 1 December 1833; d. 8 January 1862, interred in Fort Hill Cemetery. Ross, *Cemetery Records*, II:70.

did so and made some molasses candy to send to Cousin John. Finished my chemise today.

Saturday 11. Beautiful day. Mattie Reynolds spent the day here. Jimmie's fourth birthday. Lizzie Lea spent the day with the children. Uncle Caswell here this evening. Did not have fire in Mother's room so warm this morning. Mother went to Baptist Church.

Sunday 12. Pretty day, but very windy. Rhoda, Mother and I went to Baptist Church this morning. Mr. McNutt preached: 16 chapter of Luke, verse 31. Joe Lea took dinner here. Mr. Garrison and Rhoda went to the choir this evening. Mother, Mary Edwards, and I went to Baptist prayer meeting this evening. Rhoda and Lizzie went to the Methodist Church tonight. Mother and I went down to Mr. McNutt's and sat until bedtime. Mr. and Mrs. Cook were here. Rhoda, Mrs. Garrison and I were at Mrs. Cook's this evening, we had some nice apples. Sister, Mr. Carter, Annie, and Jimmie all took a walk this evening.

Monday 13. This day nine years ago Sister and Mr. Carter were married. Mrs. Bradshaw here this evening. A drizzly cold day. Helped Emeline wash, did not hang out clothes, rained some. Rhoda spent the evening with Mrs. Cook.

Tuesday 14. A cold rainy day. All the things are covered with ice. Commenced piecing my star [pattern] quilt. Sleeted all day.

Wednesday 15. Rainy day, rained hard here all night, thundered and lightninged once. Pieced on my quilt all day. Mr. Carter came back from Madisonville this evening.[4] Mr. Eldridge's boys came very near being taken by the enemy. Upton and Hughes were taken last Wednesday.

Thursday 16. Cold day. Was sick in bed this evening. Mr. Carter went down on the train this evening. Uncle Caswell took dinner here. Mrs. Cook and Ada Gaut were here this evening.

Friday 17. Pretty day. Mother, Sister, Annie, and Jimmie went up to old Mr. Carter's, Mr. William Craigmiles', Mrs. Jonas Hoyl's, and Mrs. Cook's, also at Mrs. McNutt's and Mrs. Tibb's. Heard today that Cousin Ellen and Mr. McCallie were going to marry. Anna Stuart here this evening.

---

[4] Madisonville is the county seat of Monroe County, Tennessee.

Saturday 18. Pretty day. Rhoda and Sister went around shopping, also went to Mrs. Pickens' and Cousin Mary Jarnagin's. Uncle William Lea dined with us and took tea here today. Rhoda, Adelia, and John Craigmiles took a ride this evening. Mrs. Cook and Mrs. Bradshaw and Mr. McNutt brought our breastpins which Mr. Bradshaw mended. I went up to get Mr. Cook to tell them to bring the wagon around to our house to get some victuals to take out to Capt. Jones' Company at the fairground. My mouth is very sore, can scarcely eat.

Sunday 19. Pretty day. I was sick and didn't go anywhere today. Rhoda and Lizzie went to Presbyterian School and Church. Mother and Sister went to Baptist prayer meeting at church this evening. Rhoda and Mr. Garrison went to the choir this evening.

Monday 20. Rainy evening. Washed in the forenoon. Mr. Carter went to Benton this morning. Mrs. Cook and Mother went to see old Mrs. Maples who is sick. Mrs. Maples' little girl came over after Mrs. Cook and Mother and said that her grandmother was dying. It thundered and lightninged this evening. The plum trees are budding to blossom.

Tuesday 21. Cold day. Mother went up to Mrs. Cook's to buy some sugar from her. Sister, Rhoda and I made some candy (ground nut) today. Mother and Mrs. Cook went to see J. G. Montgomery this evening. Mr. Robert Swan came to the door this evening to see Mr. Carter but he had not returned from Benton. Came back soon after.

Wednesday 22. Pretty day. Aunt Elizabeth here this evening, was brought home by Mother from "Society." Rhoda went up to see Adelia Craigmiles and took dinner at Mrs. Shadden's.

Thursday 23. Pretty day. Sister went up to see Fred Rogers, he has the fever. Mrs. Cook spent the evening here. Uncle William Lea took tea here. Heard this evening that Gen. [Felix] Zollicoffer's forces were defeated and he was killed in Kentucky. The fight took place last Sunday the 19th. Mr. Bradshaw came down after dark to hear the news. The battle of Fishing Creek or Mill Springs was a complete route [defeat] of the Southern Army.

Friday 24. Pretty day. Mother went out to Uncle Caswell's with Mrs. Bradshaw. Sister went up to Mrs. Traynor's to see Fred Rogers, he is better. Mrs. Stout was here, she told Sister that Warren Rowles died last Wednesday week ago, the 15th of January. Mr. Carter went up to Riceville[5] today, be back this evening. The choir met here tonight. Rhoda and Adelia Craigmiles took a ride this evening. Sister went up to Mrs. Cook's and took Johnnie. Messrs. J. H. Craigmiles, Garrison, Uncle William Lea, Adelia, Gussie, Mary Bradshaw, Ada Anderson, Callie Swan and Cousin Ellen Jarnagin were at the choir tonight.

Saturday 25. Pretty day. Annie spent the day at Uncle Caswell's. The cars ran off the track and did not get here until 3 this morning. Mr. Carter went up to Knoxville and back today. Cousin John Lea came down on them and stayed here until seven then went back to Knoxville on Sunday morning. Mary Edwards went to see Cousin Ellen Jarnagin this evening. Rhoda, Adelia Craigmiles, Miss Euphilia Bradshaw, and Guss Craigmiles took a ride this evening. Aunt Elizabeth and Uncle Pryor sat until bedtime, waiting for the [train] cars here. Rhoda and I called on Mrs. Bradshaw this morning. Mother and Mrs. Cook went down to see Mrs. McNutt, she has the measles. Mrs. Carol Tibbs has a boy. Sister and Mother went over to Cousin Mary's today.

Sunday 26. Pretty day. Cousin Joe Lea here, also, Alice Pickens. Mother and Mrs. Cook went to the Baptist prayer meeting, also, were down to see Mrs. Charlie Reynolds, has a girl baby. We all went to Sunday School. Rhoda and Lizzie went to the Presbyterian Church. Uncle Caswell here tonight. Wrote a letter to Cousin John Lea.

Monday 27. Pretty day. Emeline went out to get some lard. I helped Aunt Phoebe wash, had only two meals. Aunt Elizabeth, Mary Edwards and Mrs. Bradshaw here this morning, also, Bell Grant. Rhoda and Adelia took a ride this evening, went out to the "poor-house." Julius Jarnagin came down tonight and brought an invitation to attend Cousin Ellen's wedding tomorrow eve, at 3:30 o'clock. Fred Montgomery went out to Uncle Caswell's this eve sick. Bob Grant came home sick today. Cousin John came home this eve on furlough. Cousin John Lea brought Montgomery home sick from exposure. Mrs. Cook here this eve.[6]

---

5 McMinn County, Tennessee.

6 Cousin John Lea and Fred Montgomery were participants in the battle of Mill Springs on 19 January. The battle was a route of the Confederate

Tuesday 28. Pretty day. Sister and Rhoda went out to Uncle Caswell's to see Fred Montgomery this morning. Uncle William here this morning. Mother and Sister went down to Mr. Carol Tibbs this morning. Mrs. Cook here this eve. Mr. Cook gone to Atlanta, stayed all night. Rhoda, Lizzie and I went down at 3:30 o'clock to Cousin Mary Jarnagin's to see Cousin Ellen Jarnagin and Rev. T. McCallie married: went down on five o'clock train to Chattanooga. Heard this evening that England has acknowledged our independence. Messers. Ragsdale, Alexander, Gussie and Euphilia Bradshaw were at the wedding.[7]

Wednesday 29. Rained very hard for awhile today. Mrs. Bradshaw and Mrs. Shadden here this morning. Uncle Caswell took dinner here. Knitted on Cousin John Lea's socks today. Cousin John Lea took tea here this eve. Mrs. Cook stayed all night here.

Thursday 30. Pretty day. Mag Shadden here this evening, also, Mr. John Cowan to pay Mother some money. Mr. Garrison here to get us to go over to the depot to see Gen. P. G. T. Beauregard. Mother, Rhoda and I went [but] (Beauregard did not come). Mr. and Mrs. Cook sat until bedtime here. Rhoda's 19th birthday.

Friday 31. A rainy day. Mother went out to Uncle Caswell's this morning. We made Cousin John Lea a shirt today. Stepney's 8th birthday .

February 1862

Saturday 1. Pretty day. Lizzie has been sick all day. I went down to see Ada Gaut this eve. Also, Mother went up to see Mrs. Cook. Ada Gaut here this eve. Mother, Rhoda and I went to the Baptist Church this eve. Mr. McNutt read and explained John, 9th chapter.

Sunday 2. Rainy and cloudy day. Rhoda and I went to Sunday School. Went to the Baptist Church. Mr. McNutt preached from

---

forces and Gen. Zollicofer was killed. Cousin John Lea returned to Cleveland on furlough and helped Montgomery return home because he was sick after the battle.

[7] Mrs. Wheeler, Mary Pharis, Anna Anderson, and Emma Barton were boarders.

John , 17th chapter, 10th verse. Cousin John Lea dined and took tea here and stayed all night. Mr. Carter went down on the train. Gen. Beauregard passed down.

Monday 3. Rainy day. Helped Emeline wash. Cousin John dined here. Stayed all day. Mr. Carter came back this morn.

Tuesday 4. Lovely day. Mrs. Bradshaw here this morning. Mr. William Grant here this eve to pay Mr. Carter some money, he has been married 15 years today. Mrs. Cook and Rhoda went down to see Mrs. McNutt this eve. Commenced me a chemise today. Cousin Sam C. Inman was taken sick today.

Wednesday 5. A pretty day. Uncle Caswell and Uncle William Lea took dinner here. Mother, Sister and Annie went around shopping and up to Mr. Carter's. Rhoda and Cousin John Lea took a ride this morning. Mother went up to Mrs. Bradshaw's this morn. Mother and Sister went to the society this eve.

Thursday 6. Rained some today. Mr. Garrison came around and told us good-bye, he is going to Atlanta; is not coming back any more. The "East Tennessee Union Men" were let out of prison today. Mother went up to Mrs. Cook's today. Was sick last night. I am sick today with a cold.

Friday 7. A rainy day. Mrs. Cook here all day to help Mother on Uncle William's vest. Mrs. Shadden here this eve, took tea here and sat until bedtime. Mr. Carter came down to the train and brought news that the Federals had taken Fort Henry this eve. Cousin Sam C. Inman died at 10 o'clock tonight in upper East Tennessee. He came from Texas to get property left him from his Mother's estate, joined the army and died.

Sunday 9. Pretty day. We all went to Sunday School, entered Mrs. Sallie Bradshaw's class. Rhoda, Mary Edwards and I went to Presbyterian Church. Mr. Bradshaw preached from Isaiah. Cousin John to dinner and tea here. Cousin Joe here this eve. Mr. and Mrs. Cook and Henry Jones here this eve. Rhoda and Mrs. Cook went to Baptist prayer meeting. Cousin John went with Rhoda, Lizzie and I to Presbyterian tonight. Rev. Bradshaw preached from John, 2nd chapter, 15th, 16th, 17th verses. News came this morn that the enemy were in Tuscumbia, Alabama. Had landed six gunboats there.

Monday 10. A cold day. Emeline, Sues and Frank went out to Uncle Caswell's to help kill their hogs. Had only two meals today. I helped Aunt Phoebe wash today. Mother went out to Mrs. Cook's this eve, also Sister went up to Mrs. Bradshaw's, and to Mrs. William Craigmiles' to see Mrs. Pepper's baby this morn. Mr. Carter went away on the cars this evening. Rhoda and I went up to Mrs. Cook's tonight and sat until bedtime. Henry Jones came home with us. A beautiful moonlight night.

Tuesday 11. A very cold and windy day. Sister went up to see Mrs. Matt Carter (has a baby). Also up to see Lizzie Wood and old Mr. Carter this morn. Mother has been up to see Mrs. Cook all day to help make Henry Jones' pantaloons. I went up to Mrs. Cook's this morn, and also to see Sallie McMillin. Commenced a chemise today. Mrs. Cook and Henry Jones sat until bedtime tonight. Cousin John Lea took tea here this eve.

Wednesday 12. A very pleasant day. Mrs. Cook sent for Rhoda and I to come up and sit until bedtime. Henry Jones and Cousin John were there. A lovely night, moonlight. Mrs. G. W. Alexander and Miss Hannah Alexander were here this eve. Sent for Mother and Sister to see them from Mrs. Bradshaw's. They went out to Uncle Caswell's this morn, also up to see Mrs. Cook this eve. Uncle William brought in Josephus for me to read today, took dinner here.

Thursday 13. A beautiful day and lovely night. Henry Jones went with Rhoda and me to party at Judge Gaut's. Others there were Adelia and John Craigmiles, Ada and Perry Gaut, Mrs. and Col. Mills, Jessie Gaut, Nannie Johnston, Tom McMillin and Frank Ragsdale, Sallie Grant and Matt Hassle, Mollie Grant and Joe Osment, Florence Johnston and Cousin John Lea. Lucretia Tibbs and [I went] to Mrs. Cook's and baked some cake for Henry. Mother went up to pay Dr. Brown her medical bill, was not there.

Friday 14. A cold day. Mother went up to Mrs. Cook's this eve. I finished my chemise and fixed some pickles Mrs. Cook gave us. Uncle William dined here today. Valentine's Day. Received four, three were comic. I received a comic one last night at a party. Henry Jones came down to tell us good-bye tonight; he is on his way back [to] Pensacola. Some troops came down this eve on their way home; [Henry] has reenlisted, going home on 50 days furlough. Capt. Montgomery's Company started off today. Henry Jones is in Capt. Isabell's Company, "Alabama Rifles." Lizzie sent Sister a Valentine. I sent Mr. and Mrs. Cook and Uncle William one.

Saturday 15. Cold day. Commenced snowing last night. Snowed all day, three inches deep. Cousin John Lea took dinner here. John Lauderdale and Cousin John took tea here. Mr. Carter went out hunting today. Heard today that we gained a victory at Fort Donelson.[8]

Sunday 16. Snow on the ground; cold day. Cousins John and Joe Lea took dinner here. None of us went anywhere today.

Monday 17. A dark, cold, gloomy and rainy day. Sister's 28th birthday. I helped Emeline wash today. Heard this morning that Ruff Sole was dying. Mr. Cook here this eve, to hear the news that we had been defeated at Fort Donelson. Rhoda and I went up this eve and helped Mrs. Cook pack up to go to Atlanta, Georgia.

Tuesday 18. A beautiful day. We went up to Mrs. Cook's all day, helped her pack up. Uncle William took tea here.

Wednesday 19. A very windy, dark day. Rained very hard this eve. Uncle Caswell and Cousin John Lea took dinner here. We went up this morning and helped Mrs. Cook pack up. Sigh Norman and Martha Clingan were married at 4 o'clock. Heard tonight after Rhoda, Lizzie and I [had] gone to bed. (Rhoda received a letter from Cousin Mary Harrison) that Cousin Sam Inman is dead; died in Sneedville of typhoid-pneumonia on the 8th of February. He was a Capt. of a company and an excellent young man. Alas! Many a noble youth had and will fall in our struggle for our independence. How sad to think that Cousin Sam was only sick four or five days; in his 23rd year.

Thursday 20. A pretty day. Uncle Caswell and Mrs. Shadden took tea here. Mother went up to Mrs. Carter's to see about Lizzie. Took dinner at Cousin Ellen's and sat until bedtime. Mother, Rhoda and I sat until bedtime weaving some cloth at Mrs. Cook's; she sent the thread out to Mrs. White's today to get it woven. Mrs. Bradshaw here this morn. Sister and Rhoda called on Cousin Ellen McCallie, Sallie Surguine and Mrs. McGriff.

Friday 21. A beautiful day. Mother, Cousin Ellen and I spent the day at Uncle Caswell's. Mr. McCallie came up on the train, came out and took dinner. In the evening Aunt Elizabeth, Uncle William,

---

[8] This proved untrue and the Confederates under Gen. Simon B. Buckner surrendered to Grant on 16 January 1862.

Mother and I went up to see Bob Grant. Mrs. Bradshaw here, is sick this eve. Sister, Mother, Rhoda and I were at Mrs. Cook's this morning. Mother went down to see Cousin Mary Jarnagin and Cousin Ellen this morn. Cousin John Lea, Fred Montgomery, Georgie and Lizzie all sick.

Saturday 22. A very windy, cloudy and rainy day. Sister went up to Mrs. Cook's and Mrs. Worley's this eve. President Jefferson Davis[9] was inaugurated today for six years according to the Confederate Constitution. May we gain our liberty before his time expires. The Government[10] has called out the militia.[11]

Sunday 23. Beautiful day. All went to Sunday School. Lizzie, Rhoda and I went to Presbyterian Church. Mr. Bradshaw's text was Luke 21st chapter, 19th verse. Cousin John Lea took tea here. Rhoda and I went with him to Methodist Church at night. Mr. Worley preached from 2nd Thessalonians, 5th chapter, verses 11-14. Mother, Sister and I went up to Mrs. Cook's this eve. Mrs. Cook is sick.

Monday 24. A beautiful day. I helped Emeline wash today. Cousin John and Uncle Caswell dined here today. The Federal troops entered Nashville day before yesterday, or either last evening. Mr. Carter went down the road yesterday eve.

Tuesday 25. A beautiful day. Sister went up to Mrs. William Craigmiles' to see Mrs. Pepper. We all tacked a comfort for Fred Montgomery today. Uncle William took tea here. Mrs. Ewing was here to borrow a pair of cards [cotton] this morn. Mr. Carter came up this eve with a "regiment of soldiers" from Mobile; seven of them took supper here. Their names were: J. W. Steen, 2nd Lt., 23rd Alabama Reg. Co. A; W. F. Myles Ingles, Private Co., S; A.C. Roberts. 1st Lt. Company C; F. M. Jones, Lt. Co. C, 23rd Reg.; T. D. McCall, Capt. Company H; D. H. Smith, Capt. Co. D. The Colonel's name was F. H. Beck, commanding; Lt. Col. J. B. Bibb; Maj. P. F. Tait, 23rd Alabama.

Wednesday 26. A rainy gloomy dark day. Mother and Sister went up to Mrs. Bradshaw's this morn. Cousin John Lea dined here. I

---

[9] Jefferson Davis, 1808-1889. He had the distinction of having the line item veto.

[10] The Government of Isham Harris, Governor of Tennessee.

[11] The 32nd Regiment of Volunteers.

went up to Mrs. Cook's this morning. Mr. Cook is a great deal better. Uncle Caswell here this eve. Heard today that Aunt Fannie Lea (in Missouri) had gone north with all of Uncle Pleasant's property. No confidence can be placed in a Yankee. Part of 20th Alabama Reg. came up this eve.

Thursday 27. Spit snow a little today. Mother went up to Mrs. Edwards, Cousin Mary Jarnagin's, and Mrs. Traynor's, brought some shoes from Mr. Cook. Heard today that the cars ran off the track with the Alabama 23rd Reg. Killed a soldier. Part of the 20th Alabama Reg. came up tonight. Seven privates took tea here as well as Uncle Caswell, Rhoda, Annie and I went out to Uncle Caswell's this eve.

Friday 28. A beautiful day. Fast day. Mother, Rhoda, Aunt Elizabeth and I went to the Methodist Church. Mr. Bradshaw preached from Psalm 138, verse 5. Aunt Elizabeth , Uncle Caswell, Cousin John Lea, Cousin Mary Jarnagin, Helen Pharis, Callie Swan and little Anna Harris (her niece) were all here this eve. Rhoda and I went to the choir at Mrs. Pleasant Craigmiles' tonight. Miss Sallie Bradshaw here a little after tea.

March 1862

Saturday 1. Mother and Uncle Ned went out to Mrs. White's in the buggy to see about her cloth this morning. I hear a drum beating for the noble young men of our state to defend us. I am sorry to say that there are some few who will have to be dragged out in the militia (if not drafted) before they will deprive themselves of their pleasant homes to meet the invader. Miss Sallie Bradshaw and I went out to see Sallie Grant this eve, she is a little better. Rhoda and Sister went up to old Mr. Carter's this eve. Cousin James Carson came from Washington[12] tonight, stayed all night here.

Sunday 2. A hard storm this eve, rained, lightninged and thundered very hard. We all went to Sunday School. Mother, Mr. Carter, Sister, Annie, Jimmie and I went to the Baptist Church.

---

[12] Rhea County, Tennessee.

Cousin James preached from 2nd Timothy, chapter 3, verse 16. Rhoda, Mother and I went in the eve at 3 o'clock. Mr. McNutt preached from the 12th chapter of Hebrews, verses 1 and 2. A storm was approaching and we had to leave. Cousin James took tea here. Mother and Cousin James dined at Mr. McNutt's. Uncle William came in tonight to go down on the 7 o'clock train but was raining so hard he stayed here all night. Heard today that we had gained a victory in Missouri under Gen. Sterling Price.[13] Heard that [Andrew Hull] Foote was appointed as provisional Governor over Tennessee. What impudence the North [has] to think that we will be under one of their tyrants. Has also called for 50,000 volunteers. Never will he get one of my kinsmen to respond to his call.

Monday 3. A cloudy day. Helped Emeline wash today. Cousin John here this morning. Uncles Caswell and William and Cousin James Carson all dined here. Cousin John had a tooth extracted today, he and James took tea here. Cousin J. told us good-bye, is going home tomorrow. A very raw day. Snowed hard on this eve, did not lay on the ground. A soldier died at Mr. Clabe McMillin's, was buried this eve, named William Simmons from Alabama 23rd Reg.

Tuesday 4. Cold day. Rhoda, Sallie McMillin and I went out to Dr. Grant's this eve. Rhoda came 'round by Uncle Caswell's, took tea there. Sallie and I sat up all night with Virginia and Leroy, have measles. Mr. Carter went down the road tonight, he and Frank Johnson are trying to get up a company.

Wednesday 5. A very raw, cold day. Sallie and I came home this morn. Mrs. Bradshaw and Mrs. Lowe here this morn. Mrs. Bradshaw to twist some thread. Mrs. Lowe after some milk for a sick prisoner. I slept all eve, Cousin Mary Harle here while I was asleep. Mother and Sister went up to see Mrs. Worley's (Methodist minister) baby this morn, is very bad with measles, 10 months old. It died about dark. Rhoda sat up all night there tonight. Spit snow a little this morning about daybreak.

Thursday 6. A cold day, snowed very hard this morning, a real snow storm. Uncle Caswell here this morn. Sister and Mother have

---

[13] General Sterling Price, the former governor of Missouri, defeated Federal troops at Wilson's Creek. In 1862 the victory of Federal troops helped establish Union control of that state.

been up to Mrs. Worley's several times today. Commenced making me a twilled underskirt today.

Friday 7. Pretty day. Frances Craigmiles died this morning at 10 o'clock. Mother and Sister went up there this eve. Mother went to see Mrs. Worley's, Sister to see Mrs. Grant. Mrs. Traynor here this eve.[14]

Saturday 8. Pretty day. Frances was buried this eve. Finished my underskirt this eve. Rhoda, Annie and I went out to Uncle Caswell's this eve. Mr. Carter came down the road tonight and told us about Mrs. James Craigmiles' baby being burned to death last night at Knoxville. It was 7 months old, named Jeff Davis.

Sunday 9. A beautiful but windy day. All went to Sunday School. Rhoda, Mary Elizabeth and I went to Presbyterian Church this morn. Rev. Bradshaw preached from Corinthians chapter 1, verses 20 and 21. Mother went to Methodist Church. Aunt Elizabeth, Callie Swan, Samantha Swan, Mary and Helen Pharis, Anna Anderson, Mrs. Florence and Nannie Johnston were out to see them this eve. Miss Sallie Bradshaw, Rhoda and I went out to see them this eve. Julia Grant was very sick with measles. George W. Summers was out there. Oh Me!! He belongs to the 17th Mississippi Reg.

Monday 10. A rainy dark gloomy day. I helped Emeline wash today. Mrs. Cook here this eve. Rhoda received four pieces of music from Henry Lovitt Jones this morning. Rhoda received a letter from Venie [Lavena] Seavey yesterday morn. Mr. Carter went down to Ooltewah [Hamilton County] this eve.

Tuesday 11. Beautiful day. Cousin John Lea took dinner here, he's sick and has a jaw ache. Uncle Caswell and Sissy took tea here. Sallie Surguine here this eve. Mother, Rhoda and I sat until bedtime at Mrs. Cook's. Mr. and Mrs. McNutt and Mrs. Jessie Gaut were there also. Mother and Mrs. Cook went to see Mrs. Joel K. Brown this morning. Mr. William I. Campbell was here this morn to get Mother's taxes. Sister went over to Cousin M. Harle's and Mrs. Traynor's this morn. Mother went up to Mrs. Bradshaw's. Mr. H. L. Jones, 7th Alabama Rifles, Harrington, Florida, [was here possibly] to care for Capt. Isbell.

---

[14] Frances Craigmiles, daughter of P. M. and C. F. Craigmiles, was born 29 March 1858, and died 7 March 1862. Buried in Fort Hill Cemetery. Ross, *Cemetery Records*, II:97.

Wednesday 12. Beautiful day. Mother and Sister went up to Mrs. Cook's this morn. Uncle Ned brought my "Cape Jasmine" [plant] she gave me from out there. Bettie Anderson and Mary and Anna Gaut this evening. Mother and Sister went over to see old Mrs. Erwin this eve. Mother went over to the "Soldier's Aid Society" this eve. Thinking of having a hospital here. We are going to tack comforts for them poor fellows, would that we had already gained our independence! and they could return home. I finished my quilt today.

Thursday 13. A very rainy day. Twisted thread nearly all day for soldier's comforts. Cousin John took dinner here, also stayed all night. My 17th birthday, born on Thursday. Wonder if God in his providence will permit me to see my 18th. Mr. and Mrs. Cook took tea here, left on the 7:30 train for Atlanta. We are so sorry to part with them, they were such excellent neighbors. Do not know whether we will ever see them again, times are so gloomy. Uncle William Lea dined here.

Friday 14. Pretty day. Mrs. Edwards, Mrs. Bradshaw and Mrs. Shadden here today. The latter took tea. We tacked two comforts for soldiers today.

Saturday 15. Pretty day. Tacked a comfort this morning. Cousin John took dinner here. I went to Mrs. Stuart's this eve.

Sunday 16. Beautiful day. Rhoda and I went to Methodist Church. Mr. Glenn preached from Ecclesiastes, 7th chapter 5th verse. Cousin John and Uncle William Lea stayed all night here. Cousin John , Rhoda, Lizzie and I went to the Methodist Church tonight. Mr. Glenn preached from the 15th Psalm. Cousin John is going up to Raytown on 3 o'clock train tomorrow morn. Fred Montgomery going to Lynchburg, Virginia. Jim House and three other boys came here to get breakfast this morn.

Monday 17. Pretty day. Helped Emeline wash today. Mr. Bradshaw and Aunt Elizabeth Lea here this eve. Uncle William stayed all night here. Sister went up to the stores and up to Mrs. Carter's and Worley's this morn. Uncle Caswell and William Lea took dinner here.

Tuesday 18. Beautiful day. Mother, Sister and children spent the day at Mr. Carter's. Uncle William dined here and Uncles Caswell and William took tea here. Heard today the Federals had

Jacksborough [Campbell County]. This day 16 years ago we moved to the hotel. Mother colored some thread to make her some dresses. A great many soldiers went up this eve to Cumberland Gap. Have just finished *Life of Marion*. The war in which he fought was similar to our war; had to contend with Tories as we do; if we only had a second Marion.

Wednesday 19. A rainy day. Mother and Sister went up to Mrs. Traynor's and Mrs. Bradshaw's this eve. Was sick a little today. Rhoda received a letter from Cousin Mollie Harrison, she said Cousin Sam (Inman) died with congestive chills.[15]

Thursday 20. A rainy day. God defend the right. Uncle William took tea and stayed all night here also. I renewed the dirt in my Cape Jasmine this eve. Hailed this eve very hard. We tacked a comfort for soldiers.[16]

Friday 21. Spit snow some today. Mother and I went over to Mrs. Jonas Hoyl's and Mrs. Robert Swan's to see part of Floyd's Brigade of 1200 cavalry pass on their way to Cumberland Gap. We took dinner at Aunt Elizabeth's. Mary Edwards and Rhoda went up to Dr. Thompson's to choir tonight.

Saturday 22. Pretty but cold today. Rhoda, Misses Euphilia and Mary Bradshaw and I went with Cousin John Lea to a party at Mr. Jessie Gaut's. Got acquainted with Jim Hayes tonight. There was a House, Gibson, Cruse and Timmons here to get dinner. I did not get any food. Rhoda and Sister went up to Mrs. William Craigmiles' this eve. We got our new cotton dresses from weavers this eve.

Sunday 23. Cold day. Went to Sunday School and Presbyterian Church this morning. Mother and Sister went down to Mrs. McNutt's this eve. Also Rhoda and Lizzie went to choir. Cousin John took tea here. I stayed all night with Sallie Surguine tonight. Mr. Surguine was gone.

Monday 24. Pretty day. Helped Emeline wash today. Mother and Rhoda spent the day at Uncle Caswell Lea's. Sallie McMillin and Cousin John here this eve. Called on Misses Bradshaws tonight, also

---

[15] See entry for 19 February 1862.

[16] Tacking was a means of attaching the back of a quilt or comforter to the front by means of a sewing stitch that was tied on the top. Myra referred to this kind of covering as a comfort rather than the modern day comforter.

William McSpadden. Sister Myra's 26th birthday [Myra had an older sister named Myra who died as a young child].

Tuesday 25. A pretty day. Mother and Sister went up to Mrs. Onie Campbell's and Mrs. Carter's this eve. Sister and I went over to Cousin Mary Harle's. Father has been dead 11 years today. Old Mr. N. G. Burgess [age 75], was buried this eve, died last week. Rhoda, Lizzie and I sat until bedtime at Mrs. Bradshaw's this eve. Capt. Eldridge's Company started to Kingston, Tennessee at 11 o'clock. Cousin John and Walker McSpadden came and told us good-bye.[17] [No entries for 26, 27, 28, 29, 30, 31.]

April 1862

Tuesday 1. Lovely day. Mrs. Bradshaw and Sallie here this eve. Mother, Sister, Rhoda, Lizzie and I went to see Cousin Ellen McCallie this eve. Mary Elizabeth's 14th birthday.

Wednesday 2. Rained this eve. Mrs. Smith is coming tomorrow. Uncle Caswell took tea here. Lizzie Lea took dinner. Rhoda and Aunt Elizabeth Adeline went out to Uncle Caswell's to stay a while.

Thursday 3. Mrs. Smith came this morning. Beautiful day. Went over to see if Mary Hardwick or Cousin Ellen could not go after wild flowers, neither of them could go. I went out to Uncle Caswell's and got Rhoda to go out to Dr. Grant's this eve.

Friday 4. Rainy day, April showers. Uncle Caswell took dinner here. Mrs. McNutt spent the day here. Cousin Ellen McCallie here this eve. Some of the soldiers' wives tried to press some bacon today. There was a man killed over at the depot. Mrs. Shaddrick died today.

Saturday 5. April showers. I sat up all night with little Paschal Wood, who died yesterday. Mrs. McCamy, Mag Shadden, John Campbell and I sat up last night. Mother and Sister went up to Lizzie

---

[17] N. G. Burgess died 19 March 1862, and was interred in Fort Hill Cemetery, Ross, *Cemetery Records*, II:71.

Wood's this eve; Paschal was buried at 2 o'clock. Mr. Bradshaw, Sallie and Mary here this eve. Mrs. Delia Smith is still here.[18]

Sunday 6. Beautiful day. Rhoda and I commenced going to Sunday School at Baptist Church. Mary Elizabeth went to Presbyterian Sunday School. Mother went to Baptist Church, so did I. Rhoda and Sister went to Presbyterian Church. Mrs. J. J. G. Smith, Sister, Rhoda and I went out to see Ada Gaut, she is sick. Pryor and Joe Lea here this eve. Pryor brought a letter from Cousin John, he wrote that he had killed a man and wounded one in a skirmish.

Monday 7. Cloudy day. Sister and I helped wash part of the day. Rhoda went up to see Adelia Craigmiles this evening.

Tuesday 8. Rainy day. Mrs. Bradshaw took dinner here. Mr. Carter brought news this morning that there had been a large battle at Yorktown, Virginia, and Corinth, Mississippi. Gen. Johnston and Col. Bates of Tennessee killed. The regiment was cut up badly; we routed them completely. Fought on 5, 6, and 7 last.[19]

Wednesday 9. Nothing occurred. Rainy day.

Thursday 10. Beautiful day. Mr. Smith walked in the yard for the first time this morning. Mrs. Rogers called on Mrs. Smith today. Julia Tucker and Jim McGhee were married tonight.

Friday 11. Beautiful day. Anna Gaut here today. Mr. Smith is out again playing backgammon with Sister, Rhoda and I went to the choir at Judge Gaut's. Mrs. Smith, Annie, Sister, Jimmie and I went out to Mrs. Traynor's "big spring" after wild flowers.

Saturday 12. Pretty day. Mr. Smith and Sister playing backgammon today. Mrs. Smith is a very clever lady. We all like them both so much. Sue Henderson here this eve, she and Lizzie went up to see Miss Sallie Bradshaw. Cold and windy day.

Sunday 13. A rainy day. Rhoda, Lizzie and I went to Baptist Sunday School. None went to church. Joe Lea dined here.

---

[18] Paschal C. Wood, son of William and W. E. Wood, died 4 April 1862, aged 2 years, one month, 26 days. Buried in Fort Hill Cemetery. Ross, *Cemetery Records*, II:300.

[19] Yorktown, the last battle of the American Revolution, probably would have yielded to Union assaults, but General George B. McClellan cautiously put the city under siege. The Confederates abandoned the site and McClellan could write: "Yorktown is in our possession."

Monday 14. A tolerable pretty day. Sister and Mr. Smith played backgammon. The enemy has Huntsville, Alabama. Mother and I went to Mrs. Bradshaw's. Rhoda went to Mrs. Carter's this eve.

Tuesday 15. Lovely day. Mr. and Mrs. Smith started to Charleston, S. C. this eve. Cousin Mary Jarnagin here this eve. Mrs. Bradshaw and Sallie took tea here tonight. Aunt A. (Elizabeth Adeline) came in this eve. I was so sorry to see Mrs. Smith go. Feel so lonesome this eve.

Wednesday 16. Beautiful day. Rhoda and I cleaned out Aunt Adeline's room today. Gussie Craigmiles here this morn. Have a headache this eve, very bad. Mrs. Bradshaw, Mother and Sister went up to Dr. Grant's this morning to see Mollie.

Thursday 17. Pretty day. Mother was sick in bed today. I went out to Uncle Caswell's today, took dinner there. Uncle Caswell, Mrs. Shadden and Mrs. Bradshaw here this eve. Misses Sallie and Mary Bradshaw and I went out to Dr. Grant's to see Mollie this eve. She has the typhoid fever, very bad.

Friday 18. Pretty day. We have all been working out in the garden today. Little Susie Thornton died this morn at 10 o'clock with scarlet fever, and Mother and Sister went up there this eve. We are warned of our approach to death almost every day by the tolling of the bell. Sister and Mother went up in town this eve. Rhoda sat up there tonight. I stayed all night with Sallie Surguine tonight. He [her father] has gone to Richmond.[20]

Saturday 19. Rainy day. Nothing of importance occurred today. Commenced me a pair of socks today. Uncle Caswell took dinner here. Rhoda and I went over to see Mrs. Brown's cloth. I helped Aunt Phoebe milk today.

Sunday 20. Rainy day. We all went to the Baptist Sunday School. Easter.

Monday 21. Rainy and sunshiny day. I helped Emeline wash today. She took sick and had to send for Dr. Pepper this eve.

Tuesday 22. Rhoda and I ironed all morning. We went to see Miss Mattie Fout this eve. I also went to see Sallie McMillan. Rhoda stayed all night with Sallie Surguine. Sister and I went over to Mrs.

---

[20] Susie Thornton, daughter of P. L. And H. C. Thornton, died 8 April 1862, aged five years. Buried in Fort Hill Cemetery. Ross, *Cemetery Records*, II:277.

Grant's after tea. Mr. Carter started to Charleston, S.C., this eve. Pretty day.

Wednesday 23. Pretty day. Rhoda stayed with Sallie Surguine tonight. Ann Stuart was here this eve, also Julia Grant. I twisted some stocking cotton and ironed a little today. Cousin Joe was here nearly all day, took dinner here. Emeline is improving.

Thursday 24. Pretty day. Lizzie Burgis, Sue Hoyl, Ned Mayfield, Mary Hardwick, Anna and Addie Stuart and I all went fishing this eve. Aunt Elizabeth here today. Sallie Surguine came after Rhoda to stay all night with her.

Friday 25. A very, very wet, dark evening and night. Mr. Bradshaw's school[21] gave a concert tonight. I went with Cousin Joe Lea. Aunt Polly Lea stayed all night here. Mother and I went up to Mrs. Carter's (she is sick, Mag Shadden came down to tell us), also over to Cousin Mary's. I was sick in bed this eve.

Saturday 26. Pretty day. Mary and Sallie Bradshaw, Rhoda and I went out to Dr. Grant's this evening. They are better. Venie Seavey's 19th birthday. Sallie Bradshaw's 21st. Bell Grant, Annie Bradshaw and Lizzie Lea were here this eve at Annie's birthday party. Rhoda stayed all night with Sallie Surguine. Mother took dinner at Cousin Mary's with Aunt Polly Lea.

Sunday 27. Pretty day. Went to Sunday School. Did not go to church, was sick. I laid down at 10 o'clock, did not get up till 5 in the evening. Mother and Sister went up to see Mrs. Carter, she is sick.

Monday 28. Pretty day. Sister, Rhoda and I helped Aunt Phoebe wash. (Emeline is improving). Aunt Elizabeth and Lizzie Swan took tea here, also Uncle Caswell.

Tuesday 29. I went after wild flowers this evening with Miss Sallie Bradshaw's botany class. Mr. Glenn took tea here. Mrs. Bradshaw came this eve. Sallie Surguine and Mrs. Traynor came after Rhoda today to stay all night with her.

Wednesday 30. Pretty day. Mother, Annie and I went to Uncle Caswell's, came down and told us we were whipped at Porridge, would not be surprised to see the enemy here any day.

---

[21] Cleveland Masonic Female Institute.

May 1862

Thursday 1. Rained this morning. Could not have a May party. Mrs. Craigmiles, Mrs. Foute, Sallie Bradshaw took tea here.

Friday 2. Beautiful day. Rhoda, Lizzie and I went out to a May party at Candy's Creek. Tom McMillin went with me nearly all the time, he and George Summers. Tom came home with me. John Swan with Rhoda. Enjoyed myself very much. Cousin Joe Lea took tea here.

Saturday 3. Pretty day. Mr. Carter came home from Charleston, S. C. this morn. Sister has been sick all day, sent for the doctor, cannot sit up a minute. Mother and I went to the Baptist Church tonight. Mr. Kefauver preached from Matthew 17:5. Mr. Hawkins stayed here all night.

Sunday 4. Rainy day. Rhoda and I went to Sunday School. Lizzie is sick, we also went to church. Mr. Kefauver preached from I Timothy 1:15. Cousin Joe took dinner here.

Monday 5. Rainy day. Mrs. Shadden spent the day here. I helped Emeline wash. Mrs. Bradshaw, Mrs. Shadden and Cousin Mary here this eve to see Sister, she has the flu, also Eliza Wood. Johnnie has another tooth.

Tuesday 6. Pretty day. Florence Johnston, Mrs. Thornton, Mrs. Pleasant Craigmiles, Sallie McMillin and I went out to Dr. Grant's, they were all better. Johnnie was very cross last night and this morn. Mary Edwards is in bed, sick all day.

Wednesday 7. Pretty day. Mrs. Worley, Mrs. Jessie Gaut, Mrs. Bradshaw, William Craigmiles, Sallie Surguine, Euphilia Bradshaw, Mrs. White, Mrs. Reynolds, Cousin Mary, Mrs. McNutt were all here to see Sister. Mother called in Dr. Thompson for Lizzie this morn. Cousin Thomas Lea[22] arrived here this morn from Gen. Price's command.

Thursday 8. Pretty day. Mrs. Wash Alexander here this morn. This eve Mrs. Sam Smith, Judge Gaut, Cousin Mary, Rebecca Weir,

---

[22] Uncle Pleasant's son.

Mrs. Pickens, Lizzie Wood, Mag Shadden and Mrs. Bradshaw [were here].

Friday 9. Pretty day. Julia Grant here this eve, also Mrs. Bradshaw. Sister sends Johnnie up to Mrs. Reynolds and Mrs. Pepper's every day, she does not give much milk.[23] Cousin Thomas Lea stopped here a little while on his way down to his Uncle Thomas Callaway's.

Saturday 10. Pretty day. Rhoda and I took up the parlor carpet and shook it out today. Cousin Mary Jarnagin, Hattie Pharis, and Mrs. Bradshaw here after tea.

Sunday 11. Pretty day. We all went to Baptist Sunday School today. Rhoda went to Methodist Church. Callie Swan came here from Sunday School. Cousin Joe Lea here this eve.

Monday 12. Pretty day. Rhoda and I helped wash today. Cousin John Lea came home on furlough this eve. Sister tried a short dress on Johnnie this eve, he looked so sweet. Lt. Col. Dunn's reg. went down this eve. After tea Rhoda and I went up to Mrs. Bradshaw's.

Tuesday 13. Pretty day. Cousins John Lea and Tom Lea went with Rhoda and I to a party at Mr. Kenner's tonight. Will Kenner came down and invited us. Rained this eve.

Wednesday 14. Pretty day. Rained [again] this eve. Cousins Tom and John Lea spent the eve here and stayed all night. Rhoda, Cousin John and I went to hear Mr. [William Edward] Caldwell preach, his text was 1 Corinthians, 15th chapter, 55th verse.

Thursday 15. Pretty day. Mother, Sister, Rhoda, I and the children spent the day at Uncle Caswell's today. Will and Joe Kenner and Cousin Tom Lea dined there. Callie Swan stayed with us tonight. Rhoda and Children and I went to hear Mr. Wexler preach from the Gospel of John. Cousin John came home with us.

Friday 16. Pretty day. Anna Gaut and Mrs. Bradshaw here this eve, also Cousin John, Mag Shadden and John Campbell here after tea. Frank Ragsdale and Tom McMillan wrote Rhoda and I notes for us to go up to a flag presentation 6 miles above here to Herndon's tomorrow. Jim Campbell wrote Lizzie a note, she is not going. Day

---

[23] If a mother could not produce enough milk for her baby she would sometimes use a wet nurse.

of fasting and prayer. All went to church. Aunt Elizabeth and Samantha Swan came here and went to church.

Saturday 17. Pretty day. We went on the cars at 11 o'clock this morn. Came back at 4 this eve. Enjoyed myself tolerable well. Narcissa McMillin presented [a flag] to the Mountain Rangers. Cousin John Lea went with Rhoda and I to Cumberland [Presbyterian] Church tonight, came back by ourselves. Mr. Carter got back from Atlanta today, he saw Venie and Mrs. Cook down there.

Sunday 18. Rained this eve. Cousin John and Uncle Caswell here this morning. All went to Baptist Sunday School. Rhoda and Lizzie went to Cumberland Church. Cousins Tom and John Lea took tea here. Cousin John told us good-bye, is going back to Kingston[24] tomorrow.

Monday 19. Pretty day. Aunt Elizabeth and Cousin Tom spent the day here. I helped wash today. Mother and Aunt Elizabeth went up to Loudon Hospital. Heard this eve that Stonewall Jackson had gained a victory in Western Virginia.[25]

Tuesday 20. Rainy day. Received a letter and wrote one to Mary Sevier this morning. Cousin Tom took dinner here.

Thursday 22. Pretty day. Rhoda and Sister went down to see Mollie Mills, she is sick. Mrs. John Hoyl's baby died this eve. I sat up there tonight, also Mrs. Jesse Gaut, Anna Gaut, Euphilia Bradshaw and Sallie McMillin. Fred Montgomery came from Virginia this eve. After tea Rhoda and Mother went out to Uncle Caswell's. Aunt Elizabeth is going to Raytown tomorrow to see her sister Mrs. Earnest.[26]

---

24 Roane County, Tennessee.

25 George B. McClellan launched an invasion of the Peninsula in Virginia. Jackson's strategy was to strike consecutively upon the Union commanders before they could unite. He mystified the Federal forces as to where he might strike next. His activities caused the Northern press to express concern for the safety of Washington. When McClellan set out for Richmond, Jackson joined forces to strengthen the Confederate plan. Robert E. Lee was placed in command of the Army of Northern Virginia. (Randall and Donald, *Civil War*, 212, 213.)

26 Hannah E. Hoyl was born 11 January 1861 and died 22 May 1862, buried at Fort Hill Cemetery. Ross, *Cemetery Records*, II:159.

Friday 23. Pretty day. Cousins Albert Jarnagin and Houston Witt came down to see us from Charleston[27] (where they are guarding the bridge) this eve. Mother, Rhoda and them went out and stayed out all night at Uncle Caswell's. Miss Euphilia and Rhoda took a ride this eve.

Saturday 24. Pretty day. Rained this morn. I went down to Cousin Mary Jarnagin's with my two cousins, they went back this morn. Rhoda and I went to Mrs. Bradshaw's this eve. Miss Sallie and Rhoda took a ride this eve. Mother and I stayed all night at Uncle Caswell's tonight.

Sunday 25. Pretty day. Rhoda, Lizzie and I went to the Baptist Sunday School. Did not go to church. I went to Uncle Caswell's this eve, stayed all night. Came to church tonight at Presbyterian Church. Lt. Wiseman and James Crookshanks came down on the train to see Rhoda and I this eve. Called on us tonight.

Monday 26. Pretty day. Sister and I helped Aunt Phoebe wash today. Emeline is broken out with measles. Lt. Wiseman and Mr. James Crookshanks called this morn. Callie Swan and I took a ride this eve. Mother went out and stayed all night with Uncle Caswell this eve. Sent for Dr. Thompson for Aunt Adeline.

Tuesday 27. Beautiful day. Rhoda and Sister called on Cousin Ellen and Miss Hook, they came up this morn. This eve Rhoda and I went down to the rolling mill with Cousin Ellen and others. We sat until bedtime at Cousin Mary Jarnagin's. Mother stayed at Uncle Caswell's tonight.

Wednesday 28. Pretty day. Mother and I stayed all night with Uncle Caswell tonight.

Thursday 29. Pretty day. Mrs. Bradshaw here this eve. Mary Bradshaw and I took a ride. Mother and Rhoda stayed all night with Uncle Caswell. Cousin Ellen, Miss Penelope Hook and Lizzie Phillips here this morn.

Friday 30. Pretty day. Miss Sallie and Euphilia Bradshaw stayed till bedtime with us. Mother went to Uncle Caswell's tonight. Fred Montgomery sent us a fish this morn.

---

[27] Charleston, Bradley County, Tennessee, is ten miles North of Cleveland on the Hiwassee River.

Saturday 31. Warm day. Mr. Bradshaw, Mary and I went up to Benton to Mr. Reynold's this morn, 17 miles. Aunt Elizabeth came this eve.

June 1862

Sunday 1. Pretty day. A hard thunderstorm this evening in which Mrs. Reynolds' nephew, John Taylor, was killed by lightning; he was sitting by the fireplace. I went over to Callie Mayfield's and saw him. Mr. Reynolds, Mattie Reynolds, John, Mary and I went to church this morn.

Monday 2. Rained very hard today. Mr. Bradshaw, Mary Bradshaw and I came home this morn. When I got here I heard that they were fighting at Richmond, that "the Good for nothing Yanks" had killed Aunt Elizabeth's brother, George Johnson in Mississippi, went to one of his many plantations and committed some depredation, he would not suffer it, killed one of them and another low-down Irishman, such as the Northern army is composed of, shot him through the head. May his noble blood be avenged by the destruction of thousands of the cowardly and low-bred foe.[28]

Tuesday 3. Rainy day. Uncle Caswell took dinner here, had a mess of peas and some green apple pie. Mother went up to see Mrs. Dr. Edwards about sending some hospital store [supplies] to Dr. Green at Strawberry Plains. Frank [slave] cut Stephney's finger off with the ax this eve. The attack was made by our [Confederate] folks on Saturday at Chickahominy Creek, 7 miles from Richmond.

Wednesday 4. Pretty day. Wrote letter to Elvira Lea this morn. Rhoda and I were up with Stephney bathing his hand last night. Had a spring chicken for dinner today. Bathed Stephney's hand today. Our plums and cherries are getting ripe.

Thursday 5. A hard storm 'bout dark. Frank Ragsdale and Fred Montgomery sent us a card asking permission to call on us tonight.

---

[28] Myra has become harsher as the toll of the war and deaths have hurt her deeply.

The rain prevented them. Mrs. Bradshaw here this eve. Stephney did not rest well last night with his hand, pains him a good deal today

Friday 6. Rained today. I bound our fans today. Mother and Sister went over to Cousin Mary Harle's this morn and down to Cousin Mary Jarnagin's this eve. Stephney's hand has not hurt him any today. Rhoda went to the choir tonight. Fred Montgomery called on Rhoda and I tonight. Had a mess of Irish potatoes today and some dewberry pie.

Saturday 7. Mother and Annie went out to Uncle Caswell's this morn. Stephney rested very well last night. Julia and Mollie Grant, Sallie Bradshaw and Mr. John Sharp took tea here. Mr. Sharp took dinner; had cherry pie. Ben Thompson and Miss Nellie Jones were married today [at] Selma, Alabama. Some soldiers came up after buttermilk this eve. Mother cleaned out the Baptist Church this eve. We heard the Yankees were on the other side of the river from Chattanooga. Could see their camp fires last night. Mr. Carter and a good many of the citizens went down to help repulse them. Rhoda, Sister and Mother went to church at Baptist Church. Julia Grant told me this eve that she would be married before Christmas. Pretty day.

Sunday 8. Pretty day. We all went to Sunday School. Mother, Sister and Rhoda went to the Baptist Church. We all intended to have gone over to the fairground this eve, but concluded we had better let soldiers know something about it before we went. Mrs. Bradshaw and Mag Shadden here this eve. Rhoda stayed all night with Sallie Surguine last night and tonight. Mr. and Mrs. McNutt came home tonight to sit until bedtime, but we had gone to bed

Monday 9. Pretty day. Helped Emeline wash today, has quit washing for Mrs. Pepper. Rhoda stayed with Sallie Surguine tonight. The cowardly Yankees have retreated from Chattanooga. They will never fight unless they have every advantage, it shows they are cowards.

Tuesday 10. Pretty day. Rhoda and I spent the day at Mr. Robert Swan's today. Mr. Carter came home from Chattanooga this morn. Rhoda stayed all night with Sallie Surguine.

Wednesday 11. Pretty day. Heard today that Neal S. Brown hung for killing Andy Johnson last Thursday. Rhoda and I went to see Sallie McMillin and Ada Gaut this morn. This eve Mother and Sister went up to see Mrs. Bradshaw.

Thursday 12. Pretty day. Finished altering my muslin [sturdy, plain weave, cotton in fabric] dress. The soldiers were ordered away from the fairground this morn. Had new Irish potatoes today for dinner.

Friday 13. Rhoda and I went to choir with Mr. Bradshaw's folks. Pretty day. Beautiful moonshiny night.

Saturday 14. Pretty day. Ann Stuart and I went to see Josephine Middlecoff, Mary Pharis and Mag Shadden this eve. Went down to Mrs. Stuart's. Heard that John H. Morgan had camped below Tucker's.[29]

Sunday 15. Pretty day. All to Sunday School; none to church. Cousin Joe Lea dined here. Uncle Caswell took tea. Morgan's men passed through here en route for Knoxville this morn. One of his men stopped here after a drink and stayed 'bout an hour, named Allen Worth, a Kentuckian, a nice fellow. Capt. John H. Morgan passed up on the cars.

Monday 16. Pretty day. Sister, Rhoda and I all helped Emeline wash, got through 'bout 11 o'clock. Mrs. Bradshaw here this morn. Uncle Caswell and Mr. Carter went up to Cohutta Springs to get a camp, coming back tomorrow.[30]

Tuesday 17. Pretty day. Poor Matt Hassle died today at 11 o'clock; had typhoid fever. Lizzie Surguine, Ann Stuart, Addie Stuart and I spent the day at Mrs. Rutledge's; went to see Sallie Reeder. Ann and I took a short ride this eve; crossed Candy's Creek, met two soldiers. If Houston had lived he would have been 12 years old today.

Wednesday 18. Cloudy day. Commenced my cotton dress this eve. Sister intended to have gone to the springs tomorrow but heard some bad news and did not go. Mrs. Shadden and Mag here after tea. Julia and Mollie Grant here this morn. Matt Hassle was buried this eve.

Thursday 19. Pretty day. Examination commenced this eve. Mother, Sister and children went over to the steam mill and rolling mill this eve. Capt. John H. Morgan came from Chattanooga this bedtime at Mr. Bradshaw's.

---

[29] Tucker Springs.

[30] Cohutta Springs was located a few miles southwest of Cleveland. It was one of the less-well-known watering places.

Friday 20. Pretty day. Mother and I attended Mr. Bradshaw's examination this morning. Rhoda and I went around to Mrs. Hardwick's and saw Fanny Tucker before we went this eve. Mollie Grant and I went to see Ada Gaut and then went and had our fortunes told. Mollie and Virginia took tea here. Fred Montgomery went with me to the concert. Cousin Joe with Mollie. Rhoda saw Capt. John H. Morgan this eve just as he was leaving for Kentucky.

Saturday 21. Pretty day. Mr. Crookshanks called on Rhoda and I this morning. Rhoda and I went to see Mary, Sallie, and Euphilia Bradshaw this eve. Mollie Grant, Mrs. Rogers, Mary Stuart and Mrs. Bradshaw have been here. Cousin Joe Lea sent me a basketful of cherries yesterday eve. Sister ate too many and took sick, been in bed all day. Think Johnnie has whooping cough, he has four teeth.

Sunday 22. Pretty day. Uncle William Lea came up this morning, going up the road tomorrow morn. All went to Sunday School. No church in town today. Cousin Lea took tea here. Miss. Euphilia , Annie and Eddie Bradshaw, Cousin Joe Lea, Rhoda and I went nearly out to Dr. Grant's after tea.

Monday 23. Mary Elizabeth helped Emeline wash today. Rhoda went up to Mrs. Bradshaw's this morn.

Tuesday 24. Rained this eve. Miss Euphilia and Rhoda took a ride out to Mr. Joe Swan's this eve. I went up to Dr. Grant's this eve, it rained and I stayed all night. Saw a cow that was killed by cars.

Wednesday 25. Pretty day. Anna Gaut here this eve. Rhoda and I went to Presbyterian prayer meeting tonight. Rhoda and Sister went up to Mrs. Craigmiles this eve.

Thursday 26. Rained some this morn. Mrs. William Craigmiles and Mrs. Pepper spent the day here. Commenced fighting at Richmond again.

Friday 27. A rainy day. Julia and Mollie Grant spent the day here. Julia and I went up to Mrs. Bradshaw's this eve.

Saturday 28. Rainy day. Finished my cotton dress this morn. Johnnie has six teeth and whooping cough. We are whipping the Yankees badly at Richmond. Mother went out to Uncle Caswell's this morn.

Sunday 29. Pretty day. Did not go to church today. Sister, Rhoda, Mr. Carter and Annie went to church. I kept Johnnie. Mary Edwards stumped her toe on a bug under the carpet this morn. Cousin Joe Lea here this eve.

Monday 30. Pretty day. Mr. Carter's family and Rhoda went up to Cohutta Springs this morning. Took Emeline, Sues and Frank. Mary Elizabeth and I helped Aunt Phoebe wash.

July 1862

Tuesday 1. Rained very hard this eve. Mother and Mrs. Bradshaw went out to Uncle Caswell's, rode in after rain. Mr. McNutt, Anna Stuart, and Mary Bradshaw were here this eve. Cousin Joe Lea stayed all night with us.

Wednesday 2. Pretty day. I went out to Mrs. Bradshaw's this morn and Mary showed me how to make shoes. Mrs. Lowe, who keeps the jail, was here this eve. Cousin Joe Lea stayed with us all night. Heard we had gained a great victory over McClellan,[31] near Richmond, had captured all of his forces. Glad of it. Mother and I went up to Mrs. Traynor's this eve to see when they were going to springs, to meet Cousin Mary Jarnagin and Cousin Ellen McCallie.

Thursday 3. Pretty day. I went up with Mrs. Euphilia Bradshaw to invite Cousin Ellen McCallie down to spend the day tomorrow. Mr. Peter Smith and Mattie Reynolds here this eve. Mrs. Bradshaw after tea.

Friday 4. Beautiful day and moonshiny night. Cousin Mattie Lea and Lt. Fox were married tonight. Cousin Ellen and Mary had company, could not spend the day. We invited Mr. and Mrs. Bradshaw down to dinner, Mrs. Bradshaw's 43rd birthday. We had given them out and had just commenced eating when she came in. Cousin Ellen took tea here and sat until bedtime with us. Mrs. Sallie Bradshaw here after tea. Mary Bradshaw and I spent the evening at Uncle Caswell's, got some June apples.

Saturday 5. Pretty day. I finshed my shoes. Mother, Mary Edwards and I all went to church. Mrs. McGriff came home with us

---

31 Union General George B. McClellan.

for dinner, she and Mother went over to Mrs. Joel K. Brown's and Mrs. Hardwick's after dinner.

Sunday 6. Pretty day. Mary Edwards and I went to Baptist Sunday School, and then to church with Mother. No church in town except there. Aunt Elizabeth and Uncle Caswell came in and went with us. Cousin Joe Lea stayed all night with us, took tea here. I was at Mrs. Bradshaw's after tea. A beautiful night, moonshining.

Monday 7. Mary Edwards and I helped Phoebe wash today. Mr. Carter came form Cohutta Springs this morn. Aunt Elizabeth and Mother went up to Mrs. Edwards and packed up some hospital stores to ship to the Strawberry Plains[32] hospital. I was up at Mrs. Bradshaw's this eve to get Mary to take a ride to Mrs. Hughes'. Mr. Carter and Mag Shadden here after tea.

Tuesday 8. A very warm day. I went out about two o'clock after Callie Swan, she and I rode out to see Mattie Reynolds. We went to take a ride and met Scott's Louisiana Cavalry. Mr. Peter Smith turned around and came home with us. Four soldiers came here and we gave them some buttermilk. I have a headache very bad this eve.

Wednesday 9. A very rainy day. Mr. Carter and Mary Elizabeth started to Cohutta Springs at half past two this morning. I wrote to Cousin John this eve. Uncle Caswell took tea here. Mrs. Shadden spent the eve here and took tea.

Thursday 10. Pretty day. A very hard storm this eve, dreadful thunder and lightning. Mary Bradshaw here after it was over. Cousin Joe Lea stayed here all night, took tea and breakfast the next morning.

Friday 11. Some appearance of rain, but none.

Saturday 12. Pretty day. Mother went to Mrs. Carter's this eve. While there, Mary Edwards came over and told her that she had a dispatch stating there would be 300 wounded soldiers from the Richmond battle down. We baked some things and took over.

Sunday 13. Warm day. We went over to the trains again this eve, but 20 came down. Mother and I went to the Presbyterian Church this morn. Went to Baptist Sunday School.

Monday 14. Pretty day. Helped Aunt Phoebe wash a little this morn. Mother went up to Mrs. Fate Hardwick's to take some salve

---

[32] In Jefferson County, Tennessee.

for the soldiers. Miss Ellen Kendall and Emma Lea here this morn to get Aunt Phoebe to wash. Aunt Elizabeth and Uncle Caswell took tea here. We all went over to [see] wounded soldiers, 300 came today. Mrs. Bradshaw and Annie took tea, also Cousin Mary Jarnagin.

Tuesday 15. Pretty day. Mary Bradshaw and I, after we came from the train (123 wounded) went out to take a veil to Callie Swan and afterwards went out to Aunt Elizabeth's. Mary Edwards stayed all night with me. Fred Montgomery went over to the train this eve. Had our door fixed today.

Wednesday 16. Pretty day. Miss Euphilia Bradshaw called on Mrs. Kendall this morn, did not see her, was sick. Mrs. William Grant and Bob Smith's mother here this morn. Aunt Elizabeth here this eve, we all went over to train this eve. Mother, Cousin Joe and I went to Presbyterian prayer meeting. Mag Shadden and I went to see Mary Edwards. I then went back home with her. Mother and Aunt Elizabeth went up to Mrs. Horton's to see J. G. Mongtomery, Montgomery's baby boy.

Thursday 17. Cloudy day. Cousin Jimmie Harle brought up Amanda McCrosky, his bride, this noon. Rained this eve. I did not go over to the depot. Mrs. Bradshaw's girls and Mother went. They saw Maj. Jordan, a Yankee prisoner.

Friday 18. Pretty day. Rained this eve. Mother and Mrs. Shadden spent the day at Uncle Caswell's, helping make Cousin John's coat. I received a letter from him this eve. Miss Euphilia and Mary and I went to the depot. I went in the cars and handed some wine to the wounded and sick soldiers. I finished Cousin John's socks.

Saturday 19. Rainy day. We went over to the depot. Cousin Joe Lea took tea here, stays here every night.

Sunday 20. Rained this eve. I went to Baptist Sunday School. Mother and I went to Methodist Church. We went over to the depot this eve.

Monday 21. Pretty day. Mother and Mrs. Shadden went out and helped on Cousin John's clothes all day. Misses Sallie and Mary Bradshaw and I went to the depot this eve and saw ten Yankee prisoners. I helped Aunt Phoebe wash this morn.

Tuesday 22. Pretty day. Mr. Carter and Mary Edwards came from Cohutta Springs this morn.

Wednesday 23. A pretty day. Mrs. Traynor and Jim here after supper.

Thursday 24. Pretty day. Mr. Carter and I went down to Cohutta Springs today. Sister and Rhoda took me through the hotel, showed me the table service. Mrs. Spriggs came up to see me tonight.

Friday 25. Mr. Rogers left this morn for town. I stayed up all night with Mrs. Rogers. Pretty day.

Saturday 26. Pretty day. Dressed up to go down to Mrs. Spriggs but did not go, too many men there. Stayed again with Mrs. Rogers. Mrs. Richardson came to see us this eve.

Sunday 27. Pretty day. All except Rhoda went up to the free stone spring this morn. This eve Rhoda and I went to a beautiful ranch a quarter of a mile from the springs. Stayed all night with Mrs. Rogers.

Monday 28. Pretty day. Cut out my cotton dress. Mr. Rogers came. Charlie Swan died this morn.[33]

Tuesday 29. Pretty day. Made my dress body, Arthur Traynor and I played checkers this eve.

Wednesday 30. Pretty day. Rhoda and I went to Mrs. May's after eggs this morning. Mrs. Reed took dinner here.

Thursday 31. Raining all day and all last night. I was sick last night. Mrs. Jones' baby died a little while before day. Had some very nice peaches today. Mr. Carter and Mr. Wright sat up with the corpse tonight. A storm this eve.

---

[33] Charles J. Swan died 27 July 1862 age twenty-nine years, two months, five days, and was buried in Fort Hill Cemetery. Ross, *Cemetery Records*, II:270.

August 1862

Friday 1. Mr. Carter, Sister and Johnnie took tea at Mr. McCamy's this eve. Johnnie has two new teeth. Annie and I took a walk as far as Mr. Lewis Watt's. Sallie Surguine's baby died tonight.[34]

Saturday 2. Pretty day. Mrs. Thomas here this eve. Rhoda and I went down to see Ann Elizabeth Richardson this eve.

Sunday 3. Pretty day. I went to preaching two miles from here (Summer Hours Chapel) in Mrs. Richardson's wagon. This eve Rhoda and I went to the beautiful ranch and sat there a while.

Monday 4. Pretty day. Sister and I went to Mrs. McCamy's in a buggy. I drove nearly all the way. We got some cider.

Tuesday 5. Pretty day. Mrs. Spriggs, Mrs. Richardson, Rhoda and I went up to see the sugar pine tree this morn. Also Mrs. Rogers and Sister went to Mrs. Dr. May's to see about getting milk. Mr. and Mrs. Spriggs here this eve. There were four ladies came up to the springs in a carriage this evening.

Wednesday 6. Pretty day. Mrs. Russell here to see Sister. The ladies came back this morn. Mrs. Rogers dressed up her children and sent them up to the springs. After tea Rhoda and I went down and told Mrs. Spriggs good-bye.

Thursday 7. A very warm day. Mr. Carter, Jimmie and I came from the springs today. Uncle William Lea took tea and dinner here. Wrote to Cousin John this eve.

Friday 8. A very warm day. I went to Uncle Caswell's this eve. I got dinner today. Went to the choir with Miss Sallie and Euphilia. Uncle William took dinner and tea here, also stayed all night and breakfast next morning.

Saturday 9. A warm day. Mrs. Bradshaw, Mrs. Traynor and Mrs. Stout here this morn. Five soldiers took breakfast here, also dinner. Julia Grant and Mollie, also Mary Bradshaw here this eve. Mary Bradshaw and I walked home with them. I went down to Mrs.

---

[34]Jennie Surguine, born 1 August 1861, died 1 August 1862, buried at Fort Hill Cemetery. Ross, *Cemetery Records*, II:268.

Stuart's to hear some soldier playing [in] the brass band. Uncle William took dinner here, also stayed all night.

Sunday 10. Pretty day. I went to the Presbyterian Church. Cousin Joe Lea came home with me, took dinner and stayed until train time, 5 o'clock.

Monday 11. Pretty day. Mary Edwards and Aunt Phoebe washed. I got dinner. Mary Bradshaw here this eve. I stayed all night with Sallie Surguine tonight.

Tuesday 12. Rained this eve. We cleaned out the little room. I found a dress I can wear. Miss Euphilia here after tea. Mr. Carter and Jimmie started to Cohutta Springs this morn.

Wednesday 13. Pretty day. I made a dress today. Mrs. Bradshaw here this morn. Mother and Aunt Elizabeth went out to Mrs. Cannon's, Col. Lea's to see about getting provisions for hospital. Four soldiers took dinner here from Texas. Mrs. Shadden here this eve. Mr. Charlie Williams died today.[35]

Thursday 14. Pretty day. Aunt Elizabeth, Mrs. Bradshaw, Mrs. Col. Lea and Mrs. Shadden here today. They packed two boxes to send to the Chattanooga hospital. I went to Surguine's and Mrs. Parker's this morn.

Friday 15. Pretty day. Elvira Lea took dinner here. Cousin Tom[36] here also Pryor and Joe[37] this eve. Cousin Joe Lea stayed also mother. Sallie McMillin here this eve. Cousin Joe Lea stayed all night here.

Saturday 16. Pretty day. Mrs. Bradshaw here this eve. Miss Euphilia and I walked out to the fairground after pine burrs this eve. After tea, Sallie, Euphilia and I went out to Dr. Grant's. Elizabeth and Mrs. Keebler took dinner here. We have been cutting peaches all day today.

Sunday 17. Pretty day. No Sunday School at the Baptist Church. Preaching at Cumberland Church. I got dinner and Aunt Phoebe went to church. Mother and I went down to Mrs. McNutt's this eve. Cousin Joe stayed all night here.

---

[35] Charles H. Williams was born in Essex County, New York, 4 May 1829; died 13 August 1862; interred in Fort Hill Cemetery. Ross, *Cemetery Records*, II:294.

[36] Uncle Pleasant's son.

[37] Uncle Caswell's sons.

Monday 18. Pretty day. I got dinner. Mary Edwards helped wash. Mrs. Bradshaw's brother came this eve; he has been in prison. Mother put in a quilt this morn.

Tuesday 19. Pretty day. Mary Bradshaw here this eve. I went up home with her.

Wednesday 20. Pretty day. Smith's Partisan Rangers passed through here on their way to Loudon. Ate dinner at the fairground. After dinner Mother and [I] went up to Loudon. Six of them were here. Messrs. Castle and Freeman among the rest from Summerville, Georgia. Aunt Elizabeth and Mrs. Bradshaw here this morn. Miss Euphilia and Sallie went to prayer meeting; was none.

Thursday 21. Pretty day. Mrs. Bradshaw here this morn.

Friday 22. Pretty day. Aunt Elizabeth and Mother went out to Mrs. Smith's and Esq. Bates' to get something to send to the Chattanooga Hospital. Mr. Carter and Jimmie came from Cohutta Springs. Rev. Timothy Sullins made a speech at the Methodist Church this morn. A very, very hard rain this eve.

Saturday 23. Pretty day. Mrs. Traynor here after tea. Mrs. Bradshaw, Mrs. Horton and Mrs. Maj. Montgomery here this morning. I made Susan [slave] a chemise today.

Sunday 24. Pretty day. No church in town today. Mr. Carter, Mother, Jimmie and I went over across the railroad to see our corn this morn. Cousin Joe stayed all night. Mr. Carter went up the road this eve.

Monday 25. Pretty day. I got dinner. Mary Edwards helped Aunt Phoebe wash. Old Mrs. Roberts and Mrs. Cameron took dinner here. This eve Mother, Mary Bradshaw, Miss Euphilia and Sallie, Callie Swan and I went out to Uncle Caswell's and helped split [corn] shucks to fill some pillows for soldiers. Callie and I took a ride past Mr. Josiah Johnson's. It rained on us.

Tuesday 26. Pretty day. Mother and Aunt Elizabeth went to Mrs. Tucker's, Mrs. Tibbs' and Mrs. Osment's to get something for the hospital. They dined at Mrs. Jane Hall's.

Wednesday 27. Pretty day. Went out to Mrs. Frank Lea's with Emma Lea and Ella DeLano. Miss Kendell here this eve. Aunt Phoebe and I put up some fruit in cans. Mother, Aunt Elizabeth and Mrs. Bradshaw packed a box, 3 kegs, 2 bundles and 2 bags and sent them to the Chattanooga hospital.

Thursday 28. Pretty day. We took a canoe ride this morn. Mrs. Sam Smith went with us to Mrs. Traynor's to have our fortunes told. Hannah has a little girl baby. Emma, Elvira, and I stayed at the office, we never went to sleep until 'bout an hour before day. Emma was afraid.

Friday 29. Pretty day. Mr. Frank Lea came from Georgia this eve. We had a lamb supper in the office tonight. Cousin Joe Harle came in. Miss Kendall, Mrs. Sweet and Sallie McMillin rode out in a carriage this eve. George drove them.

Saturday 30. Pretty day. We went to Mrs. Carr's this morn. Elvira and I had a long talk after Emma and Ella went to sleep. Mother went to Cohutta Springs this morn with Uncle Caswell.

Sunday 31. Pretty day. I came home in a buggy with Mrs. Sam Smith this morn. Was sick this morn, laid down as soon as I got home. Mrs. Bradshaw here this eve. Mrs. Shadden and Cousin Joe Lea stayed all night here.

September 1862

Monday 1. Pretty day. I have had a headache very bad all day. Cut apples this eve. Mary Edwards helped Aunt Phoebe wash. I started to get dinner, but laid down before dinner and went to sleep. Mrs. Bradford and Euphilia here after tea. Cousin Joe Lea and Mrs. Shadden did not stay with us . Mary Bradshaw stayed all night with us.

Tuesday 2. Pretty day. Rhoda, Annie and Mr. Carter came from Cohutta Springs this morn. Mrs. Bradshaw here this eve.

Wednesday 3. Pretty day. Elvira Lea came up this morn. Rhoda and I went to hear Mr. Pitts speak at the Methodist Church; also Col. C. P. Nichols and Mr. Templeton. Elvira and I went to see Ada Anderson and Mary Kelly at Lafayette Hardwick's.

Thursday 4. Pretty day. Elvira and I spent the day at Uncle Caswell's. Anna Gaut and Mrs. Bradshaw here this eve. After tea we walked down to see Cousin Ellen McCallie. Miss Sallie and Euphilia Bradshaw sat until bedtime with us.

Friday 5. Pretty day. Cousin Porter Jarnagin, Adelia Craigmiles, Mrs. Bradshaw, Mary Edwards here this morn. Mary Shugart here this eve. Mrs. Bradshaw and Aunt Elizabeth here before dinner. We packed a box and sent it to the Chattanooga Hospital. Rhoda and Elvira went over to Cousin Mary Harle's this eve. Rhoda went to choir with Euphilia. A beautiful moonlit night.

Saturday 6. A pretty day. Elvira went to see Sue Henderson this eve. We looked for our family to come from Cohutta Springs tomorrow. Mr. Carter went up the road this eve, will be back tomorrow morning. Elvira stayed all night with Emma Lea.

Sunday 7. All went to church except Elvira Lea and I . Cousin Joe Lea dined here. Mr. Parker stayed all night here. We all went to Rebecca McGhee's burying this eve. Mrs. Hughes and Mattie Reynolds came back with us and stayed a while.

Monday 8. Pretty day. Miss Sallie Grant spent the day here. Mr. Parker took dinner. Mary Edwards, Julia Grant and Mrs. Rogers here today. I got dinner. Mary Edwards helped wash.

Tuesday 9. Pretty day. I spent the day with Mattie Reynolds, she sent a horse for me to ride. All of our family came from Cohutta Springs.

Wednesday 10. Pretty day. Mother and Rhoda went out to Uncle Caswell's to make Uncle William's pantaloons, came back to old Mr. Carter's and stayed all day. A cavalry company in town today. We unpacked today. Annie started school this eve with Mr. Bradshaw.

Thursday 11. Sprinkled rain a little rain this eve. Elvira and I spent the day at Mr. Tucker's. Mary Edwards, Martha McCarty, Mrs. Bell Hardwick and Julia McGhee were there. We had to stop in at Mrs. Stuart's on account of rain on our return.

Friday 12. Rained a little shower this eve. Sister and the children went up to Mr. Carter's and stayed until after tea. We picked wool all morning. Mrs. Carter and Miss Euphilia were here this morn. Cousin Tom and Mrs. Frank Lea stopped here on their way down to Mr. Callaway's this morn. I went up to Mrs. Bradshaw's after tea to put on Elvira's eye this eve, has a sty[38] on it. Finished letter to Cousin John.

---

[38] A sty is an inflammation of a gland in the eye lid.

Saturday 13. Pretty day. Rained a little today. We have been very busy all day knitting Elvira a pair of shoes, she went home this eve. Mother, Jimmie, and Emeline went out to Mr. Woods' to get him to card his wool. Emeline went out to check and brought it back. Jimmie is very sick this eve.

Sunday 14. Pretty day. Rhoda, Lizzie, and Mary Edwards and I went to the Presbyterian Church. Cousin Joe Lea and Fred Montgomery were here this eve. We went to the Presbyterian Church tonight.

Monday 15. Pretty day. Buck Carr died yesterday morning at 2 o'clock. Mag Shadden here this morn, she, Rhoda and I went to his burying. Elvira was here this eve. Rhoda and Mag Shadden sent out to Mrs. Hughes' to stay all night.

Tuesday 16. Pretty day. Mattie Reynolds here a little while this eve. We were weighed at Mr. Hardwick's store. I weighed 106.

Wednesday 17. Pretty day. Callie Swan and Euphilia Rutledge spent the eve here. We went to Mr. Simmons burying in the eve.[39]

Thursday 18. Pretty day. Rained all last night. Thanksgiving day. Appointed by the President. We went to church in the eve. Mr. McNutt preached at the Presbyterian Church. I went home with Ann Stuart. Mr. Schwartz talked with us nearly all the time. After tea Ann Stuart, Mary Bradshaw and I took a walk.

Friday 19. Pretty day. Mattie Reynolds came this morn, was going to spend the day with me but her father came to take her home. Knitted on my shoes all day long. Rhoda and I went to the choir tonight, a good many spectators were there. Sallie Bradshaw made a mistake in singing.

Saturday 20. Pretty day. Very busy all day knitting my shoes. Was up to Mrs. Bradshaw's this evening, helped them quilt.

Sunday 21. Pretty day. No church in town today. Cousin Joe Lea here this eve. Mary Hall and Lee Pendergrass were to have been married this morn.

Monday 22. Cloudy morn. Kate Rogers here this eve. Mary Bradshaw, Jimmie and I took a ride this eve, went in sight of Mr.

---

[39] Isaac L. Simmons born 13 June 1824, died 17 September 1862, buried at Fort Hill Cemetery. Ross, *Cemetery Records*, II:255.

Joseph Swan's. I knitted on my shoes. Heard today that Ben McCarty was accidentally shot in Kentucky.

Tuesday 23. Pretty day. Finished my shoes, made Susan three aprons. Mrs. William Grant, Mrs. Bradshaw, and Aunt Elizabeth here this eve. Sister and Mr. Carter took a ride 7 miles out in the country to find a weaver, got Mrs. Bacon. This day five years ago Brother Houston died.

Wednesday 24. Cloudy, appearance of rain this morn. Rhoda and I went to prayer meeting with Mary Bradshaw, the rest were gone. Commenced Uncle Ned a pair of socks.

Thursday 25. Pretty day. Rhoda and Sallie Bradshaw took a ride this morn. Cynthia Hardwick, Callie and Samantha Swan, John Swan, Peter Smith and I went out after muscadines [40]this eve. Went by and got Euphilia Rutledge. Mr. Smith's horse got loose. Rhoda and Sister wrote a letter to me and signed Uncle Preston's name to it.

Friday 26. Pretty day. Adelia Craigmiles and Nellie Thompson were here this morn. Mary Edwards and I went out to Aunt Elizabeth's to see Uncle Caswell, was not at home this eve. Rhoda and I went to choir tonight.

Saturday 27. Pretty day. Rhoda and I went to see Mary and Anna Gaut and Mary Edwards. Sister and Mother went down to Mr. McNutt's and Mrs. Stuart's.

Sunday 28. Pretty day. Mother, Sister, Annie, Jimmie and I went to the Baptist Church this morn.

Monday 29. Pretty day. Sister and Mother rode out to Uncle Caswell's this morn. Rhoda and I went out to see Annie Waterhouse and Mollie Jones this eve.

Tuesday 30. Pretty day. Rhoda went over to see Sallie Surguine. Sallie and Euphilia Bradshaw were here tonight. I wrote Rhoda a note this eve, she thought Frank Ragsdale and Tom McMillin wrote it, expected them to call us tonight. Mrs. Hughes and Mrs. Bradshaw here this eve. I was sick, could not eat any dinner.

---

[40]Muscadines are purple grapes that grow on woody vines.

October 1862

Wednesday 1. Pretty day. Sister and I went round shopping this eve. I went to see Sallie McMillin. Mother went up to Mrs. Bradshaw's.

Thursday 2. Pretty day. Mrs. Jessie Gaut here this eve. Sister, Mother, Lizzie, Jimmie and I went out chestnut hunting.

Friday 3. Pretty day. Rhoda and I went out to Uncle Caswell's this eve and took Jimmie. We went to choir tonight.

Saturday 4. A pretty day. Cousin Mollie Jones, Molly Pharis, Hattie Goforth, Gus Brewer, and Helen Pharis here this eve. Rhoda and Callie Swan took a ride this eve out to Mr. Reeder's. Carter and Johnnie went out in the buggy to Mrs. William Woods' after peaches this morn. Mollie, Julia, Sallie Grant and their cousin, Tom Hoge, sat until bedtime. I was at Mr. Bradshaw's and they sent for me.

Sunday 5. Pretty day. No church in town today. Pryor here all morn. "A man who does not love music is fit for treason, strategem, and spoils."[41]

Monday 6. Pretty day. Been making my stockings all day, cutting them down. Mrs. Hughes here this morn. Sallie McMillin and Anna Waterhouse here this eve. Went over to Mrs. Bradshaw's this eve. Rhoda and Lizzie went out to Uncle Caswell's to see about getting some wool to knit Cousin John a comfort. Mother went over to Mrs. McGriff's this morn.

Tuesday 7. Pretty day. Cousin Joe here this eve. Finished making my stockings, sewed on Mr. Carter's shoe sole and commenced Sister a nightcap.

Wednesday 8. Pretty day. Mother and Sister went out and spent the day at Uncle Caswell's to assist Aunt Elizabeth in making a coat for Cousin Joe. Mrs. William Grant, Mrs. Traynor and Mrs. Bradshaw here this morn. I went up to Mrs. Bradshaw's this morn to get her to show how to press Rhoda's hat. She dyed it yesterday. Mary Hardwick and Kate Britton here this eve. Rhoda and I went to Presbyterian prayer meeting. Mrs. Shadden here this eve. After we

---

[41]Myra uses this quote several times.

had gone to bed Sister came in and told us that George Summers died today at noon. Bob Grant's 20th birthday.

Thursday 9. Pretty day. Rhoda and I went to George Summer's burying this eve. I sympathize with Julia. Callie Swan and Mag Shadden here this eve. Mary Bradshaw here after tea. Made myself two nightcaps today. Mrs. Bradshaw here this morn. Sister and Mr. Carter went out in a buggy today to Mr. Hicks' to get some crabapples to color with. Mr. Carter is sick today.

Friday 10. A drizzly, dark and cloudy day. Mother and Sister went over to Cousin Mary's this eve. I assisted in putting up some apples in barrels for winter use and sewed on Sister's nightcap. Presbyterian meeting commences tonight.

Saturday 11. A cloudy, rainy day. I cut down the honeysuckle vine at Sister's porch. Finished her nightcap. Sewed the sole of Mr. Carter's shoe on the top. Rhoda and I put the carpet down in Mother's room. We had a fire in there for the first time.

Sunday 12. A dark, lonesome, rainy day. It rained all last night. Rhoda and Lizzie got ready to go to Presbyterian Church, but it rained so hard they could not go.

Monday 13. A dark, cloudy day with every appearance of rain, but none. I altered my calico dress, made it longer in the waist. Mary Bradshaw came down and twisted some thread, she took dinner here also.

Tuesday 14. A beautiful morn. Rhoda went up to see Adelia Craigmiles. Mother went to see Mrs. Dr. Edwards and Aunt Elizabeth. Rhoda and I went out to Dr. Grant's this eve, we took tea. Frank Ragsdale met us and came home with us.

Wednesday 15. Pretty day. I have been knitting Sues' stocking and her chemise. Mrs. Grant and Mrs. Reynolds here today. Heard that we had gained a glorious victory in Kentucky under Braxton [Bragg]. Rhoda and I went to Presbyterian prayer meeting with Mr. Bradshaw's folks. The soldiers from the hospital were there.

Thursday 16. Pretty day. Mother and Sister went 'round shopping this morn. Mrs. Bradshaw here this morn.

Friday 17. Pretty day. Cousin Joe here this eve. I went down to Cousin Mary Jarnagin's to see Cousin Mollie Jones. Fred Montgomery and Bob Smith came to escort us to the choir. We had gone and they came home with us. Came in and stayed awhile.

Saturday 18. Pretty day. Mollie, Sallie and Lewis Grant, Oney and Reng. McClary, Martha and Bettie Boyd, Callie Swan and Euphilia Bradshaw, Cousin Mollie Jones, Mrs. Lizzie Harris, Lizzie Lea, Fred Montgomery, Cousin Joe and I went out chestnut hunting and got back about 1 o'clock. Cousin Mollie Jones and I went to Mr. Guthman's store, and Mrs. Narritt's to get her a dress made. Caswell Shields, his father and wife stayed all night here.

Sunday 19. Pretty day. We got up at 4 o'clock, our friends had to leave on the cars. Mr. Carter, Mother, Sister, Rhoda and I went to Mrs. McCasland's child's burying this eve.

Monday 20. Pretty day. Mrs. Thompson, Uncle Caswell, Mr. McNutt, Mrs. Joel K. Brown here this morn. Elvira Lea came in this morn. She dined here. We went down to Dr. Dodson's and had a tooth extracted. Mrs. Bradshaw has a boy baby; it weighs 8 lbs., named John Neal Bradshaw. Mother has been here nearly all day.

Tuesday 21. Pretty day. Mary Bradshaw here. Sister has been up there all day. Their army is coming out of Kentucky.

Wednesday 22. Pretty day. Julia Grant took dinner here. The sick soldiers came up this eve.

Thursday 23. Pretty day. Frost for the first time tonight, ice also. I altered my blue dress today. A soldier to dinner here, J. L. Childress his name. Mrs. Heneger and Mrs. Lizzie Harris here this eve. Mother, Sister took soup to the hospital after dinner. Rhoda stayed all night with Sallie Surguine. Mr. Childress here on his horse at the gate for his bread.

Friday 24. Aunt Elizabeth and Cousin Porter Jarnagin here this eve. I altered my dress this morn. Rhoda and I went to the choir; a good many soldiers to hear us sing.

Saturday 25. Windy and raw today. Cousin Mollie Jones and Helen Pharis here a little while this morn. Cousin Mollie, Mary Elizabeth and I went out to Uncle Caswell's this eve. Fred and Joe came home with us. Fred Montgomery came in and stayed a little while. Cousin Joe Lea took dinner here. I intended to have gone to the hospital, but Mr. Carter advised me not to. Mother and Sister went.

Sunday 26. A cold windy day. Got up this morn and found snow on the ground. Been snowing all day, very hard this eve. Rhoda,

Lizzie and I went to hear Mr. Bradshaw preach. A great many strange faces there, officers and soldiers in abundance.

Monday 27. Cold day. Rhoda made Uncle Ned two shirts. Rhoda and Sister have gone every day since they came. Sister and I sat until bedtime at Mrs. Bradshaw's, the baby was crying. Uncle Caswell took tea here.

Tuesday 28. Pretty day. Cousin John Lea came this eve; we were all glad to see him. I altered my purple worsted dress. Rhoda and Sister went up to Mrs. Bradshaw's and sat until bedtime. She has the week. Received a letter from Mary Sevier. Mrs. McMillin has a girl baby.

Wednesday 29. Pretty day. Cousin John Lea took dinner here. Julia Grant came by here and asked me to walk a piece of the way home with her. I did so. Sallie Grant is sick. I made Johnnie a pair of shoes and an apron also.

Thursday 30. Pretty day. I read *Grace Trueman* all eve. Cousin John Lea here this eve.

Friday 31. Pretty day. Cousin John Lea stayed here all night. He, Rhoda and I went to the choir. Rhoda and I spent the day at Uncle Caswell's. Cousin John, Rhoda and I came round by Dr. Grant's and stayed awhile. Mary Hardwick's 18th birthday. A soldier took tea here.

November 1862

Saturday 1. Pretty day. Mother, Sister, Rhoda, Annie, Jimmie and I went to church this morn. Mr. McNutt and Mr. Stansbury took dinner here; a soldier also dined here. Wonder if I will live to see this unhallowed war over, and what will be my condition then, or even this year. Mother, Rhoda, Lizzie and I went to church tonight. Johnnie stood alone this morn.

Sunday 2. Pretty day. We all went to the Baptist Church this morn. Mother, Rhoda, Lizzie and I went to the Baptist Church tonight, also this eve.

Monday 3. Pretty day. I fixed Sues' hat today. Cousin John here this eve, also Aunt Elizabeth. She and Mother went up to Mrs. Dr. Edwards'. Cousin John took tea here. Two soldiers breakfasted here.

Tuesday 4. Pretty day. A soldier was here this morn (Mr. Hunt). Another dined here. Mother and Sister still go around every day to the hospitals. Mother went out to Uncle Caswell's this eve; he is sick. Cousin John here this eve; he told us good-bye, is going to leave tomorrow for his reg. Cousin Mary Jarnagin here this eve.

Wednesday 5. Cloudy day, rained a little this morn. A gloom was spread over the town this morn, caused by a sad accident which occurred 16 miles from here. The cable of a car broke, which caused 18 men to loose their lives, while 70 were wounded. They were brought to the hospitals. Sallie Grady here this morn. Mary Edwards here this eve. Two soldiers dined here. Mother at Mrs. Dr. Edwards' this morn. I was at Mrs. Stuart's.

Thursday 6. Pretty day. Sister was sick with a cold. I went to the hospitals with Mother for the first time.

Friday 7. Rainy day, snowed nearly all morn. Mr. McCamy and a soldier dined here. Mother and I went to the hospitals. Aunt Elizabeth here this eve, she and Mother went to the Society.[42]

Saturday 8. Pretty day. I went to the store to get Rhoda some cambric, none in town. Mother and I went to the hospitals. A soldier dined here.

Sunday 9. Rhoda and I went to the Presbyterian Church. Cousin Joe Lea took dinner here. Kate Britton and her little boy here all eve. Pretty day.

Monday 10. Pretty day. Rhoda and Mary Edwards went around to get the members of the Soldiers' Aid Society to meet. A soldier by the name of Teague ate dinner here. We tacked a comfort for George this morn.

Tuesday 11. Pretty day. Mr. Teague and a North Carolinian ate dinner here. I went down to Mrs. Stuart's to get Ann to learn [teach] me how to knit a pair of undersleeves.

Wednesday 12. Pretty day. Jimmie Thomas has returned in the garb of a Confederate soldier. He called on Rhoda and I this eve. Mattie Reynolds here this morn. Mr. Farrow here also. Sister went

---

[42] The Soldiers' Aid Society.

to see Mrs. Thompson and Adelia this morn. Mr. Teague took dinner here.

Thursday 13. Pretty day. Mr. Teague dined here. Mr. Farrow, Mr. Favor and Mr. Teague came to hear some music tonight. Adelia Craigmiles here this eve; she and Rhoda sang their old duets. Rhoda went with Jimmie Thomas up there, to Columbia, Tennessee,[43] after tea; and spend the evening. Knitted on my undersleeves.

Friday 14. Pretty day. Mr. Teague ate dinner here. Mr. Carter went out to Matt Branson's burying this morn. Mrs. McNutt, Joel K. Brown and Mrs. Heneger here this eve. Rhoda and Sister called on Mrs. Tolbert and Mrs. Tripple this eve.

Saturday 15. Pretty day. Mr. Teague diner here. Rhoda and Sallie Bradshaw called on Miss Kendall this eve.

Sunday 16. A cloudy morn, sprinkled a little. Mr. Carter, Sister, Rhoda, Lizzie and I went to Presbyterian Church. Mr. Worley preached. Mr. Noel and Mr. Teague dined here. All of us except Lizzie went over to the graveyard this eve. Rhoda, Lizzie and I went over to the Presbyterian Church tonight. Cousin Joe went with us; he did not come home with us. Mr. Jimmie Thomas came home with Rhoda.

Monday 17. A pretty day. I sat with Mrs. Reynolds' baby; it died this morning before day. Emeline Erwin and Mary Bradshaw sat up also. Mr. Noel's daughter, Mrs. Sexton, came this morn. Mr. Teague dined here.

Tuesday 18. Pretty day. I slept all morning. Mrs. McMahan took dinner here. Ann Stuart, Mary Edwards and Mrs. Matt Carter here this eve.

Wednesday 19. A cloudy day. Lizzie and I went to Mrs. Reynolds' baby's burying this morn. The wind blew very hard. Rained hard this eve. Mr. Jimmie Thomas called on Rhoda this eve.

Thursday 20. Mrs. Sexton here all eve, dined here. She assisted Sister on Mr. Carter's pantaloons. I made Mr. Carter a shirt.

Friday 21. Pretty day. Mrs. Sexton spent the day here. She and Caswell Shields took tea here. Caswell Shields stayed all night; he and Uncle William intend going to Knoxville, Tennessee tomorrow

---

43 In Maury County, Tennessee.

morn. Sallie Surguine has a baby girl. I knitted on my undersleeves all day. Have a boil coming on my leg.

Saturday 22. Pretty day. Mrs. Sexton, Mollie Jones, Hattie Goforth and Helen Pharis here this eve. I made Mr. Carter a needle case this morn.

Sunday 23. Pretty day. I could not go to church on account of my boil. My three sisters went. Mr. Teague and Mr. Robinson dined here. Cousin Joe Lea took tea here; he went with Rhoda and Lizzie to church tonight. Mr. Farrow, Mr. Skipper and Walker McSpadden here this eve.

Monday 24. A pretty day. Mr. Teague here and another soldier here a little while this morn. A great many army wagons have passed through this morn. Mr. Noel intends taking his son home this eve. I wrote a letter to Mattie Reynolds this eve; added a postscript to a letter to Venie Seavey.

Tuesday 25. Rained late this eve. Aunt Elizabeth here this morn. Uncle Caswell took dinner here. A gloomy night for us all I know. Hear the cars coming that is to bear Mr. Carter off in the "heat of war." He joined the army and is going to start to Mobile, Alabama tonight. Will we ever see him again? What will be our condition as a nation and a family this time next year? Will he be alive and at home, or have a resting place in a soldier's grave "far away" from home? Mother went over to the depot to see Mr. Carter's Reg. off; but did not get there until just now. The rest of us went to Mr. Stuart's. I finished my undersleeves tonight. Sister asked Johnnie where his father was. He looked 'round at the door.

Wednesday 26. Pretty day. I have been making my hoops smaller all day. Mr. Teague took supper here, came after a lye poultice,[44]sat until bedtime.

Thursday 27. Pretty day, very cold. I finished my hoops and twisted [thread] this eve. Mr. McNutt and Mrs. Shadden here this eve. Uncle Caswell took supper here. He came off the cars, been up to Athens, Tennessee to buy Mother a wagon.

Friday 28. A cloudy, cold day. Sister put down her carpet this morn. Mr. McNutt here this morn. Mr. Teague came here after a

---

[44]A moist, soft mass of bread, meal, clay, or other adhesive substance, usually heated, spread on cloth, and applied to warm, moisten, or stimulate an aching or inflamed part of the body.

poultice this morn. Rhoda and I went to Mrs. McMillin's this eve. I went to see Mrs. Adelia Craigmiles. Mr. Teague and Mr. McNutt here again this eve. Another unusual excitement in our town caused by two soldiers having broken out with smallpox this eve. Rhoda and I went to Judge Gaut's to the choir tonight.

Saturday 29. A pretty day. Rhoda and I went to a soldier's burying by the name of Williams this morn. Cousin Mollie Jones here, took dinner. Mr. Teague here for a lye poultice. Then came Mollie and Julia Grant. Mary Edwards, then Euphilia Rutledge. Aunt Elizabeth came in and went to the Society with Mother and I received a long letter from Emma Aldehoff.

Sunday 30. Pretty day. Rhoda and I went this eve. Mr. Mann preached. Mrs. Bradshaw here this eve. Rhoda and I went up to see Mrs. Shadden after tea, she is sick.

December 1862

Monday 1. A rainy and gloomy morning. Mr. Teague took dinner here. Callie Swan and I rode out on horseback to see Francis Tucker this eve; she had typhoid fever; can sit up now. Mr. John Sharp took tea here. Johnnie is one year old today and as sweet as he can be. Mary and Mrs. Edwards sat until bedtime with us.

Tuesday 2. Rained all eve. Mary Edwards here this eve; also Cousin John Lea took tea here. We killed hogs today; 7 only, 940 lbs. in all. I have been sewing all day on soldiers' shirts.

Wednesday 3. Rained all morning. Rhoda and Sister rode out to Mrs. Hughes' on horseback this eve. Another case of smallpox appeared in the Cumberland Hospital this eve. They moved to the Methodist Church. I sewed all day on soldiers' shirts.

Thursday 4. A cold day. Emeline went out to help Aunt Elizabeth's folks kill hogs. Rhoda and I ironed nearly all day. Julia Grant here this eve. I have just finished a letter to Emma Aldehoff and Elvira Lea. I have "ennui"[45] tonight. Cousin Joe Lea stayed all night here.

Friday 5. A cold day, rainy morning. Mother and Sister went over to the depot to see about our wagon; stopped in to see Gen. Brown. I have been fixing my riding skirt all day. Rhoda and I went to the parlor this eve and sang some of our duets. It gave me a sore throat.

Saturday 6. A cold day. Mary Edwards here this eve. Rhoda, Lizzie and I spent our time this morn knitting and playing ships coming to town, and making charades. Johnnie is beginning to talk, can say "titty" and "pretty" very plain. He is so sweet, just the age a household pet, as he is.

Sunday 7. A bitter cold day. Sister and I went to the Baptist Church. Very cold. Ate only twice today.

Monday 8. A cold day. Adelia Craigmiles sent word by her servant girl, Carolina, for Rhoda to come up there. She went after we dined, which was at 2 o'clock. Adelia gave her a canary bird. Mrs. Bradshaw here this eve. I went out to Uncle Caswell's this morn and borrowed a book to read. I found him very sick.

Tuesday 9. [Weather] Moderated considerably. Lizzie, Sues and I went over by Mrs. Johnson's and got some walnut bark to dye my riding dress. Ate only twice today. Mother spent the day at Uncle Caswell's; he is no better.

Wednesday 10. A very pleasant day. Julia Grant stayed here all night. Mr. Bob Smith called on us tonight. I went up to Mrs. Bradshaw's this eve to borrow a pattern to cut a sleeve. When I came home I found Adelia Craigmiles here. I went to town to buy some things for the canary. I could not get them. Adelia and I then went and got some miller seed. Colored my riding dress this morn.

Thursday 11. Beautiful day. Sister spent the day with Mrs. William Craigmiles and Mrs. Pepper at Mrs. Robert Swan's. I went up to Mrs. Edwards' this morning to get a sleeve pattern from Mary.

Friday 12. Pretty day. Rhoda and I went to the choir at Mrs. Thompson's tonight. John Craigmiles came home with us. Made my

---

45 Ennui is described as listlessness and dissatisfaction resulting from lack of interest or boredom. Myra uses this term several times in the diary.

riding dress today. Mother and Sister went out to Uncle Caswell's this eve; he is very sick.

Saturday 13. Pretty day. Very busy sewing on my riding habit all day. Lizzie went out to see Virginia Grant. She came back home with her and stayed for dinner. Callie Swan and I took such a nice ride this eve. Cousin Tom Lea here this morn. Cousin Joe brought me a letter from ____[blank].

Sunday 14. Pretty day. Mother, Rhoda, Lizzie and I went to Presbyterian Church this morn. Mr. Teague dined here; stayed until bedtime. Mother and Mr. McNutt went out to see Uncle Caswell this eve. He is no better.

Monday 15. Pretty day. Mr. Harrison came this morn down from the country. I intend going home, to New Market with him. Rhoda and Sister have been making my blue worsted dress. Euphilia Bradshaw and Mary Bradshaw came down tonight and told me good-bye. A very rainy night. I sent my hat over for Mary Edwards to alter.

Tuesday 16. A cold windy eve. We started on the 4 o'clock train before day. Got to Cousin Betsy's at 2 o'clock. I found her very busy spooling.

Wednesday 17. Cold day. Cousin Malvina Cochran here this morn. Cousin Betsy and Matt here very busy spooling. Wrote a letter to Mother this eve. Cousin Mary and I stayed in the parlor all morn. Cousin Han brought us in some nice walnuts. Mattie Reynolds and Peter were married this morn at Benton.

Thursday 18. A very cold day. Commenced reading *Uncle Tom's Cabin* and making my dress.

Friday 19. Cousin Livia Foust, Cal Thornbury and Lizzie Rhodefer came to see me this eve. Cousin Han went over to the store this eve, bought me some ribbon to quill in my hat and her some to make a belt.

Saturday 20. Pretty day. Quilled ribbon in my hat. Sewed on my dress. Cousin Mary went down to Cousin Sue Carson's, she sat up with Mrs. Aiken's child; it is dead.

Sunday 21. A tolerable day. Matt Mane came up with Cousin Mary. Matt and Han went to the burying. Cousin Mary and I went down to the spring. I carved my name on a rock.

Monday 22. Pleasant day. Finished my dress. Ate some walnuts this eve. Mr. McKinley here this eve for some papers.

Tuesday 23. Pretty day. Cousin Sue and William Carson, Mr. Kemper, Cousin Sallie Brazelton and Nellie Jones took dinner here. Cousins Matt and Han went to a party given to John Moffet and his bride at Mr. Moffet's. Mary and I declined going.

Wednesday 24. A very pleasant day. Cousin Mary, Matt and I spent the day at Cousin Livia Foust's. Went down to see Cal Thornbury. After tea we went over to see Dick Meek and Nellie Johns (Mrs. J. I. Carter's aunt) married at Mr. Childress'.

Thursday 25. Pretty day, cloudy. Christmas day. Cousin Juliet Gentry and Mr. George Shadden came from Dandridge; got here about when we went to bed. I did not know her; thought it was Mrs. Harrison.

Friday 26. Rained this eve. Mr. Harrison, Cousin Betsy, Juliet Gentry, Mary, Matt, Han, and I went to Col. Dicks' to a party tonight. Did not enjoy myself the least bit. Han, Mary, and I went down to Cousin William Carson's this morn; they were not at home, we rode back.

Saturday 27. Rainy morn, a gloomy dark day. I received a letter from Sister this eve. It obtained the sad news that Uncle Pleasant Lea was killed in Missouri, 12th day of September. Cousin Juliet, Han and Matt went down and stayed all night at Cousin William Carson's. Mr. Harrison went away this morn to preach.

Sunday 28. A pretty day. Juliet and Han came this morn. Matt stayed until this eve. We ate only two meals today. Mr. Harrison back this eve.

Monday 29. A pretty day. Cousin Betsy killed hogs today. Han, Juliet, Matt and I sat until bedtime with Cousin Mal Cochran tonight.

Tuesday 30. Rainy and gloomy day. I ate too many walnuts and made me sick; did not eat any supper. Went to bed very early.

Wednesday 31. Snowed today a little. Mr. Steel Shadden came for Cousin Juliet Gentry today. It is very cold. Wrote to ____ today. Mr. Harrison told us this morn that it was reported that the Yankees were at Bristol, Virginia. Laura Jones came to get Han to stay all night with her, she went. I copied off some receipts this eve.

1863

January 1863

Thursday 1. A very cold day. New year's day. Heard this morn that the Yankees are trying to burn the bridges. Cousin Mary and I rode to Cousin Will Carson's this eve, stayed all night. Matt and Han walked down there. There was a foolish man there by the name of Elisha Reed.

Friday 2. A cold day. Received a letter from home this eve. Emma Aldehoff invited me to stop at Knoxville to see her on my return home. I am a little homesick. Han and Matt returned from Cousin Sue's this eve.

Saturday 3. A pretty day. Cousin Betsy, Mary and I spent the day at Cousin Martha Dicks' today. Uncle William stayed all night here.

Sunday 4. A very rainy morn. Mr. Harrison, Uncle William, Mary and I went over to Cousin Rhoda Gentry's, got there about 3 o'clock. I was very tired. Felt very sad and lonesome all eve. Do not live in a very pretty place, very retired. I am very much pleased with Cousin Rhoda.

Monday 5. Pretty day. Juliet, Matt, Mary and I left Cousin Rhoda's. Went to Cousin Lavina Carson's this eve. We stayed all night. She lives in a beautiful house, have a view of French Broad River for a mile and a half. I enjoyed myself very much whilst there, felt loth to leave there.

Tuesday 6. A rainy morn. Cousin Sam Inman came just before dinner and invited us down to Cousin Shade Inman's. Sam Dicks and Sam Inman went with Juliet and I, we stayed all night. I enjoyed myself very much until I got restless and wanted to go to Cousin Rhoda's. Cousin Sam and Mr. Dicks are soldiers dressed in Confederate uniforms. Cousin Sam is Lt. of his company.

Wednesday 7. Pretty day. Juliet and I stayed until in the eve with Cousin Kate, she then went home. I stayed all night with Cousin

Matt Fox. Jennie and Lizzie were there. I spent a miserable night, it was very cold. Had no carpets on the floor and very poor fires. Played cards until late bedtime with Mr. Fox and Lizzie, and Cousin Matt.

Thursday 8. A very cold day. Cousin Matt Fox and I rode out to Cousin Rhoda Gentry's this morn, we spent the day there. We went after gum wax this eve. Cousin Sam Inman promised to come or send for Cousin Matt but could not. She went home by herself. Cousin Mary Harrison and I, also Matt Gentry, went over to a gum wax tree, did not get any. Cousin Juliet and Matt Fox went to another gum tree, got a good deal.

Friday 9. Pretty day. All went to town this eve except Juliet and me. Mr. Shadden came over and stayed awhile this eve. Juliet gave me some splendid cider cake and we went down to a hickory nut tree and got some hickory nuts.

Saturday 10. A very rainy day. We read magazines all day. Received a letter from Sister tonight.

Sunday 11. Pretty day. Cousin Mary and I came over from Dandridge this morn. Mary was thrown from her horse. Cousin Sue and Will Carson and Mr. Kemper here this eve. Matt Mane here all day. I received a letter from _____ and Sister also.

Monday 12. A pretty day. Copied all of "Miller's March" today.

Tuesday 13. Pretty day. Sallie Nance came this eve. Feel a little homesick.

Wednesday 14. A pretty day. Cousin Mal Cochran, Sue and Will Carson, Kemper, Emily Jarnagin, Fielding Cochran, Cal Thornbury and Lizzie Rhodefer spent the day here.

Thursday 15. A cloudy, windy morn, such a morning to produce "ennui." We can only hear the lonesome low moan and wail of the wind as it sighs through the bare branches of the catalpas and locust, reminding us that all is not sunshine in life. I have a dull headache this morn. Rained and blew hard this eve. Sallie Nance spent the day at Cousin Mal Cochran's today, had to stay all night on account of the rain.

Friday 16. A very cold day, snowed a little last night. Cousin Sue Carson, John Massingill, Mrs. Kemper and Mrs. McMurray took dinner here. Cousin Will Carson brought the carriage up. Sallie Nance, Matt and Han went down in it and stayed all night. Have concluded to go home tomorrow morn, and very busy packing up tonight after tea.

Saturday 17. Cold day. I went over to the depot this morn to go home and the cars didn't come. Cornelius Coffin and his daughter Bell dined here today. Matt and Han have not come yet.

Sunday 18. Pretty day. I got home this eve, started from New Market at 7 o'clock this morn, got here at 5. Found Emma Aldehoff here, looks like the same old Emma.

Monday 19. Pretty day. Anna Gaut here this morn. Elisha Wood here this eve to see Emma. Eliza Doss, Mr. R. W. Smith, Emma and Sue Aldehoff, Maj. Messick, Mr. Adams and Cousin Mollie Johns here and sat until bedtime. A very rainy night.

Tuesday 20. Pretty day. Emma and Sue left this morn for Knoxville. It was raining when they started. I unpacked my clothes this morn. Mr. William McNutt here this morn. Julia McGhee has a baby, a boy.

Wednesday 21. Pretty day. I spent all morning cleaning up. Mrs. Bradshaw and Sallie sat until bedtime tonight here.

Thursday 22. A cold day. Mother spent the day at Uncle Caswell's. Aunt Elizabeth came with her. Sister and they went to the Ocoee Hospital. Nep Smith, Mag [Margaret] Shadden, Mollie and Julia Grant here this eve.

Friday 23. A pretty day. The choir met here tonight. John and Adelia Craigmiles, Sallie, Euphilia Bradshaw were the only ones that met.

Saturday 24. Rained this eve and prevented Rhoda, Annie and I from going out to Uncle Caswell's. Mrs. Dr. Edwards here this eve. I wrote a letter to Ida Jarrett.

Sunday 25. Pretty day. Rhoda and Lizzie [Mary E.] went to Presbyterian Church today. Mother and Mrs. Shadden went over to Mrs. Ross' this eve. Mr. Fain and old Mr. Carter here this eve.

Monday 26. A cloudy and windy eve. Rhoda and I called on Miss Tunley and Mrs. Joe Johnson this eve. Mr. Farrow here to tell us good-bye, also four other soldiers here this eve.

Tuesday 27. Pretty day. I commenced *Vicar of Wakefield* and the cuff to Sister's undersleeves. Snowed all day but it did not lie.

Wednesday 28. Pretty day. Snowed very hard all day but melted as soon as it touched the ground. Two soldiers here this morn, one a major and the other named Harmon. Annie and Mr. Carter are both sick.

Thursday 29. A cold day. Mr. W. H. Smith called on Rhoda and me tonight. Mary Bradshaw came to see me this eve.

Friday 30. A pleasant day. Mr. Smith, Rhoda and I intended going up to the Cleveland Masonic Female Institute this eve to hear the girls read compositions, but it was too late. Mr. Bradshaw suspended school this eve for two weeks on account of smallpox. Rhoda's 20th Birthday.

Saturday 31. Pretty day. Rhoda and Mother spent the day at Uncle Caswell's. I read *Adam Bede* and performed the duties attending Saturday. Stephney's ninth birthday.[1]

February 1863

Sunday 1. A rainy and gloomy day. No preaching in town. I read Josephus' *Works* today. Heard today about the blockading fleet being destroyed at Charleston.

Monday 2. A pretty day. Mother and Rhoda went up to the Ocoee Hospital this eve. The Cumberland Hospital caught fire this eve. Mr. Smith and Rhoda called on Sallie Bradshaw tonight. Cousin Tom Lea stayed all night here, is going up the road tomorrow.

Tuesday 3. A very cold day. Aunt Adeline and Sister both sick. Mr. Tavor came this morn and told Mother good-bye, he is going to Mississippi. Mr. Smith wrote Rhoda a note this morn, asking her hand, which she rejected. Been reading [*My*] *Sister Minnie,* a novel.

Wednesday 4. A sad and cloudy eve. Aunt Adeline is no better. Finished reading *My Sister Minnie* this eve. Rhoda was called on this eve to reject another of her not very numerous suitors, Mr. Smith. I do not know why it is that he fancied her among so many girls in Cleveland. She is not so pretty as others, but I love her none the less for that. She is the sweetest sister I have, tho' not the prettiest. Mr. Smith was here this eve to see her. Oh! how utterly

[1] Stephney, old Susan's son, was a slave belonging to Mrs. Inman.

desolate he looked as he turned and bade her good-bye. I do not envy him his feelings as he returns to his home this gloomy eve, neither his lonely ride which he has to take in order to break that hearthstone which will seem so dreary to him until he finds another that is worthy of that love he placed on the shrine of my cold hearted sister. Wonder if Rhoda will ever marry, as yet she has never reciprocated anyone's [affection], neither told any they might dare to hope that has knelt to her. This world is nothing and yet we cling to it and its maddening pleasures as if they, when gained, could be retained forever in our unworthy grasp. How many hundred "castles in the air" have I built, and they all vanish, but the workman is too frail and her buildings are swept away by the first rude hand of adversity. Commenced snowing 'bout dark and before bedtime the ground was covered.

Thursday 5. The ground is covered with snow 'bout six inches deep. Aunt Adeline is better, got up this eve and put on her clothes. We saw five flocks of wild pigeons going northward this morn, a beautiful sight.

Friday 6. The snow has melted about two inches today. Mother has been in bed sick all day. I made some red pepper tea tonight for Mother. Sister, Lizzie and I all have colds. All have retired early tonight, excepting Rhoda and I, on account of colds. Rhoda is copying some pieces of poetry out of Mr. Smith's book and I am writing my diary. Have been reading *The American War* and *Adam Bede* today. Rhoda was invited to a party at D. Craighead's tonight.

Saturday 7. A cold day, the snow still melting occasionally. Rhoda received a letter from Mr. Farrow this morn. Mr. Carter's substitutes, Mr. Whipple and Mr. Boyd, stayed all night here. We, Sister, Mother, Aunt Adeline, Lizzie, Emeline[2] and I all have colds. I read in *The History of the American War* all day. Rhoda and I slept in Aunt Adeline's room tonight and had a good long talk tonight.

Sunday 8. I have had the headache bad all eve. Slept all the forenoon. Rec'd a newspaper by mail from Mr. Teague.

Monday 9. A pretty day but dreadfully muddy, the snow has not all melted yet. I wrote a letter to Cousin Juliet Gentry this morn. Mary Sevier and [Mary] Harrison tonight.

---

[2] A slave.

Tuesday 10. A pretty day. Read and practiced some today. Mrs. Bradshaw and Sallie sat until with us. Mr. Bridgers' 20th birthday.

Wednesday 11. A beautiful day. Anna Stuart here this eve. Commenced eating three meals a day. Mr. Carter went out in the country to get some corn, it is $3.00 a bu. and used to be $.10. Rhoda and Sister went over with Aunt Elizabeth to see Mrs. Ross this morn. Sister and Rhoda went to see Mrs. William Craigmiles and Virginia Harris, they took tea at Mrs. Bradshaw's. Made my cotton dress longer.

Thursday 12. A cloudy morn, rained a little, Aunt Phoebe, Uncle Ned and the two Georges went out to the farm this morn to stay all year. Susan came home sick today. I have been reading *Beulah* all day.

Friday 13. Cold day. Finished reading *Beulah*[3] this morn. Feel so lonesome this eve, always do after finishing a good novel. On the next page I will record the novels I have read. [See February 14 entry.] Sat up tonight after they had gone to bed to give Susan her medicine. Mr. Carter has gone to buy some corn and I slept with Sister. Rhoda has a cold. Florence Johnston here this eve for a piece of Rhoda's music, *The Volunteer*. Mag Shadden here this eve. Sister received a letter from Matilda Fennel. Little Tate Horton died this eve.[4]

Saturday 14. St. Valentine's day. Lizzie got a Valentine.

1. *While it was Morning,* 2. *Earnest Linwood,* 3. *Woman's Friendship,* 4. *The Two Sisters,* 5. *Beulah,* 6. *The Lamp Lighter,* 7. *Love in the Cottage,* 8. *Lady of the Isle,* 9. *Jane Eyre,* 10. *Rutledge,* 11. *Alonza & Melissa,* 12. *Children of the Abbey,* 13. *Ruth Hall,* 14. *Alone,* 15. *Nellie Bracken,* 16. *My Sister Minnie,* 17. *The Angel & the Demon,* 18. *Uncle Tom's Cabin,* 19. *Arabian Knights.*[5]

---

[3] Augusta Jane Evans, at age twenty-three produced something of a sensation when she wrote *Beulah*, her second novel. She became the foremost Southern writer. Albert B. Moore, *History of Alabama* (Tuscaloosa: Alabama Book Store, 1951) 395.

[4] John Tate Horton, son of J. M. and M. J. Horton, died 13 February 1863, aged fourteen years, four months and is buried in Fort Hill Cemetery. Ross, Cemetery Records, II:157.

[5] Myra was a member of a reading club that encouraged reading and discussing books. While they had slaves to most of the heavy work, there

A very pleasant day, like spring. A day I do dislike, it is always lonesome. I am sick today. Lt. Henry took tea here, stayed all night. Sister and I helped Emeline get supper. Susan very sick tonight. I commenced Sister a chemise band.

Sunday 15. A rainy morn. Did not go anywhere today. I helped Emeline get supper.

Monday 16. A cloudy, rainy, damp day. Wash day. Cousin Mary Harle here this morn. Rhoda and I got dinner today. Hugh Campbell brought Mr. Carter two mules from Georgetown Tennessee, he took dinner here. Mary Elizabeth started to school again today.

Tuesday 17. Rained all day. I needleworked on Sister's chemise all day. Lizzie did not go to school, it rained so much. Sister's 28th birthday.

Wednesday 18. A cloudy, muddy day. Rained very hard all last night. I needleworked on Sister's chemise all day. Sister and Mr. Carter talk a good deal of going to housekeeping in the fall. I wish I could get a letter from Wheeler and Mary Sevier tomorrow or sometime.

Thursday 19. A beautiful day. Mrs. Willis died this eve, a refugee from Nashville, Tenn., I pasted pieces in my scrapbook all eve, worked on Sister's chemise band this morn.

Friday 20. A most lovely eve, cold morn. Sister and Rhoda went out to see Mrs. Willis this morn. Dined at Aunt Elizabeth's. I worked on Sister's chemise band.

Saturday 21. A very rainy morn. Got up this morn, made up my bed, dressed, ate breakfast, worked on Sister's chemise band, ate dinner, posted my journal, read in *The History of the American War,* practiced a little, helped with supper, ate supper, washed and went to bed. This is the manner in which I usually spend my Saturdays. The evenings are usually so dull and lonesome. Wonder if I will live to see the war ended and if it will be over before this time next year. Wonder where _____ is today, they are expecting a battle there soon.

---

was more time for reading and sewing. Myra listed approximately seventy books she read during the course of the diary. It is not clear why she decided to list these nineteen here. In the entry for 13 February she said she would record the novels she had read.

Sunday 22. A cloudy, cold day. Did not go anywhere today. Mrs. Rogers here this eve. I helped Emeline get supper.

Monday 23. A cold morn, a pretty eve. I got dinner today, Sister helped me make the dessert [fried pies]. Rhoda and I got a toothbrush this eve. Uncle William sent by Jimmie Harle. Mrs. McNutt, Mrs. Kennedy here this eve, Mrs. Barksdale here to get Mr. Carter to take some clothes to her husband at Vicksburg, he is going this eve to take his substitute. Mr. R. W. Smith called on Rhoda and I this eve after tea. Cousin Joe Lea here also. I promised Mr. Smith to let him see my journal in six months.

Tuesday 24. A pleasant day. Rhoda ironed all morn. We went to the hospital to see Eliza Wood and Mrs. Cannon. Also over to see Mary Edwards. Sister sent for us. Sallie Grant and Mollie came to see us, they stayed until after tea, Mrs. Bradshaw also. Mollie told me she was to be married soon and she was going to have me for bridesmaid. Mrs. Shadden here late this eve. Rhoda, Sister and I went to church tonight to hear Mr. Kefauver preach. Received a letter from Cousin Mary Harrison this eve. Walker McSpadden's 21st birthday.

Wednesday 25. A real spring day. Florence Johnston here this morn to borrow Rhoda's saddle. A rainy eve. I needleworked this eve. Mother sewed [sowed] a few mustard seed today.

Thursday 26. A very rainy day. Read Bottas' *History of the American War* this morn. Needleworked this evening. Walker McSpadden and Pryor Lea here this eve.

Friday 27. A beautiful day. Florence Johnston here this morn. Sister went up to Mrs. Carter's this eve, took tea, brought Mrs. Shadden home with her. She stayed all night. Mr. Skipper here tonight. I read all eve in history.

Saturday 28. A rainy eve. Julia Grant here a little while this morn. Jimmie is sick. Finished reading volume I of *American History*. The two Georges and Frank [black] came in from the farm. Aunt Phoebe [slave] sent us some greens and eggs.

March 1863

Sunday 1. A beautiful spring day. Rhoda, Sister, Lizzie and I went to Presbyterian church this morn. Mr. Wexler preached. Rhoda and Lizzie went this eve. Cousin Joe Lea took dinner here.

Monday 2. A beautiful spring day. Emeline washed today. Rhoda cooked dinner. Rhoda went up to see Adelia Craigmiles this eve. Sister and I went after gum wax this eve. Rhoda got supper tonight Emeline was so tired. After tea Sister and I went to see Cousin Mary Jarnagin, she is sick in bed. Mrs. Bradshaw and Euphilia, Mary Gamble and Mrs. McNelley were there. Mr. Skipper was here when we came home.

Tuesday 3. The wind has blown some today, snowed a little this eve. Rhoda and I went out to Uncle Caswell's this morn to see Aunt Elizabeth, she is not well. Mrs. William Craigmiles and Mrs. Bradshaw here this morn. We have some little hope for peace in a few months. Rhoda received a letter from Cousin J. Lea. I received one from Mary Sevier. I helped get supper tonight. A cold night.

Wednesday 4. A windy day, very cold night. Rhoda and I went to a party at Mr. Horton's tonight with Dr. Hoyl. Rhoda and Sister went up to Cousin Ellen McCallie's and Mr. Carter's. "Old Mrs. Straley," she was buried this eve.

Thursday 5. A cold windy day. Mrs. Carter spent the day here. After tea Rhoda and Sister sent to see Cousin Mary Jarnagin. I finished a chemise band this eve. I received a letter from Mr. Meek, inviting me to _____. Where will I be this time [in] three months if I live?

Friday 6. A rainy day. I commenced me a chemise bosom today.

Saturday 7. A pretty day. Sister, Rhoda and I cleaned out the Baptist Church this eve. Mr. Bragis [a soldier] here this eve. Mr. William McNutt here this morn. Came back this eve and fixed Mother's clock.

Sunday 8. A beautiful day. All went to church except myself to the Baptist. Rhoda and Lizzie went to the Presbyterian Church in the eve.

Monday 9. A very rainy day. Mary Edwards stayed all night here. I have been diamonding my chemise bosom all day.

Wednesday 11. A pretty day. Mrs. LaFayette Hardwick here this morn. Commenced me a blue Italian Crepe bonnet this morn. Mr. Bragis here this eve, asked me to correspond with him. Mother and Sister went to Uncle Caswell's this eve. Received a letter from _____.

Thursday 12. A very windy day. Mr. Skipper here this eve. I answered Mr. Meek's letter, declining to_____. Also wrote a ballad, "Bonnie Blue." Sewed on my bonnet all the rest of the day. Cousin Joe Lea here after tea last night and tonight.

Friday 13. A cold day. Have a dull headache this morn. Finished my bonnet this morn. My 18th birthday. Sister and Mother went to Mr. Carter's this morn. Julia Grant spent the day here. Mr. Bragis here all eve.

Saturday 14. A pretty day. Mr. Wexler took dinner here. Mother and Sister went up to the graveyard this eve to plant something on Houston's and Father's graves. Rhoda and I went to a party at Mr. Thomas Johnston's tonight. Did not enjoy myself the least particle. Mr. Skipper here tonight.

Sunday 15. A lovely day. I went to hear Mr. Mann preach in the forenoon and Mr. Wexler in the afternoon. Cousin Will Carson came down on the train this eve, stayed all night.

Monday 16. A beautiful summer night and day. Cousin Will Carson went out to Uncle Caswell's to get a horse to go to Benton to get some substitutes. Cousin Ellen McCallie spent the day here with her baby. Mr. Bragis came to tell us good-bye, he started to his command today. Mother had her Irish potatoes planted and her sweet ones bedded out today, it is the dark of the moon, she had all her vegetables sowed in the dark of the moon that we eat the roots.

Tuesday 17. A beautiful summer day. I finished. Sister and myself a night cap apiece this morn. We all set out some onions this eve. Cousin John Lea came this eve. Miss Euphilia Bradshaw took tea here this eve. Rhoda and I took a walk with her, on our return I saw Maria Butner. Mr. R. W. Smith wrote Rhoda a note wishing to accompany her to a party at Mr. Spriggs', did not go.

Wednesday 18. A beautiful summer day. We all worked in the garden all day. Florence Johnston here to get flowers to set out. Cousin Will took dinner and tea here. Cousin John took tea. Cousin Will stayed all night, going up on the 4 o'clock train this morning.

Mr. Skipper here, also Mr. Willie Roland Curtis and Price were here tonight, they all think of going to their regiments tomorrow.

Thursday 19. A windy eve. Went up to Mrs. McNelley's and got some verbenas[6] this morn. Mr. Skipper took dinner here. Uncle Caswell took tea. Rhoda and Sister went to see Mrs. Miller and Mrs. Ragsdale. Francis Tucker here this eve. Mag Shadden also. Mr. Capps here to tell us good-bye. Mr. Smith called on Rhoda tonight. Cousins John and Joe Lea stayed all night with us.

Friday 20. A cloudy day, cold and windy tonight. Some rain this morn. Sallie and Annie Bradshaw took tea here. Mr. Skipper, Smith, Barnes, Roland, Daily and Price here to tell us good-bye. They are going to Tullahoma to their regiments. Mr. Wexler here this eve. I borrowed a book named *Don Quixote* from Adelia Craigmiles this eve.

Saturday 21. A pretty day. A very lonesome evening. Sallie McMillin here this eve. I did not enjoy her society at all, she was so hard to entertain. Mother and Sister went out to Uncle Caswell Lea's this eve.

Sunday 22. A pretty day. I did not go to church today, the rest went. Cousin John Lea took dinner and tea here. I assisted Emeline in getting dinner. After tea John, Rhoda, Lizzie and I took a walk nearly to Dr. Grant's.

Monday 23. A pretty day. I got dinner, Emeline washed. Sallie Grant and Florence Johnston stopped at the gate and talked this eve. Rained late this eve.

Tuesday 24. A hail storm this eve. Rhoda and I went up this morn to call on Maria Butner. Mother, Sister, Rhoda and I spent the day at Uncle Caswell's today. Mattie Smith stayed all night with me. Received a letter from Mr. Bridges this morn. In February He was 20.

Wednesday 25. A windy day, frost tonight. I went out to Mrs. Hughes' with Mattie, stayed all day. Mr. Hughes came home this eve. I stayed all night. Mrs. Hughes, Mattie and I went down to Mr. Woods' to see about getting a loom, they informed us of Sue Kenner's marriage.

---

[6] A flowering ground cover.

Thursday 26. Pretty day. I came home at 10 o'clock. Cousin John, Rhoda, and I went out to Dr. Grant's after tea, stayed until 8 o'clock. Major Messick and Mr. Glass were there, did not enjoy myself very well. Mother went out to Mr. Joe Swan's to see about getting a loom, took dinner there.

Friday 27. A windy eve. Cousin John stayed here last night. Fast day. Mother, Sister and Rhoda observed it. We went to church in morn. Dr. Curry preached. Mrs. Dr. Brown was there. Julia Grant, Mollie, Sallie, Virginia, Ann and Ada Stuart, Sue Hoyl and Lizzie Burgis and I went up to the graveyard to plant some shrubbery on George Summer's grave. Mrs. Pierce was buried while we were there. After, Rhoda, Cousin John and I went over to Cousin Mary Harle's.

Saturday 28. A beautiful day. I wrote to Mr. Bridges this morn. Received one from Ida Jarrett. Rhoda went to see Mollie Johns this eve, also Sallie Bradshaw. I went to see Mary Bradshaw. We went over to the Academy, looked at the apparatus, pianos, etc. It made me feel so sad, everything reminded me of my school days. Rhoda borrowed "Lorena" and "All Quiet Along the Potomac tonight."

Sunday 29. A very windy day. Rhoda and I went to church this morn. Cousin John Lea came to the gate with them. I helped Emeline get dinner.

Monday 30. It turned cold last night, also snowed, rained and sleeted. Very disagreeable and windy. Emeline did not wash today. I patched my cotton dress, and commenced knitting Mrs. William Hughes a pair of slippers.

Tuesday 31. A cold day. I knitted on Mrs. Hughes' shoes and read *Don Quixote*. Rhoda got dinner. Emeline washed. Mr. R. W. Smith called Rhoda and me tonight. The 10 pin alley[7] fell on a man, liked to have killed him this eve. Sister and I went to Mrs. Reynolds'.

---

[7] Tin Pan Alley, also tin pan alley, is a district associated with musicians, composers, and publishers of popular music or the group as a whole. Earlier, tin pan referred to noisy, tinny, sounding. In Myra's time she was speaking of a place that was built for the musicians to gather, play, or write music of songs. This was not usually a very sturdy building but some type of open-air structure. These alleys were usually at the springs of watering places where people went in warm weather.

April 1863

Wednesday 1. A cold morn, tolerable pleasant evening. Snow on the ground this morn when we got up. Lizzie's (Mary Elizabeth's) 15th birthday. Cousin Joe Lea sent me an "April Fool" this eve. Rec'd a letter from Mr. Farrow, do not intend answering it. I churned and dressed the butter this eve for the first time in my life. Tried to milk "Old Red" but couldn't. Cousin John and Rhoda went down to Judge Gaut's this eve after tea to sit awhile. I have been reading *Don Quixote* all day. Rhoda and Sister went up to the hospital to see Mrs. Cannon and up to old Mr. Carter's this eve. Mother is talking about buying a farm.

Thursday 2. A beautiful day. Adelia Craigmiles and Florence Johnston here this morn. Mrs. Hughes, Mr. and Mrs. Smith here this eve. Cousin John took tea here, told us "good-bye," he is going to his command tomorrow. Mr. Ragsdale and Sallie McMillin were married tonight.

Friday 3. A pleasant day. Have been sick all day with a cold, laid down this eve. Emma Lea came to see me. I had to get up and entertain her. Sister and Mr. Carter went out to the farm this eve.

Saturday 4. A pretty day. Lizzie went up to see Sue Henderson. Mollie Johns is sick. My cold is some better.

Sunday 5. A pretty day. Rhoda, Lizzie and I went to Baptist Sunday School this morn. I did not go to church. Mother and I went down to Mrs. McNutt's this eve.

Monday 6. A pretty day. Emeline washed today. I got dinner with Rhoda's and Sister's assistance. Mrs. Joel K. Brown and Mrs. McNutt spent the day here. I went up to Mr. Hacker's shop with Mattie Smith to get some music. I then went up to see Mollie Johns, she is better. I rec'd a letter from Mr. Skipper asking me to stay here.

Tuesday 7. A pretty day. Rhoda and I called on the bride (Mrs. Frank Ragsdale), Miss Mattie Wilson, Mary Edwards and Mag Shadden. Cousin Will Carson came this eve and stayed all night. Sallie Bradshaw and Euphilia here after tea.

Wednesday 8. A delightful day. Mrs. Cannon, Mr.Wexler, Sister and I spent the day at Mrs. Hughes' today. Rhoda and I went to a party at C. H. Mills' with Mr. Henry Cate and Mel Osment. We dressed in low neck and short sleeve dresses. Did not enjoy myself much. Lieut. Clyde informed me they were fighting at Charleston, [S.C.] commenced yesterday, also at Port Henderson.

Thursday 9. A pretty day. My cold is worse from my dissipation[8] last eve. Rhoda and I went out to see Callie Swan this eve. Lizzie Burgis and Miss Mattie Wilson were there. Sister and Mr. Carter went out to the farm to stay all day.

Friday 10. A beautiful day. Mr. Carter and Sister went out to the farm again today. Mother, Johnnie, myself and Sues went out to Mrs. Traynor's big spring to get some "never wet lillies" to put on Sues' burnt leg. Rhoda and I went up to the choir at Mrs. Bradshaw's, Mrs. Bradshaw had gone to Chattanooga and we stayed all night, enjoyed myself very much.

Saturday 11. A windy morn. Cousin John Lea came back yesterday eve, came in this morn. Cousin John dined here. I rec'd a letter from Mr. Bridges this morn. I am very lonesome this eve. Mrs. Shadden took tea here. Mary Gaut here this eve. Rhoda and Sallie Bradshaw went out to Uncle Caswell's to call on Miss Jennie Smith. Rhoda also went to see Anna Waterhouse, Florence Johnston and Fannie Kingsley. Heard this eve that the hospital is to be moved away from here. Rhoda and I have the "blues' very bad this eve, about a certain Dr. (Rhea) going to leave.

Sunday 12. A beautiful day. I went to Baptist Sunday School and Presbyterian Church. Mr. Bradshaw preached. Cousin Joe, Rhoda, Lizzie and I went to Methodist Church at night. I went without my hoops. Mr. Worley preached.

Monday 13. A pretty day. Emeline washed, Rhoda cooked. Cousin John here this morn. Elvira Lea came in before dinner. After dinner, she and I went out and spent the evening at Uncle Caswell's, took tea. Cousin John came in with us and stayed all night.

Tuesday 14. A rainy morn and cloudy. Cousin John, Elvira and I read magazines all morning. Elvira went home this eve, Cousin John also. Florence Johnston here this eve. I ironed some late this eve. Mother is sick, went to bed before supper. A lonesome and dull day,

---

[8] A dissipation is an amusement. Myra is probably referring to the party she attended the evening before.

haven't enjoyed myself any at all with John and Elvira. Mr. Carter's 40th birthday.

Wednesday 15. A rainy morn and cloudy, damp and muddy eve. Rhoda and I ironed this morn. Emeline is not very well. Sister and Rhoda got dinner.

Thursday 16. A cloudy day. Miss Jennie, Annie and Ellen Smith were here this eve, also Aunt Elizabeth and Cousin John. Uncle Caswell, Aunt Elizabeth, Cousin John took tea. Sister and I helped get supper.

Friday 17. A warm day. Mr. Carter, Sister, Cousin John, Rhoda, Jimmie and I went out to where Aunt Phoebe is fishing. Ate our dinner down at the spring. Rhoda and Cousin John went to the choir tonight at Dr. Thompson's. I was very tired, stayed at home and mended my shoe. Mr. Curtis here to tell Mother good-bye

Saturday 18. A warm day. Rhoda and I went to a picnic on Candy's Creek. Dr. Rhea, Mr. Wexler, Anna Gaut and Mary, Dr. Hoyle, Tom McMillin, Cousin John, Rhoda and I all ate together. Dr. Rhea came home with Rhoda, Dr. Hoyle with me. We got up early and prepared victuals [provisions; food supply] to take with us.

Sunday 19. Pretty day. I did not go anywhere today. Slept about two hours this eve. Cousin Joe Lea here this eve.

Monday 20. Pretty day. Emeline is very sick, had to send for Dr. Thompson and Ford, thought she would die. We all spent a miserable day. Malinda (black) helped Rhoda and me get dinner. Cousin Mary Harle dined here. Cousin Joe took tea. Have been tying harness after Emeline got better. Cousin John brought me in some cotton thread to knit George a pair of socks.

Tuesday 21. A pretty day. Aunt Milly (Mrs. Col. Lea's black woman) came this morn to stay until Aunt Phoebe got well. We cleaned up the parlor today, took up the carpet. Old Mrs. Reynolds took dinner here. Mollie Johns and Pauline Hereford took tea here. Mrs. Hughes and Mattie Smith here this eve.

Wednesday 22. A rainy and cloudy day all day. Rhoda and I have been very busy making harness[9] for loom, a thing I detest. Cousin

---

[9] A harness is a device that raises and lowers the warp threads on a loom.

Joe here this morn. Rhoda and I went up and talked to Emeline after and before tea awhile.

Thursday 23. A beautiful day. Rhoda has just rec'd a letter from Mr. Bridges asking her to correspond with him. I think my letters to him will be like "angel visits," few and far between.[10] Sister and I changed work, she is going to finish the harness and I am to make Annie two aprons. Eliza Keebler and Mrs. Wilson stopped at the fence this morn.

Friday 24. A pretty day. Rhoda and I went to the choir at the Presbyterian Church with Cousin John.

Saturday 25. A pretty day. Nothing of importance occurred today. The day passed away as Saturdays usually do, very dull.

Sunday 26. A cool day. We went to Sunday school and church at the Presbyterian
Church. Mother, Mr. Carter and Annie went down to Frank Lea's to see Uncle Pleasant Lea's children, they got here from Missouri Friday eve.

Monday 27. A rainy day. Commenced altering my buff muslin dress. Cousin John here this morn.

Tuesdsay 28. A cloudy day. Cut out and fitted my dress body. Cousin John and Tom Lea took dinner here.

Wednesday 29. A pretty day. Sister has been sick (in bed) all day, has the toothache very badly. Cloudy and muddy day.

Thursday 30. A pretty day. Rhoda and I spent the day at Uncle Caswell's. I helped Aunt Milly take some cake, etc, up to the May party. Mrs. Bradshaw, Mary and Sallie took tea here. Mattie Foute and Mollie Johns here this eve. Mr. R. W. Smith called on Rhoda and me tonight.

May 1863

Friday 1. A pretty day. Mr. Bradshaw's school, Cleveland Masonic Female Institute, and the young ladies and gentlemen of

---

[10] Mr. Bridges had written Myra on 11 April 1863. She was probably upset with him because he was now writing to Rhoda.

this place went up to Charleston to a May party. Mr. Wexler went with Rhoda, Francis Tucker and I. Mary Edwards, Laura and Leigh Stout, Julia, Nannie and Sallie Grady, Francis Tucker, Mr. Wexler, Barrett and Capt. Burris, Rhoda and I all ate together. I went to preaching at the Baptist church. Had a very bad headache after I came home. Mr. Wexler took tea here.

Saturday 2. A pretty day. Mr. and Mrs. Kennedy and Sallie took dinner here. Mrs. Kennedy came back from church with Mother and stayed all night.

Sunday 3. A rainy morn, was very pretty day after 10 o'clock. I went to church both noon and eve. Cousin John stayed here all night. Mrs. Kennedy, Nannie and Johnnie took dinner here.

Monday 4. A pretty day. Mr. Wexler here this morn. I cleaned up the parlor this morn when they had all gone to church. Mother's loom was finished this eve, got it this morn. Mr. R. W. Smith and Dr. Martin called on Rhoda and me tonight. Mrs. Kennedy here, stayed all night.

Tuesday 5. A pretty day. Cousin Alfred Lea and Cousin John here this morn. Messrs. Kefauver, Kimbro, Kennedy, McNutt and Mrs. Kennedy dined here. Sister and Mr. Carter went out to the farm today. Have been altering my dark calico dress.

Wednesday 6. A rainy, damp, disagreeable day. Cousins John and Alfred took dinner here. Received a letter from Mr. F. E. Bridges.

Thursday 7. A cloudy day, cold rain and gloomy, wish it would clear off. Went over to Mrs. Frank Hardwick's and to see Mary Hardwick. Cousin Alfred and John Lea here this morn.

Friday 8. A windy and cloudy day. Rhoda, Sister, Mother, Mr. Carter, Cousin Alfred and I spent the day at Uncle Caswell's. Rhoda and I called on Emma and Sue Aldehoff and Mary Mee at Mr. Pleasant Craigmiles, on Cleo Watkins at Dr. Thompson's. Mr. Smith went to Miss Euphilia Bradshaw's concert with Rhoda, Alfred Lea with me. Cousins Alfred and John Lea took tea here. Enjoyed the day very much. Cousin Alfred is going to leave tomorrow morn before day for Knoxville.

Saturday 9. A pretty day. A very lonesome day indeed. Rhoda and Sister went to Presbyterian Church this morn. Cousin Alfred did not leave this morn as he thought of doing last night, will leave tomorrow morn. He and Cousin John took tea here, went with Rhoda, Lizzie and I to Presbyterian Church at night, told us good-bye at the gate. Rhoda and I went up to see Florence Johnston this eve. Mary Mee, Emma Aldehoff, and Ada Stuart here this eve.

Sunday 10. A pretty day. Sister, Mr. Carter, Annie, Jimmie, Lizzie, Rhoda and I all went to the Presbyterian Church and to Sunday School. Cousin John took tea here, went with us to church.

Mother went out to see Aunt Elizabeth this morn, took dinner there, she is very sick.

Monday 11. A pretty day. Callie Swan here this morn. Rhoda went to see Emma Aldehoff and Sue, they are going to Atlanta this eve. I commenced reading *Esperanza* this eve, felt quite lonesome all eve. Emma and Sue did not go, Emma here this eve. Mr. R. Smith here tonight.

Tuesday 12. A pretty day. Sister and Mr. Carter went out to the farm this morning to spend the day at Martha Hall's. Mother has been spooling[11] all day. Emma Aldehoff came for Rhoda to go to see Adelia Craigmiles. Dr. Rhea and Cousin John called on Rhoda and me tonight.

Wednesday 13. A pretty day. Mary Mee and Florence Johnston here to get Rhoda and me to spend the day at Mrs. Tucker's. Did not go on account of a soldier being there sick. Rhoda and I walked out to Uncle Caswell's after tea, Cousin John came home with us. Rhoda then went and stayed all night with Mary Edwards.

Thursday 14. A pretty day. Rhoda stayed all night with Mary Edwards again tonight.

Friday 15. A pretty day. Cousin John went with Rhoda and me to the choir tonight. Rhoda commenced altering my dress bonnet today. Miss Mattie Wilson here this eve. Uncle William came this eve and stayed all night.

Saturday 16. A pretty day. Mrs. Lea, Carrie and Annie here this morn. Cousin John took dinner here. Mr. Carter and Sister went to see Mrs. Rogers today at their farm. Cousin John, Rhoda and I sat out under the honeysuckle bush after dinner. After he left I had the blues about something he said about A. C. L. Twisted thread for Mother to weave.

---

[11] Spooling was a term used for winding thread on spool.

Sunday 17. A pretty day. Mother and I went up to the graveyard and down to Mrs. William McNutt's this morn. Rhoda and Lizzie went to hear Mr. Douglass preach. Cousin John here this eve. Cousin Joe here after tea.

Monday 18. A pretty day. I went to see Mary Edwards at Mrs. McNelley's, Mrs. Frank Hardwick's and Cousin Mary Harle's to get roses to bud. Mr. Smith came and showed me how this eve. Cousin Joe Lea took tea here, he intends leaving for the army tomorrow, told us good-bye. He dislikes leaving so much, wish the war was over so he could remain at home always.

Tuesday 19. Cool morning, had to have fire. Been sewing on Frank's shirt. Mary Lea, Carrie and Johnnie came this evening from Mr. Callaway's, intend staying several days with us.

Wednesday 20. A beautiful day. Elvira Lea came up this morning from Mr. Frank Lea's. She has the headache very bad, laid down nearly all evening. I sewed on her bonnet for her, we then went over and stayed all night with Emma Lea. Enjoyed myself very well. Capt. Manville and Florence Johnston were married this evening at 3 o'clock, went off on the [train] cars.

Thursday 21. A pretty day. Elvira, Mary, Carrie, Johnnie and I spent the day at Uncle Caswell's. Sister and Rhoda came out in the evening. Drs. Rhea and Hoyl called on Rhoda and me tonight. The children stayed all night at Uncle Caswell's except Elvira.

Friday 22. A warm day, have the headache this eve. Mary Hardwick, Mary and Carrie came in this eve. Rhoda and Elvira went over to Cousin Mary Harle's. Dr. Rhea went with Rhoda to the choir tonight. Mary Elizabeth, Carrie and I went together.

Saturday 23. A pretty day. This morning Elvira and I went to a fortuneteller to get our fortunes told, she was not at home. We then went to Mr. Demour's (the guard halted us there) and Mr. Horton's stores after paste board, did not find any. We went to see Julia McGhee and Mary Hardwick. The girls went home this evening, Uncle Caswell took them. Sister and I commenced tying a seven hundred harness.

Sunday 24. A warm day. Rhoda, Lizzie, Annie and I went to Sunday School. I went to church with Sister, Rhoda and Lizzie. Mr.

Bradshaw preached Stonewall Jackson's funeral. [12] Mother, Lizzie, Rhoda and I went to church. Dr. Rhea came home with us.

Monday, 25. A pretty day. I have been sick all day, laid down on the lounge a great portion of the day. Sister is sick too. Mr. Smith called on Rhoda and me tonight.

Tuesday 26. A warm day. Lizzie came home and told us that the hospital was going to be moved next Monday. Rhoda and I went out to see Callie Swan and Lizzie Burgis this eve. Cousin Joe stayed all night here. Cousin Mary Jarnagin here after tea. Borrowed *Not a Ripple on the Stream* from Anna Gaut, been reading it all morning. Mrs. Bradshaw at the fence this morn. Rhoda has the blues this eve.

Wednesday 27. A pretty day. Rhoda sent a bouquet to _____ this morn. Sewed some on Frank's [shirt] today. Wrote a letter to Cousin Mary Harrison this eve.

Thursday 28. Rained nearly all morn, a very cloudy eve and rainy night. Dr. Hoyl and Dr. Rhea called on Rhoda and me tonight. He told me that this night two years ago was the first night he ever spent in camps. Finished Frank's shirts and twisted some thread this eve. Uncle William Lea stayed all night here, took tea also. Mr. Carter got home from Alabama this eve.

Friday 29. A very rainy morn. Uncle William took breakfast here. No choir tonight. Cousin Joe here after tea.

Saturday 30. A rainy day. Fixed my bonnet and skirt this eve. Cousin Joe here this morn to see me weave. I learned how yesterday.

Sunday 31. A pretty morn, rainy eve. We went to church this morn and tonight to hear Mr. Edward Caldwell preach.

---

[12]After forcing a union retreat at Chancellorsville, Virginia. Thomas J. "Stonewall" Jackson was accidentally wounded by confederate pickets and died of pneumonia shortly thereafter. Mr. Bradshaw, the principal of the local Masonic Institute, preached the funeral service in Richmond. He was buried at "Lexington in the Valley of Virginia." Morris, *Encyclopedia of American History*, 1068-1069; Henry K. Douglas, *I Rode With Stonewall* (Greenwich, Conn: Fawcett Pub., 1961) 222-223.

June 1863

Monday 1. A warm eve. Mrs. Rogers, Mary Shugart, Martha Hall and Capt. Bill Brown took dinner here. I assisted Emeline in getting dinner. Rhoda and Sister called on Mrs. Creavy and Harding. I feel so lonesome this eve. Mr. R. W. Smith called after tea, brought his guitar and left it.

Tuesday 2. A rainy day. Fixed my slippers and read *The Ancient Mariner* and *Christabal.* Wove very little today. Mr. Carter and Mother went out to the farm and spent the day.

Wednesday 3. A very rainy morn. Read some of Shelley's *Queen Mab.* Wove a little while this morn and wove all eve.

Thursday 4. A pretty day. Mrs. Hughes and Mrs. Morrison here this eve. Sister, Jimmie, Johnnie and Mr. Carter went to Mr. Hall's today. Dr. Rhea and Dr. Hoyl called on Rhoda and me tonight. Uncle William stayed all night here. A cold meeting last night at Mr. Stewart's. Mother intended going to the Baptist Church, but it commenced so late she came home.

Friday 5. A pretty eve, rained this morn. Had a mess of Irish potatoes for the first time today. Wove some this morn and this eve. Dr. Rhea and Dr. Hoyl with Rhoda and me to the choir tonight. The Sunday School scholars went with us to sing for the celebration.

Saturday 6. A pretty day. I went to see Mollie Johns this eve. Rhoda went to see Ada Gaut, we both took tea at Mrs. Bradshaw's, I enjoyed myself very much.

Sunday 7. A pretty day. Rhoda, Lizzie and I went to the Presbyterian Church to hear Dr. Lapsley preach and to Sunday School. The other members of the family went to hear Mr. William McNutt. Rhoda and I went with Cousin Joe to the Presbyterian Church at night. Dr. Rhea went home with Rhoda. We had a mess of beets for dinner today.

Monday 8. A beautiful but cold day. I helped Emeline wash today. Dr. Rhea here this evening to tell us good-bye, he left for Chattanooga, Tenn. this eve. I went over to Cousin Mary Harle's this eve with Mollie Johns, we took tea. She promised to let me see some notes she received from Dr. _____ . Mr. McNutt and Mr. Hendricks here this eve. Mr. R. W. Smith here this evening, he stayed so late we got very sleepy.

Tuesday 9. A cool day. Mr. Hendricks and Mr. McNutt here this morn. Took dinner and left this eve for Rome, Ga. I went out with Mollie Johns to Uncle Caswell's and took tea. We had a mess of peas today for the first time.

Wednesday 10. A rainy day. Rhoda and I intended to have walked out to see Aunt Phoebe this morn but the rain prevented us. Cousin Joe Lea here after tea. Darned my stockings this eve.

Thursday 11. A rainy morning. Rhoda and I called on Mrs. Capt. Manville. Dr. Hoyl called on Rhoda and me tonight. I wove all morning. Dr. Hoyl spoke of the Fishing Creek [or Mill Springs] affair, he described Gen. [George B.] Crittenden to us, said he was very eloquent.

Friday 12. A pretty day. Rhoda is making herself a white jaconet[13] body. I rubbed the spoons, castor tea pots, etc., this morn, went in our room and sat on the lounge. Rhoda and I talked about Cousin Alfred, Dr. Rhea, Mr. Teague, Mr. Hendricks and others, had quite an interesting conversation about what will take place after the war is over. Mollie Johns took tea here, she showed me some notes of hers and left them here with me.

Saturday 13. A pretty day. We cleaned up Aunt Adeline's room. I went over to see Mollie Johns this eve. She gave me some notes to read. Old Mrs. Hameltree stayed all night with Mother.

Sunday 14. A pretty morn. A heavy rain this eve. Cousin John Jarnagin [Sallie Whitlock's father], Uncle William and Mollie Johns took dinner here. Uncle William and Cousin John stayed all night. Cousin Joe here after tea. Aunt Phoebe sent us a mess of beans.

Monday 15. A cloudy morn. Emeline told me something this morn that surprised me. Frances Tucker wrote me a note asking me to go with her down to Mrs. Frank Lea's next Thursday. Mr. Smith called on Rhoda and me tonight. I have been weaving all eve and had on my cotton dress. Have the headache. Mr. Carter started over to the Winchester Convention [Franklin County, Tenn.] this eve.[14]

---

[13] Jaconet is a cloth with a soft finish resembling rainsook. The jaconet body refers to the torso of the dress.

[14] On 15 June 1863 a group of Confererates, including John G. Carter, left Cleveland to attend a political convention at Winchester. They were to

Tuesday 16. A pretty day. Mrs. Harris and Sallie Swan spent the day here, she and Rhoda went to call on Miss Mattie Wilson. Rhoda is not well today, ate too many cherries.

Wednesday 17. A pretty day. Read *Nemesis* by Marian Harland all day, and diamonded [sewing stitch] my chemise band.

Thursday 18. A pretty day. Frances Tucker and I went out and spent the day at Mrs. Frank Lea's today. Carrie is sick with fever. Cousin John Lea here after tea.

Friday 19. A pretty day. Concert tonight at Mr. [G. R.] Knabe's; a very good one[15]. Miss Kennedy came in and stayed all night with us, she, Lizzie and I went together. Mary and Mr. Smith and Rhoda went together. Rhoda and I called on Miss Lou Parker and went down to Mrs. McNutt's, they sent for us. Mattie Smith and Ellen Cowan here, the latter and Uncle Caswell took tea. Heard this evening the enemy were at Lenoir's Station.[16]

Saturday 20. A pretty day. Sunday School celebration out at Mr. Peters' old place conducted principally by Lincolnites. Mr. Carden (a Tory by the way), delivered an address.[17] Miss Kennedy and her two little sisters (Sallie and Jennie), Rhoda, Annie, Lizzie and I all went, they dined here. I went to see Ophelia Rutledge this eve.

Sunday 21. A pretty day. I slept nearly all morn. None of us went to church or Sunday School. Mrs. Mary and Jimmie Bradshaw dined here, they, Mother and I went over to the depot to see her brother, Gen. Brown. I was introduced to him, also to Major Roy, Lt. Brown [Gov. Neil S. Brown's son], and Mr. George McCollum. Rhoda and I

---

nominate Confederate candidates for the August elections. Governor Isham G. Harris issued a call for the meeting. They nominated a candidate for governor and a full slate of congressional hopefuls. An election was held in August but some candidates were unable to serve because they lived in areas of the state that were under Union control. (Murray, *Bradley Divided*, 106).

[15]He was born in Saxony and was in charge of the music department at the institute

[16] Anderson County, Tennessee.

[17]Mr. Carden was the one who said, in the fall of 1863, when a rebel raid came in town, that it was only a little Southern Cavalry, as he was hurrying to make his escape in a cornfield. Mr. Carter would mock him, "He had a halt in his step--was getting away as fast as he could."

went up to the choir, there was none. We then walked out to Uncle Caswell's.

Monday 22. A pretty day. Mollie and Hetty Grant here this morn. Rhoda and I helped Emeline wash this morn. Cousin Joe Lea here after tea. Mr. R. W. Smith called on Rhoda and me tonight.

Tuesday 23. A pretty day. Sister, Mr. Carter, Johnnie, Rhoda and I all went out to Aunt Phoebe's today. They have a splendid swing, it made Rhoda and me both sick swinging in it. Sister, Johnnie, Rhoda and I went up to Mrs. Hall's this eve. Miss Martha, Rhoda and I went from there to Mr. Allison's, his youngest is dead. We came and stayed all night with Miss Martha.

Wednesday 24. It commenced just before dinner, rained all the rest of the day and all night very hard. Sister, Jimmie, Johnnie and Mr. Carter came back this morn. Rhoda and I came back to Aunt Phoebe's and spent the day. Mr. Carter took Rhoda and Jimmie home and left me, Sister and Johnnie to stay all night at Mrs. Hall's, very much against my will.

Thursday 25. A rainy morning. Mr. Carter came this morn and brought us home. I read some in *The Black Baronet*, sewed on my dress and put some puffing in my chemise bosom [dickey or front of dress] this eve.

Friday 26. A rainy eve. Commenced harvesting our wheat. Four soldiers dined here. I sewed on my chemise bosom. Uncle William here this eve.

Saturday 27. A pretty day. I sewed on my chemise band all day and read in *Black Baronet*. Brother Houston would have been 13 years today.

Sunday 28. A pretty day. Rhoda and I went to Sunday School, also Lizzie and Annie. I went to hear Mr. Bradshaw preach. After tea Dr. Rhea and Cousin Joe Lea came down here for Rhoda and me to take a walk, we went nearly up to Dr. Grant's. A beautiful moonlight night. This afternoon all of us except Mother and Johnnie walked over to the field and nearly up to Dr. Grant's.

Monday 29. A pretty day. Eliza and Mrs. Keebler spent the day here. Two soldiers that came to cut our wheat took dinner here. I sewed on my dress. Dr. Rhea here this eve, he went to Ringgold, Ga. this eve. We had fresh cucumbers today for dinner.

Tuesday 30. It rained this eve. Julia Grant stayed all night with me. Sister went to Bradshaw's examination this morn. Great excitement in town, heard that Dan Trewhitt was bringing a force of Yankees across the river at Harrison.[18] Rhoda and I helped Emeline wash today.

July 1863

Wednesday 1. A very warm day. Sister, Rhoda and I attended the examination this morn. Rhoda and I this eve. Dr. Hoyl delivered a short address. Dr. Hoyl went with me up to the Presbyterian Church to hear the compositions read. Wonder what events will transpire between this and next June.

Thursday 2. A pretty day. Been very busy putting puffs on the skirt of my dress. Cousin Joe Lea went with me to the concert. Walker McSpadden came home with me.

Friday 3. A pretty day. Mary Day and Helen Pharis here this morn. Ellen Cowan here this eve. Walker McSpadden here this eve. Uncle William stayed here all night.

Saturday 4. A pretty day. Finished puffing my dress and sewed it on the waist. Sister commenced weaning Johnnie this morn, did very well all day.

Sunday 5. A pretty day. I stayed at home all day, got dinner. Emeline went to see Aunt Phoebe this eve. We all took a walk over to the field and up the railroad. Johnnie cried a good deal last night.

Monday 6. A pretty day. I feel very lonely today, nothing of importance to engage my attention. Cousin Joe Lea here until late after tea.

Tuesday 7. It rained this eve. Emeline and Lizzie washed this eve. I assisted in getting dinner. Sewed the sleeves in my dress. Dr. Hoyl here tonight. Uncle Caswell took tea here. Heard today that Vicksburg has fallen.[19]

---

[18] Hamilton County, Tennessee, near Chattanooga.

[19] Vicksburg was the last city by which the Confederates controlled the Mississippi River. Gen. Grant demonstrated his daring and resourcefulness

Wednesday 8. A pretty day, very unsettled weather, showers all throughout the day for several days. Sister cut us all out some collars. I commenced making hers this eve. Pieced my chemise sleeves on, wrote a long letter to Cousin John Lea at Knoxville. Rhoda and I received cards from Walker McSpadden and Bob Grant inviting us to attend a party at Mr. Frank Hardwick's. We declined.

Thursday 9. A pretty day. Been sewing on Sister's collars all day. Heard yesterday glorious news for Lee's army in Pennsylvania and that Vicksburg had fallen. I feel very lonesome this eve. Wonder what will take place between this time next year. Mr. Wexler here this morn. Rhoda and I talked of going out to Dr. Grant's this eve and then to Uncle Caswell's and stay all night, but have given it out. Ada Stuart here this eve. Uncle Caswell, Aunt Elizabeth and Lizzie Lea took tea here. Rhoda and I went home with them and stayed all night.

Friday 10. A warm day. I came by Mrs. Bradshaw's this morn. I have sore throat today, do not feel well. I borrowed some music

---

in the campaign. In 1862 the Union mounted an unsuccessful naval expedition against the city. Memphis was captured on 6 June 1862. Gen. William T. Sherman led a hopeless assault against Chickasaw Bluffs in December 1862.

At last Grant threw military theories aside and cut loose from Memphis. Within three weeks Grant's troops were closing in on Gen. W. H. Pemberton's troops and successfully invested the city of Vicksburg by 19 May 1863.

After two unsuccessful assaults upon the city, Grant laid siege to the city. On 25 June the Union forces exploded a powder charge. The Confederate soldiers and civilians were largely living underground and were very short on rations. The naval units and Grant's artillery kept the pressure upon the city. Unable to escape, Gen. Pemberton surrendered his whole force of over 30,000 on 4 July 1863. Instead of taking them captive, Grant released them as prisoners under parole. The fall of Vicksburg came at about the same time as the Union victory at Gettysburg, Penn. These events marked the convincing turning point in the war.

After the surrender of Vicksburg on 4 July 1863, some Southerners refused to celebrate that historic date in the nation's history. Fireworks for the Fourth became a noisy celebration at Christmas time. It would be a long time before the Fourth would be celebrated by Southerners.

from Miss Euphilia Bradshaw to learn. Cousin Joe Lea here until ten o'clock.

Saturday 11. A pretty day. Rhoda, Lizzie, Mr. Carter and family and Lizzie Lea all went out to see Aunt Phoebe, rode back in the wagon. I have been sick all day. Laid down the greater part of the day.

Sunday 12. A pretty day. No one except Rhoda went to church. A thunderstorm this eve. I laid down and took a short nap this morn, was not very well.

Monday 13. A rainy and cloudy day with some sunshine, a day suited to my life. Rhoda read some in *Bertha Pearcy* this eve. I have been stitching Mother a collar. Mr. Farrow and a soldier named Kay here to see us this morn.

Tuesday 14. A shower or two today. Rhoda assisted Emeline in washing. She and Mother went down to see Horace Gaut this morn. I have been sewing some edging on some of my nightcaps and a chemise [loose, shirt like undergarment]. Mr. Farrow and Mr. Kay called after tea, stayed until 10 o'clock. Rhoda and I received a letter from Cousin John this eve.

Wednesday 15. A pretty day. Received news that Port Hudson, La. has fallen, where is Henry Jones? Fallen too, probably. Oh! this life! I sometimes feel as if I would willingly die if I were prepared and give up this dull life, it is so intermingled with grief and sadness. Feel very sad this morn, but what day does pass that I do not feel sad? None. This life is wisely compared to sunshine and rain. How many thoughts I would like to commit to these pages for future reference, but as I wish no one to see them but myself I will desist. Wonder in after years if I will remember them when I read these few lines I have named. I read some in *Bertha Percy* every day. Julia called at the door to return Sister's collar. I walked out home with her and stayed a while, came back after tea and took my supper in the kitchen, then Rhoda and I sat on the doorstep and I read *Bertha Percy* to her.

Thursday 16. A pretty day. Mr. W. R. Smith called this eve to tell us good-bye. Rhoda sat up at Judge Gaut's tonight, Horace is very bad with scarlet fever. Dr. Hoyl called on me tonight, stayed until half after eleven, I was very sleepy.

Friday 17. A pretty day. I got up this morning with a dull headache. Mother and I went down to see Horace Gaut this morn, he died while we were there, suffered inexpressibly. This eve Rhoda and I went to his burying at 4 o'clock. I finished *Bertha Pearcy* this eve. Oh! if our household was like hers. I feel so lonesome this eve.[20]

Saturday 18. Cool mornings. Sister and Mr. Carter got up and left the table this morn very quick, do not know why. I reproved Mary Elizabeth very gently last eve about something she did at the supper table. She did the same thing over this morn, Sister reproved her this morn. Rhoda and I are going to clean up the little front room today. I dread it, wish it was over. Johnnie has a sore on his neck caused from a chigger bite. We are very uneasy about it, it is spreading on his face. Sister, Mr. Carter and all the children went out to see Aunt Phoebe. Aunt Elizabeth came in and reeled [winding thread] some, stayed for dinner. Cleaned Aunt Adeline's room, sewed Emeline's dress and skirt on the waist, helped her get dinner and took up the butter and dressed it. Uncle Caswell took tea here. Cousin Joe here after tea a while. Rhoda went up to see Adelia Craigmiles this eve.

Sunday 19. A pretty day. No preaching in town today. The town is full of soldiers getting the hospitals ready for the sick. Mr. Carter, Sister, Annie and Johnnie spent the day at old Mr. Carter's. Peyton came home yesterday, he gave an awful account of the Vicksburg siege.[21] Gave a dollar for a handful of greens, $12 lb. for butter. $8.00 gal. buttermilk. (in Confederate money.) George Tucker was married a few days ago, on the 15th.

Monday 20. A pretty day. I helped Emeline wash and Sues get dinner. Mrs. Bradshaw here all morn. We had tomatoes today for the first time. Samantha Swan here this eve. Johnnie's face is very sore, I fear Sister will lose him before the summer is over, he is falling off [losing weight]. These days are so lonesome and long to me. I am attempting to finish Botta's *History* but read very little in it.

---

[20] Horace C. Gaut, son of John and Sarah A. Gaut, was born 19 December 1856; died 17 July 1863, of scarlet fever; buried in Fort Hill Cemetery. Ross, *Cemetery Records*, II:126.

[21] See 17 July 1863 entry.

Tuesday 21. A pretty day. Mrs. Prudence Brown and Mrs. Col. Johnson here this morn to see Mother and Sister. I made a fire screen for Mother's room this morn. Rhoda answered two letters this morn, received one from Bob Smith. Sister went down to see Mrs. Jessie Gaut's twins yesterday eve.

Wednesday 22. Emeline went after berries for Rhoda and me to put up in cans. We put them up this eve. A sad accident happened this eve. A stray cat caught Tully this eve about 2 o'clock, we feel very sad about it.[22] Mrs. William Craigmiles here this eve. I got dinner today, like to have never got the cornbread baked. Sister went over to Cousin Mary Harle's to twist some thread and took dinner. Rhoda and I took a walk over to the railroad with Johnnie, he was delighted. Poor little fellow! he is looking so badly.

Thursday 23. A pretty day. I finished Annie a bonnet and made her a nightgown today. Mrs. Shadden here this eve. Johnnie Lea here this eve.

Friday 24. A pretty day. Rhoda and I spent the day at Uncle Caswell's, we mended Uncle Caswell's and Cousin John's coats. Dr. Gregg, the surgeon of the camp of instruction, boards there. I enjoyed myself very much. After tea Cousin Joe was here.

Saturday 25. A pretty day. Sister and Mother have gone up to Mrs. Carter's to warp [straighten] some cloth. I have been digging some grass off of the sidewalk. Mother is talking of taking some day boarders. I assisted Sister to twist some balls of thread this eve.

Sunday 26. Rained all night, a pretty day. All except Mother went to the Presbyterian Church this morn. I slept nearly all evening. Cousin Joe here after tea, we did not go to church, had no one to go with us.

Monday 27. A pretty day, rained just after breakfast. I read in Botta all eve. Mr. R. W. Smith called tonight, I was indisposed, did not go in.

Tuesday 28. A pretty day. Adelia Craigmiles and Sallie Grant here this morn. Mr. Smith, here this eve to tell us good-bye, is going to Atlanta, Ga. Mary and Sallie Bradshaw and Sallie Ragsdale here.

---

[22]Tully was a pet canary which had been given Rhoda by Adelia Craigmiles.

Dr. Hoyl called on us tonight. Rhoda and I went up to Cousin Mary Jarnagin's and played for her.

Wednesday 29. A pretty day. Adelia Craigmiles here again this morn. Also Aunt Elizabeth and Uncle Caswell. Sister went over with them to see Aunt Fannie Lea, she is very sick. I commenced Mary Lea a pair of stockings this morn. Received an invitation to Mollie Grant's and Joe Osment's wedding. Rhoda and Mother went over to see Aunt Fannie this eve. Mother says the South will be subjugated [subdued] in 12 months. She is subjugated now.

Thursday 30. A rainy evening. Rhoda and Sister went up to see Mrs. Dardis [Mrs. Traynor's sister], a refugee from Winchester, Tenn. George took Rhoda and me out to Joe's and Mollie's wedding, they were married about the setting sun by Mr. George Caldwell. I formed Lt. Rucker's acquaintance. Rhoda and I came home in Mr. Tibbs' carriage. I enjoyed myself much better than I anticipated.

Friday 31. A pretty day. Joe and Mollie Osment went up on the train this morn to Strawberry Plains. Another one of my particular friends entered into the matrimonial state, wonder who will be next. I have been combing back the rods while Mother wove all day, and knitting. Rhoda has been staying over to Cousin Mary Harle's with Aunt Fannie Lea, she is no better. Uncle William Lea took dinner here. Received a letter from Dr. Rhea this morn. Uncle William told us that Cousin Albert Jarnagin was killed in the battle at Big Black River.

August 1863

Saturday 1. A pretty day. Rhoda received a letter. Mr. Smith is in a great deal of trouble about going in the army. Mrs. Carter, Sister and the children have gone out to the farm to spend the day. Mother and I went to the Baptist Church this morn. Mr. and Mrs. Kennedy came home and took dinner. I went up to Mrs. Bradshaw's this eve and then went down to Mrs. McNutt's and brought Misses Sallie Walker and Nannie Kennedy home with me to stay all night. After tea Lizzie, Sallie, Nannie and I took a walk round the [Masonic]

Institute. Cousin Joe Lea here when we returned. He informed us of his Uncle Joe Johnson's death and that Cousin Alfred Lea was wounded in the shoulder in Mississippi. He may be dead before now. Wonder when we will hear from him again, probably never, wonder if when.

Sunday 2. It rained very hard this eve. This morn Lizzie, Sallie and Annie went to Sunday School. Mother, Lizzie, Rhoda and Annie went to the Baptist Church, brought Nannie and Sallie home with them. It rained and they had to stay all night. A very gloomy eve. I have the "ennui" so bad, feel like I wanted to go off and never see anyone again. Tonight Cousin Joe went with us girls to Presbyterian Church. If I could get to write what I wish to in my journal, but someone might see it. We had two muskmelons today.

Monday 3. A pretty day. Excessively warm. Rhoda received a letter from Bob Smith, asking her hand, only for a second refusal. Nannie Kennedy and Sallie Walker left this morn. I feel free and foot loose once more, although with a sad heart. I expect if I live, to look over this and smile at my folly. I wove three yards today.

Tuesday 4. A pretty day, very warm. I knitted on Mary Lea's stocking this morn. Went over to see Aunt Fannie Lea this eve. Cousin Joe Lea here after tea. Alice Brown arrived in Cleveland this morn. Heard that Scott's Brigade were taken prisoners.

Wednesday 5. A very warm day. I wove all day, got a piece of cloth out this eve. I took a ride on horseback with Callie Swan this eve, went out by Mr. Osment's. I enjoyed the ride very much.

Thursday 6. A warm day. Mrs. Warner and her father came here this morn, intend staying a week. Mr. Warner is sick in the hospital, she came to see her husband. They have a nurse and a baby with them. It is very inconvenient to board them, but in preference to turning them out of doors we will have to try and do the best we can. Uncle Caswell here this eve. I wrote to Cousin John and enclosed it in his letter. I have been knitting all day. Election day. A case of smallpox in town. I cannot tell how we will accommodate Mr. and Mrs. Warner and her brother tonight, we have so little room. They are all from Alabama, live 15 miles from Montgomery.

Friday 7. A pretty day. Ann McNelley and Sue Henderson here this morn. D. Hoyl called, stayed until (after tea), very much to our discomfiture. Mr. Knight had to sleep with Mr. Carter. Cousin Joe here after tea. Cousin John sent down something which he got in Kentucky.

Saturday 8. A pretty day. Aunt Elizabeth came in and brought us some hairpins, needles, pins, me a comb and Rhoda a pair of shoes, Mother also a pair which Cousin John sent us. A very busy day with us, we are threshing out our wheat and are expecting Uncle Caswell's hands to dine with us. We are very tired of our boarders. Uncle Caswell's Phoebe is here helping us cook. Rhoda and I called on Florence Manville, Cousin Ellen McCallie and Mattie Foute. Miss Martha Hall took tea here. Mrs. Warner and the rest stood out in the front yard and heard the brass band play at the Ocoee House.

Sunday 9. A warm day. Rhoda and I went to Presbyterian Church, Mrs. Warner, Mr. Knight, her baby [Virginia Elizabeth] and their nurse [Sylvia] left on the 5 o'clock train. We hated to see them leave, not knowing whether we would ever see them again or not. Sister and I went over to Cousin Mary Harle's to see Aunt Fannie. Mother and Rhoda went down to see Rose Gaut, they are expecting her to die with scarlet fever. Rhoda sat up there tonight. Cousin Joe here after tea.

Monday 10. A pretty day. I helped Emeline wash. Cousin Albert Jarnagin, Sallie Hook, Cousin Ellen McCallie, Joe Lea here after tea. John Gaut came down for me to sit up at Mrs. Jessie Gaut's, Rose died this eve.[23] Dennis Isbell, Mary and Charlie Hardwick, and Mary Bradshaw sat up. We looked for Cousin John this eve, but were disappointed.

[*Tuesday 11.* No entry for this date]

Wednesday 12. A pretty day. John Gaut here to get boarding for Emma and Laura Callaway, we cannot take them. We had a very nice muskmelon this morn. Uncle Caswell was here.

Thursday 13. A warm day, been excessively warm for several days. Rhoda and I called on Mollie Osment this morn. I went to see Ann Stuart this eve. Mr. Schwartz was there. Ann and I called on Ada Gaut's sister, Julia. Mother, Mr. Carter, Annie and Jimmie went out to the farm today. Mr. Wexler here this morn.

---

[23]Rose Gaut died 10 August 1863 of scarlet fever aged three years, two months, four days. Ross, *Cemetery Records*, II:126.

Friday 14. A pretty day. I wrote a letter to Mr. Bridges this morn. Mother and Sister went out to Aunt Elizabeth's this morn. Mr. Farrow here this eve.

Saturday 15. A pretty day. Mary Shugart here this eve. I bathed all over in a wash tub this eve. Sister, Mr. Carter and Johnnie spent the day at Aunt Phoebe's.

Sunday 16. Rained a little this eve. Mr. Warren and Mr. Farrow here this eve. Rhoda, Sister, Mr. Carter, Annie and I went to the Methodist preaching in Presbyterian Church. Cousin Joe Lea took Rhoda, Lizzie and me to church at night. Cousin John's 23rd birthday.

Monday 17. A pretty day. Had a dull headache all day. Miss Sallie Bradshaw here this eve. She and I went over to Mrs. Miller's, came 'round by Cousin Mary Harle's. Mrs. Shadden took tea here.

Tuesday 18. A pretty day. Mother went up to see old Mrs. McCallie at Cousin Mary Jarnagin's. Rained very hard tonight. Rhoda and Mother stayed at Cousin Ellen's all eve. Rhoda sat up there tonight.

Wednesday 19. A pretty day. Mollie Osment, Sallie Grant, Anna Gaut and Miss Emma Metcalf here this morn. Rhoda and I went out to Uncle Caswell's this eve. Mr. Wexler went with us from there to see Callie Swan.

Thursday 20. A pretty day. Mr. Carter and family went out to the farm today, they left Jimmie there. I have been very busy mending my stockings and sewing on my white body.[24] Mrs. Dr. Nash returned Rhoda's call this eve. Lizzie went up to see Sue Henderson, she got her leg broken yesterday eve. She and Mother also went out to Uncle Caswell's.

Friday 21. A pretty day. Fast Day. I did not eat any breakfast, had a headache and ate an apple. Mr. Carter came and informed us that Gen. Bragg was making a move into Middle Tennessee. We are expecting a battle there soon. I await the event with mingled hope and fear for our safety. All the town is in confusion, the hospitals are being broken up and the sick are leaving as fast as possible. They are expecting the Yankees in here very soon. They are attempting to cross the Tennessee at Harrison, Blythe's Ferry and Chattanooga.

---

[24]Body or bodice, is the part of a garment covering the torso.

They have been shelling Chattanooga all day. The casualties on our side at the last account were 7 men killed, one woman and a child's leg shot off, it has since died. Mrs. Stout here after tea, she was very much excited (as we all are). Mr. Carter, Rhoda, and I went up to Cousin Mary Jarnagin's to see if we could hear any news from Chattanooga. Bragg arrived from Cherokee Springs yesterday eve, they were completely surprised at Chattanooga. We all sat up until after eleven o'clock last night, hiding things. Waited until after the Negroes went to bed.[25] I went to see Fannie Lea this eve, she is better. Rhoda and I went up to see Mrs. Horton's baby, it died last night. Rhoda went up to see Anna Waterhouse, Cousin Ellen's baby and Mary Edwards.

Saturday 22. A pretty day. Mr. Carter, Sister and Johnnie went out to Mr. Hall's to get Jimmie this morn. The wagons are lumbering along towards Chattanooga, they keep up a noise nearly all day. I am going to make pockets in my chemise so if the Yankees come I can hide some things from them. If this war was only over. I am so tired of the suspense we are always in, but I fear our scourge[26] is just commencing. I nearly made Susan a dress today. Mr. Warren and Mr. Farrow here this morn. After tea Sister and I went up to see Cousin Ellen's baby and up to old Mr. Carter's. We took Johnnie with us.

Sunday 23. A warm day. Sister, Annie and I went to Presbyterian Church to preaching. This eve Mr. Warner was here. Sister, Mother, Annie and Jimmie went out to Uncle Caswell's to see William Lea, Uncle Alfred's son. Our suspense is so great, looking for the Federals.

Monday 24. A pretty day. Rhoda is sick and I washed in her place. Capt. Blair dined here, intends staying all night. Capt. Blair took tea here, went up on the train this eve. Mag [Margaret] Shadden and Euphilia Bradshaw here this eve. I made up biscuit dough this eve for Emeline, she was so tired of washing.

Tuesday 25. A cloudy morn. Rhoda is no better. The Yankees are not here yet and I am in hopes never will. Cousin Mary Harle here

---

[25] Uncle Ned and Aunt Phoebe were trusted slaves and Mrs. Inman got them to help her hide valuables and food.

[26] Scourge is the cause of widespread and dreaded affliction, as pestilence, or war.

this morning. I commenced a pair of socks for George [slave] today. Sister, Mr. Carter and Johnnie went out to Aunt Phoebe's in the buggy this eve. Mother sent for Dr. Thompson for Rhoda this eve, he pronounced her case intermittent fever. A cold, cloudy day very much like fall, the fall crickets have been singing all eve a song, which I do not like to hear.

Wednesday 26. Another cold, cloudy fall day. Rhoda is much better this morn. I wrote a letter to Mattie Smith this morn. Cousin Thomas and Cousin William Lea took dinner here. I made Cousin William a haversack[27] and fixed him up a needle case. They came back after tea to stay all night but we had retired for the night, they went back to Uncle Caswell's.

Thursday 27. Another cool, fall day. Cousin William Lea dined here, he started to his command this eve. I knitted on George's socks all day. Sister, Annie and I went up to Mrs. Stuart's, Cousin Mary Jarnagin's to see Cousin Ellen's baby, and to Mrs. Bradshaw's. Uncle Caswell here this morning and this evening. Heard this eve that Mary Pharis and Dr. Dunlap were married last Monday.

Friday 28. A cool, cloudy morn, the air feels like autumn, a season which always brings sadness with it to me. I dislike to see winter coming, it lasts so long. Rhoda is better. Mother has been complaining for several days with something like flux. We feel considerably easier in regards to Yankees getting East Tennessee, Bragg intends to try to hold the southern part. I do wish we could get them this side of the river and then run them back into the river and drown them all. Tonight Mr. Carter, Lizzie, Sister, Rhoda and I _____ . We have been hiding all eve.

Saturday 29. A pleasant day. Mrs. Hughes here this morn. We have been very busy all day changing the things in the porch room into Aunt Adeline's room. We papered it for her and fixed it up nice, feel very tired tonight. Had a fire in Mother's room for the first time tonight, looked quite cheerful. Mr. Carter, Sister, Jimmie and Johnnie went out to see Aunt Phoebe this eve.

Sunday 30. Nearly cold enough for frost. All of the black ones [Negro slaves] have gone out to the farm today. Mr. Warren here this morn, he took dinner. We were all very busy getting dinner as

---

[27]A haversack is a one-strapped canvas bag worn over the shoulder

we are inexperienced cooks. Cousin Joe Lea took tea here, and stayed all night.

Monday 31. A pretty day. Emeline sick with flux. Rhoda and Mother had to get supper. I have a violent headache tonight, went to bed early. Johnnie has intermittent fever. Our forces have fallen back from Lenoir's [see June 19.] to Charleston, Tenn. I received a note from Julia Grant asking permission to call tomorrow eve, with a friend, she cannot come as we are nearly all on the sick list. We all feel very gloomy about the Federals getting in.

September 1863

Tuesday 1. A pretty day. I spent a miserable night last night, have had the headache all day and have been lying down. Miss Lou Swan and Sallie Bradshaw here to see me this morn. Johnnie is better. Emeline has been in bed all day. Six Lincolnites got out of jail last night.[28]

Wednesday 2. A pretty day. I have been suffering with the headache all day, sent for Dr. Thompson this eve. Did not eat any dinner or supper.

Thursday 3. A pretty day. I am better but have sat up very little. Anna Stuart and Mary Bradshaw here, cannot sleep, we are looking for the Yanks. The cavalry is passing through continuously en route for Chattanooga. Mr. Stuart's family are to leave tomorrow.

Friday 4. A pretty day. Dr. Thompson came to see me this morn and eve. I was very sick all this morn, have the intermittent fever. I did not rest well last night. A great confusion among soldiers retreating to Georgia. Cousin Joe stayed all night here.

Saturday 5. A pretty day. I feel considerably better but can sit up to do no good. Mother went to church today. Mrs. Kennedy, Mrs. McNutt, Aunt Elizabeth here this eve. I did not rest well, have the intermittent fever.

---

[28] Lincolnites were local citizens who supported the president's efforts to preserve the Union.

Sunday 6. A pretty day. I feel better today but have a slight headache. Ate some tomatoes today. Cousin John Lea came today, took tea here. Pryor came with him. Mary Bradshaw here to see me after tea. Mrs. Hameltree and Mr. Jones dined here. Had all our darkies packed up to send off and concluded to send only the [two] Georges.

Monday 7. A pretty day. I spent a bad night. Cavalry passing all night long. I feel better, have sit up nearly all day. Cousin John here this morn and this eve. Mr. Carter left with black George this morn. Yellow George failed to come up, but came at night. Our soldiers like to have pressed him[29], we cannot get him to Mr. Carter, he is just hiding out.

Tuesday 8. A warm day. I feel nearly well. Rhoda had a chill today, has a very bad headache. All of the southern soldiers have left today. Oh, I feel so sad to think the southern army [has] left and left us to our fate. We are looking for the Yankees in soon. Mr. Farrow was here this morn. We are very busy baking biscuits for some soldiers, the last we will cook for them in a long time, I am afraid. When will we see peace again? I never wish to pass such a week as the last has been, such confusion and noise I never witnessed. Cousin John Lea came and told us good-bye about 2 o'clock; he went on down to Dalton, Ga. I am very lonesome this eve. The soldiers have all left and everything is quiet, looking for the Yankees in every minute. When will we see another southern soldier, we are now in the federal government, how I detest it. I do wish we could whip them. We are cut off from all of our friends and relatives. The town looks deserted. I took a good cry this eve about our fate.

Wednesday 9. Warm day. Mother and Sister have gone down to Mr. William McNutt's. Uncle Ned came in this morn to see if he might move Aunt Phoebe in here, she is afraid to stay out there, they are coming today. The rear guard has not left yet, I saw a soldier this morn. Everything quiet, just waiting for the Yankees. I have been reading *The Life of a Hunter in the West* nearly all day. Aunt Phoebe came in this eve.

Thursday 10. A warm day. Sister went out on Mr. McNelley's horse to Mr. Cowan's to tell George to come in. Mrs. Shadden and

---

[29] Press: from impress, meaning to force to serve with the military.

Miss Lou Swan here this morn. It is so dreadfully lonesome now, the town is so still. I finished George's pair of socks this eve. Been reading *The Perils and Pleasures of a Hunter's Life.* Rhoda had another chill this morn, a very bad headache. Sister went up to see Mrs. Hardin this eve, she is very low with typhoid-pneumonia. Mr. Carter came in and took dinner. We thought the Federals were coming and he slipped out.

Friday 11. A warm day. We all got up with sad hearts, longing for the return of our army. Everything is so still, no [train] cars and very few persons passing about. We look for them, the Yankees, every day and wonder what will be our fate. Numbers of southern families have left. Mother and Sister have gone up this morn to see Mrs. Hardin. Oh, it is so lonesome. We have no life about us, no encouragement to work. Do not know how long we will get to keep what we have even. We are needing rain very badly, everything is perfectly parched up. Aunt Elizabeth sent in word for us to fast yesterday, but we did not. I have a slight headache and sore throat and concluded to eat. I never felt so sad in all my life, we hear nothing from our army, do not know what it is doing. We are cut off from all news. Mrs. Hardin died this morn about 4 o'clock. Sister and Mother have been there nearly all day. Rhoda has been sick all day in bed. I risked and helped eat a water and muskmelon this eve. Mrs. Miller here this eve. I laid down before dinner and took a short nap. The Yankees' cavalry came in a while after dark tonight. I read a book through titled *What Will Women Do?* this eve. Mother went down to see Capt. Grant this morn. He is very low, do not think he will live throughout the night. These are sad days for secessionists, but we hope for brighter.

Saturday 12. These days pass and I hardly know what day of the week it is. A warm day. (About 200 of) the Yankees' cavalry rode in from the fairground where they bivouacked last night, the "stars and stripes" floating above their heads, I could not realize they were our enemies and had come to deal death missiles amongst us. Anna Gaut here this eve. Another lonesome eve. We all feel so lonesome, everything is so quiet. I have not been doing anything today, only reading *Esperanza* a little. Isabel has a girl baby. A warm day. The Federals left town this morn.

Sunday 13. A warm day. If we could only hear what our army is doing. I ate a musk and watermelon this morn. Mrs. Shadden and Mrs. Rogers here about supper time. I felt so lonesome I laid down after dinner and slept till about 3 o'clock. When will I go to church again? Annie went to Sunday School this morn. Sister and Rhoda went over to Cousin Mary's and Mrs. Grant's this eve. Johnnie sat up to the table and fed himself at tea.

Monday 14. A cool morning. Rhoda and I went over to see Mary Edwards this morn, from there we went down to Robert Swan's. Aunt Elizabeth was there. We then went down to Aunt Elizabeth's and spent the day.

Tuesday 15. Morning cool. Wish this suspense was over and the battle was won. Mrs. Ryan here to get that house out at Mr. Hall's for Mrs. Braxtel, we do not wish to let them have it. Mr. Hall and Francis Tucker here this eve. Scott's Cavalry made a dash in here with the intention of finding some Yankees but only shot at some renegades. The men ran in every direction. I was very much excited. Mrs. William Grant here this eve. Aunt Elizabeth and Uncle Caswell here this morn. They received some bad news and went home. Sister took dinner at Mr. Caswell's. She and he started to see Mr. Carter but gave it out. I am afraid we will have a battle here in Cleveland one of these days. Aunt Elizabeth left a dress for me to make for Lizzie. I have been sewing on it. Johnnie sat up to the table in his chair and fed himself today.

Wednesday 16. A pretty day. The Yankee cavalry came in last night. The Lincolnites are gallanting[30] them round to breakfast. I made Johnnie a dress today. Capt. William Grant died at 1 o'clock today[31] Mother went up to William Campbell's to get George and Uncle Ned passports out to the farm. Rained a very hard shower for a little while this eve. Washed the dust off of everything.

Thursday 17. A pretty day. Mother went up with Mr. William Campbell to the Ocoee House to get George and Uncle Ned a passport. Mother and I went out to Uncle Caswell's this morn. Mary Elizabeth came out and told us they were looking for 10,000 rebels, she and I stayed out there all day. Rhoda came out in the eve. Mr.

---

[30]Gallanting is the act of proudly escorting the soldiers to show them off.

[31]Capt. William Grant, born 25 Feburary 1792, d. 16 September 1863, interred in Fort Hill Cemetery. Ross, *Cemetery Records*, II:134.

Robert McNelley came home this eve. Mother and Sister went there after tea, they arrested him whilst they were there. Dr. Hughes here tonight to tell Sister and Mother that they are to be arrested tomorrow morn for being at Mr. McNelley's.

Friday 18. A cloudy, raw day. This morn the Confederates had a skirmish with the Yankees' cavalry here. Commenced about 5 o'clock, killed 3, wounded some, took some prisoners, and ran the rest towards Charleston. A Kentuckian took breakfast here; Hodge's command. Sister and Mother went out to Uncle Caswell's after the fight. We all went down in the cellar during the fight. We anticipate a greater conflict soon. Francis Tucker here this eve. Cousin Mary Jarnagin and Mrs. Traynor here after tea, sat until bedtime. The Yankees and Lincolnites left for Athens in a hurry this morn.

Saturday 19. A pretty day but cool and windy this eve. I finished Lizzie Lea's dress this morn. Rhoda and I took it out to her this eve. Miss Lou Swan was there. We heard cannons [in the direction of Ringgold] from 10 to 12 o'clock without ceasing this morn. We are very anxious to know the result. The town looks gloomy and deserted, see just a few men standing on the corners of the streets. The southern men and Lincolnites have all run.

Sunday 20. A cold day. A heavy frost and some ice this morn. No church or Sunday School in town, everything so still. We tremble at the result of this battle, if we can only win it. Mr. Carter came in this eve. After tea he and Mrs. Traynor sat until bedtime.

Monday 21. A pretty day. I chilled today. Rhoda spent the day at Uncle Caswell's. Fighting at Chattanooga. Soldiers passing into Charleston.

Tuesday 22. A pretty day. Mother and Uncle Ned went out to the farm today. We received news that the Yankees were coming. Our forces fell below town. We got up from the table at dinner and went over to Mrs. Miller's each with a sack. Mr. Carter went down to Mr. McCamy's. We came back about 2 o'clock, finished our dinner and packed our clothes in sacks and all (16 of us) went out and stayed all night at Mr. Reeder's. Sister, Johnnie, Annie and I rode in the buggy. We had some apprehensions of them shelling the place.

Wednesday 23. A pretty day. I chilled this morn. Have had a severe headache all day. Mr. Reeder started after his sister today. Mother, Uncle Ned, Aunt Phoebe, Susan, Stephney and Frank all went home this eve. Sister and Mary Elizabeth rode Mr. McNelley's horse in to our house to see if everything was right. Sister took Aunt Eliza Adeline in to Uncle Caswell's this eve in buggy.

Thursday 24. A pretty day. Sallie Reeder and I went down and got some gum wax this morn. Sister, Sues, Emeline, and Johnnie walked to town this morn. Mr. Carter sent for Sister to come home, heard that Mr. F. Carter was killed last eve by our scouts. This eve Sallie and Rhoda went up to Mr. Fate Hardwick's to hear some news. Mr. Hardwick and Ham Rossen called and told us we had a fight above town with the Yankees and ran them [off].

Friday 25. A pretty day. I chilled today, had a very bad headache all day. Rhoda, Annie and Johnnie walked home this morn. I wanted to go very much but was too unwell. I slept by myself tonight.

Saturday 26. A warm day. I walked with Sallie, Phil and Mat Reeder as far as Mrs. Johnson's this morn and met Mr. Carter coming after me in a buggy. Cousin John came up here this eve, went on up above. Cousin John Lea belongs to Scott's Cavalry Brigade of 500 men and Capt. Kuhn's company of 100 men. A great many soldiers passed Mr. Reeder's this morn going on to Knoxville, Tenn., some took breakfast. The town is full of them going to whip the Yanks. Rhoda went out and stayed all night at Uncle Caswell's.

Sunday 27. A pretty day. I chilled today, been in bed all day. Mr. Carter, Sister and Johnnie went to Mr. McCamy's this morn. Julia and Sallie Grant here this eve.

Monday 28. A pretty day. Aunt Elizabeth here all day to get Mother to show her how to make harness. Julia and Mattie Grant dined and spent the eve here. Mr. Carter, Sister and Johnnie returned this eve with George and the wagon. I feel a little better today. Have eaten very little. A soldier dined here, three took breakfast.

Tuesday 29. A pretty day. I missed my chill today. Callie Swan, Mrs. Hughes here today. Uncle Caswell took tea here. Gen. [Nathan Bedford] Forrest is here now, two regiments of his cavalry are encamped at the fairgrounds. Four took tea here, we cooked a great many of their rations. Had to turn off quite a number. Rhoda chilled this eve.

Wednesday 30. A pretty day. Aunt Phoebe has been cooking and washing hard all day for soldiers, a great many have eaten here today. Cousin John Lea came in this eve, he came this morn, intends remaining awhile at home, is afflicted with boils.

October 1863

Thursday 1. Rained all last night, rained this morn without ceasing, cloudy all eve. Been cooking and washing for soldiers all eve. I knitted on Susan's stockings all morn. Rhoda chilled today. I practiced a little on the piano last eve, the first time since our army retreated. It is very much out of tune and consequently did not make much melody.

Friday 2. A pretty day. Cousin John Lea took dinner here. Mrs. Smith[32] here this eve. I knitted all morn. Mr. Carter and Sister went out to Mr. Reeder's after our clothes this eve. Cousin John took tea here this eve. Rhoda and I went out and stayed all night at Uncle Caswell's. Mother stayed all night with Cousin Mary Jarnagin.

Saturday 3. A pretty day. Rhoda chilled at Uncle Caswell's and we stayed all day and all night. Mother and Callie Swan out there in the eve.

Sunday 4. A cool day. We came home this morn. Rhoda and I went to the Baptist Church, also Mother and Rhoda in the eve. Mr William McNutt here this eve. Cousin John Lea took tea here.

Monday 5. A cool morn. Cousin Mary Harle here this morn. Mother spent the day at Uncle Caswell's. Cousin John took tea here, also Capt. Dale and another soldier.

Tuesday 6. A pretty day. Mother and I went out to Uncle Caswell's this morn to assist in putting in Aunt Elizabeth's cloth. I chilled in the eve and had to stay all night, slept with Lizzie. Will Kenner stayed all night here. I did not eat any supper.

Wednesday 7. A rainy morn. Pleasant eve. Sallie Grant came down to see me this eve. She stayed all night. Julia and Lieutenant Rucker came down and remained a few minutes. Will Kenner and two soldiers stayed all night here. I was very sick awhile this morn

---

[32] Bob's mother.

from taking pills. I sat up this eve nearly all eve. Did not eat any breakfast or dinner.

Thursday 8. A windy and cold day. Mother came out and stayed all day. A large number of soldiers at Uncle Caswell's all day. I chilled and have been in bed nearly all day. Mr. Varnell stayed at Uncle Caswell's all night. Cousin John read to me this eve. Aunt Elizabeth went up to Mrs. Swan's this eve.

Friday 9. A pretty day. Mother came out and I went home this morn. Cousin John came in this eve and brought us two squirrels. He took tea here. Capt. Pierce and two other soldiers here until late bedtime. I finished putting a binding on my gingham dress tonight.

Saturday 10. A pretty and pleasant day. I missed my chill today. Have been mending some of my clothes today. Two soldiers came in to hear me play this eve. Mr. Carter has been very busy hauling our corn. Mr. Morgan's men are taking it.

Sunday 11. A pretty day. No church in town. Three soldiers here this eve. Cousin John Lea took tea here. I have been reading all morn. I received a note from Elvira Lea and answered it this evening.

Monday 12. A very windy day. Three soldiers dined here. Albert Blackman dined here. Rhoda and I played a good deal for him stayed until 3 o'clock. Sister and Rhoda went up to Mrs. Guthman's this morn. Sister and Rhoda went to see Callie Swan this eve. Mother and Sister went out to Uncle Caswell's this eve. I bound me a collar this morn. I feel lonesome this eve. Capt. Dale here, took breakfast this morn. Cousin John Lea took tea here. Four soldiers came tonight to hear us play on the piano. I knit this eve, on Susan's stockings. Dr. Long and another soldier here this eve.

Tuesday 13. A very rainy and gloomy day. The mails have commenced coming. The soldiers are dealing very badly, taking corn, leaving down fences, stealing horses, chickens, hogs and everything else they see. We turned off several that wanted dinner. I have been knitting all day. Mrs. Dr. Edwards here in the rain this morn. Mother commenced putting corn in the little front room this eve. (Mother was hiding corn, which broke the floor down and filled the house full of mice.) I have had a headache all eve.

Wednesday 14. A rainy morn. Beautiful evening. Rhoda and I both chilled this morn. Rhoda in bed all eve, I only part. Albert

Blackman here this eve. I went in the parlor and played some for him Dr. Long and Adj. Perry called on Rhoda and me tonight. I had to entertain them as Rhoda was indisposed. Three soldiers dined here. I altered me two collars this morning. Mr. Barker here this eve to hear me play.

Thursday 15. A dark, rainy and gloomy day. Rained all last night. Capt. Nolen here this eve to bring a letter from Cousin Joe Lea. I wrote to him this eve. Capt. Dale and three more soldiers took tea here.

Friday 16. A pretty day. Rhoda and I both chilled today. Cousin John and Capt. Dale dined here. Albert Blackman here awhile this eve. I was in Annie's bed nearly all eve. Two soldiers here this eve to see Rhoda and me. I was indisposed.

Saturday 17. A pretty day. I chilled a slight chill this morn. Four soldiers dined here this morn. We had a serenade from the soldiers tonight. Cousin John Pryor and George Lea, Mrs. Traynor and Kate Rogers here until bedtime. Johnnie chilled today.

Sunday 18. A rainy morning, pleasant evening. I chilled this morn. Forrest's men left this morn for Loudon. The brass band played "Dixie" and "On to the Field of Glory" as if it was not Sunday--how can we gain our independence when our soldiers regard not the Sabbath? Cousin John took tea here, stayed all night. Some soldiers came up on the train tonight en route to Loudon. Capt. Dale and two more soldiers breakfasted here. Mr. Byers came and bade us good-bye.

Monday 19. A pretty day. Sister and Cousin John went out to Mr. Reeder's after the rest of our clothing this morn. Johnnie chilled this morn. I have been knitting on Aunt Phoebe's stockings. Gave two soldiers their breakfast this morn. We baked some ginger cakes this eve. Cousin John, Thal Crozier and Mr. Cassly were here tonight. Mrs. Capt. Grant, Mrs. Alex Davis and Cynthia Hardwick here this eve. Cousin John told us good-bye. He is to leave for Loudon tomorrow. Johnnie chilled today.

Tuesday 20. A pretty day. Mother and Sister went out to Uncle Caswell's this morn. I laid down this morn to keep from chilling, got up with the headache. Mother and Sister have gone out to the woods to get some pine resin for us to take to cure the chills. Johnnie chilled today. Lt. Fox took tea here and stayed all night. Mr. McNutt here this eve.

Wednesday 21. A pretty day. Rained a little this eve. Cousin John Lea took tea here, he came down from Charleston to get his regiment flour. Rhoda and Sister went down to Mrs. McNutt's this morn: She gave them some furs to make us some muffs. I made them this eve. Johnnie had a very hard chill in my lap this morn. Mrs. Rogers here this morn. Rhoda and I sat up until 9 o'clock to give Johnnie some oil. Mrs. Fox dined here, left on the evening train. Two soldiers came here to get Uncle Ned to dig Mr. Hendrick's grave.

Thursday 22. A cloudy morn. Cousin John dined here. Rhoda and I went out to Uncle Caswell's and took tea. Will Kenner and Cousin John came home and stayed until 8 o'clock. A beautiful eve and moonshiny night.

Friday 23. A very rainy and gloomy day. I footed Sues a pair of stockings. Mr. Blair took tea here.

Saturday 24. A cold, windy, cloudy, muddy and gloomy day. I looked over my clothes and mended the ones that needed it. Mr. Blair took tea here.

Sunday 25. A cloudy morn. Mother, Rhoda and I went up to the graveyard this eve. I read *Irish Amy* all Morn. Cousin John here this morn on his way down to his regiment, his wagons were ordered back to Candy's Creek and he went on out there.

Monday 26. A pretty day. Our folks are very busy hauling in our corn. We will have plenty of corn, potatoes, tallow, pumpkins and nearly enough meat to do us another year if we can only keep it from our soldiers. How thankful we should be for our blessings. The soldiers are ruining Uncle Caswell, taking his corn, burning his rails and killing his hogs. Mrs. William Craigmiles here this eve, also Cousin John Lea. I ate a walnut last night and it made me sick, have been in bed all day. Rhoda is busy altering her traveling dress to go to see Lavena Seavey.

Tuesday, 27. A pretty day. Armstrong's Brigade is encamped here. Mr. Carter has the blues about it. I commenced [altering] my blue dress this morn. Lt. Fox took tea and stayed all night. Sister went to see Mrs. Mills, Mrs. William Craigmiles and Mrs. Shadden this eve. Mother heard a snowbird today.

Wednesday 28. A pretty day. I chilled today. Mr. Fox went up to Charleston this morn. Sister went up to Mrs Traynor's this eve. I sewed on my dress this eve.

Thursday 29. A pretty day. I finished my cape this morn. Sister and Mother went up to Mrs. Carter's and warped a piece of cloth.

Friday 30. A very rainy evening. I chilled this morn. Cousin Sam M. Inman took tea here,[33] Lt. in Davidson's Division, Carter's Regiment.

Saturday 31. A cold day. Cousin Hamp Rice here this morn and all eve, took tea and dinner here. Cousin Sam Inman took tea. Uncle Caswell and Mrs. Rogers dined here. We killed a hog this morn., will have some nice pork to eat for awhile. Mother commenced weaving hers and Sister's dresses this morn.

November 1863

Sunday 1. A lovely day. Cousin Sam Inman took breakfast, dinner and tea here. His company is stationed in front of our house in Judge Grant's lot.

Monday 2. A beautiful and moderate day. Cousin Sam Inman took breakfast here. Julia Grant, Mollie Osment and Anna Gaut here this eve. Rhoda chilled today. I have been very busy puffing my dress skirt with black silk.

Tuesday 3. We made the soldiers some shirts today. Cousin Sam Inman took dinner and tea here. After tea we went into the parlor and stayed until about 8 o'clock. A pretty day. Mr. Caldwell here this eve.

Wednesday 4. A warm day. Cousin Sam Inman took breakfast, dinner and supper here. He, Rhoda and I spent a very pleasant eve in the parlor. I finished putting the puffing on my blue dress. Mr. Caldwell here this eve, he gave me an orange.

---

[33] Another cousin by the same name—Sam Inman—had died on 8 February 1862.

Thursday 5. A rainy day. Cousin Sam and I intended to take a ride this morn but on account of the rain we did not go. He took breakfast, dinner and tea here, also Capt. Dale and Lieutenant Maynard. Rhoda, Cousin Sam and I stayed in the parlor until after seven. I enjoyed myself very much. I like Cousin Sam very much. Mr. Hardwick here this eve.

Friday 6. A pretty day. Cousin Sam and Cousin John Inman took breakfast here. Cousin Sam, Mr. Hardwick, Mr. Swan and a Capt. in Hodge's Brigade dined here. Cousin Sam and his brigade left for Tunnel Hill about 2 P.M. Cousin John Lea left also. Sallie Reeder and her father took dinner here this eve. Cousin Joe Lea here this eve, took tea and stayed all night here.

Saturday 7. A pretty day. I mended some of my clothes today. A very lonesome eve. Cousin Joe Lea here this eve, he went down to Cassville this eve.

Sunday 8. A pretty day. Mr. Bradshaw came up this morn. Mag Shadden here this morn to go to the Baptist Church with Mother and Rhoda, but went back and went to hear Mr. Bradshaw preach. Mr. McNutt and Mr. Jones here this eve. A great deal of cavalry passed through en route for Sweetwater[34] Mr. John Wesley Harle took tea here.

Monday 9. A pretty day but quite cold. I cut out my blue merino[35] dress sleeves today and have been very busy sewing on them. Seven of Gen. James Longstreet's men took tea here. We gave up the table to them.

Tuesday 10. A cold day. Finished my dress, wore it out to see Miss Nannie Kennedy with Rhoda this eve. Four soldiers from Charleston, S. C. here all morn. We are troubled a great deal by them asking for something to eat. Four took tea here. Lou and Callie Swan here this morn. Cousins Mary and James Jarnagin here tonight.

Wednesday 11. A pretty day. I commenced making Sues a calico dress this morn. Georgie Lea's 15th birthday.

Thursday 12. A pretty day. Aunt Elizabeth spent the day here. Mollie Osment and Mattie Grant here this eve. Cousin James

---

[34] Monroe County, Tennessee.
[35] Merino is a soft, light weight wool material.

Jarnagin here after tea, stayed until 8 o'clock. Mother and Aunt Elizabeth have been making harness all day. A concert in town tonight, did not go.

Friday 13. A pretty day. I finished Sues' dress this morn. Helped Mother make harness this afternoon for Aunt Elizabeth. Mel Osment called on Rhoda this eve. (One night when Mel Osment was calling on Rhoda, Mother came in and said, "Mel, are you going to let the Yankees take you?" He jumped up and flew on his horse with the guns popping after him, and we heard nothing of him for a long time.)

Saturday 14. A rainy day. I looked over my clothes this morning in my wardrobe, basket and drawer, then bound a collar for Emeline, after noon put new wristbands to Mr. Hardwick's shirt and mended my dress, after tea washed and retired to rest. Mr. Hardwick here this eve.

Sunday 15. A pretty day. Rhoda, Lizzie and Annie went to Sunday School at Presbyterian Church for the first time. All of us went to hear Mr. Bradshaw preach except Mother, Aunt Adeline and Johnnie. Rhoda and Mother went down to Mrs. McNutts' this eve. Five soldiers from North Carolina ate supper here. Mr. Carter and Sister went up to Mr. Carter's after tea and stayed awhile. Uncle Caswell came down for Mother, Rhoda and Lizzie to go to church tonight. Rhoda received a letter from Venie and Mr. Smith this morn. I one from Cousin Joe Lea and a piece of poetry from Mr. Smith. Mother received a letter from a soldier by the name of Smith.

Monday 16. A pretty day. Mrs. Carter spent the day here. Sues went out to the farm to pick up potatoes [they finished digging today] and Mary Elizabeth helped Emeline wash. I put on a cotton stocking to knit for myself this morn. Mother and Annie went out to Aunt Elizabeth's this morn. Uncle Caswell and Mag Shadden here this eve.

Tuesday 17. A pretty day. Rhoda, Annie, and I stayed at Uncle Caswell's all night. He intended going down to Ringgold to see Cousin John but there was no train and he came back home. Lieutenant Myers boards there. Helped Sister make Mr. Carter a pair of drawers and Annie a petticoat today. Sister and Annie went out to Uncle Caswell's this afternoon. Mr. Carter commenced sowing wheat today.

Wednesday 18. A pleasant day. Rhoda, Annie and I stayed until nearly dinner time, spooling Aunt Elizabeth's cloth. Uncle Caswell took dinner here. Rhoda and Annie stayed there all night tonight. Mother and Aunt Elizabeth warped her cloth at Mrs. Shadden's this eve. I went up there and from there home with Aunt Elizabeth. Uncle Caswell did not get off on the train tonight.

Thursday 19. A pretty day. Uncle Caswell went down this eve. Mother and Annie went out to beam[36] Aunt Elizabeth's cloth. Rhoda and I went out and stayed all night with Aunt Elizabeth, Miss Lou Swan and Nannie Kennedy were there, after tea we went home with them as it was too late for them to go alone. I helped Sister make another pair of drawers for Mr. Carter.

Friday 20. A windy day, rained this eve a little. Mother, Sister, Annie and Jimmie spent the day at Uncle Caswell's. Rhoda and I went up and spent the day at Mr. Kennedy's. After dinner Sister, Lizzie Lea and Annie came up to Mr. Kennedy's and stayed until it commenced raining. Mr. Carter finished sowing his wheat today. Miss Nannie treated me to some such new hickory nuts in the dairy. I have enjoyed the last 5 days and nights finely, hope I will get to enjoy myself next week as well as I have this week. Lt. Loury, Mr. Traynor, Mrs. Rogers, Mollie Dardis and Mary Shugart here tonight.

Saturday 21. A rainy day. I made my cotton jockey this morn, pasted pieces in my scrapbook this eve, washed in Mother's room by the fire and retired to rest early.

Sunday 22. A pretty day. Rhoda and I went to Sunday School. I went to church to hear Mr. Bradshaw preach. Heard cannons nearly all day.

Monday 23. A pretty day. Mrs. Kennedy dined here. Commenced me a pair of cloth shoes this morn, stuck the awl in my hand and laid them aside. I heard a good deal of cannon this eve. Read some in Miss Edgeworth's writings this eve. We killed our calf this morn.

Tuesday 24. A pretty day. I have been reading some in Sister's journal today and knitting some. I beat up some red pepper this eve to put in our meat. Tonight I entertained Annie and Jimmie by telling them of Santa Claus.

---

[36]A beam is a roller with flanged edges on which the warp of material is wound on the loom.

Wednesday 25. A pretty day. We killed 8 of Mother's hogs today. A raid of Yankees came in this eve. They took two hogsheads [37]of our corn this eve and are all over in everything else. We go to bed with sad hearts. Mr. Carter and George left with the mules this morn. They came in at 3 o'clock. Mel Osment here today. We have heard hard cannonading all day.[38]

Thursday 26. A cold day. The Yankees are taking our corn, potatoes, pork, salt, and never pay a cent and besides talk very insulting to us. Rhoda, Sister and I went up to the crib and got two bags of our potatoes for Johnnie. We try to look on and see them take our things and try to give them up but it is so hard to see it done and can't help our selves. They burnt Mr. Raht's wagon and the railroad and some cars. Two took supper here. Aunt Elizabeth sent Malinda in here and I went out and stayed all night with her. Oh, how I wish I had power. A union man stayed all night at Aunt Elizabeth's, Mr. McLeod.

Friday 27. A pleasant day. Our forces[39] attacked Gen. Long's forces, 13 hundred strong, and whipped them. We had 2 cannon and a howitzer, 2 or 3 killed on both sides, several wounded. We were at breakfast when the fight commenced. All of us ran up to get in Mrs. Morrison's cellar. Aunt Elizabeth then came in with me. Mrs. Mary Smith was here. We feel very sad this eve, as sad as we were joyous this morn. The soldiers all left town this eve, ordered to Spring

---

[37]A unit of capacity used in liquid measure in the United States, equal to 63 gallons.

[38]In and around Chattanooga, Tennessee, a three-day battle was taking place. Gen. U. S. Grant had 60,000 troops to Braxton Bragg's 30,000 troops. The battle had three main phases. Gen. W. T. Sherman crossed the Tennessee River and attacked the Confederate right at the North end of Missionary Ridge. Gen. Joseph Hooker challenged the Confederate's extreme flank. The main portion of the campaign occurred on the afternoon of 25 November 1863 when two of George H. Thomas's divisions demonstrated to take pressure from Sherman's troops. Sherman's troops were to carry the rifle pits at the base of the ridge. Upon completing this order, the men, without orders ascended the mountain and dislodged the Confederates and increased the Federal hold on Chattanooga and Tennessee. The shelling by the artillery was heard in Cleveland thirty miles distant.

[39] five hundred strong, commanded by Gen. John H. Jolly.

Place, Ga. We expected the enemy in tonight. Bragg has fallen back. Lizzie Lea and I went out this eve and I stayed all night with Aunt Elizabeth. Miss Nannie Kennedy also. Capt. Nichols, a Lt. from Kentucky, and 4 other soldiers stayed all night at Aunt Elizabeth's. I feel so sad about Bragg's army.

Saturday 28. A pretty day. Mr. Cox came in a hurry and got his clothes this morn. We heard the Yanks were at Mr. Clingan's coming on. Mr. Carter came in and got his hogs this morn and drove them into Georgia. I am so glad. Aunt Elizabeth, Lizzie and I went up to Mrs. Kennedy's this eve, after we ate out dinner, (had only two meals). Miss Nannie came down with us and remained all night. Two Kentucky soldiers stayed here all night.

Sunday 29. A very cold day. Malinda came in town with me. Sister went down to see Mr. Carter at Mr. Carr's today. Came back this eve. The Yanks came in town this evening about 3 o'clock. Gen. William T. Sherman's Company camped all around us tonight, robbing us of our corn, potatoes and taking all our chickens, left only two. A brigade surgeon, Dr. Abbott, took tea and stayed all night. A very cold night and we have very little wood. The soldiers are in Uncle Ned's house and in the kitchen stealing and taking everything they can get. Took Aunt Phoebe's quilt off of her bed. Mrs. McNutt and Kennedy, Cousin Mary Harle and Mrs. Grant here today. The Yanks took George's and our two best mules, but let George's loose. We sit in the house with bowed down heads while the victorious army passes along with raving manners, and offer up a silent prayer for our country whilst we hear nothing but the exultant shouts of our enemy. They came in town playing "Yankee Doodle." We go to bed with sad hearts but still hoping God has better days for us.

Monday 30. Very cold indeed. The enemy left early this morn, en route for Knoxville, Tenn. in order to capture [Gen. James] Longstreet's Army. It is said about 2 corps are to go up. The wagons are passing through under whips and lash whilst the infantry are double quickening it.[40] Mother went out to Uncle Caswell's this morn. Rhoda went out to Aunt Elizabeth's with Malinda to stay all

---

[40] Double-quick is a very quick, rapid marching cadence.

night. Mother moved the trundle bed in Sister's room to sleep in this eve.

December 1863

Tuesday 1. [Weather] moderated considerably. We shelled some corn and sent it to mill by Tom Pasley. I put two new sleeves in my night-gown this eve. Mr. McNutt here this eve. Johnnie's 2nd birthday. Mr. and Mrs. Ervin and Mrs. Lowe here this morn. Sister went out to Uncle Caswell's this eve. He, Georgie and Pryor have come home, the Yanks have laid his farm waste. Wilder's Yankee Cavalry camped on our lot from sun down until 12 o'clock, took corn, potatoes and straw and burnt a great number of our rails. The major's headquarters were near the pig pen. He appointed a Mr. Brown to guard us. Two soldiers came in and talked to us until late.

Wednesday 2. A pretty day. Sister was very anxious to get off down to Mr. Carr's to see Mr. Carter, but George [colored] refused to go with her and she had so many other crosses [trials, frustrations] she concluded not to attempt it. Annie, Sues and I went out this eve to take Jack's horse back. I feel so sad this eve about our condition. I often wonder what will be the end of all of this. If we were only away from all of this trouble in some quiet retreat I would be willing to go anywhere, I think. Lizzie Lea stayed all night with Annie. I went up to see Cousin Mary Jarnagin, she came home with me to get George to kill her hogs she got from the Yanks this morn.

Thursday 3. A very pretty day. Rhoda came home from Uncle Caswell's this morn. Pryor came in and helped me shell corn this morn. Miss Nannie Kennedy here this eve, also Sallie. A few Confederate soldiers came in this eve and took a few Yanks prisoners this eve. Sister and Rhoda went up to Mr. Carter's this eve.

Friday 4. A pretty day. Mr. Carter came this morn and Sister and the children went down to Mr. Carr's with him. We are very busy this eve packing up some things for Pryor Lea to take down to Mr.

McCamy's for Sister. He stayed all night with us. Will Kenner here this morn. The Rebel soldiers came in this eve and drove off some hogs. Mag [Margart] Shadden, Mrs. Davis and Mrs. Rogers here this eve.

Saturday 5. Rained some this morn. Pryor started this morn early. The Confederate soldiers still in town. Mrs. and Mag [Margaret] Shadden here this morn. I made my cotton dress larger in the body this eve. Rhoda and I took a regular cleaning up this morn. Rhoda went out to Cousin Mary Harle's this eve. Cousin Mary Jarnagin here until late this eve. I made me two shoestrings this eve.

Sunday 6. A pleasant day. Mr. McNutt here this morn. Mother went up to Dr. Thompson's this morn to get a vial of laudanum [a tinture of opium] for Uncle Ned. Mrs. Dr. Edwards and Mrs. William Grant here this eve.

Monday 7. A cold day. Pryor came back last night. he started down there again this morning with Emeline, Sues, Frank and George. I went out to Uncle Caswell's house this morn. Mother, this eve. We got the walnuts off of the house this eve. Lt. Fox stayed all night.

Tuesday 8. A rainy day. Rhoda and I washed this morn, did not hang them out. Mrs. Shadden here this morn. Pryor came back this eve cold and wet, he stayed all night here. We shelled a little corn this eve.

Wednesday 9. A lovely and very pleasant day. Rhoda and I, after finishing hanging out the clothes, went up to Dr. Grant's to tell them good-bye, they are going to move to Georgia to live. I hate to see them leave so much, never expect to see them again. We then went down to Uncle Caswell's where we met Mother and came on home. Mrs. Rogers and Mrs. Traynor here tonight. We expect the Yanks in tomorrow.

Thursday 10. A lovely day. Early this morn we put Sister's bed in the parlor and changed Mother's room into a dining room, took her bed out and put it in Sister's room for her to sleep in. I cleaned out the press in Mother's room this eve.[41] Rhoda put down a carpet in the dining room. Cousin Mary Jarnagin stayed all night with us.

---

[41]A press is an upright closet or case used for storing clothing, books or other articles.

Friday 11. A cloudy day. The wind sighs so mournfully this eve, in unison with my depressed spirits. Mother and Rhoda went out to Aunt Elizabeth's today to assist in putting in her cloth. I have been reading the 18th volume Waterly novels, *Red Gauntlet.* I felt so lonesome this eve I went and played on the piano a little to drive off "ennui." Wonder where all of my friends are that belong to the Rebel army, wonder if I will ever see them again. Oh, I feel so sad and gloomy this eve, wish I could hear some good Southern news. I hope that God has brighter days in store for us.

Saturday 12. A rainy day. Mary Elizabeth and I cleaned off Sister's porch and her room. The rest of the day I read *Red Gauntlet.* I ate some walnuts, Mother and I went out to Aunt Elizabeth's to weave. I commenced me a chemise this eve. Rained in torrents tonight.

Sunday 13. A pretty day. O. O. Howard's Corps are in camp near town. Several Yanks were here for bread this eve. A very hard rain tonight, accompanied by thunder and lightning.

Monday 14. A pretty day. A few Yanks here for something to eat. Dr. Thompson brought Lt. Thomas here this eve and he gave us a guard, Conrad Lewis. I have been sewing on my chemise today. The soldiers here to hear us play this morn.

Tuesday 15. A cold day. Two Yanks breakfasted here, one a Kentuckian. Two took dinner. Two officers from New York took tea here. Lt. Thomas, from Massachusetts, here this morn.

Wednesday 16. A pretty day. The Yanks have all left this morn early except a few stragglers. Mother went out to Uncle Caswell's this eve. I sewed on my chemise this eve. I carried some wood for Uncle Ned.

Thursday 17. A windy day, rained this morning a little, the wind howls so mournfully around the house. Aunt Elizabeth gave us some wool this morn. Rhoda and I washed. Mr. McNutt here this morn. I have been sewing on my chemise all day, very windy tonight. Mother went to Mrs. Thompson's and Mrs. Carter's this eve. A few Yanks were fired on by two of our soldiers this morn.

Friday 18. A very cold and windy day. I rinsed our clothes and hung them out this morn. I sewed on my chemise, finished it by noon. I ironed my clothes this eve. Uncle Caswell here, took dinner,

I carried wood in for Uncle Ned this eve. Yanks are looking for Confederates in today.

Saturday 19. Cold day. We killed two hogs this morn. I went up to Cousin Mary Jarnagin's and Mrs. McNelley's this morn. Four Yanks from New Jersey breakfasted here. Looking for a "Rebel raid" today. A very cold night.

Sunday 20. A pretty day, very cold day, a very cold night. Mr. McNutt here this eve, he feels quite sanguine in regard to the next battle.

Monday 21. A cold day. Rhoda and I washed this morn. Mr. Kennedy, Mr. McNutt, Cousins Mary Jarnagin and Mary Harle were here today. Uncle Caswell took dinner here today. I commenced me another chemise today, sewed on it steadily all eve. Rhoda stayed all night with Cousin M. Jarnagin tonight. Grandmother has been dead 11 years today.

Tuesday 22. A pleasant day. Rhoda has been out all day weaving for Aunt Elizabeth. She stayed all night there. Mother went out to Aunt Elizabeth's, Mrs. Carter's, Mr. McNutt's, Mr. Kennedy's [he was here this eve], Dr. Long and Mr. Demour's today. I ironed my clothes this morn. Been needleworking on my chemise this eve. Mrs. Pickens here this morn. The Confederates made a raid in here this eve, took a few horses, guns, and wounded one on each side. The Yanks have returned this eve. Kuhn's Company came in about 200 in all. We could hardly get the trap door open and the kitchen door unlocked. Mother was away from home.

Wednesday 23. A cold day. I went up to Mrs. Edwards to get her to go to Mrs. Erwin's to see a wounded soldier. Mary and I went, I sat up tonight. I went to see Julia Grant this morn. Mr. McNutt laid our hearth over this eve.

Thursday 24. A pretty day. I slept all this morn. Sallie and Jeanette Grant here this eve. We went over to see Mr. Walcott [the wounded soldier]. He is worse this eve. It looks so gloomy and cheerless over there, I have felt so sad ever since I was there. Oh, if he would only get well. Lt. Bradford shot him. What a gloomy Christmas eve this; how unlike other Christmases I have passed. Will I ever enjoy myself as well again? Rhoda came in from Aunt Elizabeth's this eve to enjoy, no not enjoy, but pass Christmas. She is now reading our hero *Stonewall Jackson's Life* to Mother. Rhoda and I fixed up a few ground nuts, walnuts and hickory nuts for Stephney's stocking. Oh, so sad is our life at this time. If I could only see into our future, but it does no good to record sad thoughts and gloomy scenes, so I will close my journal, hoping when I take my pen again tomorrow I will have some good news to record. Mother heard cannon this morn. The Yanks have reinforced, and are looking for the "Rebs" tomorrow.

Friday 25. A cloudy, though pleasant day. Christmas Day, but I could not realize it, so unlike other Christmas days, so still and sad more like Sunday. Mr. Kennedy took dinner here. Julia Grant stayed all night with me tonight. Rhoda and I went over to see Mr. Walcott this morn, he was some better. I sat up there tonight; needleworked on my band as usual.

Saturday 26. A rainy and gloomy morn. Some Yankee Infantry came in about noon. Julia left about 11 o'clock. I have been needleworking on my chemise band all day. Julia Grant came and we went over and sat up tonight with Mr. Walcott. He rested badly, was very restless.

Sunday 27. Rained very hard all day. Julia took breakfast here. Two Yanks also. Mr. McNutt here this eve. I slept some this morn. I laid down but did not sleep this eve. We had an alarm and fled to the cellar this eve. Caused by two of our men firing on the Yankee pickets. Mrs. Alexander has a boy, born yesterday, also Mrs. Harris.

Monday 28. Windy and cloudy day. The Rebels fired at the Yanks about 4 o'clock this morn. About daylight the Rebels came in town and fought a while. The Yanks repulsed them. I cleaned out Sister's press this morn. Rhoda and Lizzie went up to see Mr. Walcott this morn. He is improving. I sat up with Mr. Walcott tonight. He is better, slept very well.

Tuesday 29. A pretty day. I slept all this morn. Cousin Mary Jarnagin here, spent the day. I went up home with her and practiced some. Mother and Rhoda went over to see Mr. Walcott this eve. Mary Hardwick, Nannie Kennedy and Sallie Swan here this eve. I borrowed the *Bride of Lammermoor* of Cousin Mary Jarnagin this eve.

Wednesday 30. A cloudy eve, cold morn. I went to Mrs. Erwins, Cousin Mary Jarnagin's and Dr. Grant's today. Rhoda went out to Aunt Elizabeth's to weave this morn. Mrs. Nannie Kennedy came home with her. They, Rhoda and she, sat up with Mr. Walcott tonight. I have the blues tonight about something I dare not commit to paper. Wheeler was repulsed at Charleston, Tennessee yesterday. Wonder where I will be this time two years. Suspense is awful. Miss Nannie and Rhoda came back; there was someone there to sit up. Lizzie Lea stayed all night here. Sallie Reeder's 16th birthday.

Thursday 31. A rainy day. Miss Nannie Kennedy and Lizzie stayed all night and all day here. It rained so they could not go home. Julia Grant and I sat up with Mr. Walcott tonight.

1864

January 1864

Friday 1. New Year's Day. A very cold day. Colder than it has been this winter. The wind whistles around the house so cold. I slept from 10 until 2 o'clock. Aunt Adeline has been in bed sick all day. Nannie Kennedy, Julia Grant, Lizzie Lea and the rest of us were sitting around the fire this morn. We wondered where we would all be this time next year, if we would be permitted to live until then.

Saturday 2. A very cold day, colder than yesterday. It is intense cold. Cousin Mary Jarnagin here this eve. I finished my chemise sleeve this eve. I think it is about the coldest day I ever experienced. The Yanks have been skating all day on Mrs. Traynor's pond.

Sunday 3. Another cold day. Rhoda went out to Mrs. Erwin's, Mrs. Grant's and Cousin Mary's today. Messrs. McNutt, Kennedy, Mary Edwards here this eve. Sallie Ragsdale's 18th birthday.

Monday 4. A cloudy and rainy day. I finished my chemise this eve. About 100 more Yanks came in this eve. One here for milk and another for butter. How I long for peace or even to see our Army back here again. This is the darkest hour our Confederacy has ever seen. About two thirds of Georgia has given it up. They are putting every man from the age of 15 to 65 in the army. A great many of our soldiers are deserting. How disgraceful. Wonder if the yoke of bondage will be on our necks this time next year. I feel so impatient to see the end of all this strife and bloodshed. If I could only see into the future 6 months, but I presume I will be jogging along the even tenor of my way, anticipating yet never realizing my wishes.

Tuesday 5. A cold day, very muddy. I went over to Mrs. Erwin's and to Cousin Mary Jarnagin's this morning. They were both here today, also Mr. McNutt. The Yanks all left this eve, looking for Rebels in tomorrow. Rhoda and I went up late this [evening] to Mrs.

Edward's. Mary came home with us and stayed all night. I cut myself out a petticoat this eve.

Wednesday 6. A very cold day. I took some potatoes over to Mr. Walcott this morning. Mrs. Shadden here all this eve; she took dinner here. I sewed on my underskirt all eve. Finished it tonight. I wish so much I knew where Cousin John is tonight. I would write him a long letter.

Thursday 7. A very cold day; rained (rather misted) all day. We washed today. Rhoda and I went to see Anna Gaut this morn. About two regiments of Indianians and Ohioans came in this eve. Nine took supper here. Two from Indiana sat up until bed time.

Friday 8. A cold day. We got up this morn and found snow on the ground. The Yanks left this morn. I feel so relieved when an army passes. Mother always explains, "Behold one woe has passed and another cometh quickly." I went up and spent the day at Uncle Caswell's today. I found Cousin Mary Jarnagin here when I came home. I went over to see Mr. Walcott. He is a little better. He has the neuralgia. Mother has been spinning some candlewick for Cousin Mary Jarnagin. John Kennedy's 16th birthday.

Saturday 9. A very cold day. I went over to Mr. Demour's and to see Mary Hardwick this morn. I dried my clothes and ironed them this morn. Gid (our dog) died this morn. I washed this eve and then went to see Mrs. McNutt. Mary Elizabeth went over to see Virginia Grant. Sallie came with her. She and I went over and sat up with Mr. Walcott. John Swan here this eve.

Sunday 10. A cold, cloudy day. The snow is still on the ground. Sallie Grant breakfasted here. Cousin Mary and Julia dined here. I slept this morn and this eve.

Monday 11. A cold, cloudy day. Mother is busy carding and spinning candlewick. Mr. Cam Johnson here this morn, brought a letter from Sister. Jimmie's 6th birthday. I went over to see Mr. Walcott. He is much better. Mrs. Traynor here this eve. We heard some cheering news from [General] Longstreet.

Tuesday 12. A pretty day. Mother went out to Uncle Caswell's this morn. Ada Gaut and her sister Julia Anderson here this eve. Uncle Ned has been sick in bed all day. Rhoda borrowed *The Household of Bouverie* from Cousin Mary Jarnagin this morn. We finished spinning the candlewick tonight. I commenced an underskirt today.

Wednesday 13. A very pleasant day. Mother went out to Mr. Kennedy's this morn. He and John were here tonight. I finished my underskirt tonight. Mr. McNutt and Pryor Lea dined here. Rhoda went out to Aunt Elizabeth's to weave tomorrow. Julia Grant, Mr. and Mrs. William and Bell Grant were here this eve. Sister was married 12 years ago tonight.

Thursday 14. A pretty day. I wrote a long letter to Cousin John Lea this morn. After that I shelled some corn. In the evening I made Mr. Walcott a blackberry pie and took it over to him. Mary Jane Tucker and Sallie Reeder here this eve. Sallie stayed all night. Rhoda came in this eve. She expects to go to Georgia tomorrow with John Swan.

Friday 15. A pleasant, though cloudy day. Sallie Reeder and Lizzie went over and took dinner at Dr. Grant's. Sallie stayed all night here. The Rebels came in this morn and remained only a few hours. Pryor and Uncle Caswell Lea and Cousin Mary Jarnagin here this eve; sat until bedtime. We all shelled corn this eve. Uncle Ned is still in bed but he is better.

Saturday 16. A pleasant, though cloudy day. Mr. Reeder came for Lizzie before dinner. Nannie Kennedy and Lizzie Lea here this eve. Rhoda went with Nannie over to Mr. Erwin's and then went out home with her and stayed all night. I mended my hoops, chemise and drawers today, also made me a silk nightcap. Mr. Kennedy here this eve. Pryor Lea here this morn. I put some steel beads on my net; have been very busy all day doing small jobs. Sallie Reeder and Lizzie went over to see Mr. Walcott this morn. He was better. Mrs. Jack Henderson died last night.[1]

Sunday 17. A beautiful day. Rhoda and Pryor Lea started to Georgia this morning. Uncle Caswell and Margaret (Mag) Shadden here this morn. I feel so lonesome this eve. When will I see Rhoda again and what will we have passed through? I hated to see her leave. I will be so lonesome here. Late this eve I went over to see Mr.

---

[1]Mrs. John [Sandney] Henderson was born 16 October 1796, and died 16 January 1864, and was interred in Fort Hill Cemetery. John and his wife, had A. E. Blunt living in their home at the time of the 1860 census, Ross, *Cemetery Records*, II:151.

Walcott. After I returned Mother and I then went over to Mr. William Grant's and sat until nearly 9 o'clock.

Monday 18. Rained very hard this morn and the sun shone out beautifully, then closed in and commenced raining late this eve. I went over to Cousin Mary Harle's this eve also, to see Julia Grant. She read some to me in her journal. I have been reading *The Household of Bouverie* today. Mrs. Rogers, Mary Sugart and William Traynor here until bed time. Uncle Ned is a little better; sat up some today.

Tuesday 19. We found the ground covered with snow this morn. It nearly all melted today. I read *The Household of Bouverie* all morn. Went up to Cousin Mary Jarnagin's this eve. Sallie sent *Hal's Travels* and some popcorn tonight by Bill. Lizzie and I have been reading some in Amos and Joel tonight to Mother. These days are so sad and gloomy. I feel as if we were only camping and were waiting for something dreadful to occur to change our situation. Emma Lea and Ella DeLano here this morn. Cousin Mary's 17th birthday.

Wednesday 20. A beautiful but muddy day. Mother went out to Aunt Elizabeth's this morn to assist in making George a coat. I washed this morn. After dinner I went out to Aunt Elizabeth's and Miss Nannie Kennedy's. She stayed all night with me at Aunt Elizabeth's. I have the "ennui" this eve.

Thursday 21. A beautiful day. I wove all day for Aunt Elizabeth. I stayed all night with Nannie Kennedy tonight.

Friday 22. A beautiful day. I wove all day today for Aunt Elizabeth. I came home tonight. Was really glad to get home once more. Felt as if it had been a month or two since I left. Two Yanks took dinner at Aunt Elizabeth's.

Saturday 23. Another delightful day. I went out to Aunt Elizabeth's early this morn and wove all day for her and came by for Nannie Kennedy and she came home and stayed all night with me.

Sunday 24. A most lovely day. We all went to the Presbyterian Church in the morn and eve and heard Mr. Kennedy preach. Nannie and I went over to see Mr. Walcott this morn. He is improving. This eve Sallie, Virginia, Julia and Jeanette Grant went with Lizzie and me over to the graveyard. Mrs. Shadden stayed all night with us.

Monday 25. A most beautiful day, more like summer than winter. Lizzie and I washed today. Mother went to church this morn. Mrs. Kennedy came home with her and took dinner. After we dined I took my music up to Cousin Mary Jarnagin's and practiced nearly all eve. I washed the window glass, looking glass, today, it was such a mild day.

Tuesday 26. A beautiful day. The loveliest weather I ever saw in winter. I went out to Aunt Elizabeth's this morn, wove all day, stayed all night. I made up some light rolls this eve for breakfast. Aunt Elizabeth is giving me lessons in bread making. I went out and took a seat on the log at the spring-house and read some in *The Household of Bouverie.*

Wednesday 27. Another beautiful day, very pleasant without fire. I wove all day, finished my three yards late this eve and then went up to see Mrs. Nannie Kennedy. There I met Miss Laura Garder, Miss Lou and Callie Swan. Miss Eliza Wood was married to a cousin of her's this eve.

Thursday 28. A most beautiful day. The mornings are so pleasant that I have taken up my morning's ablutions[2] again, which refreshes me considerably. After finishing my three yards and partaking of a nice glass of milk and a loaf of bread, I in company with Pryor and Lizzie Lea went up to Dr. Grant's and brought Julia back to stay all night with me. They moved back to their old home yesterday. They were perfectly delighted to get back once more. I feel so glad to see them back there again.

Friday 29. Another lovely day. As the sun ascended the Eastern Horizon, Julia and I arose, performed our toilet, came down stairs and were greeted with the joyful intelligence that France had recognized us [which proved to be untrue] and that Longstreet had gained a great victory over Foster near Knoxville. I wove two yards today. I had a slight chill this morn.

Saturday 30. Old Sol [sun] has not made his appearance today; the clouds have intervened between us and the rain has once more blessed the earth with her genial showers. I wove about two yards today. Mother came out this eve and I came home with her. Was

---

[2]Ablution was a washing or cleansing of the body, especially with religious connotation.

very glad to see "Home Sweet Home" once more. Went out and looked in the garden to admire Uncle Ned's horticultural talents. He had planted onions, sewed [sowed] cale, mustard, etc. Everything looks very cheering; reminds me that there is "Life in the Old Land Yet." A few Rebels in town this eve though I never saw them. Rhoda's 21st birthday. I posted my journal late this eve. Will now go and make up some hop yeast bread Aunt Elizabeth gave me.

Sunday 31. Just as grey dawn streaked the leaves, I arose, donned my apparel, and made up my rolls. They were very nice. Sol has not cheered us with his bright rays today, but moves majestically along behind the clouds. Stephney's 11th birthday. What I will record in these subsequent pages, no one can tell, but I fear I will have dark deeds and gloomy scenes to sully these fair leaves with. Mrs. Traynor sent for me to come and stay with her tonight. I went. Mother and Lizzie went to church this morn. Some Federals passed down this eve.

February 1864

Monday 1. A lovely day. I went out to Aunt Elizabeth's and wove; finished her piece. We then went to visit Nannie Kennedy and also to Mrs. Rob Swan's. I came home and found Cousin Mary Jarnagin at our house. We then went over to see Mr. Walcott. He was sitting up. Mr. Davis was at Uncle Caswell's this morn. Mr. Clingan died of smallpox at 5 o'clock this morn.[3]

Tuesday 2. A beautiful morn, windy and cloudy this eve and tonight. Lizzie and I washed this morn. Mrs. Shadden and Mrs. McNelley here this eve. This eve I went out to Dr. Grant's and from thence to Aunt Elizabeth's where I stayed all night. Uncle Caswell went down in Georgia to get two mules back the Confederates took from him.

---

3 A.A. Clingan was born 20 February 1801, and died 1 February 1864, and is interred in Clingan Cemetery. Ross, *Cemetery Records*, I:158. Mr. Clingan filled the unexpired term of William Carter, who was the first sheriff of Bradley County, 1836-1838; Clingan served again from 1842-1846.

Wednesday 3. A pretty but rather windy day. A large number of Federals passed Aunt Elizabeth's this morn, going to and from Charleston, S. C. and Chattanooga. A Lt. Simmons came in and stayed about an hour and talked. Miss Nannie Kennedy here a while this morn. Julia and I have been fitting and making Aunt Elizabeth's cotton dresses all day. She went home this eve. John Waterhouse stayed with Georgie tonight.

Thursday 4. A beautiful but rather windy day. Julia came down this morn and we sewed all day. The brigade of Federals that passed up yesterday came back today. Lt. Simmons dined with Aunt Elizabeth. John Waterhouse stayed again tonight. Sallie Grant came to Aunt Elizabeth's this eve and Julia and I walked part of the way home with her.

Friday 5. A cloudy day; disagreeable this eve, so windy. Julia and I finished Aunt Elizabeth's dress this eve and she went home. Mother came out this eve and I came home with her. I was disappointed that Mother did not let me go home with Julia. Federals in town; come to work on the railroad. I made up some hop yeast bread tonight for breakfast. Mr. Kennedy here this eve. I feel so dejected this eve, what is to be our fate? Our sentence has gone forth, if it is only executed. I tremble for our future. God can alone protect us and soften the hearts of our foes. Uncle Caswell returned this eve with a sad countenance. He thinks [Joseph E.] Johnston's army is falling back, it may be, but cheer up, better days are in store for us.

Saturday 6. A cloudy, gloomy and dark rainy day, which adds more to the sorrow and gloom of our hearts. Mrs. Shadden here this morn. The cars have commenced running here today.[4]

Sunday 7. A pretty day. Miss Nannie Kennedy here, her mother and brother this morn, also Mr. McNutt. They came to go to church but concluded to have prayers here and then went home. Nannie

---

4 Reportedly some of the rails near Cleveland had been removed and the trains were unable to run. Myra's comment about the cars running indicated that the rails had been repaired. As early as 28 November 1863, Maj. Gen. William T. Sherman had heard that the Federal cavalry had "already destroyed a large part of the railroad" near Cleveland. A good many Federals camped on the hill near the graveyard.

stayed all day with me. She and I went over to see Mr. Walcott in the eve; found him out in the yard.

Monday 8. A pretty day. This is now Monday and it has been some time since I unburdened my heart to you, old journal, so I will enumerate the scenes through which I have passed since my last communication to you in the regular order. This Monday morning finds me busy collecting our soiled garments for the washtub. After Lizzie and I finished our chore of washing we went in and assisted Mother entertain Mrs. Kennedy and Aunt Elizabeth. After we dined, I walked out to Mrs. Kennedy's to get Nannie to color some bonnets for Lizzie and me. Three soldiers were here tonight to get the girls to play for them; they treated us with disrespect as much as they could. We entertained them to the best of our knowledge and I think softened their hearts toward "us Rebs."

Tuesday 9. A pretty day. I have been picking wool all day excepting the time I prepared my hop yeast for drying and also played for soldiers. The Yanks are looking for our Southern hero, Gen. Morgan;[5] they have moved their commissary alone to headquarters to Dr. Shugart's.

Wednesday 10. A lovely though rather cold day. I attempted to write a letter to Mrs. Gamble but gave it up in despair, my mind is in such a confused state these latter days, and days of trouble. I can write to do no good. Hundreds of ideas crowd my mind in one minute, but vanish when I attempt to commit them to paper, leaving my imagination a perfect vacuum. The Federals hoisted their flag this morn. It now floats over Cleveland. Sad emblem of what once was. Once happy and beloved United States, never will liberty and freedom be perched on the banner as it was when thousands of patriots poured out their life blood under the sacred folds. Grant how soon, God, that our gallant Stars and Bars supplant that now deserted flag. Mr. and Mrs. Bradford dined here today. I sent Mr. Walcott over a piece of blackberry pie Caperanza this eve by Lizzie.

Thursday 11. A pretty day. Washington's birthday. How we have abused the liberty he fought for. Cousin Mary Jarnagin took dinner here. She and I went out to Mr. Kennedy's this eve. There were three very mean Russians there. I became so infuriated at some of the

---

5 General John Hunt Morgan, CSA.

things they said. I wrote to Uncle Alfred Lea for Mother by Mr. Bradford. I heard that Brownlow's[6] Regiment came this eve, but proved to be a false rumor. Mother went out to see old Mr. Wood this eve. He died this morn.[7]

Friday 12. Clouded up this eve. Five soldiers ate here today. I had an argument on slavery with one this morn. Mother went to Mr. Wood's burying this eve. I quilled some ribbon for my hat this morn. This world! I feel so tired and perfectly exhausted with its troubles sometimes, and feel almost tempted to retire to a hermitage and pass the remainder of my days a recluse. I practiced a little at Cousin Mary Jarnagin's this morn. I am so fond of music, what Shakespeare says does not apply to me: "The man that has no music in his soul, nor is not moved with concord of sweet sounds, is fit for treason, stratagem, and spoils, and his affection dark as Erebus. Let no such man be trusted." Mother breakfasts and dons her walking costume, shawl, bonnet, and stays a large portion of the day and comes back late in the eve to report and lodge for the night. She visits like she used to when Sister went to Charleston, S. C.

Saturday 13. A pretty day. John Kennedy came and told me this morn that my hat was finished. Mary Elizabeth went out and brought it in and I trimmed it in canary-colored ribbon and black velvet. Mary Elizabeth wiped up Mother's floor this eve.

Sunday 14. Rainy morning. We did not go to church. A chaplain preached in the Presbyterian Church. I read in *Hal's Travels* through Egypt and Palestine, all day.

Monday 15. Rainy morning. I spun nearly all day for Mary Elizabeth's dress. Our cat "Tom" climbed to the top of the shop and cannot get down.

Tuesday 16. A real Norther [a sudden, cold gale from the North] has come. This morning it was very pleasant and tonight it is freezing cold. The wind darts around the house in low mournful wails, playing the deuce with our unprotected fingers and noses. Lizzie and I wrote a letter to Sister tonight. Mother sits in one

---

6 William Brownlow

7 John Wood, Sr. was born 5 April 1800, in Tennessee, and died 10 February 1864. He is buried in Fort Hill Cemetery. Ross, *Cemetery Records*, II:299. Wood, a carpenter by trade, was listed with his wife Polly and five children in the 1860 census. Also listed in his household was Meridith Legg.

corner, slowly masticating her cornbread and drinking her milk, whilst every now and then she stops to relate some event of the day. Aunt Eliza Adeline sits in the other, holding her hands and baking her feet to the large wood fire blazing the hearth. Mr. McNutt and Cousin Mary Jarnagin here this eve. Lizzie and I washed this morn, a very bitter pill as the wind cut keenly around our unprotected arms.

Wednesday 17. A cold day. Sister's 30th birthday. Some of Gen. Sherman's men are camped here. Some soldiers ate here today. Cousin Mary Jarnagin and I went to Mrs. Ragsdale's this eve, Mother to McNutt's. Joe Lea was at home tonight.

Thursday 18. A pretty day, but windy. Snowed a little this morn. I received a letter this morn from my cousin. Mr. Sam died this morn at 2 o'clock. Mother went to Mrs. Kennedy's this morn. Aunt Elizabeth here this morn. Eight soldiers dined here today. Uncle Caswell took the oath this morn, dined here this eve.[8]

Friday 19. A windy day. I went over to get Mary Edwards to trim Lizzie's hat. This eve I went out to Aunt Elizabeth's and I remained all night. Also, Misses Nannie Kennedy and Julia Grant. Lts. Miller and Simmons took tea and remained until after 11 o'clock. Three officers of Sherman's men came in just after I went out to Uncle Caswell's to take some suspenders this morn. Uncle Caswell went to see about some cloth this morn.

Saturday 20. A windy, but milder day than yesterday. To you, old journal, I am indebted for many a pleasant moment. I can unburden my heart to you, not feeling betrayal. I came home this morn. Mrs. Pickens here with a major this eve. How I dreaded the interview but it passed off at last, when I donned my hat and hied [to go quickly] to Mr. Craven's to see Mr. Walcott. It is quite refreshing to talk to a Confederate and unburden our hearts to

---

[8] The oath was required of every civilian or military officeholder, either "for honor or profit." Commonly called the "ironclad oath," it was passed by Congress on 2 July 1862. It required the individual to pledge allegiance to the Constitution of the United States and declare that the swearer had never voluntarily borne arms against the Union, or aided in any way such a rebellion. On 11 March 1864, Mrs. James W. Inman, Myra's mother, was required to take the oath. Failure to do so would have meant imprisonment.

friends, after being surrounded by blue coats and hearing their taunts and jeers. George Lea here until bedtime.

Sunday 21. Snowed very briskly this morn, but when old Sol started his effluent rays on the beautiful little gems they quivered beneath his gaze a moment and melted away. Mr. McNutt here this morn. Mary Hartley died last night with consumption, poor girl.[9]

Monday 22. A beautiful and pleasant day. We washed this morn. I felt so lonely this eve. Just after sundown, when the last rays of our bright luminary gilded the western horizon, our old faithful servant, Aunt Phoebe, was suddenly called away from this wicked and tumultuous earth to inherit the blessings that are prepared for those who love and serve our Master. She went to milking in her usual health. I went up to her house and was sitting by the fire. (She asked me to stay in the house to prevent the soldiers from taking anything). I told her I was hungry. She made a fire and split up some pieces of bread and then stooped down and complained of a swimming in her head. I looked at her and then resumed reading in *Rob-Roy.* She then arose and sat on a chair. She then says, "Miss Myra, do get me something!" I ran for Mother and I got the camphor. When I reached her, her hands were drawn, her features convulsed, and death was depicted in her distorted countenance. She then closed her eyes and after drawing a few long sighs as if bidding us "Long Farewell," her soul had pinioned its flight into vast eternity. Uncle Ned was in the woods at the time, came in, in a few minutes after she was dead. He takes her death very hard. Lizzie and I went out to Aunt Elizabeth's by ourselves, just as the moon arose in all its grandeur and majesty, to communicate the sad intelligence to them. Pryor came in and stayed all night. Mr. Chambers brought a letter from Rhoda informing us of the birth of Sister's little girl, born the 18th of this month. I can never forget this night. Poor Aunt Phoebe, words cannot express the grief her death has cause us. Just as we are made to weep over the death of an old one. From the time she was taken until she died, it did not exceed three minutes.

P.S. Aunt Phoebe baked 450 biscuits today with Lizzie's assistance. I peeled the parsnips and potatoes for her dinner. She was so

---

[9] A Mary Hartley (eighteen years old) was listed among the family of James G. Hartley, a tailor, in the 1860 census. She would have been approximately twenty-two years old at the time of her death.

kind to us, treated us like children and indulged us in every whim. We went to her like a Mother and she took such an interest in us and indulged us all our foibles; but she is no more and it does no good to lament her death, but should take it as a warning and prepare to meet her in heaven.

Tuesday 23. A lovely day. The sun wanes in the West; the moon ushers up from the lovely East and this long, sad, dreary and lonesome day has passed at last. It seemed as if it would never end. How utterly desolate I feel. Aunt Phoebe seemed like a mother to me. Truly we have lost a friend. She was a bright star for any of us to take pattern after. Numbers have been here to look on her form for the last time. She was put in the coffin about sundown. It was such a sad and solemn hour. She looked like she was asleep. Uncle Ned says he is broken up.

Wednesday 24. With sad hearts we arise, make our fire and I assisted Susan ("big Susan") prepare our breakfast. We paid the last and sad rite to our old and faithful Aunt Phoebe, that of depositing her remains in her cold and lonely tomb at 9:30 o'clock this morn. After we came back I assisted Susan get a plain dinner. Mr. Kennedy, Cousin William Shields and son dined here. This eve we scoured the buckets at Uncle Ned's house. Uncle Ned seems nearly heart broken. He sat by the smokehouse and then would walk about for a while and then sit at the pigpen and look over the fence. I know it has been a long eve to him. I am glad the long, long weary day has passed away. Mrs. Robert McNelley sat until bedtime with us. A lovely day.

Thursday 25. This morn I assisted Susan in getting breakfast and went up and tried to milk the cow, but I haven't enough strength in my hand to milk to do any good. I then scoured the safe table and a few other things this morn and this eve helped Susan scour the kitchen. We miss Aunt Phoebe so much. Mother helped Uncle Ned pack away her clothes this morn. Susan washed up her things this morn. I was invited to a musical entertainment at Mrs. Traynor's tonight, but did not go. Lt. Simmons called on me this eve. I went up this eve with Susan and milked some. It tires my hands so I cannot milk to do much good. The wind blows like it would rain soon.

Friday 26. A pretty day. I have been very busy all day. Got breakfast, dinner, and supper. Susan went home after breakfast.

Mary Hardwick here this morn. Mr. William Grant brought a Mr. King here to hear me play this eve. I was invited to a party at Mrs. Hardwick's this eve but did not go. Aunt Elizabeth here this eve.

Saturday 27. A pretty day. I cleaned up the hall and Mother's room this eve. I got up this morn and dressed myself, came out and got breakfast for the first time in my life. Mary Edwards here this morn. Nannie and Mrs. Kennedy here this eve. Cousin Tom Lea brought Miss Callie Callaway here this evening to stay all night. Mother and I milk every day. Only milk one of our cows. Lt. Simmons called on me tonight. Sent me a paper.

Sunday 28. A windy day. Pryor Lea, Georgie and Tom, William Shields and Callie Callaway dined here. The wagons left from off Judge Grant's lot this morn. A great many troops passed through town. I feel so lonely this eve. They had a fight near Dalton, Ga. Our troops repulsed them. They have come back here and encamped.

Monday 29. A rainy, dark, cloudy and gloomy day. I feel so very lonely this eve. I practiced a good while this morn. The last day of winter and a wet and gloomy day it is. I have been reading a good deal in *Waverly's Magazine* [that] Lt. Simmons sent me. How lonesome I feel this eve. Aunt Phoebe died this evening a week ago.

March 1864

Tuesday 1. A very rainy and gloomy day. Three soldiers here today. I made molasses pie this morn for dinner by a new recipe. Succeeded admirably. A good many soldiers (several regiments) left on the train this morn and evening. Father would have been 55 years old today.

Wednesday 2. A lovely day. We received a letter from Sister describing little Rhoda. I wish we could see her. Mr. Bradford dined here. Miss Callie and I took tea at Aunt Elizabeth's. We came home and went up to Mrs. Traynor's. Lts. Riley, Pappon, and others were there, also Mary Hardwick and Mollie Dardis. I played a few pieces for them and came home.

Thursday 3. A pleasant day. Miss Callie and I went over to see Mr. Walcott. I took him a paper and some pie. We enjoyed the jaunt. It is so refreshing to see a Rebel and talk our sentiments freely. Lt. Simmons called and brought me two papers this morn. I am better pleased with him than any so far, but there is something repulsive in a Yankee's look. Not like the bold candor, handsome and brave heart of Southern heroes. If we can only gain our independence, it is all I ask. I would willingly sacrifice everything. Col. Champion and two of his staff were here this eve to hear me play. Maj. Lefever and Surgeon Woods called on me tonight. I do not like their assurance a bit.

Friday 4. A rather cloudy and windy day. Miss Callie Callaway started home this morn with Mr. Robert Pickens. Mrs. Reeder here this morn. Mother got a guard this morn. I played for some soldiers this eve. I altered my corset this morn and eve. Red (the cow) has a son.

Saturday 5. A pretty day. I scoured the pails, table, etc. this morn. Lizzie got corn out of the loft and we wiped up Mother's room and porch this eve, beside performing other Saturday duties. Lt. Riley here this eve. Mrs. Traynor came down this eve to get me to go up and play for the Col. and staff. I went. Several soldiers were there and I stayed until 9 o'clock. An officer came home with me. If I could [I would] lie down and sleep away the time they are here and wake up when our troops come, which I hope will be soon. I am almost worried to death entertaining Federal officers. If I could send them all adrift. Maj. Lefever called tonight. I was not at home.

Sunday 6. A cloudless day. I have been at home all day. Mrs. Kincannon here this eve. Mother and I went over after tea to Cousin Mary (Harle's) to see Aunt Fannie Lea. She is very sick. Two soldiers here this eve, Jimmie Smith, William Mite. A Mr. Widows sent me some apples by Arthur Traynor. Mother and Lizzie went out to Uncle Caswell's this eve. We received good news from [Joseph E.] Johnston's army. They are moving. We are expecting an attack every day.

Monday 7. A pretty morn. Rained a little this eve. Lt. Simmons and Lt. Walters called this eve. Lizzie and I washed this morn. Had two weeks washing on hand. I went out and remained at Aunt Elizabeth's tonight.

Tuesday 8. This morning is lovely. I rode with Pryor and William Shields from Uncle Caswell's and Dr. Grant's this morn where I spent a nice day. Capt. Chewey and three other officers called while I was there. Lizzie Lea called for me and I, with Julia Grant, went down and spent the night at Aunt Elizabeth's. Miss Nannie Kennedy was there when we came. We heard this eve that Sherman was cut to pieces, and several other things that I hope are true.

Wednesday 9. A lovely day. Aunt Elizabeth came home with me this morn and remained a little while. Mrs. Shadden stayed with us tonight. Surgeon Woods called tonight. We played backgammon in Mother's room. I crocheted on Lizzie's net most all day. We received a letter by Mr. Chambers that Sister's family wanted to come home. Jimmie Smith and William Mite here this eve for me to play. Mother and I went up to see Cousin Mary Jarnagin. She has just returned from Chattanooga.

Thursday 10. A beautiful day. I marked some pocket handkerchiefs this morn. Mother has been trying to obtain a passport to go through the lines to see Sister, but failed. Mr. William Campbell here this eve. Uncle Caswell here this eve. He is in trouble about Cousin John. Morgan captured a letter Uncle Caswell wrote to Cousin John about him. Miss Nannie Kennedy and her father here this eve. I took a long cry this eve. Mother went up to see Mrs. Pickens this eve. She was telling her something that William Mite said about me relative to inviting Mr. Walcott down here. I heard they had sent Mr. Walcott to Chattanooga. How I sigh for independence; my spirits feel crushed. In vain I sigh for peace and find none. My very soul is depressed and weighed down with grief. I have no alternative left but to pray to God in the language of our psalmist when he was oppressed by his enemies, in Psalms 8:9: "Deliver me from mine enemies, O my God; defend me from them that rise up against me." Judge [Gaut] and his lady here tonight. Such a trade of abuse I never heard as he pronounced against our beloved South. Mrs.___ said she was truly sorry for the Confederate army. He said they were forced to fight at the point of bayonet and spoke of them being urged on by a few fanatic demagogues. He denounced the Confederate lying newspaper in the bitterest terms. How my heart ached for revenge. O, our Father, if it is Thy will, let us gain our independence. Truly I thought he would spare our feelings, but alas, he bridled not his tongue, neither spared he our feelings. I could only sit and deliver up a feeble prayer to God for our deliverance. We are done with peace. Maj. Lefever called to escort me to a party at Mr. Callaway's, but I did not go.

Friday 11. A windy day. I wrote a letter to Sister this morn. I got up this morn with a sad heart and longing for the return or our brave heroes, but almost in despair of ever seeing them. If I could only express the deep gloom that envelops my heart, but alas, it is too deep for utterance. Mother took the oath today. Mrs. Swan and Mrs. Grant and Mrs. Shadden here this morn.

Saturday 12. A pretty day. I cleaned up the floors, press, buckets, etc. this morn. Uncle Caswell and Mr. Shields here this eve. Mr. and Mrs. Headrick here this morn. Ada Anderson has a baby boy.

Sunday 13. A lovely day. My 19th birthday. Mother and I went over to Cousin Mary Jarnagin's to see Aunt Fannie this morn. Mary Edwards, Lt. Simmons, Bell Grant and Mr. Wilson here this eve to pass my birthday.

Monday 14. A lovely day. I washed today. Lizzie and I, Cousin Mary Jarnagin and Aunt Elizabeth here this eve. I went with Mr. Widows to a grand military ball tonight at the Peat residence. Saw more bluecoats, shoulder straps and brass buttons there than was agreeable. Cousin Mary Jarnagin went. The house was decorated with pine nicely.

Tuesday 15. A pretty day, but very cold. I slept this morn. We did not come home last night until 3 o'clock. Jimmie Smith here this eve to hear me play.

Wednesday 16. A cold day. Lt. Simmons here this eve. He gave me his photograph, his 31st birthday. I ironed some this morn. Mother and I went over to see Aunt Fannie this eve. She is no better.

Thursday 17. I read in a book this morn. Lt. Simmons lent me, *Was He Successful?* This eve I went up with Mr. Smith to see Mattie and the baby, little Ada Barton, born December 22nd. I then went down to Cousin Mary Jarnagin's, where I remained until after tea. I then played on the piano for some Federal officers. I got into a discussion with a surgeon relative to slavery.

Friday 18. A cold, windy day. I have a sore throat this morn. I wrote off my "first impressions" of Lt. Simmons this morn. I finished *Was He Successful?* tonight. Sallie Ragsdale has a girl.

Saturday 19. A rather unpleasant day. My cold has troubled me a good deal today. Emeline, Jimmie, Sues and Frank came up this morn from Sister's. Aunt Elizabeth here this morn. She and Mother went over to see Aunt Fannie. I went up to Cousin Mary Jarnagin's this eve. She, Miss Lou Swan and I went down to see Mrs. Williams' goods. Jimmie Smith and William Mite here this eve.

Sunday 20. A pretty day. Aunt Elizabeth, Lizzie, Mrs. Shadden and Mrs. Kincannon here this morn. The Yanks are looking for the Rebels in today. Mother and I went over to see Aunt Fannie this eve. Mary Elizabeth and Mother went to see her tonight. She died at half past 8 o'clock at night.

Monday 21. A cold, cloudy, windy day. I finished Lizzie's net this morn. Mother and Jimmie went out to Mr. Joe Swan's this morn. She went to Aunt Fannie's burying this eve. Lt. Simmons called on me this eve. We exchanged "first impressions." He also brought me several papers. Uncle Ned is sick. Cousin Mary Jarnagin here tonight. My cold is some better.

Tuesday 22. This morn, after waking, the first thing I heard was Sues making on a fire as Uncle Ned is sick, in bed. I arose and looked out of the window on a white world. This is 4 o'clock and it is still snowing. Has not ceased a minute today. Several cargoes of Yankees have passed on sleighs today. I finished off Mary Elizabeth's net and made Aunt Elizabeth a little shawl this morn. Jimmie is very restless all day, as Mother keeps him indoors to prevent him eating snow. This day, one month ago, Aunt Phoebe died. Georgie and Pryor Lea here this eve. Snow is about a foot in depth.

Wednesday 23. The sun shone out and the snow is melting very fast. Lt. Simmons here this eve. I needleworked on Lizzie Lea's pantalettes this morn.

Thursday 24. A pretty day, but very windy. The snow is melting very fast. I needleworked on Lizzie Lea's pantalettes today. I cut out a cape for my calico dress this eve and nearly finished it. Sister Myra would have been 27 years old, if she had lived.

Friday 25. A cloudy, wet, disagreeable and gloomy day. It snowed some last night. I finished altering my dress this eve. Lt. Simmons sent me two papers and a piece of poetry of his own composition, headed "Twilight Musings," this evening. Father has been dead 13 years today.

Saturday 26. A beautiful day. Julia and Sallie Grant here this eve. Then Surgeon Woods called; then Lts. Riley and Simmons. Two East Tennessee renegades took supper here. I cleaned up the parlor, hall, etc., this morn, also wiped around the dining room carpet, hall and porch.

Sunday 27. A lovely day. The sun arose in resplendent glory this morn, auguring [to predict as from signs or omens] a beautiful Sabbath, but how marred is the terrestrial world. We heard not the clear chimes of the bell peal forth, but in its place we are greeted by the oaths and curses of our fellow men. Sad degeneracy of human nature, caused by war! Two East Tennessee renegades here this morn. If this war were only over. Why are we scourged so bitterly? My conscience answers for our sins. Bitter indeed is the chalice. What will be another year hence? I am in hopes the wheel of time will in its revolution bring peace, but my hopes are very shallow. It seems hardly possible. Miss Nannie Kennedy and her mother came for us to go to church. Mother went with them. Mary Edwards, Mrs. Kincannon and Cousin Mary Jarnagin here this eve.

Monday 28. A windy morn; rained some this eve. Five soldiers here; two dined. I played for Jimmie Smith. I put a new band in my worsted dress. Cousin Mary Jarnagin here this eve. I went home with her.

Tuesday 29. A pretty day. I finished my worsted dress this morn. I copied off a discussion for Lt. Simmons today. Mary Hardwick and Sallie Reeder here this eve.

Wednesday 30. Snowed this morn. The sun shone out a while, then clouded up again. Lizzie and I spent the day at Aunt Elizabeth's. Lizzie went up to Mrs. Dr. Grant's and stayed a while and brought Julia home with her to stay all night.

Thursday 31. A pretty day. Julia Grant went home this morn. I went down to see Sallie Surguine. Lt. Simmons here this morn. He took dinner and left at 2 o'clock. Four soldiers here this eve for me to play. Aunt Elizabeth here this eve. I went with her as far as Cousin Mary Jarnagin's. We heard some good news from Mrs. McNelley. We received a letter from Sister telling us she was coming home.

April 1864

Friday 1. A dark, cloudy, windy and cool day. Lizzie's 16th birhtday. I felt so lonely this eve. I ate some walnuts to employ my time. Cousin Mary Harle here this eve. Uncle Caswell took dinner here.

Saturday 2. A cloudy, wet and rainy day. Uncle Caswell here this morn. Mother and Jimmie went out there this morn. I helped wipe up the floor and helped Emeline to scour the kitchen furniture. I feel so lonesome this morn. If I could only see my dear Cousin John, but when will that be, no one can tell under what circumstances. Something tells me [that it will be] after peace is made. That seems so long and in the future so far. I feel as if I were writing this for nothing. What is my future to be? No one can tell, but as I write it through life as it occurs, as the present, and read in the future, as the past, it will be revealed to me. Mrs. Kennedy and Jennie here this eve. We heard this eve that the Rebels are very near here. They are looking for them tomorrow.

Sunday 3. A pretty day. We went to church this eve. The house was crowded with soldiers. Nat Carson and Green Craigmiles called on me this eve. Mrs. Shadden here this eve.

Monday 4. A rainy day. Lt. Simmons here this eve. We exchanged, which exerts the greater influence, the hope of reward or the fear of punishment. I went in an ambulance to the military ball at the Simmons' Hall. Capt. Hancock accompanied me.

Tuesday 5. A pretty day. Capt. Hancock called on me tonight. I went up to Mrs. Shadden's and to see Mary Edwards this morn.

Wednesday 6. A pretty day. Virginia and Jeanette Grant here this morn. I went with Cousin Mary Jarnagin and Mrs. Rumple and Col. Waters to have my ambrotype [picture] taken this eve. Lt. Simmons, Adj. Douglas, Surgeon Woods, Capt. Chewey and Lt. Cashan here this eve, also Nannie Kennedy and Mollie Dardis.

Thursday 7. A very, very windy day. I took dinner at Aunt Elizabeth's today. Lt. Simmons and Adj. Douglas, also Aunt Elizabeth and I went up to Mrs. Kennedy's this eve. We were joined there by Mother, Jimmie and Lizzie.

Friday 8. A cloudy, rainy, windy and gloomy day. Fast day appointed by President [Jefferson] Davis. I fasted. I copied off, "Home, what is it, what ought it to be?"

Saturday 9. A beautiful though windy day. Miss Nannie Kennedy, Sallie and Lizzie spent the day at Mrs. White's. I cleaned up Mother's room and Aunt Elizabeth's this morn.

Sunday 10. A pretty day. I wrote a letter to Sallie Shields this morn. Mattie Reynolds and Mrs. Hughes here this eve. Mattie's father and all the family are going to Nashville, Tenn. tomorrow.

Monday 11. A lovely day. I got dinner today. Emeline washed. I went up to see Mattie Smith this eve, told her good-bye. She and her father intend starting to Nashville tomorrow. Lt. Simmons called on me this eve. We exchanged, "Home, what it is and what it should be." Sgt. Douglass here this eve. We spoke of going down to see Sister.

Tuesday 12. Rained this morn. Surgeon Woods called on me this eve. I faced my petticoat this morn.

Wednesday 13. A pretty day. I went out to Aunt Elizabeth's this morn. Julia and Sallie Grant came down and spent the day. We commenced making Lizzie's dress. Nannie Kennedy came down and I spent the night with her. A picket base[10] was captured by our forces last night. Yanks excited.

Thursday 14. A pretty day. I went down to Aunt Elizabeth's this morn. Sewed on Lizzie's dress until about two. I came home, Aunt Elizabeth with me. We stopped at Mrs. McNelley's. I then went up to Cousin Mary Jarnagin's. There I met Col. Waters. Sgt. Douglass and Jimmie Smith here this eve. Sgt. came to see about going to Sister's tomorrow.

Friday 15. A lovely day. I prepared to go to see Sister but we could not go. Jeanette and Virginia Grant and Willie dined here. Lt. Riley and Surgeon Woods called here this eve, Miss Nannie and Mr. Kennedy, also Sgt. Douglass, to see if I would go to see Elvira Lea tomorrow.

---

[10] A picket base is a detachment of one or more soldiers advanced or held in readiness to give warning of enemy approach.

Saturday 16. A pretty day, but cold and windy and sometimes cloudy. Sgt. Douglass, Lizzie Lea and I went out in a buggy to Mr. Lea's. Lt. Trimble called this eve.

Sunday 17. A lovely morn. We are expecting a battle near Richmond soon. Both sides tremble for the result. Oh God, give us the victory, although neither of us deserve it, we are so wicked. Probably we will have a battle here in this department. How I long for the time to come when we will be free and see our friends once more. The Copperheads are rising and giving them some trouble. They had a fight a few weeks ago at Charleston, Illinois. This eve we were much excited; heard that Sister was at the lines and could not get in. We sent her a pass by Uncle Ned (a family slave), but it would not bring her. George and Pryor Lea and Sgt. Douglass here this eve.[11]

Monday 18. A pretty day. Mother and Sgt. Douglass went out this morn to Mrs. Simpson's and brought Sister, Rhoda, Annie and Johnnie and the baby in. We were all delighted. The baby, Rhoda Lea, is very pretty and sweet. Lt. Simmons called this eve to see Sister and family.

Tuesday 19. A pretty day. Lt. Simmons called this eve.

Wednesday 20. A pretty day. Surgeon Woods and three other Federals called on us this eve. Surgeon Woods gave me a copy of Shakespeare's plays. Rhoda, Annie and I went out to Uncle Caswell's and spent the night. Surgeon Woods says he wants to see me when the war is over. He says my opinions will have changed. Surgeon Woods says he would as soon think the heavens would fall as for us to gain our independence.

Thursday 21. A very windy eve. We remained at Aunt Elizabeth's until eve and then Aunt Elizabeth, Mrs. Kennedy and we went up to Dr. Grant's and remained a short time. Pryor came home with us.

Friday 22. A very windy eve. Julia and Virginia Grant and Mag Shadden here today. I wrote a little for Lt. today.

Saturday 23. A lovely day, very windy. Nannie Kennedy stayed all night here last night. She and Rhoda went up to Mr. McNutt's

---

[11]Copperheads was a contemporary term of reproach for those Democrats who were outspoken in their opposition to Abraham Lincoln's administration. It was also used to classify supporters of the Confederate cause.

this morn. A Yank fixed Sister's clock this morn. Surgeon Woods and Maj. Lefevre here this afternoon.

Sunday 24. A lovely day. I ate some walnuts this eve. Elvira Lea came home this eve. Woke me up from a pleasant nap. I got Rhoda to sleep three times today for the first time. I felt very proud.

Monday 25. A lovely day. I did not eat any breakfast this morn. Feel too unwell. Elvira went to Dr. Dodson's and had her teeth operated on this morn. I got dinner. Rhoda and Sister helped Emeline wash. Mr. Davis, William R. dined here. I feel so lonesome and blue this eve. Elvira went over to Mrs. DeLano's and stayed all night.

Tuesday 26. A pretty day. Elvira came back after dinner. Lt. Simmons here this eve. Elvira and I then went out and spent the night at Aunt Elizabeth's. I gave Lt. Simmons an answer at home.

Wednesday 27. A lovely day. Elvira left at 3 o'clock this eve. I was so sorry to have her go. Sister, Rhoda, Elvira and Jimmie all had their ambrotypes taken this eve. Rhoda and Lizzie went to the Baptist Church with Mr. Raymond tonight. Sgt. Douglass here this eve.

Thursday 28. A beautiful day. I went up to Cousin Mary Jarnagin's this eve. Annie and Lizzie Chambers stayed all night here. Mrs. Grant here this eve. They have Sister's case up in court, whether to send her off or not.

Friday 29. Rained this morn. I got up this morn and helped Sues get breakfast. Emeline is sick. Annie's 9th birthday. The Chambers left this morn. Lt. Simmons called this eve. I feel very, very blue this eve. I confided my whole heart to Rhoda. Inclination and duty is at war.

Saturday 30. A pretty eve. Lt. Simmons and Surgeon Woods here this eve. Lt. Simmons bade me "farewell," going on to fight our friends. God grant that he may be failed in his purpose. Emeline has a boy, born at 3 o'clock this morn. Lt. Simmons says that war will be terminated by this time next year, but he can't say how.[12]

---

[12]Lt. Simmons' statement was prophetic. The war ended, for the most part, with the surrender of Gen. Robert E. Lee to Gen. Ulysses S. Grant at Appomattox Courthouse on 9 April 1865.

May 1864

Sunday 1. May Day. How differently we spent our May Day to last May Day. We were then surrounded by our gallant southern friends; now we frown on our enemies. Julia Grant here this eve. Lt. Kirby and Capt. McNeely called on them here. Kentuckians.

Monday 2. Rained a little this morn. Lt. Simmons called on me this eve. He loves me. I dislike him. He is a Yank. He filled my heart with doubt as regards Gen. Johnston's success. I sewed a button on his coat for him. He bade me good-bye. Mr. McNutt and John Swan here this eve. Surgeon Woods called on Rhoda and me and bade us good-bye this eve. They are all ordered to march on our small, gallant, brave heroes. This eve late Rhoda and I took a letter up to Dr. Grant's from Mother and remained all night. We washed today.

Tuesday 3. A lovely day. Will I ever, can I ever, forget this day? Never, never. Our hearts all bowed down in grief. I am sitting at the parlor window. I hear the drums beating, the bands and fifes playing and ever and anon I let my eyes wander over the once beautiful country, I behold the foes marching and their guns and bayonets glistening in their onward march to desolate our country and rout our high spirited but downtrodden friends. I have (yes, we all have) mingled many a tear with our fervent prayers to God for our success. Fifteen thousand, they say, are to march from here. Whilst thousands are going from this vicinity, and thousands are to flank our poor boys; God have mercy on their souls. If it is Thy good pleasure,let us be caused to rejoice at Thy interposition in our behalf; let our enemy be totally routed, driven back, and their baggage captured from them. Let Lee in Virginia achieve a glorious victory over Grant. Let peace soon dawn on us and we be made to rejoice and praise God for giving us victories and causing us to establish our independence. Humble the hearts of all the people in the Southern States; cause them to feel that with Thy help alone we can gain the battle and establish our independence. Oh, our Father! Give us the victory if it is Thy will. I feel that it is our sins alone that will prevent us from being the victors. Watch over and guard and protect our friends in this coming struggle. Save the souls of those whose lot it is to fall in the impending battle. Sherman is marching on Gen. Johnston with an army of one hundred and fifty thousand strong. Such an army has never been mustered in these United States. We wish and tremble for the result. A few weeks will decide it. Sgt. Douglass came and told us good-bye. Thousands of cavalry have passed here this morn, going on, on to kill our beloved friends. Rhoda and I came around by Aunt Elizabeth's with Julia Grant. Uncle Caswell has no hope for our success. Aunt Elizabeth here this eve. Mrs. Mary Rumple and Cousin Mary Jarnagin here a while after tea. We finished the ironing today.

Wednesday 4. A lovely day. This eve Rhoda and I went over to Mary Edwards'. Callie Swan was there. We went out home with her and remained to tea. Nannie Kennedy came over. We talked over our hopes and fears in regard to the coming battle. Oh, our Father! Be with our poor soldiers, nerve their arms to strike our freedom. Grant that we may soon see our dear, dear friends. Sister, Rhoda and I fasted today. Mr. Knabe had a concert in town tonight. Two settlers took tea and stayed all night here. Gen. Schofield's[13] staff took tea here, three in number.

Thursday 5. A pretty day. Those five gentlemen breakfasted here. We have concluded not to board them. We have taken two other settlers[14] to board with us; they dined here. A Mr. Page and a Mr. Crocker. Mrs. Russell and Uncle Caswell here this eve. I feel so lonely this eve. We can hear nothing from the front officially. No regular engagement, however, as yet. The suspense we are in. If we are only successful. There is not an hour in the day that I do not pray to our Heavenly Father for our success and the protection of our friends whose mission it is to face Sherman's terrible army of rag jackals, ground hogs, etc. I feel sad, gloomy, depressed, heart sick when I picture the battlefield and the terrible carnage that is soon to ensue. If I could only be there to lend a feeble hand but stout heart to the assistance of our brave heroes whose lot it will be to fall pierced by the balls of our unfeeling, relentless foe. I do not think about Gen. Lee's army very much as Gen. Johnston's is so much nearer home and our interest is in this army more than our brave

---

[13] General John M. Schofield.

[14] Settlers were those who followed an army and sold provisions or liquor.

and gallant Gen. Lee's. Two more men have come to tea and to lodge for the night.

Friday 6. A lovely day. Those two gentlemen left this morn, one before and one after dinner. I went out to Aunt Elizabeth's and got some hop yeast this eve. Mr. Page left on the [train] cars before tea. Rhoda and Lizzie went to church with Mr. Kennedy's family.

Saturday 7. A lovely day but rather warm this eve. Sue and I wiped up the floors this eve. Three commissariats[15] are boarding here. Three took tea. Two remained all night. We do our own work. Rhoda is the main cook; I am the chambermaid; Mother acts as housekeeper, whilst Sister performs sundry duties. It fatigues us a great deal as we are not accustomed to it.

Sunday 8. A pretty day. One of our new boarders breakfasted here. Three dined. Sister, Mother, Rhoda, Lizzie, Annie, Jimmie and Alice Pickens and Mr. Crocker went up to the graveyard this eve. I have been thinking of poor old Aunt Phoebe this eve. Sometimes I feel as if it were almost cruel she died. I am in hopes that she is better off than if she were in the wicked and troublesome world. Mr. Robinson left this morn. Capt. T _____ and his clerk dined here. The clerk took tea here. Mr. and Mrs. Kennedy and Sallie took tea here.

Monday 9. Mr. Page came back this morn in time for breakfast. Sister, Rhoda and Sues washed this morn. Lizzie and I got dinner. A warm day. Lizzie Lea and Annie came in this eve for Annie's clothes. They took tea and went back.

Tuesday 10. A pretty day; rained this morn. We baked some biscuits for some soldiers this morn. Mr. Crocker sent us some soap and mustard this morn. Sister and Rhoda went out to Aunt Elizabeth's this morn.

Wednesday 11. A sad, gloomy and cloudy day. It is disagreeably cold this eve. They have been fighting ever since Saturday. It is still undecided. Oh! our poor soldiers, how many are suffering. Give us the victory, our Father, if it is Thy will. Capt. Hending and his clerk dined here. Capt. took breakfast and remained all night last night. We heard this eve that yesterday the Federals drove our forces back

---

[15] Commissariats are officers in charge of supplying food and supplies for the troops

and captured a great deal from them and Gen. Johnston drove their left wing back four miles. Our poor, poor, suffering soldiers. God is alone able to save us. Be with our suffering soldiers, and raise up our friends to alleviate their pains and administer to their wants. If I could only be there to wait on them. I feel unusually sad this eve, and you, old journal, are the friend that I will confide in.

Thursday 12. Rather cold this morn. The woods are green and beautiful; our roses are in bloom. I feel so sad when I think probably they will fade and none of our Confederates see them. I would be so happy if I could only see them or if I even thought I would have the pleasure of presenting my sweetheart with a bouquet. Julia, Jeanette Grant and Mag Shadden here this eve. Report says that a raid of our Confederates is coming. Welcome, brave heroes, to the land of your nativity! Thrice welcome, stalwart sons of freedom!

Friday 13. A pleasant day. Mr. Crocker here nearly all eve playing backgammon. Sues and I scoured up the hall and the two porches and around carpets in the front room, dining, and Sister's room this morn. This evening I feel so sad, when I think of the awful carnage that is now going on at Richmond, Va. and Dalton, Ga. They have had desperate fighting near Richmond, beginning last Thursday and still continuing, from what I can learn. Lee, our Garibaldi of the South, is holding Grant at bay very well. If they can obtain Richmond and Atlanta, they will wade through blood to get there. God grant that they may be foiled in the attempt, but not our will but Thine be done. No news from the front at Dalton. God preserve our brave heroes and let them achieve a great victory. The reports are so contradictory that I rarely ever attempt to publish any war news.

Saturday 14. A lovely day. Julia and Sallie Grant stayed all night here. Mr. Crocker and Mr. Milligan were in the parlor after tea. We had a nice eggnog and quite a debate on the war. Mr. Crocker said he thought, this eve in Sister's room, that the Confederacy would go by the board in two months. Mrs. White was here this morn. She also remarked that she thought the Confederacy was on its last leg. After tea, Julia, Sallie and I went up to Mrs. Long's for a while.

Sunday 15. A bright, lovely and beautiful morn. Sister and Mother are both sick this morn from eating eggnog last eve. Julia and Sallie Grant went home early this morn. I feel both sick and tired of this automaton existence[16] I am leading now. We hear all kinds of reports relative to Lee's army. The news is rife that his army is completely routed and driven back to Richmond. We can hear nothing from Johnston's army. Our only Creator and Preserver, assist and nerve them to repulse the foe. Annie, Jimmie and I helped in the pasture tonight as Mother, Sister and Johnnie are all sick.

Monday 16. A lovely day. Sister, Rhoda and Sues washed; Lizzie and I got dinner. Mr. Crocker sent to Dalton this morn. Heard this morn that our brave and noble chieftain Longstreet was dead; died from a wound in the neck received at the Richmond battle. Heard this morn that the bridges at Strawberry Plains, Jefferson County, Tenn. and Loudon, Tenn. were burned by the Rebels. Mr. Crocker came from Dalton and brought me a bouquet that came from Gen. Johnston's headquarters, also a letter. Old Uncle Joe Hatcher died.

Tuesday 17. A lovely day. Nothing of importance occurred today. Our boarders left this morn, Mr. Milligan and Capt. Hending. Uncle Ned is sick.

Wednesday 18. A pretty day. Rhoda and I went over to Mrs. Grant's this eve. We feel very much encouraged with the news. Uncle Ned is very sick. We hardly think he will live. About 12 o' clock last night we were sent for by Emeline; he was delirious from pain. We sent for Dr. Long and we remained up for the rest of the night.

Thursday 19. A lovely day. Rhoda and I went over to Mrs. Grant's this eve. We are rather low-spirited this eve; heard that Johnston was still retreating. Uncle Ned is some better today. We sent for Mr. Daily and Mr. Campbell and made his will this morn.

Friday 20. A pretty day. Uncle Ned is still better. We think probably he will get well. Aunt Elizabeth here this eve.

Saturday 21. A lovely day. Uncle Ned is no better than yesterday. I spent the eve in rubbing the spoons, scouring the knives and forks.

Sunday 22. A pretty day. Mr. Crocker spent all the forenoon here. Mrs. Kennedy here this eve. I went up to Cousin Mary Jarnagin's this eve.

---

[16]Automation here means one that behaves in an automatic or mehanical fashion. Perhaps Myra felt that she was just going through the motions of living rather than enjoying life anymore.

Monday 23. A pretty day. Rhoda and I are sick today. Sister and Sues washed today. I got breakfast. After tea I played backgammon with Mr. Crocker. He and Mr. Walsh have a room.

Tuesday 24. A pretty day. Sister and I baked some sweet cakes this eve. Mr. Crocker and I played backgammon after tea. Rhoda is quite sick with flux. Rained this eve.

Wednesday 25. A lovely day. Julia and Virginia Grant here this morn. Uncle Ned is better. Mother is sick in bed. Mother sent for Dr. Thompson for Rhoda this eve. Invited to a soiree and promenade[17] this eve at the Peters' place. Mr. Crocker and I went to the soiree tonight. Jimmie started to school for the first time this morn to Miss Nannie Kennedy. He and Ann board at Aunt Elizabeth's.

Thursday 26. A pretty day. Rhoda is no better. Rained this morn. Mr. Crocker rose early this morn in obedience to Sister's command.

Friday 27. A pretty day. Aunt Elizabeth and Mrs. Kennedy here this eve. Adelia Craigmiles here this morn.

Saturday 28. A pretty day. I finished a letter to F.B.? and Mrs. Crocker.

Sunday 29. A pretty day. Mr. Crocker and Mr. Walsh left this eve on the 3:30 o'clock train for Chattanooga. We regretted seeing them leave. Mr. Kennedy and Uncle Caswell here this eve.

Monday 30. A lovely day. Sister and I helped Emeline wash this morn. Aunt Elizabeth and Mrs. Russell here this morn. Rhoda was taken suddenly worse this eve. We were very much alarmed about her. Cousin Mary Harle came over and we applied poultices to her bowels and it relieved her very soon.

Tuesday 31. A pretty but very warm day. Aunt Elizabeth spent the day here. Sister took the baby and went out and spent the night at Aunt Elizabeth's. Rhoda is better. Mrs. Edwards, Cousin Mary Harle, Mrs. William Craigmiles, Anna Grant, Callie Swan, Mary Edwards, Nannie Kennedy and Mrs. Grant here today; also Sallie Grant and Millie Dement.

---

[17] A promenade is a formal ball or dance.

June 1864

Wednesday 1. A pretty day. Sister remained out all day at Aunt Elizabeth's. Annie is out there sick. Rhoda is better. Mr. Crocker came this morn from Chattanooga. Cut me out two nightgowns this morn.

Thursday 2. A pretty day. Mr. Crocker and I went up to Mrs. Rumple's after tea. Have been making a nightgown today.

Friday 3. A pretty day. Rhoda is still improving. She walked in the hall this morn.

Saturday 4. A lovely day. Julia and Sallie Grant here this eve. Mr. Crocker gave us all a photograph of his sister and I baked cakes this eve. Rained so this eve that Lizzie Lea stayed all night.

Sunday 5. A pretty day. Mary Edwards and Mrs. Britton here this eve. Curled my hair this eve and Mr. Crocker made a good deal of sport of me. He is such a tease.

Monday 6. A pretty day. Sister and I washed this morn. Julia Grant dined here. Mr. Crocker brought us down some nice pickles, canned tomatoes. We had some nice canned blackberries for dinner. Mr. Crocker and I went out to Uncle Caswell's this eve.

Tuesday 7. A pretty day. Mrs. Smith here this eve. Rained very hard this eve. I wrote a letter to Cousin John to send through to some exchanged prisoners.

Wednesday 8. A pretty day. Mr. Crocker and I went out to Dr. Grant's, Uncle Caswell's and Cousin Mary Jarnagin's this morn. He came home with a severe headache and laid down. Mr. Crocker left for Chattanooga this eve.

Thursday 9. A lovely day. I slept this morn and eve. I commenced me a nightgown this eve. They commenced fighting at Altoona Mount[18] last Sunday week, and are engaged everyday. Hundreds are being killed everyday, horrible thought. If we can only gain the victory.

Friday 10. Rained this eve. Sister, Rhoda, Johnnie and the baby spent the day at old Mrs. Carter's. I made Lizzie Lea an apron today. Between 75 and 100 wagons passed this morn en route for the front.

---

[18] Near Atlanta, Georgia.

Saturday 11. A rainy day. Julia and Mollie Grant spent the day here. I finished my nightgown this eve. The bell has just rung for tea, so goodnight, old journal.

Sunday 12. A cool morn. Sallie and Virginia Grant here this eve. Sarah Roberts sent over to borrow my riding habit. Such a piece of insolence I never heard the like.

Monday 13. A pretty day. We deferred washing this morn on account of rain, but it cleared off beautifully.

Tuesday 14. A pretty day. I got dinner. Sister and the rest washed. Rhoda and I went out to Aunt Elizabeth's and spent the night.

Wednesday 15. A lovely day. We went from Aunt Elizabeth's to Dr. Grant's and spent the day. Had new Irish potatoes and a spring chicken for dinner. Enjoyed myself very much. From there we went to Mr. Kennedy's and spent the night; Callie Swan also.

Thursday 16. A warm day. We went from Mr. Kennedy's to Mr. Robert Swan's and spent the day. Had nice new beets and peas for dinner. Julia and Virginia Grant came and we then went down to Aunt Elizabeth's from there to see Mattie Foute and then home. Found all well. I enjoyed the trip very much.

Friday 17. A pretty day. Sallie, Virginia and Jeanette Grant came by for me and we went out to Mr. Reeder's this morn. Ham Rossen went with us. Sallie and I, after going upstairs and taking an evening siesta, went up to Mr. Hardwick's and took tea. We came back to Mr. Reeder's, dusty and tired. After taking an evening ablution, we retired to bed. Rhoda, Sister and Callie Swan spent the day at Mr. Miller's. We had some such nice raspberries and cream for dinner, also beans.

Saturday 18. A pretty day, cloudy. We came back this morn; stopped a few minutes at Mrs. Emmet Johnson's. We had pickled pork, green apple pie and peas for dinner for the first time. We have enjoyed ourselves so much this week. Quite an excitement in town last eve caused by the Rebs coming very near town and picking up about 45 scouts. Rhoda gave Lizzie Lea and Annie a music lesson this morn. I gave them one this eve. I feel so lonely this eve. Little Rhoda is sick with a cold.

Sunday 19. A pretty day. I slept nearly all morn. I feel so lonely this eve. Mr. and Mrs. McNutt here this eve. A Dr. Smith came here to board this eve.

Monday 20. A pretty day. Sister and I helped Emeline wash this morn. I gave Annie a music lesson this eve. The Yanks are looking for Wheeler[19] in soon. I feel so, so lonesome this eve.

Tuesday 21. Some appearance of rain this morn. I feel so fretted this morn, it is wrong, I know. I wish I could tell you, my old friend journal, the source of my troubles, but for fear some truant might peer behind these leaves, I will desist. Mother and Sister intend attending a sale at Mr. Cruvey's this morn. Mrs. Craigmiles, Mattie Foute and Mollie Gallagher intend spending the day here. I cleaned up the house this morn; felt more like sitting down crying than anything else. Rhoda went down to see A.G. yesterday eve. She plays so well on the piano and we play so miserably. Mother could have let us take music lessons until we were proficient before the war, but now we have nothing. What little property we had is gone since the Yanks have come. These days are so sad. What selfish creatures we are. I am selfish, I know, but I try a little (very little, though, I am afraid) to master the passion. The old adage is that we keep our own faults behind us and those of our neighbors before us, but my faults are so numerous they will sometimes loom up before me. If I could only have more patience. This world has so many pleasures for some and so few for others. I find more pleasure this morn in writing in this complaining style than anything else. I cannot say it is "nursing my wrath to keep it warm." "All is well that ends well," and I think that sometimes I will peruse these pages and laugh at my folly and wish I could erase some of this sin, for I feel it is sinning to sigh and regret over things we cannot help. Is this not our day of adversity and will not prosperity dawn on us sometime? When I build air castles I picture them so different from what my real life is. Mattie Foute and Mrs. Craigmiles spent the day here. I enjoyed the day finely. This eve Mattie, Rhoda and I went in the parlor and played on the piano. Mrs. Traynor here this eve. Look for the Rebels in every day.

---

[19] General Joe Wheeler, CSA.

Wednesday 22. Rhoda and I took up the parlor carpet and sunned it today.

Thursday 23. I finished crocheting Annie some lace for pantalettes. Dr. Smith here this afternoon. Finished making Mag Shadden's tape points. Uncle Caswell dined here.

Friday 24. A very warm day. We shelled corn some, and then tacked down the parlor carpet this morn. This eve I washed and put on clean clothes and went to see Mary Edwards and then to Cousin Mary Jarnagin's and took tea with Miss Sallie Gamble. Lizzie went up to see Gussie Craigmiles and Sue Henderson this eve.

Saturday 25. A pretty day. Rhoda and I took up the carpets in the dining room and Sister's room. I washed all the windows and looking glasses this morn. Wiped up the porch floor and Sister's floor. Sister put a short dress on the baby for the first time this eve. Our plums, cherries and June apples are ripe. Miss Martha Hall stayed all night here tonight. Nannie Kennedy here this eve. Saturday eves are always so lonesome to me. Several families in Athens were arrested and sent off to Nashville for trial a few days ago. I would not be surprised if we were arrested soon.

Sunday 26. A very, very warm day. Nannie Kennedy, Julia and Virginia Grant and Pryor Lea here this eve. Dr. Lecher brought me a letter from Lt. A. Simmons this eve, written June 23. We had beans for dinner the first time.

Monday 27. A very, very warm day. Sister and I washed this morn. This eve I spooled some thread. A thundershower this eve. The Federals have Mr. McNutt arrested. They compelled him to sweep out the courtyard. Houston, if he had lived, would have been 14 years old today.

Tuesday 28. A very warm day. I spooled thread all morn. Have a boil on my leg that troubles me a good deal. Uncle Caswell here this morn. The Yanks took Mr. Pryor's beautiful little horse last Tuesday. If I could only see my dear cousins in the rebel army, Cousin John, Joe and Alfred Lea. Emeline is busy baking pies, bread and meat for the harvest hands tomorrow. They have been constantly fighting for 40 days, Johnston and Sherman; sometimes all night. Sister, the baby and Rhoda went out to Aunt Elizabeth's and stayed all night.

Wednesday 29. A pretty day. I answered Lt. A. Simmons letter this morn. Sewed on Johnnie's apron the remainder of the day.

Sister and Rhoda spent the day at Mr. Robert Swan's. I felt so lonely this eve, and not only this eve but all the time. If my dear friends were only here.

Thursday 30. A very warm day. Dr. Dwyre and Chaplain Spence commenced boarding here this noon. Sewed on Johnnie's aprons all day. Mag Shadden, Sue Rowan and Ada Anderson here this eve. Sister went up to Dr. Grant's to see how to make Blanc Mange.[20]

July 1864

Friday 1. A warm day. Sewed on Johnnie's apron today. My boil troubles me a great deal. We had cucumbers for dinner for the first time. Mother put her loom up in the porch this eve.

Saturday 2. A warm day. I finished Johnnie's three aprons. After tea we went in the parlor and played for our boarders. We received a letter from Mr. Crocker that he is coming up tomorrow.

Sunday 3. A very pleasant day; rained this eve. Mr. Crocker came this morn. We were glad to see him. Brought us three calico dresses, box of hairpins and two pairs of kid gloves.

Monday 4. The fourth day of July. The Federals fired a salute of thirteen cannons before breakfast. At noon 35 are having a celebration. We are invited to a ball at Mr. Farroe Callaway's tonight. Mr. Crocker and Rhoda went out to Aunt Elizabeth's this morn. Mr. Crocker went down to Chattanooga this eve. I feel so lonely this eve, having no particular work to do. Uncle Caswell, Mr. and Mrs. Simpson dined here. Had beets for dinner; first mess. A pleasant day. Sister and Rhoda came back from Cousin Mary Harle's and told us sad news. Mattie Smith died in Edgefield last Saturday morn at 6 o'clock with cholera. Capt. Peak is dead also. I feel afraid to hear from our friends in Dixie. I fear some of them have gone to their last homes. Rhoda and I played for our boarders after tea.

---

[20]Blanc Mange is a flavored and sweet milk pudding thickened with corn starch.

Tuesday 5. Rhoda and I helped wash. I did sundry little jobs. I spent a miserable night last night. A rat got in Sister's and my bed in the night. We moved our boarders into the other room across the hall and passed the remainder of the night. I feel unusually depressed and low spirited today. Mattie Foute stayed with us tonight. Why was it God took my classmate, Mattie, and left me? When she was so loved and will be so missed. Her poor little babe, how she will miss her mother. Was it to warn me to be ready, too, that she was taken? It should teach me a lesson. Be ye also ready, for in an hour when ye know not the Son of Man cometh. A warm day.

Wednesday 6. A pretty day. I feel unusually sad this morn. Mattie went home this morn. Uncle Caswell here this morn. Said the Provost Marshal was inquiring who the Miss Inmans were. Aunt Elizabeth here this eve. Cleo Watkins, Nannie Kennedy and Aunt Elizabeth took tea here. I went out and stayed all night at Aunt Elizabeth's. Mr. Spence went to Knoxville this morn. I feel very, very gloomy this eve.

Thursday 7. A warm day. Aunt Elizabeth and I went up to Mrs. Kennedy's and stayed awhile. I came home this eve and found Julia and Sallie Grant here. They took tea.

Friday 8. A warm day. Mrs. Shadden here this eve. Cousin Mary Jarnagin came down this eve in a tremendous state of excitement and informed us that she was ordered to report to Gen. Steedman at Chattanooga Monday; that all the Rebel sympathizers were to be separated from their homes, sent North, or either sent down the Mississippi River. Chaplain Spence returned this eve, perfectly elated with the news that Atlanta had fallen. I feel very miserable this eve, but had to stifle back my tears and play backgammon with Dr. Dwyre.

Saturday 9. A warm day. Uncle Caswell dined here. He is ordered to Chattanooga. Mollie Grant and Julia Grant came this morn; they are in a great deal of trouble in consequence of being notified to report to Chattanooga. We are making some new calico dresses in case we have to desert our homes. The order was read to us by a sergeant in the dining room just as tea was ready, stating that all Rebel sympathizers had to report at Chattanooga Monday. Through the assistance of Chaplain Spence we have been released. How sad I feel to think even if we are permitted to stay our friends will go, and we cannot even bid them farewell or else we will be accused of sympathizing with them and plotting against the government and be sent off without a thing in the world. Cousin E. McCallie here after tea, she and Cousin Mary Jarnagin.

Sunday 10. Rhoda and I went to church to hear Chaplain Spence preach. Rained this eve. Dr. Dwyre and Chaplain Spence stayed nearly all eve. We retired to rest early this eve.

Monday 11. We had an early start and finished our washing by 9 o'clock. No one left for Chattanooga this eve. Mr. Smith here this eve. Received a letter from Sallie Shields this eve. Mr. Swan's folks reported at the depot but were sent home.

Tuesday 12. A warm day. Cousin Ellen and little Mary spent the day here. Chaplain Spence started north this eve. I played backgammon with Dr. Dwyre until nearly eleven o'clock tonight. I am so uneasy for fear something will recur to make me burn or lose my journals.

Wednesday 13. A warm day. Mr. William Campbell here to get Sister to take the oath this morn, also this eve to tell us that Uncle Caswell was ordered to report to Chattanooga tomorrow. Uncle Caswell came in and took tea this eve.

Thursday 14. A warm day. We baked some cake for Uncle Caswell this morn. Uncle Caswell, Dr. Dwyre, Julia, Sallie, Virginia, Mattie, Jeanette Grant, three McGriff girls, Mr. Reeder, Hardwick, Mr. Hartley and son went down to Chattanooga on train this eve. Rhoda went out and spent the night with Aunt Elizabeth. Mrs. Grant and Mary here after tea.

Friday 15. A warm day. Cousin Ellen was telegraphed to this eve to come home, that they were ordered north Saturday. Uncle Caswell wrote back they were all released except the McGriffs. I feel very, very lonely this eve. But what eve is it I do not feel lonely; if I were to write an everyday life it would be one repetition of the blues.

Saturday 16. A pretty day. Uncle Caswell and all except the Misses McGriffs were released. Aunt Elizabeth, Uncle Caswell and Lizzie dined here and took tea. Pryor took tea. Dr. Dwyer brought his mockingbirds last eve.

Sunday 17. A pleasant day. I went to sleep this morn. Dr. Dwyer went to Tyner's station[21] this eve, coming back tomorrow. Lt. Trimble called on me this eve. Read in a paper where the [Clement L.] Vallandigham men had chosen their standard for the Northwestern Confederacy.

Monday 18. What will I record in these pages? No one but our Heavenly Father can tell. We washed this morn. Emeline cooked. Dr. Dwyer brought two more mockingbirds this eve. Mrs. Shadden here after tea. We went in the parlor this eve and we played. A soldier came in and Rhoda played for him. I retired to rest. A beautiful moonshiny night. After I blew out the candle I opened the window blinds and let the rays of the brilliant moon stream across the floor. Uncle Caswell went to Chattanooga this eve.

Tuesday 19. A pretty day. I finished Sues a cotton dress this eve. Cousin Mary Jarnagin here this eve. We retire to rest very early these nights if we have no company to entertain. Heard yesterday afternoon that Petersburg was taken.

Wednesday 20. A very cool and pleasant morn. It is reported that several thousand cavalry are to be encamped here, coming from the front. I have just finished cleaning up the house. If my friends were only here; there is not an hour in the day that I do not think of them. The brass band belonging to the 2nd Ohio Heavy Artillery plays every evening at the Raht House on the hill. I like to hear it, yet it makes me very, very sad. I hear it now playing in the distance. After Rhoda and I go to bed in our snug little domicile, we hear them beat the tattoo [a call on a drum shortly before taps]. After that dies away the sound of the bugle pierces our ears. When the last blast is heard all is still for the night, and we sink to rest with a heavy heart amid fortifications and cannon ready to deal deadly missiles among our hearts' idols who are banished and exiled from their homes. I commenced stitching some collars this morn.

Thursday 21. Rained a heavy shower this eve. Eliza Keebler here this eve. Been making us some plain linen collars. I played backgammon with Dr. Dwyer this eve until late.

Friday 22. Today has been very pleasant; more like fall than summer, cool winds. Aunt Myra died this morn. Sallie Surguine here

---

[21] Tyner's Station is located nine miles east of Chattanooga.

this eve. Sister went with Dr. Dwyer to the Provost Marshal's to get a pass for Annie and Jimmie to go to school. Rhoda and I went up to Mrs. Carter's, Trewhitt's and Dr. Thompson's this eve. Persons are required to have street passes. We were advised by some friends not to visit Southern families, that we are watched by secret policemen.

Saturday 23. A cool and pleasant day. Sister spent the day at Mrs. Carter's today and stayed all night. Mrs. Shadden has typhoid fever. Rhoda and I went up to see Sallie Surguine this morn. She and Rhoda swapped dresses. Aunt Myra was buried this eve. I received a letter from Surgeon Woods this eve.

Sunday 24. A pleasant day. I wrote a letter to Sallie Shields this eve. Received one from her yesterday eve through her father who is here with Hester Henderson's children. Hetty [Hester] died last Monday. Lt. Burke here this eve with Dr. Dwyer to see the birds. Mother and I went up to see Mrs. Shadden this eve.

Monday 25. A pretty day. We washed this morn. Sister went up and stayed all night with Mrs. Shadden. Capt. Gifford and Sue Henderson called on us this eve. I went up to Cousin Mary Jarnagin's this eve. Mr. Shields here to see us.

Tuesday 26. A lovely day. Cousin Mary Harle, Mr. Sutherland, Lt. Burke and Mr. Kennedy here this afternoon.

Wednesday 27. Rainy and cloudy morn. Rained some this afternoon. The sun shone also. I finished stitching our collars this eve. Nannie Woods here this eve. A Southern man cannot live over at Georgetown.[22] They are hung nearly every night; their houses robbed and they are compelled to lie out at night.

Thursday 28. A pleasant day; rained a light shower this eve. We scaled[23] this morn in Sister's room. Mrs. Kennedy, Miss Leony Garnold, Julia and Sallie Grant spent the day here. Uncle Caswell and Cousin Merill Witt dined here. Chaplain Spence came back from Cincinnati, Ohio this morn.

Friday 29. A pretty day. Aunt Elizabeth and Mrs. Morrison came in this morn. I went with Mrs. Morrison down to Mrs. McMillin's to see Aunt Wood and to see Mrs. Shadden. She is very low with typhoid fever. After the rain this eve, Sister and I went over near the

---

[22] In Bradley County, seven miles northeast of Cleveland.

[23] Practicing scales on the piano.

steam mill [near the depot] to see some poor sick refugees. Took them some meal and a can of beef soup. We then stopped at Mrs. William Grant's. Lincoln has called for 500,000 more men. The opinion is they are needed to suppress the Copperheads.

Saturday 30. A warm day. Mother is sick this eve. I wrote a letter to Surgeon Woods and Lt. A. Simmons this morn.

Sunday 31. A warm day. Col. Gibson's 2nd Ohio Heavy Artillery had grand inspection in Uncle Caswell's field this morn. How vain they looked with their flaming sashes, brass buttons, flashy red side stripes and glistening bayonets, but the nerve of these ones United States was not there; no, it is in Atlanta, clothed in dirty grey and dingy shoes. They are the ones that can try steel with steel. These are the band-box soldiers. Wrangling with the clear peals of the church bell was the distant roar of the drum, one calling the worshipers of God to the sanctuary, the other waking the soldier up from his lazy resting place and calling him to the place of assemblage before going to inspection. Rhoda and Lizzie went to church this morn. Sister went up to see Mrs. Shadden.

August 1864

Monday 1. A cool, pleasant day. Lizzie and I, with the assistance of two of the hostlers [24]at the livery stable trimmed up the rose bushes and cut the grass down in the yard. I feel very tired this eve. Rhoda and I wondered what we could be doing this day next year.

Tuesday 2. A pretty day. We washed today. I feel very sore this morn from my yesterday's work. Julia Grant here this morn.

Wednesday 3. A lovely day, cool night. Gen. Steedman ordered all the men to board within the fortifications. They have moved their headquarters from the Raht House. Chaplain Spence and Dr. Dwyer stayed here tonight. Sister, Rhoda and I went this eve to the Daguerrean Gallery. Rhoda and I had our ambrotypes taken.

---

[24]A holster is one who takes care of horses at livery stables.

Thursday 4. A pretty day. I made Cousin Mary Harle's dress sleeves this morn, needleworked on Lizzie Lea's pantalettes this eve. Dr. Dwyer stayed all night here.

Friday 5. Rained very hard just before day. I feel sad and gloomy this morn. I remarked to Rhoda this morn when were dressing how happy I would feel if we could never hear the drum beat anymore, calling the soldiers to their tasks. How long, our God, will this war continue, until we are all destroyed? I fear it is torture. I walked out home with Julia Grant; came back just after tea.

Saturday 6. A lovely morn. This eve quite a hard rain accompanied by thunder and lightning. Night closed around with her sable mantles [covering] whilst ever anon we hear the pattering rain singing a quiet and lonely requiem for the departed day. I feel sad and lonely this eve. Why is it? Oh pen, canst thou not tell? No! for thy controller dost not know herself, in order to wield thee to write an answer. Dr. Dwyer left this eve on a leave of absence for 20 days for his home in New Petersburg, Highland County, Ohio. Chaplain Spence left this morn for Charleston, Tennessee. Rhoda and I went over to Mrs. Grant's this eve. Adelia Craigmiles has a girl, born last eve. Mother has spent a good portion of the day looking for her calf.

Sunday 7. A lovely morn. We were awakened in the night by the ringing of the church bell, caused by the burning of Mr. Gallaher's dwelling house. They saved very few things. Aunt Elizabeth, Lizzie and Pryor came in and all except me went to church. They dined here. Pryor and I ate some peaches and grapes; they are ripening. Mother and Lizzie went over to see Tommie Grant this eve. Sister and Rhoda went up to see Mrs. Traynor.

Monday 8. A pretty day. We washed this morn. Cousin Tom Lea here this eve. Read us a letter from Missouri, written by Cousin Esther Ann. Cousin Julia died last winter. She informed us of the prison at Kansas City, where Cousin Julia was at one time confined a month, being undermined and blown up. All the ladies that were prisoners were either killed or crippled for life. One of her acquaintances was killed. They entreated the Federals to let them out, but their reply was, "Your friends will take care of you." Uncle Alfred and family were ordered to leave home and move to some military post at 8 o'clock.

Tuesday 9. Rained this eve. About 9 o'clock tonight we felt and heard an earthquake. Emeline went up and ironed for Mrs. Trewhitt today. We have been busy making Cousin Mary, Phoebe and Lucy some dresses. Rhoda sold her muslin robe this eve for $10. Sister bought Mother a calico dress yesterday eve and Lizzie a hoop skirt.

Wednesday 10. A pretty day. We have been busy making Bettie's and Lucy's dresses. Uncle Ned sent us in a piece of watermelon this eve. After tea Sister and Lizzie went up to Cousin Mary Jarnagin's.

Thursday 11. A pretty day. I went up this eve to [see] Callie Callaway at Mr. Farroe Callaway's. Rhoda and I stayed all night at Uncle Caswell's tonight. Quite an excitement in regard to Mr. Low whipping a Negro for stealing.

Friday 12. A pretty day. Mrs. Craigmiles and Mrs. Miller here this morn. I have been busy making a bonnet for Mrs. Gallaher. Elvira dined here on her way to her Aunt Susan's. Our wheat is all spread out on the floors to rid it of weevils. Chaplain Spence dined here. The baby has a tooth.

Saturday 13. Cloudy morn. Rhoda sat up last night at Mrs. Grant's. Tommie died at 4 o'clock this morn. I have just finished reading an account of the terrible assault at Petersburg, Virginia, on the 30th day of July, where one of our forts was undermined and blown up by eight tons of powder, but they were desperately defeated by our gallant men. The 22nd South Carolina Regiment was blown to atoms; very few escaped. The Yankees are very much dispirited on account of the Stoneman and Petersburg reverse and the disturbed affairs in the Northwest, but how's it with us? Jubilant, joyful and full of hope and confidence that God is our ruler and will overrule this struggle for independence, for our good. I feel gloomy this morn, not with regard to our nation particularly, but home affairs and domestic matters. I went over to Mrs. Grant's this morn. Cynthia Hardwick, Callie Swan, Andy Russell, Mary Edwards, Laura Stout and I sat up at Mrs. Grant's tonight with Tommie's corpse.

Sunday 14. Rained this morn; very hard rain this eve. I slept three hours this morn. Chaplain Spence dined here. Rhoda and Sister went to church. Lizzie and I intended going to the burying, but it rained. Mary Edwards and I stopped at Mrs. Hardwick's. John

Campbell and Mag Shadden here this eve. We had peaches for dinner. The baby has another tooth.

Monday 15. Rained today. We washed this morn. Uncle Caswell and the boys fanned out our wheat and put it in [a] hogshead[25] this morn. Chaplain Spence dined here; brought us two watermelons. Looking for the Rebels every minute. News is that they have captured Dalton and Athens.

Tuesday 16. We were awakened last night at 1 o'clock from our slumbers, by the hurrying to and fro of army wagons, horses, men, etc., caused by an alarm given that the Confederates were coming. Rhoda arose, dressed. We all packed some few clothes to take in case we were ordered out of town. About 4 o'clock we all dressed, put on our bonnets and ate a little cold breakfast and were ready to start to the country when the first gun was fired. Cousin Martha Howell and a Mr. Norris and Uncle Caswell dined here. I received a letter from Lt. A. Simmons, in answer to two I had written him. It was rather caustic and bitter. Rhoda says it made her feel very blue. I will acknowledge I felt rather pikered and sad after I read it. Cousin John's 24th birthday.

Wednesday 17. Rhoda and I took up the dining room carpet this morn. I am so sad this morn about this war. Rhoda has just remarked that she is the saddest creature in the world, the most miserable. I told her something about—that Callie Swan had said; she has been sad ever since. We sunned our winter clothes today. I wonder if we will not feel more cheerful when winter comes. Chaplain Spence repeats to us often, "Do good and ye shall be happy." That is so, if we would only yield up this world and think and prepare for the future, but we are too sinful. I take no pleasure in anything; the world looks dark to me. This is a sad journal for a girl out of nineteen to write. It is sinful for me to be wearing and fretting my life out about my friends. I should improve these golden moments and turn them to some good and wise account. Sadness seems stamped on everything to me. At noon the alarm was given that "The Rebels were coming." We were eating when the first cannon fired. We all fled to the cellar, leaving the table just as it was. We then concluded it was not safe even there and we left (all except

---

[25] A large barrel or cask with the capacity of about sixty-three gallons.

Sister, baby, Mother and Aunt Elizabeth) and went to Mr. Reeder's. Hundreds of persons joined us (with bundles) in our march for the country. We went to Mr. Reeder's and stayed all night. In due time Mother and the rest joined us there. I will always remember the night. Between 40 and 50 persons were there and nearly as many Negroes. The children and the grown people lying stretched on the bare floor. I was ensconced in a large feather bed where I nearly suffocated from heat. Mrs. Col. Gibson and I went out on the veranda at 2 o'clock and not a breeze was stirring; there was not a quiver of the leaves. The full moon rose majestically, yet sadly to me, through the clear with vapory clouds. Silence reigned in the direction of our lonely and deserted homes. Not more than half a dozen families remained at home. Occasionally we could hear the booming of cannon firing from the fort of the Confederates, who were peering at them saucily from the woods beyond the fairground. They tore up the railroad and left about dark. I felt considerably disappointed; was in hopes they were going to pay us a visit of two or three days and we could get to see all our friends. We heard the Bradley boys were along. Mrs. Col. Edwards' family, Mrs. O'Neil's, Mrs. Sample's, Mrs. Ware's, Mrs. Col. Gibson's, Sue Henderson's mother, Mrs. Williams and Mrs Walker, also Mrs. Capt. Grant stayed all night at Mrs. Reeder's. Aunt Elizabeth stayed at Mr. Hardwick's.

Thursday 18. A warm day. Lizzie and I came in town this morn. We stopped at Mrs. Emmet Johnson's and there saw Mrs. McGriff and Mrs. Alex Davis. Just as we unlocked the doors at home three cannon fired. We hurried and gathered up a few things and beat a hasty retreat in the direction of Mrs. Johnson's. When we got to Mrs. Howard's we saw them moving the hospitals and we then went to Aunt Elizabeth's where we took dinner. Mother came out in the afternoon and we came home. The rest of the family arrived in due season, when we retired to rest. We felt very much jaded and worn out.

Friday 19. A warm day. Pryor's 18th birthday. I needleworked on Lizzie Lea's pantalettes; finished them.

Saturday 20. A pretty day. Sewed some on Lizzie Lea's dress, cut me off a bustle to hem, helped make a nightgown for the baby. We sent two trunks of clothes down to Mrs. Lea's by Cousin Tom. Rained very hard about dark.

Sunday 21. A rainy day. Elvira came up from Mr. Callaway's this morn, went down home this eve. Mr. Kennedy dined here. Elvira told us all about seeing the Confederates, Cousin John Lea, Capt.___, Dr. Goodman, Lt. Maples. They are en route to Knoxville to make junction with Longstreet. Cousin Mary Harle here this eve. Uncle Caswell's 62nd birthday.

Monday 22. A pretty day. I started to help wash this morn and tore part of my fingernail off with the washboard and quit. Little Rhoda is sick, teething. Read the rest of the day *Rob Roy.*

Tuesday 23. A pretty day. Read in *Rob Roy* this morn. Spooled thread the rest of the day. Sallie Reeder and Mollie Dardis here this eve. Nannie Kennedy stayed all night with us. I slept with Johnnie in Sister's room. The baby and Johnnie were sick. Great excitement in town; the streets full of troops going to capture Wheeler's forces. Chaplain Spence [here] after tea. His regiment went up this eve.

Wednesday 24. A pretty day. Finished spooling thread this morn. Sgt. Douglass took tea and spent most of the afternoon and evening here.

Thursday 25. A rather warm day. I finished reading *Rob Roy* this morn. Bound Sister's, Rhoda and my dresses with braid this eve. Mag Shadden, Sallie Surguine and Mrs. Dr. Edwards here this eve. Mrs. Reynolds sent for Mattie's ambrotype this eve.

Friday 26. This is Monday and it has been sometime since I recorded the few events that have occurred in my life drama. This Friday morn I went up to Mrs. Shadden's and Cousin Mary Jarnagin's. I have the headache. Mother put a piece of cloth in loom this eve. Sgt. Douglass here this eve. We sang some pieces in the "Jubilee."

Saturday 27. A pretty day. Mrs. Smith's little girl Lilly and Windsor dined here. I went to the Daguerrean Gallery with them. I then went over to see Mrs. William Grant. Sgt. Douglass and Aunt Elizabeth took tea here. Lizzie went out to see Mary Smith this eve; will remain with her until Monday.

Sunday 28. A pretty day. I went nowhere today. Sgt. Douglass and Pryor Lea dined here and spent the afternoon here. Mrs. Miller and Martha Hall here this eve. The town in confusion; soldiers parading the streets in search of supper. We fed seven. Just returned from an unsuccessful chase after Wheeler.

Monday 29. A pretty day. We deferred washing on account of much cooking to do. Fed nine soldiers at breakfast; gathered tomatoes to sell them. This eve I worked on Elvira's collar.

Tuesday 30. A pretty day. Callie Callaway came up this morn for me to [go] down home with her. Sgt. Douglass brought me in a frame he made. He dined, took tea here and remained all night. Callie and I went around shopping this eve. I enjoyed the day very much although I have felt a little blue at times. We washed this morn.

Wednesday 31. A pleasant day. Sgt. Douglass took tea here. We repaired the frame this morn. After I arose this morn I felt very blue. I cannot tell why, probably because Mother is not exactly willing that I should go to Mr. Callaway's. Mrs. Harris and Anna here this eve, also two Federal soldiers here this afternoon. Mrs. Eliza Woods and her husband here to hear us play after tea. It is now about ten o'clock at night. Callie and I have both undressed. She is sitting at the piano playing. I am sitting at the table with my old friend journal in my lap to entrust to his kind care the events that have occurred since we last met. I will now close these sacred pages (sacred to my eyes alone, for no one has the same friendship with them that I have, its guardian) and read a chapter in the Bible and consign myself into the luxuriating and peaceful arms of Morpheus. This is the last day of summer and Atlanta and Richmond are still ours. Yes, for our Confederates brave, and our kind friends are still contending with the foes for their homes in both of these strongholds.

September 1864

Thursday 1. The first day of fall and a gloomy eve it is. Sgt. Douglass and his friend Mr. McDougal here nearly all day. Sgt. Douglass dined here, left this eve on the cars for his home at 4 o'clock. I feel sad this eve. I thought this afternoon that I would sit down and write a good deal in my diary, but since I have washed I do not feel like writing. Sister is sad this eve and when I see the rest sad I feel so too. I have done comparatively nothing this week and cannot tell when I have been so miserable. I expect to go home with Callie tomorrow. Mother has not yet given her consent and I am afraid she will oppose it so much I will not enjoy myself even if I go. When will I write in you again, old journal? I am in hopes time will have chased away the blues before then.

Friday 2. A pretty day. I put up seven cans of tomatoes this eve; then Callie and I went out to Aunt Elizabeth's. When we came back we were greeted with the sad intelligence that Atlanta had fallen. Lizzie is playing on the piano. Callie is lying on the lounge, whilst I lounged on the floor and indulged in a very quiet cry over our country and absent friends. Callie and Lizzie went out to Mr. Joe Swan's this morn to see when John Swan is going home.

Saturday 3. Rained this eve. Mr. Swan brought Mr. Callaway's carriage around for us and Callie and I came out to her father's this morn. Had a very pleasant ride and feasted extensively on a very nice watermelon.

Sunday 4. A pretty day. Mrs. Callaway and Bell went down to Mrs. Coffee's this eve. Mr. Callaway came and brought Mr. McClain home with him this eve; he remained all night. Dr. Hill here this morn. John Swan here this eve. I like Mrs. Callaway very much. Bell is mischievous but bright and comprehensive. Callie and I, after tea, walked down to the river.

Monday 5. A pretty day. I read some in *Rural Life in America* and cut Elvira Lea out some collars. I felt sick and laid down this morn. Was ushered up early by Mr. Cal Campbell presenting himself at the door.

Tuesday 6. A pretty day. This morn I was awakened by my bed fellow Callie who was up and toilet made before I was aware Aurora[26] had revealed his smiling face to the world. We went fishing this eve; did not catch anything. We then went to the field and assisted Mrs. Callaway gather beans. I saw some women shear sheep this eve. We came back from our jaunt and I performed my evening ablution, made my toilette for tea. After partaking hastily of some nice biscuits and cold beans I doffed my dress, petticoats, etc.,

---

[26]Poetically, "aurora" means dawn

donned my nightgown and sat down quietly in my dishabille [loose negligee] to posting my journal.

Wednesday 7. A pretty day. Callie and I went over to Cousin Betsy Shields' this morn. We had a nice treat of peaches, musk and watermelons. I ate some honey; it made me sick. I laid down in the eve a little while. Cousin Martha Howell went to the river with us. We waded the river coming home.

Thursday 8. A pretty day. John Swan brought me home this eve. Sister informed me that the report was that John Morgan was killed. I do not believe it. Wheeler is playing havoc with the railroad in North Tennessee. When I came home I found a letter from Lt. A. Simmons.

Friday 9. A pretty day. I canned some peaches this eve. Cousin Ellen McCallie came from Chattanooga this morn. Sister and Lizzie went up to see her after tea. Rhoda stayed last night with Nannie Kennedy.

Saturday 10. A pretty day. Mr. John Swan here this eve. Sgt. Douglass came from Chattanooga this morn; took tea here. He told us this eve we had as well pray for the success of the Yankee Army, for they were bound to succeed.

Sunday 11. A pretty day. I went up after tea to see Cousin Ellen McCallie. Pryor and Sgt. Douglass took tea here. Mr. Ham Rossen here after tea.

Monday 12. We washed this morn. Aunt Elizabeth and Sgt. Douglass came in this eve. He went home this eve to Hillsdale, Michigan. I went up to Mrs. Edward's and Mrs. McNelley's this eve. Mrs. Smith here this eve.

Tuesday 13. I finished needleworking Elvira Lea another collar. Cass Shields returned from his banishment in the North this morn; dined here. He brought good news in regard to the Copperheads and Southern sympathizers. Mother out to Aunt Elizabeth's this morn and cut apples to dry. Rhoda, Sister and the baby went out and took tea at Aunt Elizabeth's. I took Johnnie and the rest of the children and walked and met them. Johnnie enjoyed it very much.

Wednesday 14. Sister and I went up to Mrs. Craigmiles' this eve and got some nice peaches. Nannie Kennedy stayed all night with Rhoda and me. Cousin Ellen and Mary came down and sat until bedtime. Sister and I went up to see Adelia's baby. Rhoda commenced crawling today.

Thursday 15. I moved nearly all day. Made catsup this morn. Pauline Hereford and Lizzie spent the day at Mrs. Smith's. Pauline stayed all night with Lizzie. Julia and Mattie Grant here this eve.

Friday 16. Mother went out visiting today; made the rounds Generaly. Mrs. Pickens here this morn to show Sister how to make apple butter. Aunt Elizabeth here this morn. Julia McGhee has a boy, born Wednesday. I wove three yards today.

Saturday 17. I have been sick all day. Took too much laudanum. Have sat up very little. Dr. Dwyer came from his home, New Petersbourg, Ohio, this morn, dined, took tea and stayed all night here.

Sunday 18. Dr. Dwyer and a soldier by the name of Erwin took tea here. John Swan here after tea. Sister received a letter from Mr. Carter this eve, written from Purdy, Tennessee, on July 26th. Pretty day.

Monday 19. We washed this morn. Sister went up to the store with Cousin Mary Harle this eve and got a bolt of calico.

Tuesday 20. A pretty day. Mrs. Shadden spent the day here helping Mother make a coat for Pryor. Dr. Dwyer dined here. Aunt Elizabeth here this morn. I bought myself a corset this morn.

Wednesday 21. A rainy day. Dr. Dwyer took tea and stayed all night here. I made myself a nice linsey underskirt and swapped it off with Sister for a flannel one.

Thursday 22. Rained this eve. I have been darning my stockings and preparing my winter clothes for use.

Friday 23. Rained nearly all day. Sallie Reeder came in this eve to stay until tomorrow eve. I cut me out a pair of drawers and made them this eve. This night our dear and only brother left this world of sorrow to dwell in realms of eternal bliss. Gently and softly the sad new came of Gen. Morgan's death, tempered from a thunderbolt to a mournful regret that our Southern Marion had fallen. Killed in Mrs. Williams' garden at Greenville, Tennessee. A woman by the name of Mary Henderson rode 13 miles in the night and reported where he was. Mollie Osment has a boy.

Saturday 24. A pretty day. The day the militia of Tennessee are enrolled. Uncle Caswell is very much troubled for fear Pryor will have to go. Sallie Reeder went home this eve, Lizzie with her. Rhoda and Sallie Reeder went out to Mrs. Kennedy's this eve. Cousin Ellen here this eve.

Sunday 25. A pretty day. Rhoda and I went to Dr. Grant's this eve. Rhoda and I went to church this morn.

Monday 26. A pretty day. We washed this morn. Rhoda and I went out to Mrs. Kennedy's this eve to see about them.

Tuesday 27. A pretty day. Dr. Dwyer here, took dinner here. I have been making tape points to trim Elvira Lea's collar.

Wednesday 28. A pretty day; rained this eve. Aunt Elizabeth spent the day here. Mrs. William Craigmiles here this eve. I trimmed a net this morn. Made a sliced potato pie the first time this morn.

Thursday 29. A rainy day. Commenced my dark calico dress this morn. Sewed on it all day. The Rebels have destroyed two bridges in Middle Tennessee.

Friday 30. A pretty day. Sewed on my dress all day; finished it this eve. Julia Grant here this eve. Rhoda, Sister and the baby went out after dinner and stayed all night at Aunt Elizabeth's.

October 1864

Saturday 1. A pretty day. Elvira Lea came in this eve. She and I went to Mrs. Dr. Edwards' this eve to get her hat. We then went over to see Ella DeLano. She has fever; was some better when we came home. Sister and Rhoda have returned home from Uncle Caswell's. Mrs. Smith and Mrs. Shadden here this eve. I crocheted some on my net this morn; wove a little this eve.

Sunday 2. A pretty day. All went to church except baby, Johnnie, Elvira and me this morn. Elvira left for home this eve. Cousin Tom came for her. Mr. Ham Rossen, Julia and Jeanette Grant and Cousin Mary Jarnagin here this eve.

Monday 3. Rained some today, enough to prevent our washing. Sister and Lizzie went up to the store this morn, bought me a pair of shoes, gave $5 for this, Lizzie a dress. Mother went to see Mrs. Cowan, spent the day there. She is very low with consumption [tuberculosis] . Some excitement in town, looking for Wheeler and [Nathan B.] Forrest. Pryor came in this eve and said Cousin John Lea sent for him to be at Dr. Shugart's at dark last night, that he would be there with 50 men.

Tuesday 4. A pretty day. Great excitement in town tonight. It is reported that Forrest and Wheeler are three miles from town. Rhoda and I packed up our clothes to be ready if we had to leave town. I crocheted on my net all day. Mrs. Cowan died last night, buried this eve.[27]

Wednesday 5. Rained some this eve. Mother went out to Uncle Caswell's this morn, took dinner. I wove 2-3/4 yards today.

Thursday 6. A pretty day. Uncle Caswell here this eve. I crocheted on my net today. Rained very hard this morn.

Friday 7. Pretty day. I finished and trimmed my net today. Aunt Elizabeth here this eve. She and Lizzie took tea here. Rhoda and I then went out home with her. Pryor and Georgie had a candy stew. We sat up until 11 o'clock. Heard this eve that Lt. Simmons had gone home in very bad health. The Col. and Surgeon of First Heavy Artillery took tea.

Saturday 8. A cold, windy day. The Second Heavy Artillery is to be transferred to Knoxville. Four or five took tea. Mother retired to rest early this eve, suffering with toothache and cold. Rhoda and I went up to see Mrs. McCulty, Mary Edwards and Mollie Shugart this eve. Such an eve as this I take the blues. I have felt lonely, blue and uncomfortable all day.

Sunday 9. A pretty day. Mother is better, sat up all eve. Uncle Caswell here this morn and eve; brought me a letter from Sallie Shields. Sister went up to Mrs. Shadden's this eve.

Monday 10. A pretty day. We washed this morn. Rhoda and Cynthia Hardwick went out to Dr. Grant's this eve. After that Rhoda and I went out to Mrs. Kennedy's to see Cleo.

---

[27] Mrs. James M. (Nancy M.) Cowan was born 7 April 1830, in Tennessee, and died 3 October 1864, and is interred in Fort Hill Cemetery. She was the wife of James M. Cowan, a brick mason, and the mother of three children: John M. (five), Andrew (three), and Nannie A. who was four months old at the time of the 1860 census. Ross, *Cemetery Records*, II:295.

Tuesday 11. A pretty day. I have been ironing all this morning, mending my clothes this eve. I feel sad and lonely this eve.

Wednesday 12. A pretty day. I went out to Mr. Frank Lea's this morn in the wagon with Joe Harle. Rhoda went out to Mr. Reeder's this morn.

Thursday 13. A pretty day. I came back this morn from Mr. Lea's with Luke Harle. I made me a grey worsted underskirt today.

Friday 14. A pretty day. A great confusion in town. The Yankees have evacuated this place. The town is perfectly quiet this eve; all the Union men have left. I went out to Aunt Elizabeth's this morn, and up to Cousin Mary Jarnagin's this eve. The Confederates have captured Dalton; we are looking for them here.

Saturday 15. A pretty day. Sister, Cousin Mary Jarnagin, Mrs. Rumple, Lizzie, Rhoda, Jimmie and I went up to view the fortifications and deserted Yankee encampment this morn. I have the headache this eve and laid down to take a nap. I will be so disappointed if the Rebels do not come. I still look for them a little.

Sunday 16. A pretty day. Read in *Key to Popery.* Ham Rossen, Julia and Jeanette Grant, Cousuns Mary Harle and Mary Jarnagin and Mrs. Rumple here this eve.

Monday 17. A lovely day. We washed this morn.

Tuesday 18. Pretty day. Cleo Watkins here this morn to tell me she was going home and she wished me to go down and give her music lessons. Sallie Reeder, Laura Stout, Cousin Mary Jarnagin and Mrs. Rumple here this eve.

Wednesday 19. A pretty day. I mended my hoops today and went up to Cousin Mary Jarnagin's this eve. Rhoda and I went out and stayed all night at Aunt Elizabeth's. John Swan was there. We made candy.

Thursday 20. This eve Lizzie, Jimmie and I went out to Uncle Caswell's and Pryor and Georgie went chestnut hunting with us. After tea Rhoda and I went over to Mrs. Grant's a little while.

Friday 21. I went up and got Mrs. Rumple to show me how to knit the baby a shirt out of yarn. Pretty day. Rhoda and I put a carpet down in the dining room made of sacks.

Saturday 22. A pretty day. Nannie Kennedy and Sallie took tea here. I went out home with her and stayed all night. Knitted on the baby's shirt all day.

Sunday 23. A lovely though windy day. I spent the day at Aunt Elizabeth's. She and I went up to Mrs. Morrison's this eve. Mr. Davis came in with me. Capt. McNeely and Julia Grant here this eve.

Monday 24. Pretty day. We washed today.

Tuesday 25. A pretty day. Julia Grant stayed all night with me tonight.

Wednesday 26. Rained a little today. Mrs. Kennedy and Jennie dined here. Jennie is to take music lessons from Rhoda. Mr. Reed came for me to go down to Mrs. Watkins' this morn. We started about 2 o'clock this eve in a buggy. Got there about dark. I could not realize I was leaving home and friends to go out into the cold and cheerless world. It makes my heart ache, when I think of it, but I try to banish all gloomy thoughts and consider it is nothing but a school girl freak.[28] May God protect me from dangers of every kind and raise up friends to love me and assist me. Can I realize this is only the beginning of my separation from my dear friends and may it not be. Everything and every person is so strange except Cleo.

Thursday 27. Rained nearly all day. Gave Cleo a music lesson this morn. Read some in magazines today, commenced reading *Scottish Chiefs*. It has been a long day for me. May God in his goodness unite our household once more and may we spend many bright days in each other's society again. I like Mrs. Watkins very much, and pray to our Father above that I may give them no cause to dislike me.

Friday 28. Gave Cleo a music lesson this morn. Read in *Scottish Chiefs* this morn. Hemmed a ruffle this eve. Pretty day.

Saturday 29. Pretty day. Mrs. Watkins and the little girls went to church and brought Mr. Bower, Mr. Daily and Nannie home to stay all night. Nannie Daily, Cleo and I went over to the railroad to see if Nannie Kennedy came down. She did not.

Sunday 30. Pretty day. I went to church with Cleo, Lena and Tack this morn. This eve Mr. Reed, Cleo, Lena, Josie and I went over to the railroad where we saw some Rebel prisoners. Mr. Daily, Nannie and Mr. Bowers stayed here all night.

Monday 31. Lovely day. Mrs. Watkins told Mr. Daily Saturday that the Rebels were gentlemen by the side of the Yankees and that

---

[28] A sudden capricious turn of the mind.

they took 13 wagon loads of corn and said after she bemeaned them the Yankees took all the rest. And that she wished the Rebs had taken it, that she would have given it to them willingly. That she never thought of hiding from them, that the Rebs would leave enough for her family, and the Yanks left none at all. Sherman's men took from her 21 bed quilts, 4 head of horses, 8 milk cows, 18 hogs, 100 chickens and turkeys, every knife and fork, broke the locks in all the doors, 1 bag of salt, flour all, meal all, took all of the jewelry, watch, all of Cleo's gloves, handkerchiefs, stockings and some of her underclothing, and knocked Mrs. Watkins down because she tried to get her shawl from him. Kicked her bureau and sewing machine to pieces. Injured her $5000.00 worth. Lovely day. Mrs. Watkins went to church this morn. I wrote Rhoda this morn. Gave Cleo a music lesson this morn.

November 1864

Tuesday 1. Pretty day. Mrs. Watkins and Bruce went to Harrison this morn. Cleo and I cut her out a morning dress in Mrs. Watkins' absence. Cleo and I took a ride this eve. Rode down to Mrs. Igou's. Gave Cleo a music lesson this morn.

Wednesday 2. Rainy day. I sewed on Cleo's morning dress a good deal today. Gave her a music lesson.

Thursday 3. Gave Cleo a music lesson. I commenced Laura an apron this eve. A rainy and gloomy day.

Friday 4. A rainy day, dark. Cleo and I went in to the parlor and sewed on her morning dress this eve. Reese went after Tack this eve. Rumored that Sherman is falling back from Atlanta. Hope it is true.

Saturday 5. Pretty day. Cleo and I took a ride this eve. I received a letter from home this eve. Wrote that Uncle Caswell had received a letter from Cousin Joe Lea by "flag of truce." I feel sad this eve. I showed Tack how to make a picture frame this eve. Gave Cleo a music lesson this morn.

Sunday 6. Cold day, rainy and windy. Lena, Tack, Josie and Mr. Reed went to church this morning. Mr. Igou dined here.

Monday 7. Pretty day. Gave Cleo a lesson this morn. We commenced Cleo a worsted apron dress this eve.

Tuesday 8. Rainy day. Election day for President[29]. I wrote home this eve. Been sewing on Cleo's dress. Gave her a lesson this morn.

Wednesday 9. A blustering, windy and rainy day. Gave Cleo a music lesson. Made Mrs. Watkins an underskirt. Read *Scottish Chiefs* this morn.

Thursday 10. Cold day. Gave Cleo a music lesson this morn. Lena and I took a walk this eve.

Friday 11. A pretty day. Gave Cleo a music lesson. She and I went to Harrison after Tack this eve.

Saturday 12. Pretty day. Mr. Igou came this eve, stayed all night. Laura and I took a walk to the railroad this morn.

Sunday 13. Cold day. Mr. Igou and the boys went to preaching this morn. Two boys dined here and stayed here all eve. Received a letter from Sgt. Woods and home this morning.

Monday 14. Pretty day. Gave Cleo a music lesson this morn. Sewed on the skirt of Lena's dress today.

Tuesday 15. Rainy day. Finished reading *Scottish Chiefs* this morn. Commenced reading *Woodville* this eve.

Wednesday 16. Rained a little this eve. The boys went partridge driving this morn. Laura and I went to the railroad this eve. Gave Cleo a lesson this morn.

Thursday 17. A pretty day. I feel lonesome today. Been making pincushions out of aprons this eve.

Friday 18. Gave Cleo a music lesson this morn. Knitted on my stocking today.

Saturday 19. Rainy day. I finished Josie a pair of drawers and made four pincushions this eve.

Sunday 20. Rainy day. Wrote to Sallie Shields this eve. Tack went off to school at Harrison this eve. I have been reading in Moore's *Poetical Works* today. Received a letter from home which made me feel very blue.

Monday 21. Snowed all this eve, rained this morn. Mr. Yarnell and Mr. Hall dined here today. Gave Cleo a music lesson.

---

[29]The President of the United States. Abraham Lincoln defeated George B. McClellan

Tuesday 22. A cold day. Mrs. Watkins killed 3 hogs this morn. We have nice ribs and sausages now. Knitted and read some in *Thaddeus of Warsaw.* Gave Cleo a music lesson.

Wednesday 23. Colder than yesterday. I finished my letter to Sallie Shields and wrote to Rhoda this eve. Knitted most all day.

Thursday 24. Gave Cleo a music lesson. Mr. Guthrie started to Monroe County this morn. Pretty day.

Friday 25. Pretty day. Tack came home this eve. Cleo and I fixed Mrs. Reed's sheet tonight.

Saturday 26. Rained a little this eve. Washed this eve, mended my clothes this morn.

Sunday 27. Pretty day. Cleo, Josie, Lena and I went to the railroad this eve. Mr. Guthrie brought me a calico dress from home this eve.

Monday 28. Pretty day. Gave Cleo a music lesson this morn. Cut out my morning dress this morn.

Tuesday 29. Pretty day. Sewed on my morning dress all day.

Wednesday 30. Pretty day. Finished my dress this morn. Dr. Rhoddy dined here. Lena and I went down to Mrs. Reed's this eve.

December 1864

Thursday 1. I ironed my clothes today. Johnnie's 3rd birthday. Knit[ed] some today.

Friday 2. Pretty day. Mr. Reed and Mr. Guthrie went to Chattanooga this eve. Cleo and I were disappointed about going for Tack this eve. Gave Cleo a music lesson.

Saturday 3. Rained a little this morn. Doug and Sam Igou dined here; killed a beef. Cleo baked some cake this eve. Mr. Yarnell here last this eve. Cleo and I sewed up Mrs. Reed's and Tack's coats this eve. I washed and retired to rest early tonight.

Sunday 4. Pretty day. All went to church except Mrs. Watkins and me. We stayed at home and got dinner. Mr. Igou dined here. He, Cleo, Josie, Lena and I walked with Tack as far as the railroad. Mrs. Watkins sick tonight. Mr. Yarnell stayed here all night.

Monday 5. Pretty day. Gave Cleo a music lesson. Commenced her a pair of undersleeves.

Tuesday 6. A pretty day. I finished Cleo's undersleeves tonight. Knitted them out of yarn.

Wednesday 7. Pretty day. The Rebels came in Ooltewah[30] last night and sacked the place. Mr. Guthrie and Mr. Reed left tonight to go over the river, for fear they would return. Gave Cleo a music lesson this morn.

Thursday 8. Cold day. Reese and Bruce started to school to Mr. McNabb yesterday.

Friday 9. Cold day. Tack came home from school this eve. Mr. Guthrie got in this eve. A very cold day, rained this eve. Mr. Dan Yarnell and Doug Igou stayed all night here. Cleo had to get supper for them. I commenced me a pair of stockings. Gave Cleo a music lesson.

Saturday 10. Cold day. I knitted some today. Tack put up a new swing this eve. We swung nicely in it. Mr. Reed and Mr. Guthrie left this eve.

Sunday 11. Cold day. Mr. Reed and Mr. Guthrie came in today. Cleo and I went in the kitchen after dark and talked until bedtime.

Monday 12. A very cold morning. I knitted all day. Three men from McElwee's cotton factory stayed all night.

Tuesday 13. Cold and windy day. Knitted and read all day. Gave Cleo a music lesson.

Wednesday 14. A cloudy and windy day. Knitted and read all day. Read some letters from Lt. A. Simmons.

Thursday 15. A pleasant though cloudy day. After dark we swung. I knitted all day. Wrote to Julia Grant. Gave Cleo a music lesson.

Friday 16. A cloudy but warm day. Assisted Cleo in making her chemise band and bosom. Went to the walnut tree and ate a great many walnuts.

---

[30] Hamilton County, Tennessee.

Saturday 17. Rainy day. Miss Lemira Yarnell came up this morn to see me. Mr. Igou came in with her and took dinner.

Sunday 18. Cloudy day. Mr. Yarnell and Mr. Igou here this eve. Miss Mira went home this eve. Dr. Rhoddy stayed all night here. Received a letter from home this eve.

Monday 19. Cloudy day. Rained today. Dr. Rhoddy dined here.

Tuesday 20. The wind blew this morn; rained this eve. I went up home with Mrs. Igou on her wagon. Sam Igou and Yarnell went with us. We got there at 5 in the eve; found all glad to see me. I was delighted to get home. Rhoda had a nice "shaker" for me. Gave Cleo a music lesson this morn.

Wednesday 21. A very, very cold day. I spent the day at home; packed up some things to take down. Uncle Caswell dined at our house. There was a bushwhacker hung near here today. Rhoda and I went out and stayed all night at Aunt Elizabeth's.

Thursday 22. An extremely cold day. We came back to stay; got to Mrs. Watkins' at 5 o'clock. Sallie Kennedy came with us. I felt very bad when I got there; had to wade the branch to get there. Mother's 55th birthday.

Friday 23. Cold day. I knitted some today. Cleo and I went this eve to Mrs. Barnes' after the washed clothes. Met Tack and the two Messrs. Igou.

Saturday 24. [Weather] moderated some. Ironed this eve. Trimmed Josie's net this morn and helped Cleo starch the clothes. Reese went to Mrs. Igou's this eve.

Sunday 25. A pleasant day. Christmas day. I wrote home this morn.

Monday 26. A cloudy day. Mr. Igou came this morn. Cleo, Tack and I went home with him this eve.

Tuesday 27. A pretty day. We knitted on some undersleeves for Miss Lena today. Mr. Yarnell took tea here. We played blindfold.

Wednesday 28. Cold day. Mr. Guthrie, Reese, Tack, a Mr. Bell, Monroe and Doug Igou, Miss Lemira Yarnell, Sallie Kennedy, Cleo, Ellen Igou and I all spent the day at Mrs. Dr. Reynolds'. We then came back and stayed at Mrs. Igou's.

Thursday 29. Pretty day. Mr. Yarnell came up and brought some whiskey and we had a nice eggnog this morn. We came home this eve. Monroe Igou stayed all night here.

Friday 30. Cold day. Mr. Igou left for home just before dinner. I commenced altering my brown worsted dress.

Saturday 31. Cold day. I sewed all day on my worsted dress. I feel very sad to see the departure of this year. Snowed last night.

1865

January 1865

Sunday 1. A very cold day. New Year's Day. Wonder if I will see my Rebel friends by next New Year's. God grant that next New Year's day we will all be home again.

Monday 2. A pretty day. I finished altering my dress this eve. Gave Cleo a music lesson this morn.

Tuesday 3. A pretty day. Sallie Surguine's nineteenth birthday.

Wednesday 4. A pretty day. Finished Josie's shaker this morn. Lena, Laura, and I went after gum wax this eve. Gave Cleo a music lesson.

Thursday 5. Pretty day. Mrs. Watkins started to Chattanooga this morn. Mr. Guthrie with her. I doubled thread all day. The wind is blowing very hard tonight.

Friday 6. A rainy and gloomy day. Gave Cleo a lesson this morn. I have been knitting and doing small jobs all day. Tack came home this eve. Mr. Guthrie and Mrs. Watkins came home also drenched with rain.

Saturday 7. A pretty day. I finished Lizzie's stocking this morn. I ironed a little this eve. After dark I washed and went to bed. I received a letter from Julia Grant this eve.

Sunday 8. A pretty day. Cleo, Josie, and I went with Mr. Reed to hear Mr. Daily preach. Hugh Bell and Doug Igou dined here. Tack went with them over to Harrison.

Monday 9. A rainy and gloomy eve. I wrote to Rhoda today. I commenced footing my yarn stockings this morn. I feel so lonesome this eve. Gave Cleo a music lesson this morn. Had a nice mess of partridges for dinner.

Wednesday 11. A pretty day. Mr. Reed came back this morn.

Thursday 12. A pretty day. Cleo and I rode down to Mr. Ritchey's this eve to get some shoes mended. No one was here for dinner except Josie, Lena, Mrs. Watkins, Laura, Cleo, and I. I gave Cleo a music lesson this morn.

Friday 13. A pretty day. Sallie Kennedy and Sam and Ellen Igou came up this morn, intended remaining until Sunday eve.

Saturday 14. A pretty day. I wrote to Julia Grant this eve. I finished Cleo's slippers this morn. I feel so lonesome this eve. I get very homesick sometimes and wonder when we will all be together again. Did I say all? Yes! I mean all. Mr. Carter, cousins John and Joe Lea. My happiness would be complete if we could all assemble around the fireside as of old. Maybe that happiness will always remain untasted. Sister and Annie, I presume, are out at Mrs. Cannon's, also the baby and Jimmie. Rhoda probably is at Uncle Caswell's whilst Mother, Lizzie, Johnnie and Aunt Elizabeth are at home sighing for the return of the absent members of the household and wishing the day may soon come when we will all be gathered together. Mother wrote me, she had rented her kitchen and dining room to two families who have fled from the guerillas who are committing depredations in the country. How earnestly I wish this war was over. Tack [Watkins], Reese, Sam Igou, Cleo and I swung this eve. Two Yankees stayed all night there.

Sunday 15. A pretty day. Ellen and Sam Igou, and Sam Kennedy went home this eve. Two soldiers took tea here. I commenced reading *Washington and His Generals* this eve.

Monday 16. A pretty day. I commenced Josie's undersleeves. Mr. Yarnell and Mr. Igou here today. Gave Cleo a music lesson.

Tuesday 17. Pretty day. Finished Josie's undersleeves and commenced Mother a pair of stockings.

Wednesday 18. A pretty day. Mr. Igou, Dan Yarnell, and Mrs. Yarnell dined here.

Thursday 19. A pretty day. Knitted all day.

Friday 20. A pretty day. Cleo, Bruce and I went over to Mrs. Smith's examinations at Harrison. Dined at Mrs. Caldwell's.

Saturday 21. A rainy day. Tack came home this morning. I received a letter and a pass to go home this eve.

Sunday 22. A rainy day. I came home this morn. Tack brought me over to the depot and Mr. Mat Parker brought me home. Mr. and Mrs. Grant and Bell here this eve.

Monday 23. Snowed and hailed this morn. Turned off cold and cloudy.

Tuesday 24. A very cold day. I went out and spent the day at Uncle Caswell's. I went up to Mrs. Kennedy's to see if she would board Tack. Nannie Kennedy stayed all night with me tonight.

Wednesday 25. A cold day. Rhoda and I dined at Cousin Mary Harle's today, also went this eve to Mrs. William Grant's and Mrs. Dr. Edward's. A great deal of talk of foreign recognition and Mr. Blair's mission to Richmond being a visit of note.

Thursday 26. A very cold day. Rhoda and I, in company of Julia Grant, spent the day at Mrs. Cannon's. We went to see Sister and the children. Johnnie is the only one remaining at home. Callie and Lou Swan came back to town with us. Rhoda and I stayed all night at Dr. Grant's; enjoyed it finely. Had boiled custard as a lunch before going to rest.

Friday 27. A very cold day. We came home this morn and went over to Mrs. William Grant's this eve.

Saturday 28. A very cold day. I finished a cotton nightgown this eve. Rhoda and I went up to the store this eve.

Sunday 29. A tolerable pleasant day. Rhoda and I went up to see Nannie Kennedy this eve, then we went to Mr. and Mrs. Igou's.

Monday 30. A pretty day. Rhoda's birthday. We cleaned up every room about the house. We also moved the tables, etc. back in the dining room. Tack Watkins here this eve to see me. He came up this morn to go to school.

Tuesday 31. A beautiful and pleasant day. Sister and Jimmie came in and spent the day with us. Mrs. William Grant and Bell here this eve. Rhoda and I took Johnnie and went nearly to the mill with sister. Johnnie is so sweet. He is just beginning to prattle so sweetly. "Gut" is his exclamation for disgust. Julia Grant came in and stayed all night with us.

February 1865

Wednesday 1. A pretty day. Julia and I went 'round shopping and went to see Ada Grant. She then went home. Rhoda and I went up to see Adelia Craigmiles. We got some music for Cleo, then out to see Callie Swan. Took dinner with Aunt Elizabeth and then up to see Nannie Kennedy. Then we came back and met Nannie at Bug Cate's. She and Nannie had been down to see us. We then stopped in there for a while. After that we went over to see Sallie Ragsdale and Sallie Surguine.

Thursday 2. A pretty day. Rhoda received a letter from Lt. Henry Jones. He is at Johnson's Island, [located in Lake Erie, near Sandusky], a prisoner, taken December 22. How rejoiced we were to hear that Henry was living well. Rhoda, Lizzie, Lizzie Lea, and Johnnie had their hats on to accompany me over to the depot for me to go to Ooltewah, but the whistle blew and Uncle Caswell and I had to skedaddle so quick they could not go. Cleo and Josie met me at the depot. It rained on us all the way coming to Mrs. Watkins'. Dan Yarnell and three other men stayed all night here. Mother and all the rest got up last night and dressed, looking for the Rebels.

Friday 3. I knitted some this morn and played some pieces over for Cleo on the piano. A pretty day. We played for Mr. Yarnell this morn.

Saturday 4. A beautiful day. Cleo and I pasted pieces in our scrapbooks this morn and eve. Mr. Reed has quit boarding here. He was here awhile tonight.

Sunday 5. Rained a little this morn. Two regiments of Yanks came to repulse the Rebels. They stole some of Mrs. Watkins' corn, four pigs, three or four chickens, two hams of meat and burnt a great many rails. I finished reading Pope's *Essay on Man*.

Monday 6. A pretty day. I cut and commenced me a cashmere jacket.[1] Gave Cleo a music lesson. Heard this eve the Rebels were coming.

---

[1] Cashmere is fine, downy wool growing beneath the outer hair of the Cashmere goat.

Tuesday 7. A cold day. Snowed last night and some today. I finished my jacket this morn and knitted some this eve.

Wednesday 8. A very cold day. I cut Rhoda a jacket this eve. Knitted some this morn. Gave Cleo a music lesson. Tack's eighteenth birthday.

Thursday 9. A cold day; spit snow this morn. The sun shone out this eve. I made me a silk apron this morn. Wrote Lizzie this eve.

Friday 10. A cold day. Made Rhoda a cashmere jacket today.

Saturday 11. I ironed and mended my clothes. Beautiful day. Mrs. Igou spent the day here. Cleo and I rode part of the way home with her. I enjoyed the ride very much.

Sunday 12. Pretty day. Cleo, Lena, Laura, and I went to church and there was none. I received a letter from home.

Monday 13. A pretty day. Gave Cleo a music lesson. Mrs. Watkins and Laura went over to Mrs. McNabb's this eve [and] to Mrs. Ragan's this morn.

Tuesday 14. Cloudy day. I knitted today. We swung this eve. Mr. Yarnell here this eve. St. Valentine's Day.

Wednesday 15. A rainy day. Gave Cleo a music lesson. Helped make Josie a dress.

Thursday 16. A pretty day. I ironed this morn.

Friday 17. Pretty tho' windy day. Mr. Guthrie started to Chattanooga this eve. Gave Cleo a music lesson. Sister's 31st birthday.

Saturday 18. A pretty day. Three soldiers were here this morn, took dinner. Cleo and I went to Mrs. Barnes' with some carpet rags; came by the railroad to see the passenger car go down. We made up some garters this morn. Rhoda's first birthday.

Sunday 19. A beautiful day. Cleo, Josie, Lena, Laura, and I took a walk to the railroad this eve. Mr. Guthrie came this morn.

Monday 20. A pretty day. Gave Cleo a music lesson. Wrote out my article for school. Mrs. Young here this eve. I made Josie a pair of sleeves for her dress. We had a nice swing this eve.

Tuesday 21. A pretty day. We went after some sassafras roots this eve. Mrs. Poe and Rebecca Caruthers here this eve.

Wednesday 22. A pretty day. Gave Cleo a music lesson this morn. We commenced Cleo a morning dress this eve. This day, a year ago, Aunt Phoebe died.

Thursday 23. A pretty day. We sewed constantly all day on Cleo's morning dress. Reese could not come home tonight, it rained so hard, so Mr. Reed had to come up and feed and stay all night. Mr. Guthrie is gone.

Friday 24. A cloudy day. We finished Cleo's dress this morn.

Saturday 25. A very, very rainy day. I knitted all day. I went out and milked a cow this eve.

Sunday 26. A beautiful day. I finished reading *Washington and His Generals* this eve. Two Yanks here this eve, one, a Mississippian, deserted from our army, served two years. I took a cry this eve about my loneliness, etc. I milked the cow alone this eve, the first time in my life.

Monday 27. A beautiful day. I gave Cleo a lesson this morn. I read a book entitled *The Prairie Missionary* this morn; liked it very much. It almost made me feel like going out on the prairie and assisting in the great work myself, although she (the author) had enumerable trials to endure, but cannot I be of use to my fellow beings here at home? Yes, of more service than my poor sinful nature will undertake, every day. I feel more like I have a duty to perform in this world and that I am far from it. I feel as if I am very remiss in the duties I owe my Creator and repining over my gloomy life, when I should be thanking Him for giving me so many friends to make me happy. I feel the conviction that I should be a Christian, but the way is so hard for me to renounce the world and live a life of holiness. It is so much easier to think evil than good, so much easier to serve Man than God. I went out and assisted Cleo in the yard this morn. We all went out this eve and gathered some shrubs in the woods and set them in the yard. After tea we played Caste [a game.]

Tuesday 28. A pretty day. Cleo and I went out to Mrs. Whittenburg's to rent a house for me to teach school in.

March 1865

Wednesday 1. A pretty day. Cleo and I went out this morn to get me a school. I gave her a music lesson this morn. Mrs. Watkins and

Lena went this morn to Mrs. Conn's. I commenced reading *Prairie Flower* this morn. Three men from McElwee's factory stayed here all night.

Thursday 2. A rainy day. I knitted some and finished *Prairie Flower* this eve.

Friday 3. A pretty day. I wrote some this morn. Gave Cleo a music lesson. I took a cry this morn about Mr. McDaniel saying that Mr. Carter was the means of having [his] father arrested and his brother killed. I have the blues miserably this eve. If I only felt assured all would be well, I would feel perfectly happy, but everything looks so dark. Mr. Brown here this eve, a refugee from Georgia.

Saturday 4. Pretty day. President Lincoln's second inaugural day. Wrote to Sallie this eve. Wonder who will be the next President of the United States.

Sunday 5. A beautiful day. Discovered this morn the mice had ruined my blue worsted dress. Cleo, Josie, Laura, and I heard Mr. Douglass
preach.

Monday 6. A pretty day. Gave Cleo a lesson. Knitted all day.

Tuesday 7. A rainy day. Knitted today and read in a Roman history [book]. I hemmed some ruffles for Josie. Cleo wounded my feelings by saying she wished the Yanks would get old Gen. Longstreet at Knoxville. Gave Cleo a music lesson.

Wednesday 8. A cloudy day. Wrote some this morn. Knitted some this morn. Mr. Guthrie has a very bad felon[2] on his finger.

Thursday 9. A cold day. I knitted some today. I have been reading in *Whelply's Compendium.* Cleo and I sang her songs over this eve.

Friday 10. A pretty day. Mr. Reed brought a letter to me from home.

Saturday 11. A pretty day. I ironed and mended my clothes today. Dr. Rhoddy and Mr. Reed here this eve.

---

[2]A felon is an inflammation of a finger or toe, normally in the cuticle at the edge of the nail.

Sunday 12. A pretty day. Bettie Jarrett's 23rd birthday. Cleo, Josie, Lena, Laura, and I went up to the Yankee encampment and old fort this eve.

Monday 13. A pretty day. My 20th birthday. Cleo and I both wondered where we will be when I am forty years old, if we will live that long or not. This birthday has passed like all other days, sad and lonely. I had hoped last year on my 19th birthday that ere another would roll around; the war would be ended, but alas, my hopes and wishes were vain, for still the war is raging much the same as on my 17th birthday. We ate three meals today for the first time. Gave Cleo a music lesson this morn. We had cornfritters for dinner.

Tuesday 14. Pretty day. Uncle Pryor's birthday.

Wednesday 15. Gave Cleo a music lesson. Mr. Yarnell came from Nashville this morn and brought Cleo and me some music. Mr. Reed brought me a letter and a package from home.

Thursday 16. A pretty day. We practiced a great portion of the day. Mr. Yarnell stayed here all night.

Friday 17. Pretty day. I needleworked on Cleo's chemise band all day. Gave Cleo a lesson.

Saturday 18. Pretty day. Mrs. Watkins and Lena went to church this morn. Brought Mrs. Igou, Sam, and Mr. Yarnell home to dinner.

Sunday 19. Lovely day. Cleo, Josie, Laura, and I went with Mr. Reed to church. Mr Igou, Miss Lemira, Sis, and Mrs. Yarnell dined here.

Monday 20. Pretty day. I needleworked on Cleo's chemise band all day. Gave her a lesson. Wrote a letter home. Mr. Yarnell here this eve.

Tuesday 21. I needleworked this eve. I ironed this morn.

Wednesday 22. Pretty day. Mr Yarnell and Mr. Harvey Johnson here this eve. He was awfully "bad off" on account of Miss Lou Evans giving him the mitten.[3] Lt. B. passed up the road today.

Thursday 23. Pretty day but very windy. Cleo wounded my feelings by saying the Yankees ought to go to the Rebels forever, that they brought the war on. I ironed my dress this eve.

Friday 24. Pretty day. Mr. Harvey Johnson here this eve. Tack came home from Cleveland this eve. Gave Cleo a music lesson.

---

[3] A breakup to their relationship, telling them good-bye.

Saturday 25. Windy day. Cleo and I made up some geese hoops[4] and played this eve.

Sunday 26. Lovely day. Tack, Mr. Reed, Lena, Cleo, and I went to hear Mr. Burns preach. Cleo, Mr. Reed, Tack, and I rode to the cave this eve.

Monday 27. Windy day. Mr. Yarnell here this eve. I gave Cleo a lesson. Needleworked on Cleo's chemise band.

Tuesday 28. Windy day. I diamonded on Cleo's chemise band.

Wednesday 29. Windy day. Nannie Kennedy came up this morn. Doug Igou came with me. I was sitting in the portico with a heavy heart, writing home, when she rode up. My joy was unbounded. I forget everything in my joy to see her. I have felt so sad for the last few weeks. Cleo, Nannie and I took a walk this eve to the rock bridge.

Thursday 30. Windy day. Josie, Nannie, and Mr. Yarnell went over to the depot to go on the train to Cleveland and they would not take them on. They came back to wait until tomorrow morn. Tonight Nannie and I walked to the wagon with Tack after rails. We have romped considerably since Nannie has been here.

Friday 31. Pretty day; Rather cool this morn. Cleo and I went to the depot with Mr. Yarnell. Nannie and Josie off to Cleveland. A man by the name of Rogers wished me to teach school in his neighborhood. I think I shall go, although it is such a treat to myself.

April 1865

Saturday 1. Pretty day. Cleo and I went down to Mrs. Igou's this morn to see about Mr. Roger's family. Mr. Igou came home with us late this eve. Cleo and I received some April Fools this eve. Lizzie's 17th birthday. Tack went to Cleveland today.

Sunday 2. Warm day. Cleo, Mr. Igou, and I went over to the graveyard this morn. Mr. Yarnell came this eve and brought me a letter from Rhoda and Nannie.

---

4 Probably a game, see 14 April.

Monday 3. Pleasant day. Mr. Chambers, Methodist preacher, stayed here tonight. Gave Cleo a music lesson. I wrote out my article this morn and sent it to Mr. Rogers. We killed a snake this morn.

Tuesday 4. A pretty day. Cleo and I went over to the depot to meet Mrs. Hall, but she did not come this eve. Mr. Guthrie went to Chattanooga this eve.

Wednesday 5. Windy day. I gave Cleo a music lesson. Tack sent me an April Fool this morn. Mrs. Hall and little Jimmie Yarnell stayed here tonight. News is that Richmond is captured.[5]

Thursday 6. Rainy day. Mrs. Hall and little Jimmie went to Mrs. Igou's this eve. Reese took them. He stayed all night. I finished diamonding Cleo's chemise.

Friday 7. Rainy day. I read in the magazines most all day.

Saturday 8. Pretty day. Mr. Guthrie came home this morn. I wrote home this eve. Needleworked on a chemise bosom for myself. Bruce, Lena, and I played ball this eve.

Sunday 9. Rainy day. Very, very long morning. Cleo and I went in the kitchen this eve; sat by the fire and talked of Lt. B.

Monday 10. Rainy day. Gave Cleo a music lesson. Needleworked on my chemise all day. News is that Gen. Robert E. Lee has surrendered his army.

Tuesday 11. Cloudy day. Commenced knitting Mrs. Watkins' a pair of slippers. Mr. Yarnell here this morn.

Wednesday 12. Pretty day. Gave Cleo a music lesson. Knitted on Mrs. Watkins' shoes.

Thursday 13. Pretty day. This day four years ago Fort Sumter fell. The Union flag was again hoisted on it today. We heard heavy cannonading in the direction of Chattanooga in honor of it.

Friday 14. Lovely day. Knitted on shoes today. Played geese hoops and ball this eve. Reese hid them from Lena and me.

Saturday 15. Rained very hard, accompanied by thunder and lightning. I finished Mrs. Watkins' shoes this morn.

Sunday 16. Pretty day. Easter Sunday. Mr. Guthrie came over from town this morn, informed us that [President Abraham] Lincoln was shot Friday night at the theater; died at 7:30 o'clock Saturday

---

[5]On April 3, Union troops under Gen. Weitzel occupied the Confederate capitol. A fire broke out and consumed most of the business district. Randall and Donald, *The Civil War and Reconstruction*, 527.

morn. Secretary Seward was stabbed whilst in bed; was not killed. Wilkes Booth was the perpetrator of the deed, assisted by others whose names as yet are not known. Cannons were fired every half hour at Chattanooga all day. Mr. Reed dined and spent the day here.

Monday 17. Pretty day. I received a pass to go home tomorrow. Hannibal McNabb and Mr. Goulding, telegraph operator, brought it. Laura, Lena, and I went up after gum wax this eve. Mrs. Barnes scouring up the boys room this eve.

Tuesday 18. Pretty day. Cleo and I went to town this morn. I came up home, found sister in from Mrs. Cannon's. Mr. Petty and Mr. Crowson are living in the kitchen and dining room of our house. We did not go to sleep until 12 o'clock. I went up to see Josie this eve.

Wednesday 19. Aunt Elizabeth spent the day here. Nannie Kennedy stayed here all night. Rained this eve. Tack Watkins here this eve.

Thursday 20. Rhoda and I went out to Mrs. Cannon's this eve and spent the day and stayed all night. Pretty day.

Friday 21. Mrs. Cannon and Jimmie spent the day with Mrs. Davis. Sister and little Rhoda spent the day at Mrs. Col. Lea's. Rhoda and I spent the day with Callie Swan. Rhoda and I came to Uncle Caswell's this eve. There we met Lt. Simmons and Cousin Caswell. We stayed all night.

Saturday 22. Rhoda and I went up to see Miss Nannie Kennedy this morn; then we came home. Josie Watkins spent the day here. Lts. Simmons and Caswell here this eve. Lt. Simmons took tea. Lizzie Lea spent the day here. She and Lt. Simmons went out to Uncle Caswell's this eve.

Sunday 23. I slept nearly all morn. Mr. Petty, John Swan, Ham Rossen, Josie Watkins and Pauline Hereford here this eve.

Monday 24. Adelia Craigmiles, Sallie Surguine here this morn. Sister spent the day here. Lt. Simmons came and told us good-bye this eve. Julia and Virginia Grant dined here.

Tuesday 25. I have been making me a calico dress this morn; Busy sewing all day. Adelia Craigmiles here this eve.

Wednesday 26. I cut out another calico dress and sewed all day.

Thursday 27. Pretty day. Rhoda and I went out to Mrs. Smith's this eve. Uncle Preston Lea came this eve. We were rejoiced to see him. He says the Confederacy is undoubtedly a failure. I am completely subjugated for the first time and have utterly given it up, although I know first, Providence will work it out alright and be glorified in the end and will not forsake His followers.

Friday 28. Mother and I went out to Uncle Caswell's with Uncle Preston Lea to spend the day there. We met Sister; we came back with her and spent the day. We stopped at Mrs. Shadden's. Rhoda and I went as far as Aunt Elizabeth's and spent the night.

Saturday 29. Rhoda and I came by to see Nannie Kennedy, also Miss Lou Swan. Mother met us and I went back to Mrs. Gain's and spent the day. There we met Mrs. Cannon with little Rhoda and Jimmie. We went with them over to Mrs. Cannon's. We then sent for Sister and she brought Johnnie. Then mother and I came on and stopped in to see Josie Watkins. Annie's 10th birthday. Bob Smith's 24th birthday. Rhoda went up to see Adelia this eve.

Sunday 30. Bob McCamy and Mr. Harris here this morn. Mr. Abbott, Cousin Tom, Pryor, and Uncle Preston Lea dined here. Mr. McCamy took tea here and stayed all night, also Uncle Preston.

May 1865

Monday 1. Uncle Caswell and Uncle Preston Lea dined here. Sister came in and spent the day here. She and I went up to the stores. Rhoda and I spent the afternoon and took tea at Dr. Grant's. Two Yanks killed tonight.

Tuesday 2. Mary Smith spent the day at our house and stayed all night.

Wednesday 3. Mrs. Cannon, Mother, Rhoda, Annie, Jimmie, Johnnie, Uncle Preston, and I spent the day at Uncle Caswell's. Had an excellent dinner. Had a spring chicken and strawberries. Nannie Kennedy and Mrs. Harris came down in the eve.

Thursday 4. Pretty day. Mother, Lizzie, Uncle Caswell, and I went over to Mrs. Watkins' this eve. Found Mrs. Watkins and Lena from home; had gone to Mrs. Igou's to spend the day. Received a magazine from Lt. Simmons this morn.

Friday 5. Gave Cleo a music lesson. I helped milk this eve. Cleo and I went to see Lettie Barnes this morn; she died last night. We sat up there tonight. Came home at 12 o'clock with Mr. Reed and his sister.

Saturday 6. Cleo and I went over the mountain to Lettie's burying. I slept nearly all eve. We got up and helped milk.

Sunday 7. Cleo and I went to hear Mr. Hall preach. Mr. Reed came home with us and dined. In the eve Cleo and I went down to the creek and we then came back and milked.

Monday 8. Gave Cleo a music lesson. Made me a chemise. These days are so sad and lonely to me. Not until my friends returned did I fully realize that my long cherished schemes were thwarted, my brightest, fondest, dearest hopes and wishes blasted forever--the independence of the South. Mysterious it is to me why God permitted such a sad calamity to befall our South. Why He permitted the noblest blood of the South to be sacrificed for the bondage of the sable race. Many a bitter tear and sad regret has the termination of this unhappy ending caused me--unjust as I would deem it, if I did not believe God has decreed it thus. "Air Castles," which my imagination has erected for the last four years, are crushed and only their memories live to remind me of their existence. It seems to me as if a wild infatuation possessed the minds of the people of the Southland and rendered their reasoning facilities dormant, which caused us to boast and dream vain dreams of our independence until our last weapon was wrested from our hands and our great leader, Gen. Robert E. Lee, rendered powerless. Jefferson Davis, Thaddeus of Warsaw--like, then I hope ere this has eluded the vigilance of his enemies and retired beyond the limits of the United States, where I trust he may breathe out his life in a peaceful asylum, for I still love and revere him as I did when we looked to him for guidance and protection. I often wonder if my love for the "Old Flag" will ever be as great as it once was, if I will ever have the same interest in its promotion as I did for the "Stars and Bars"—for my every hope, wish and plan was clustered around its sacred folds. It is so hard for me to relinquish my dreams of our Confederacy without a sigh and I often repeat, as if in amelioration, these lines from Moore:

Let Fate do her worst, there are relics of joy,
Bright dreams of the Past which she cannot destroy
And which come in the night time of sorrow and care,
To bring back the features that joy used to wear.
Like a vase in which roses have once been distilled,
You may break, you may ruin the vase if you will,
But the scent of the roses will hang 'round it still.

So it is with our Confederacy. We often explain, "It might have been," and the phantom of what might have been arise from its charred remains, which causes our sadness and melancholy to be deeper. But gradually I hope this night will wear away and stay even more brilliant for our Confederacy than we had anticipated, and will illuminate our lives and cause us to feel that it were better that it was not as we would have had it.

Tuesday 9. Posted my journal this eve. Sewed on my chemise all day.

Wednesday 10. Pretty day. Tack Watkins came from Cleveland this eve. Mr. Blunt has suspended school for a week on account of smallpox. Gave Cleo a music lesson.

Thursday 11. Pretty day. Mrs. Watkins went over to Mrs. Young's this eve.

Friday 12. Gave Cleo a music lesson. Mary Ragan took tea here. Jimmie Bell stayed here all night. So cold we had a fire tonight.

Saturday 13. Pretty day. Tack Watkins went to Cleveland this eve.

Sunday 14. Pretty day. Mr. Reed came up and sat awhile this eve. I was lying down in Cleo's lap.

Monday 15. Gave Cleo a lesson. Cut out my pink morning dress this eve. Received a letter from Rhoda and Lizzie this morning stating that Cousin John Lea had come home. I packed up to go home this eve. Heard this morning that Jefferson Davis was captured.[6]

---

[6]President Jefferson Davis was captured at Irvinville, Georgia, and later imprisoned at Fort Monroe (1865-1867). He was indicted for treason in 1866, released on bond in 1867, and the trial was dropped. He lived out his years at Beauvoir, Mississippi and died in 1889.

Tuesday 16. I came home this morn. Met Uncle Caswell at the depot. I went out to Uncle Caswell's and took dinner. I met Cousin John. Sister brought little Rhoda in this eve from Mrs. Caswell's, sick with flux. Cousin John and Uncle Preston took tea here. Cousin John stayed all night.

Wednesday 17. Pretty day. Mr. Petty left this morn and I cleaned up the dining room for mine and Rhoda's room.

Thursday 18. Rained a little this morn. Rhoda and I spent the day at Uncle Caswell's. Rhoda has been teaching Uncle Caswell's boys since last Monday eve.

Friday 19. Pretty day. Sister and little Rhoda are both very sick with flux. Sent for Dr. Long this morn. Cousin John spent the day here. I helped Mrs. Petty's black woman clean up the kitchen for our dining room, Aunt Adeline's room and the porch. We ate in the dining room this eve. Mr. Harris has eaten here every meal since Mr. Petty left.

Saturday 20. Rhoda and Sister have not sat up any today. Little Rhoda is very sick. Mrs. Shadden, Bug, and Mattie Cate and Callie Swan here this eve. I put a carpet down in mine and Rhoda's room. A pretty day.

Sunday 21. Pretty day, very warm. Mrs. Adelia Craigmiles, Mrs. Callaway, Mrs. Shadden, Mrs. Traynor, Mrs. Ford, Mrs. Kennedy, Cousin Mary Harle, Pryor and Lizzie Lea all here this eve. Uncle Preston here all day; stayed here all night last night. Mr. Harris and Mr. Petty left this morn. Mr. Petty came yesterday at noon. Wrote a letter to Cleo this morn. Our Confederates are returning from the South and from Northern prisons, one by one. Lts. Charlie Hardwick and Dick Harris, Joe and Will Osment and Bob Grant have already come. Miss Lou Swan here this morn. Charlie Gibbs, Bob and Julia Grant here this eve. Uncle Preston stayed here all night. The sick folks are all convalescing a little.

Monday 22. Pretty day. I cleaned up today. Mr. Parks here this morn. Little Rhoda and Sister are no better.

Tuesday 23. Pretty day. I have been busy cleaning up. The sick are improving.

Wednesday 24. Rhoda is a good deal better. Walker McSpadden dined here. I moved Aunt Adeline's bureau in her room. Julia Grant and Mr. Ben Crawford here this eve. I helped get supper. Emeline is sick. Capt. Murphy here drunk this eve.

Thursday 25. Pretty day. Mr. Petty and Mr. Harris left this eve. Rhoda went out and taught the boys today. Mother went out to see Mr. Ramsey Swan this eve.

Friday 26. Cold day. I cleaned up in the yard today. Mary Hardwick here this morn; says Mr. Carter will be at home in a few days.

Saturday 27. Pretty day. Rhoda and I went to see Adelia Craigmiles this eve. She is going North Monday. We also went to see Nannie Kennedy and Mr. Ramsey Swan. I cleaned up the yard this morn.

Sunday 28. Pretty day. Mr. Carter came this morn. We were all delighted to see him. Rhoda would have nothing to do with him at first. Mrs. Shadden, Mrs. Traynor, John Swan and Campbell, Mr. William Grant, and Dr. Shugart here to see him. Mr. Carter was here Capt. and Cousin John, Lt. Uncle Preston here this eve; dined here.

Monday 29. Pretty day. Sister and Mr. Carter went up to old Mr. Carter's and Mrs. Campbell's this eve. Cousin John went down to Chattanooga this eve to get his horse back, his own private property that the Yanks took. We put a piece of cloth in to weave this eve.

Tuesday 30. Pretty day. Mr. Petty here for dinner and Mr. Henry.

Wednesday 31. Lizzie wove all day. Mother and Sister spent the day at Mrs. Cannon's. Cousin John dined here; did not get his horse. Had a green apple pie for dinner.

June 1865

Thursday 1. Pretty day. Cousin John, Aunt Elizabeth, Uncle Caswell, and Pryor Lea spent the day here. We had a cherry pie and new potatoes for dinner. Cousin John and Uncle Pryor stayed here all night.

Friday 2. I wove all day. Have the blues terribly today about a heap of things. Julia and Virginia Grant here this eve.

Saturday 3. Very warm day. I scoured knives, buckets, etc. this morn. Rode Mr. McNelley (on a rail) this eve.[7] Uncle Preston and Pryor Lea dined here. Mr. Roberts and his two children stayed all night here.

Sunday 4. Warm day. Mother and Sister spent the day at Mrs. Cannon's. Uncle Preston and Pryor Lea dined here.

Monday 5. Warm day. Sister, Lillie, Rhoda, and I went out to stay a few days with Mrs. Cannon this morn. Mr. Roberts' children are sick.

Tuesday 6. A very warm day. Rained a little this eve. Still at Mrs. Cannon's.

Wednesday 7. Warm day. Willie Roberts and I rode in the buggy with Dr. Long up to Mrs. Col. Lea's for some raspberries this morn. Cousin John came out to Mrs. Cannon's this eve. Sister, Rhoda, and I came home this eve. Were delighted to get home.

Thursday 8. Warm day. I wove all day. Sat up at Mrs. Huff's with Hannah tonight.

Friday 9. I slept all morn. Rhoda and I, also Cousin John rode in a buggy to Mrs. Smith's this eve. I feel lonesome, sad, and everything else this eve.

Saturday 10. Pretty day. Rhoda and I papered the dining room today. I sat up at Mrs. Huff's tonight. Dr. Long, Cousin John, and Tack called this eve.

Sunday 11. Warm day. I stayed all day at Mrs. Huff's. Sister spent the day at Mrs. Cannon's.

Monday 12. Wove all day. Had the blues all day.

Tuesday 13. Went to see Miss Tennie Yarnell this eve and Aunt Elizabeth. Hannah Huff died this eve. I sat up there tonight. Mary Gaut died in Nashville yesterday.

Wednesday 14. Warm day. Cousin Dick Jarnagin and Mr. Scruggs here this morn. I slept this morn. Sister and I went up to see Mag Shadden and Mrs. Hughes this eve. Cousin John and Uncle Preston here tonight.

Thursday 15. Pretty day. I took up the parlor carpet today and cleaned up the parlor.

---

[7] Union troops put Robert McNelley on a rail and carried him to the town limits. This harsh action was due to McNelley's support of the Confederacy.

Friday 16. Pretty day. Cousin John and I made a dining room fire screen this morn, put the parlor carpet down this eve and cleaned up the dining room. Had beans for dinner first time.

Saturday 17. Warm day. Circus show in town. Adelia and Nina Craigmiles[8] spent the day here. Cousin John and Pryor dined here. Cousin Shade Inman came on the train this eve. He and Uncle Pryor stayed all night here.

Sunday 18. Cousin Shade and Uncle Preston Lea spent the day here. Cousin John Lea and Cousin Shade stayed here all night. Rhoda stayed with Sallie Surguine tonight.

Monday 19. Very warm day. Cousins Sam and John Inman and Mr. Swan came down on the train this eve. They and Cousin John Lea stayed here all night. Mrs. Shadden and Mag here this eve. Mr. Fox, Cousin John Lea and Shade dined here.

Tuesday 20. Mr. Hugh Martin, Cousin Shade, Sam and John Inman, John Lea, Uncle Preston, Mr. Fox, Mr. Swan dined here. All left this eve. Sister and Rhoda went up to Mrs. Shadden's this eve.

Wednesday 21. Sister and Mother spent the day at Mrs. Cannon's. Uncle Preston and Mr. Fox dined here. Capt. Wallace of [the] Confederate Army here this eve. Uncle Ned moved to Dr. Prues' this eve. Mr. Fox and Uncle Preston stayed here this eve.

Thursday 22. Uncle Preston and I went over to the depot and met Cleo this morn. Sister and I went for Lizzie and me a hat this morn. Lizzie got her one at Mrs. Trewhitts this eve. Cleo and Lizzie went to Mr. Blunt's exhibition tonight. We are extremely anxious to keep hotel.

Friday 23. I got a hat from Mrs. Trewhitt's this morn. Cleo dined here. Adelia Craigmiles, Nannie Kennedy, Mr. Cate, John Kennedy, and Tack Watkins here today. Cleo stayed all night with me.

Saturday 24. Pretty day. Cleo and I went up to see Adelia Craigmiles this morn. Lizzie called on Gussie and Sue Henderson this eve. I went out to Mr. Kennedy's this eve. I then went out and took tea at Aunt Elizabeth's this eve. Walker, Mr. Swan, and Johnnie were there. Mr. Fox and Uncle Preston came home with me and stayed all night.

---

8 Nina Craigmiles, born 5 August 1864, was the daughter of John H. and Adelia Craigmiles. At the age of seven she was killed in a buggy accident, 18 October 1871.

Sunday 25. Pleasant morn. Cleo came in this morn. She went home this eve. I went over to the depot with her. Mrs. Traynor, Laura Stout, and Mrs. Francisco here this eve.

Monday 26. Pretty day. Miss Lemira Yarnell spent the day with us. Elvira Lea stayed all night with me. Mrs. Smith, Windsor and Cousin Mary Harle here this eve. Uncle Preston and Mr. Fox stayed here tonight.

Tuesday 27. Had Houston lived he would have been 15 today. Cousin Ellen McCallie and her children and Gus Jarnagin came on the train this eve. Adelia Craigmiles here this morn; tuned our piano. Rhoda stayed all night with her tonight.

Wednesday 28. Cousin Martha Fox came on train this eve and went out to Uncle Caswell's. Cousin and little Mary dined at Dr. Jordan's. Cousin Ellen and her two children, Sister and Johnnie took tea at Mrs. Robert Swan's. Rhoda and Adelia Craigmiles assisted Prof. Blunt and Mrs. McNutt in a concert tonight. Lizzie, Annie, and I went with Uncle Preston and Cousin John. Elvira Lea here this eve.

Thursday 29. Warm day. I wove all day. Mother, Cousin Ellen, Mary, and Gracie spent the day at Aunt Elizabeth's. Mrs. William Craigmiles here this eve.

Friday 30. Cousin Martha, Mr. Fox, Uncle Pryor, Miss Lou Swan, Gus Jarnagin, Cousin Ellen, Cousin John, and Uncle Preston dined here. Cousin Mary, Miss Lou, and I went over to the depot with Cousin Ellen. She left this eve. Mr. Fox and Cousin Mary stayed all night here.

July 1865

Saturday 1. Rained all night and this morn. Cleared off this eve. Miss Lemira Yarnell, Cousin John, Mr. Fox, and Cousin Mary spent the day here. Cousin Mary was telling us about letting a hot lid fall on a Yank's hand when he attempted to take some biscuits out of an oven, also about them attempting to search her when she had three gold watches and four thousand dollars belted around her and her taking out her pistol and daring them to touch her. Cousin John Lea stayed here all night. Sister, Rhoda, and little Rhoda went out to Mrs. Cannon's this eve.

Sunday 2. Uncle Preston stayed all night here; dined here. Julia and Jeanette Grant here this eve. Rhoda and Sister came home this eve.

Monday 3. I commenced altering my muslin dress this morn. Lizzie and I wove all day. Cousin John stayed here last night.

Tuesday 4. Very, very warm day. Thermometer at 102 [Fahrenheit]. I wove all morn. Cousin John and Uncle Preston and Johnnie Lea dined here. Cousin John, Sister, Jimmie, Rhoda, and I went over to Emmett Johnson's to see Frances Tucker. Rhoda and I went with Gid Thompson and John Traynor to a Fourth of July party at Dr. Preus' tonight.

Wednesday 5. Very warm day. I sewed on my dress all day. Cousin Martha and Mr. Fox spent the day here. Uncle Preston stayed all night.

Thursday 6. An extremely warm day. Cousin Joe Lea and Cousin Frank Lea of the Confederate Army came this morn. Joe Callaway brought them down. Uncle Preston, Cousin Frank, Tom, John and Joe Lea took tea here. Cousin Frank and Joe Lea stayed here all night. Yesterday, four years ago, Frank and Tom Lea separated in the Rocky Mountains.

Friday 7. We finished the clothes this eve and took the loom down. We are glad it is out, I finished my dress this eve. Uncle Preston dined here. Cousin John stayed all night here.

Saturday 8. Rhoda, Lizzie, and I scoured both porches this morn, also Mother's room. Mrs. Bell Hardwick spent the day here. Uncle Preston has sick headache; he stayed here tonight.

Sunday 9. I finished the first volume of Washington Irving's *Life of Washington.*

Monday 10. I commenced me a jaconet [body] this morn. Cousin Joe Lea and Joe Callaway here after tea. They went on out to Uncle Caswell's. Rained this eve.

Tuesday 11. Mr. Carter came last night. Cousin Joe Lea here this morn. Rained some this eve and morn. I have been sewing on my [dress] body all day. Feel miserably blue today. Mr. Carter will not hear us going to a hotel.

Wednesday 12. Sister and I went out this eve to see about taking music lessons from Mrs. McNutt. Uncle Preston started to Aunt Charity's this eve. Mr. Carter, Sister, Jimmie, and I took tea at Mrs. Carter's.

Thursday 13. Pretty day. Rhoda and I took a music lesson this morn. I paid Mrs. McNutt $12.00. Mrs. West and Mrs. William Craigmiles here this morn. Sister, Rhoda, Jimmie, Annie, and I went up to Charlotte's to see Susan and Tom married, after tea. Finished my body this eve.

Friday 14. Pretty day. Hemmed my Swiss[9] skirt and bound it today. Sister made some plum jelly this eve. Mrs. Smith brought Rhoda some peaches this morn.

Saturday 15. Mrs. William Craigmiles, Mrs. West, Cousin Betsy Shields, Mary Dunlap, Helen Pharis, and Cousin Joe Lea spent the day here. Lizzie and I called on Miss Preus this eve.

Sunday 16. Rained this eve very hard. Cousin John Lea took tea and stayed all night.

Monday 17. Commenced me a white Swiss body this morn. Cousin Joe Lea, Sister, Lizzie, and I went out to Mrs. Traynor's big spring for some blackberries. Cousin Joe took tea here. Adelia Craigmiles gave Rhoda a fan and two bells this eve.

Tuesday 18. Took a music lesson this morn. Mother and Sister spent the day with Mrs. Cannon. John Swan and Cousin Gid Lea here this morn. Cousin Frank Lea's 22nd birthday.

Wednesday 19. Miss Lou Swan and Francis Tucker here this eve. Cousin John Lea stayed here all night.

Thursday 20. Warm Day. Cousin Joe Lea and I went out in a buggy to Mrs. Fate Hardwick's this eve. Cousin Joe Lea went with Rhoda, Joe Callaway, and me to a party at Mrs. Farroe Callaway's. Mr. Carter came from Georgia tonight, Uncle Preston from Alabama. Cousin Frank Lea here this eve and after tea.

Friday 21. I took a music lesson this morn. Rhoda, Lizzie, and I went to a party at Mr. Pleasant Craigmiles' this eve. Mr. Carter took us. Jim Campbell came home with us. Col. Brownlow and Miss Mary Brownlow were there.

---

[9] Swiss is a crisp, sheer cotton cloth used for light garments or curtains which was originally made in Switzerland.

Saturday 22. Pretty day. Cousin Martha Fox spent the day here. Cousin Frank and Cousin Martha took tea here.

Sunday 23. Cousin Dick Jarnagin spent the day here and all night. Warm day. Cousin Frank here this eve.

Monday 24. Mr. Carter started to New York this morn before day. Cousin Dick left on the same train. Cousin Frank took tea here. I went out to see Miss Lemira Yarnell. Aunt Elizabeth went with me this eve. Cousin Retta dined here. A great many families are going to South America. I would like to go.

Tuesday 25. A warm day. Rained this eve. Took a music lesson this morn. Cousin Frank and Joe Lea stayed all night here.

Wednesday 26. A very, very warm day. Mother, Aunt Elizabeth, Uncle Preston, and Cousin John all went down to Cousin Betsy Shields' this morn. Mrs. McNutt, Mattie Foute, and Mrs. William Craigmiles here after tea. Cousin Joe Lea stayed here all night.

Thursday 27. Very warm. Mother and the rest came back this eve. Mrs. Shadden and Mag took tea here. I was sick this morn. Laid down and went to sleep.

Friday 28. A Warm day. I took a music lesson this morn. Posted my journal all morn. Mother, Sister, and Johnnie spent the day at Mrs. Cannon's. Aunt Elizabeth, Lizzie, Rhoda, and I the only ones here for dinner. Cousin Joe Lea and Uncle Preston stayed here all night. Rained this eve. Mr. Callaway and wife and Belle stayed here tonight; went up on 12 o'clock train.

Saturday 29. A pretty day. I have felt sad all day. Uncle Preston stayed here tonight.

Sunday 30. Pretty day. Cousin Shade Inman came this morn; took breakfast here. Cousin John Lea dined here and took tea. Had peaches and cream. After we had gone to bed, Cousins Tom and Joe Lea came down. Cousin Shade Inman and Uncle Preston stayed here tonight. John Swan and Willie Cannon here this eve.

Monday 31. Rained this eve. Uncle Preston left for Dandridge on 12 o'clock train. Cousin Shade and Sister went out to Uncle Caswell's this eve. I received a letter from Charlie Gatrel this morn. I got dinner today. Cousin Martha and Mr. Fox and Cousin Shade stayed here all night. They are to leave for Atlanta tomorrow morn before day.

August 1865

Tuesday 1. I went out to Uncle Caswell's this morn. Mrs. McNutt sick. I did not take a lesson. This eve Rhoda, Cousins Joe and John Lea, and I rode out to Mrs. Smith's. Had a real treat of peaches, grapes, pears, and almonds. Mattie Foute and Cousin John Lea stayed here tonight. Warm day.

Wednesday 2. Cousin Hugh Inman came this morn. Mrs. Cannon spent the day here. Cousin Hugh and I went out to Uncle Caswell's this eve. Sister, Johnnie, and I took tea there. We went out and helped milk. Cousin Hugh is to leave tomorrow morn. He and Cousin John stayed here tonight. Very warm.

Thursday 3. Warm day. Cousin Joe Lea here this morn. Mrs. Traynor and Eliza Keebler spent the day here. Took a music lesson this morn.

Friday 4. Pretty day. Tack Watkins here this morn, also Cousin Frank Lea. Cousin Joe Lea and Rhoda, Cousin Frank and I went to a party at Mr. William Craigmiles' tonight. Cousins Joe and Frank stayed here all night.

Saturday 5. Warm day. Cousin Ben Lea came this morn before day on 12 o'clock train from Ohio. I took a music lesson this morn. Maston Henry here this eve. Mother and Cousin Ben went out to Uncle Caswell's this eve.

Sunday 6. A warm day. Cousins Ben, Frank, and George Lea dined here. Rhoda, Sister, Mother, and the children went to the Baptist Church this morn and eve. I read *The History of South America* all day.

Monday 7. A pretty day. Mr. R.W. Smith and Cousin John Lea dined here. Cousin John stayed all night. Aunt Elizabeth and Cousin John took tea here. Cousins Joe and Frank Lea here this eve. Cousins Joe Lea and Joe Callaway here after tea. We took a walk by moonlight to the railroad. Cousin Ben Lea left this morn on the 11 o'clock train.

Tuesday 8. A cool and pleasant day. Cousin Joe Lea dined here. Rhoda and I went over to see Bug Cate and Mrs. Grant, took little

Rhoda. I feel sad and lonely this eve; do all the time. I fear if I indulge too much in "ennui" I will become a settled hypochondriac as well as a misanthrope. Cleveland has no charms for me. I wish we could leave here and go somewhere else. New York, South America or anywhere from here. If no one but myself were to read this I would unburden my heart to you, my friend, but knowing to keep them pent up within the narrow cell of my heart, hoping and wishing a brighter day may be in store for me. Mother and Sister, with the children, have gone to Uncle Caswell's, so there is no one here but Rhoda, Lizzie, Aunt Adeline, and myself. I do feel so lonesome and miserable this eve. Cousin John Lea, Cousin Tom, and Joe Callaway here after tea. Cousin Joe told us good-bye; he is going to Louisiana tomorrow morn. Cousin John stayed here all night. Rhoda stayed all night with Mattie Foute.

Wednesday 9. Pretty day. Mrs. Kate Rogers and her two children, John and Mary, spent the day here. I went out to Aunt Elizabeth's this eve. She and I went to see Miss Lemira Yarnell. She is to go home tomorrow. Callie Swan took tea here.

Thursday 10. A pretty day. Cousin Frank here this eve. I practiced.

Friday 11. A pretty day. Sallie Reeder stayed all night here. Cousin Frank Lea, Rhoda, and I went out after tea and spent the eve at Mr. Robert Swan's. Mattie Foute and her brother Bob, William, David, and Ham Russell were there.

Saturday 12. Pretty day. Adelia Craigmiles here this eve. She brought Rhoda a set of jewelry. Cousin Frank here this eve.

Sunday 13. A warm day. Rhoda, Sister, Mother, Annie, Jimmie, Johnnie, and I went to hear Mr. Kennedy's preaching. Cousin John stayed here tonight.

Monday 14. A very, very warm day. I took "Last Rose of Summer" this morn. Sister, Johnnie, and Jimmie went out to Uncle Caswell's this eve, also to Mrs. Frank Hardwick's. Jimmie and I went up to Mr. Kennedy's after pears.

Tuesday 15. A warm day. Sister, Rhoda, and I have been busy moving the things out of the storeroom and tore down the partition and made a larger room. No one here today for the first time in weeks.

Wednesday 16. A warm day. Mother, Annie, and Lizzie spent the day at Mrs. Reeder's today. Rhoda, Sister, and I have been busy all day preparing the room opposite the parlor for a reception room. Lizzie stayed all night at Mr. Reeder's.

Thursday 17. A pretty day. Rhoda and I received some new pieces of music from Cincinnati. Nannie and Sallie Kennedy dined here.

Friday 18. A pretty day. Rhoda and I practiced all day. Emeline left today. We have no servants to eat here, the first time such a thing occurred since I can remember. It seems so strange we have to do our own work. Susan washes and milks for us. Sister and Mother cook. Aunt Adeline and Lizzie iron. Rhoda and I clean up the house. Mrs. Shadden here this eve.

Saturday 19. A pretty day warm day. Rhoda and I went down to Mrs. Hardwick's to see Lucretia Tibbs and over to see Mary Edwards. Cousin Frank Lea here this eve.

Sunday 20. A pretty day. Mrs Callaway and Bell came down on the train this morn before day. She and Rhoda went up to Mr. R. J. F. Callaway's to get a conveyance to take her home. Mr. Petty and his brother and Mrs. Callaway and Bell stayed here all night. Nannie Kennedy here this morn.

Monday 21. A very warm day. Rhoda was sick all last night. Cousin John and Mary Edwards here this morn. Lucretia Tibbs here this morn. I did not see her; was taking my music lesson.

Tuesday 22. A pretty day. Rained this eve. Rhoda went around this eve with Mrs. McNutt to get some music pupils. Cousin Frank Lea and Joe Callaway here this eve; took tea.

Wednesday 23. A pretty day. Rhoda went with Mrs. McNutt again this morn. Sister and Mother went up to Mr. Robert Swan's this eve. I have been reading *Guy Mannering* this eve.

Thursday 24. Pretty day. Rhoda and I went out and called on Mrs. Bob Smith this eve. Mr. Smith came home with us.

Friday 25. A pretty day. The nights are becoming cold, a precursor of fall. Cousin John took tea here. I have the sore throat; feel quite unwell. Mr. Carson called after tea. Cousin Frank here after tea. We changed mine and Rhoda's room into the dining room this morn. Rhoda has been complaining of feeling unusually blue today.

Saturday 26. Pretty day. I do not feel like doing anything today. Oh! that I could have things my way. Prepare my own station and duties in this life. Willie Cannon brought us three muskmelons this morn. I feel lonesome this morn. Cousin Joe Lea came from Virginia this morn. He, Cousin John, and Aunt Elizabeth took tea here. Gussie Craigmiles and Sue Henderson here this morn. Cousin Frank Lea stayed here all night. Rhoda and Sister went up to see Mag Morgan.

Sunday 27. Uncle Wood came this eve to stay all week. I went with the rest to the Baptist Church. Cousin John Lea took tea here. Mr. Blunt has come with his wife, also Will Russell and Lizzie Burgess are married. Pretty day.

Monday 28. Pretty day. Aunt Wood came this morn.

Tuesday 29. Pretty day. Aunt Wood went to Charleston this eve. We are thinking of going to the hotel. I finished *Guy Mannering* this eve.

Wednesday 30. Pretty day. Aunt Wood came back this morn. I finished reading *Valley of the Amazons* this eve. Cousin Frank Lea here after tea.

Thursday 31. Rained a little this eve. Rhoda and I canned some peaches this eve. The last day of the Summer 1865. I dislike to see winter coming on. In a month we will have cold weather.

September 1865

Friday 1. A pretty day. The first day of Fall. I feel sad all the time; our family are so unsettled. Aunt and Uncle Wood left this eve. Bob Smith and his wife here after tea. Mother went to Aunt Elizabeth's this eve to put in a piece of cloth.

Saturday 2. Pretty day. I finished making Jimmie a body this eve. Mother spent the day at Aunt Elizabeth's.

Sunday 3. Pretty day. Sister, Mother, and I went to the Baptist Church this morn. Mary and Carrie Lea, Mrs. Rogers, Mary Shugart here this eve. Cousin Frank and John took tea here.

Monday 4. Pretty day. Mr. and Mrs. Carr came this eve to stay two or three days. Mrs. Windsor Smith here this eve.

Tuesday 5. Pretty day. Cousin John dined here. Mr. and Mrs. Carr did not take tea here. Cousin Mat Harrison was married this eve 2 P.M. at New Market, to Mr. Talbot Naff.

Wednesday 6. Pretty day. Mr. and Mrs. Carr left this eve. For the last time I have been sewing for Sister. I sat up with Julia McGhee tonight.

Thursday 7. A pretty day. Mr. Carson and John Traynor here tonight. I did not see them. Retired to rest early on account of sitting up last night. I slept this morn.

Friday 8. Pretty day. I practiced most all day.

Saturday 9. Pretty day. Mr. Reed here this eve. I was not at home. Julia McGhee died last night. [10] Rhoda, Annie, and I went to her burying this eve.

Sunday 10. Pretty day. Mr. Kennedy dined here. We went to the Baptist Church this morn and afternoon.

Monday 11. Pretty day. Mother, Johnnie, and I took dinner at Uncle Caswell's. Julia and Jeanette Grant took tea.

Tuesday 12. Pretty day. I commenced the baby a flannel petticoat. Rained this eve.

Wednesday 13. Rained this eve. We took down the bedstead in Mother's room and sold it and put up Aunt Adelia's. Received and wrote a letter to Cousin Mary Harrison.

Thursday 14. Pretty day. Rhoda and I spent the day at Mrs. Reeder's. Sallie, Rhoda, and I went over to Mrs. Russell's to see Lizzie.

Friday 15. Pretty day. I practiced all day. Rhoda and I, accompanied by John Traynor, went to the choir. Adelia Craigmiles and Nannie Kennedy here this eve.

Saturday 16. Pretty day. Cousin Mary Jarnagin spent the day and night here.

Sunday 17. Pretty day. I had a severe spell of cramp colic last night; sick all day. All but me went to church this morn. Mr. Goings and John Kennedy here this eve.

---

[10]Julia Tucker McGhee, wife of James McGhee, b. 27 June 1840, d. 9 September 1865, Fort Hill Cemetery. Ross, *Cemetery Records* II:212.

Monday 18. Rainy day. Cousin John dined here. I do not feel well today. Two Mr. Goings here this eve.

Tuesday 19. I went up and took a music lesson this morn. Rhoda and I went up to the Presbyterian Church this eve and practiced on the organ. Adelia came whilst we were there. A real fall day. Cousin Mary stayed here tonight. Mr. Shields brought us a large watermelon.

Wednesday 20. Rainy day. Mother and Sister spent the day at Mrs. Gallaher's.

Thursday 21. Cousin Mary stayed with us tonight. I went up and practiced on the organ this eve. Aunt Elizabeth here this eve.

Friday 22. Pretty day. I had another spell of the cramp colic last night. Cousin Mary Harle here this morn. Cousin Frank took tea and stayed here all night. Nat Carson and John Traynor took Rhoda and me to the choir. I played on the organ.

Saturday 23. Pretty day. This day eight years ago Houston died.

Sunday 24. Pretty day. Cousin Mary Jarnagin spent the day with us. Mother, Annie, Jimmie, and I went up to the graveyard and the forts this eve.

Monday 25. Pretty day. Cousin Mary Jarnagin spent the night with us. Sister and I went up town and got me a cloak this eve.

Tuesday 26. Cousin Mary [stayed] all night with us. Rhoda sick all day from eating grapes. I went up to Mary Edwards' this morn.

Wednesday 27. Pretty day. I went up to Mrs. Shadden's to get her to assist me in pleating a black silk dress. Cousin Mary left this morn for Athens on the train. We received some books and shoes from Mr. Carter this morn.

Thursday 28. Pretty day. Cousin James Brazelton came this morn; took dinner, tea and stayed all night here. He is going to Texas soon. John Traynor went with Rhoda and me to the choir.

Friday 29. Pretty day. Cousin John Lea and Rhoda are thinking about going to Texas with Cousin James. He left this morn. Cousin John took Rhoda and me to church tonight.

Saturday 30. Pretty day. Rhoda has given out going to Texas. I think of going in her place.

October 1865

Sunday 1. Pretty day. Rhoda and I went to the Presbyterian Church this morn. Uncle Preston and Mr. Calvin Nance came up last night.

Monday 2. Pretty day. We have been very busy preparing for my trip to Texas. Cousin Joe, Uncle Preston, and Cousin John dined here. Uncle Caswell here this eve.

Tuesday 3. Pretty day. Mother, Sister, and Uncle Preston went to Ringgold on the two o'clock train to see a house we think of buying. They came back at ten o'clock tonight. Our trip to Texas is bursted up. Cousin John is indicted for treason. I went out and took tea at Uncle Caswell's this eve. Mrs. Cannon spent the day with us. I went with her up to see Eliza Wood and Katie Rogers.

Wednesday 4. Pretty day. We are so anxious to go to Ringgold to live. We are in suspense; do not know whether we can get the house or not.

Thursday 5. Pretty day. Sister, Rhoda, Annie, and the baby went out to Mrs. Cannon's this afternoon to stay all night. Uncle Caswell and Preston and Cousin Joe Lea took tea here. Uncle Preston stayed all night. I made coffee the first time tonight.

Friday 6. Pretty day. Sister and the rest came back late this eve. Mother spent the day at Aunt Elizabeth's. I got dinner for Aunt Adeline, Lizzie, Jimmie and Johnnie. Cousin Joe and Uncle Preston took tea here. Uncle Preston stayed all night. We went to the choir but there was none.

Saturday 7. Pretty day. Mrs. Kennedy dined here. I have had the blues for the last two days. Mrs. Dr. Brown and Mrs. Hughes here this morn. Miss Nep Smith here this eve. Uncle Preston and Cousin Joe took tea here.

Sunday 8. Pretty day. Mary Lea and Uncle Preston spent the day here. Mrs. Shadden here this eve. Uncle Preston stayed here all night.

Monday 9. Pretty day. Uncle Preston and Callie Swan dined here.

Tuesday 10. Pretty day. Uncle Preston stayed here all night. Cousin and Uncle Preston took tea. Cousins Joe, Frank, and Pryor [here] awhile after tea.

Wednesday 11. Pretty day. Cousin James Brazelton, Mary Ann, Sallie, Joe, Johnnie, Florence, and Frank all dined here. They are on their way to Texas. Uncle Caswell, Preston, Aunt Elizabeth, and Mr. Carter dined here. We received a letter stating that we could not get the Inman house at Ringgold for less than $ 5,000.00. Uncle Preston and Frances Tucker stayed here all night.

Thursday 12. Pretty day. Cousin John came from Knoxville this morn. Sister and I went up to Mrs. Shadden's this eve after a pattern for my worsted dress. Came home this eve and cut out the sleeves. Rhoda and Mother spent the eve at Uncle Caswell's. Uncle Preston stayed all night here.

Friday 13. Rained very hard this eve. I finished my worsted dress this eve. Mr. Kennedy at our home this eve.

Saturday 14. Rained some this eve. Mrs. Watkins, Lena, and Miss Bettie Carter came to our house to get me to go home with them. I packed up and came home with them this eve.

Sunday 15. Pretty day. Bettie Carter, Cleo, and I went over to Ooltewah to Sunday School. We took a walk this eve.

Monday 16. Pretty day. I gave Cleo a lesson this morn. Cleo, Bettie, and I went over to Mr. Guthrie's store and Mitch Stone's. There we saw Dr. Rhoddy and we [each] got a piece [of music].

Tuesday 17. Pretty day. Gave Lena a lesson. Cleo, Bettie, and I went down to the horse lot this eve. Reese came this eve from Concord.[11]

Wednesday 18. Rained some this morn. Gave Cleo a music lesson. Helped sew on her calico dress.

Thursday 19. Pretty day. Bettie and I went after gum wax this morn. I gave Lena a music lesson this morn Cleo, Bettie, and I went over to Mr. Guthrie's store this eve. We got some mugs full of sugar. The moon was in eclipse this morn. I received a letter from home this eve.

Friday 20. Pretty day. This eve Bettie and I went and got some hickory nuts. Gave Cleo a music lesson this morn.

---

[11] Concord is in Hamilton County, Tennessee.

Saturday 21. Pretty day. Gave Lena a music lesson. This eve Cleo, Bettie, and I dressed up and went over to the stores. We then came back and took a ride through Ooltewah.

Sunday 22. Pretty day. Cleo and I went to Sunday School this morn. Bettie did not go. I wrote to Cousin Joe Lea this eve. Dick Arnett here this eve. After he left, Cleo, Bettie, and I walked nearly over to town.

Monday 23. Pretty day. Gave Cleo a lesson. I tucked my pantalettes this eve.

Tuesday 24. Pretty day. Cleo, Bettie, and I went over to town this eve. We took tea at Mrs. Ragan's. Gave Lena a music lesson.

Wednesday 25. Pretty day. Bettie, after dark, dressed up in Reese's clothes and came in Mrs. Watkins' room. I hemmed my dress this eve. Gave Cleo a lesson.

Thursday 26. Pretty day. I gave Lena a lesson. Bettie, Cleo, and I took tea at Mrs. Parker's this eve.

Friday 27. Rained this morn. Gave Cleo a music lesson. Ironed my clothes this morn. Bettie, Cleo, Reese, and I went over to Mrs. Ragan's after tea to meet Josie and Pauline Hereford. We looked for them on the train. They did not come. Cleo baked cake for them. Bettie and I had a scuffle over an apple.

Saturday 28. Gave Lena a lesson. Bettie and I trimmed Cleo's hat. I received a letter from home saying we had bought Farroe Callaway's house[12]

Sunday 29. Pretty day. Mrs. Watkins, Bettie, Cleo, and I went and heard Mrs. Douglass' funeral preached. I suffered with cold. I received a letter from home saying for me to come home. Mr. Reed dined and stayed here all night.

Monday 30. Pretty day. Bettie, Cleo, and I went with John Kennedy down to Mrs. Igou's this morn.

Tuesday 31. Pretty day. Miss Lemira Yarnell came back with us this morn.

---

[12]On Lea Street which later became Broad Street. Mrs. Inman bought the home for $3,300.00. The house was built on a one-acre plot of land in Lot 71. The transaction was completed on 26 October 1865. Bradley County Deeds, A. 132.

November 1865

Wednesday 1. Pretty day. Cleo, Reese, and I got up before day and went over to the train with Bettie; she went home. Miss Lemira and John went to Cleveland. Gave Cleo a lesson.

Thursday 2. Rained this morn. Gave Lena a lesson. I received a letter this eve from Lizzie saying I must come home. A rainy eve. I gave Cleo "Smith's March."

Friday 3. Rained this morn. Cleo and I took a ride this eve.

Saturday 4. Rained a little this morn. Cleo and I went up to Mrs. Barnes' this eve for stone dye, and then took a ride.

Sunday 5. Cold day. Cleo and I went to church today. Doug Igou, Dick Arnett, and Mr. Reed dined here. Cleo packed my trunk for me to go home this eve. I feel sad to leave Mrs. Watkins and her family.

Monday 6. Cold day. Cleo, Mr. Reed, and I came over to Mrs. Ragan's to wait for the train. I came up home this morn. Found everything torn up preparatory to moving to our new home where Farroe Callaway lives.

Tuesday 7. Pretty day. Cousin Joe Lea and Cousin Frank came to tell us good-bye. They are going to start to Louisiana tonight. Elvira and Emma Lea came with them.

Wednesday 8. Pretty day. We commenced moving this eve. Rhoda and Lizzie and Cousin John Lea stayed at home tonight. Mother, Sister, little Rhoda, and I spent our last night at our old home in the kitchen.

Thursday 9. Pretty day. We finished moving today.

Friday 10. Pretty day. We commenced washing the window glass this morn. I tacked down carpet in Mother's room. Rhoda, Lizzie, and I went with Dr. Carson tonight to the church.

Saturday 11. Pretty day. We have been very busy all day cleaning up. We got the window sashes all washed this eve.

Sunday 12. Pretty day. Rhoda, Lizzie, and I went to the Presbyterian Church. Nat Carson went with us tonight to church.

Monday 13. Pretty day. Mother and I planted out shrubbery in the yard today. Mrs. Sallie here this eve. Mrs. Harris came to board with us this eve.

Tuesday 14. Pretty day. Mr. Nelson, Mr. Rice, and Mr. Sam Haynes stayed here last night. Rained this eve. Callie Callaway came this eve.

Wednesday 15. Pretty day. Mossalana Gerr commenced papering our dining room this eve. Elvira, Aunt Elizabeth, and Martha Boyd here this eve. Samantha Swan's 28th birthday.

Thursday 16. Pretty day. Callie Callaway left this morn. Miss Lemira Yarnell here; spent the day. We heard today that Henry Jones is dead; died in Newnan, Georgia. We all feel so sad to hear of his death.

Friday 17. Pretty day. Finished papering our room this eve. Rhoda, Lizzie, and I went to the choir this eve. Wrote to Cleo Watkins this morn.

Saturday 18. Pretty day. Been sewing on parlor carpet today. Adelia and Nina Craigmiles here this eve, also Mrs. Traynor and Kate Rogers. Samantha Swan died last night at one o'clock. Rhoda and I sat up there tonight.

Sunday 19. Pretty day. Mrs. Cannon dined here. Cousin Mary Harle, Mrs. Norwood, and Mrs. Callaway here this eve. Rhoda, Lizzie, and Mother went to hear Samantha Swan's funeral preached. Old Mr. and Mrs. Carter here this eve after tea. Mother, Lizzie, and Rhoda went to church tonight.

Monday 20. Rained this eve. Sister and I got dinner today. Mr. Harris came down in the parlor and we played for him this afternoon. I feel sad and blue and lonesome this eve. Mrs. Thompson and Adelia here this eve.

Tuesday 21. Pretty day. Mr. Harris left tonight for the North. Mrs. Craigmiles and Mattie Foute sat until bedtime with us. Sister and I went out to Mr. Ross' after carpeting, Mrs. Swan's and Uncle Caswell's this eve.

Wednesday 22. Pretty day. Nannie Kennedy here this eve. I walked out to Uncle Caswell's with her and came back with Rhoda and Lizzie who went out there this eve. Mother, Annie, Jimmie, and I went down to Mrs. Carter's and sat until bedtime.

Thursday 23. Pretty day. Rhoda, Sister, and I went over to Mrs. Thompson's and sat until bedtime. Mary Smith and Maston Henry here this eve.

Friday 24. Pretty day. Nannie Kennedy took tea here and went with Rhoda, Lizzie, and me to the choir. Rhoda and I went to see Mattie Coulter, Cynthia Hardwick, Sallie Ragsdale, and Ada Gaut this eve.

Saturday 25. Pretty day. I finished reading *Oliver Twist* tonight.

Sunday 26. Pretty day. Rhoda, Mother, Lizzie, and I went to hear Mr. Edward Caldwell preach this morn. Rhoda and I [went] to hear him tonight. Mother, Sister, and all the children except little Rhoda went out to Uncle Caswell's this eve.

Monday 27. Pretty day. Lizzie and I went out to Mrs. Smith's this morn for rose slips and grape cuttings. We moved Aunt Adeline's bed out of our room this eve and put a carpet down in our room of tousles.[13]

Tuesday 28. A dull, cloudy day. Sister and I went around to the stores and down to Mrs. Ramage's and Mrs. Traynor's this morn. I sent Cleo a sleeve pattern this morn. Sister and Rhoda went out to see Mrs. Lizzie Harris this eve. She is going to Alabama soon.

Wednesday 29. Cold day. Mr. Dennison from Michigan came here tonight.

Thursday 30. Pretty day. Sister and Mrs. Gallagher went over to see Emeline this eve. Dr. Carson and John Traynor called on us tonight.

December 1865

Friday 1. Pretty day. Sister and Rhoda spent the day at Mrs. Cannon's. Adelia Craigmiles here this eve. We went to the choir at the church.

Saturday 2. Rhoda, Mattie Foute, and I spent the day at Mrs. Swan's. We helped Callie sew. The Baptist meeting commenced at the Presbyterian Church tonight. Mr. Russell, the minister, stayed here all night. Mrs. Giddings left here this eve.

---

[13]The word tousles refers to a room that is in disarray.

Monday 4. Rained this morn. Mr. Carter came last night. We went to church tonight. I went down to the drugstore and got a jubilee[14] and some kerosene oil.

Tuesday 5. Rainy day. I altered my dark calico dress. Mr. James Carter left tonight.

Wednesday 6. Pretty day. We went to the choir at Dr. Thompson's tonight.

Thursday 7. Rainy day. I went to Mrs. Swan's and got Mrs. Massengill to cut out my cloak this eve. Thanksgiving Day.

Friday 8. Pretty day. I sewed on my cloak all day. Cleo Watkins came this eve. She and I went down to the stores. We went to the choir at Dr. Hunt's.

Saturday 9. Rainy day. Eight persons from the North came this morn to board with us. Rhoda and I laid [made fire] the parlor hearth; we tacked down the carpet this eve. Mr. Reed took tea here.

Sunday 10. Pretty day. Cleo and I went out to see Jennie Kennedy this eve; she is very sick. We then went to see Uncle Ned at Dr. Jordan's. He is not expected to live.

Monday 11. Rainy day. Cleo and I went down to the stores to get her a clock. Got it from John Traynor.

Tuesday 12. Rainy night. A sad and gloomy eve to all of us. This afternoon at two o'clock another one of our old and faithful family servants, Uncle Ned, bid adieu to this terrestrial sphere and joined our friends in another world. When I reflect on past scenes and my mind reverts to memories of "auld lang syne" I feel sad, sad. Never, no never, will we see Uncle Ned's and Aunt Phoebe's cheerful faces again, spreading ease, comfort and happiness wherever they go. It seems as though two grandparents had left us since they have been called away, for a parent would not have cared more for our comfort and pleasure than they did for "Miss Annie and her children," as they called us. It is growing late, and fain would I dwell on their virtues if I had the power to do them any good, but alas, the only duty left us is to be ready to join them in the spirit world when our hour comes, where there is no distinction of color or rank. Mother

---

[14] A jubilee is an ice cream sundae with cherry sauce and whipped cream.

was there all day. I went over this morn and eve. Mr. Lea here, took tea. Cleo and I cut her cloak out this eve.

Wednesday 13. Muddy today. I have been sewing on Cleo's cloak all day. This eve Rhoda, Lizzie, and I went over to Dr. Jordan's to see Uncle Ned.

Thursday 14. A cold day. Sister and I went around shopping this morn. Uncle Ned was buried this morn at ten o'clock. Mr. Carter went to his burying. It is so cold, we did not go.

Friday 15. A very cold day. I feel sad and blue and lonesome this eve. Have nothing particular to do and do not feel like doing anything; Rhoda went down to see Adelia Craigmiles this morn. She was sick and said the choir would not meet there. She was telling Rhoda about Gussie Craigmiles spending Christmas at the "White House" and her preparations, getting a white velvet cloak for a reception cloak, and another to go out in.

Saturday 16. Cold day. Cleo went to Mr. Edwards' this morn; came back this eve.

Sunday 17. Rainy day. Mrs. Col. Lea stayed here last night.

Monday 18. Rainy day. Cleo and I called on Mrs. Harris from Ohio this morn. Cleo went and stayed with Nannie Kennedy tonight. Mr. DeLany commenced boarding here this eve.

Tuesday 19. Rainy day. Mrs Ewing and Mrs. Riddle went to housekeeping [home making] this eve.

Wednesday 20. Rainy day. Mrs. and Mr. Harris called this eve. Lizzie and Sallie Jones have been making a doll for Rhoda.

Thursday 21. Cold day but clear. Adelia Craigmiles spent the day here and tuned our piano. Cleo went to stay with Bug Cate tonight. I feel sad this eve, sitting in mine and Rhoda's room over the kitchen. Sister says she believes Mother will have to break up housekeeping, that she cannot support herself and family keeping [a] boarding house. It makes me feel sad to hear her talk so. "Poverty is a rigid school and the sessions are long." I am now reading Burns' *Life* and heartily do I sympathize with him in his poverty and pride. I want to take music lessons next session and I fear, yes, I do not even hope that I will get to take them. Good-bye, old journal, Lizzie has called me to set the table, and as that is my only task I should perform it willingly.

Friday 22. Pretty day but muddy. The choir met here tonight. Cleo and Lizzie, with Mag Cate, went to the academy this eve. I enjoyed the choir meeting very well. I played on the piano for them.

Saturday 23. Very muddy but mild day. Cleo went home this eve. Lizzie went to the depot with her. Rhoda and Adelia Craigmiles went to Mary Gaut's burying this eve. I went over to the church and practiced this eve. I ironed all eve. Rhoda stayed all night with Adelia tonight.

Sunday 24. Rainy day. Rhoda and I went to the church this morn and tonight. I played on the organ. Mr. Carter came home this morn.

Monday 25. Rained some today. Christmas Day. The children were delighted with the presents Kris Kringle brought them. Rhoda and I dined at Dr. Thompson's. Dr. Carson was there. I enjoyed the day pretty well. Tonight we went to a ball at the Ocoee [House]. I was introduced to Mr. Rusber Ruder and Mr. Lillard. I enjoyed myself only tolerable well; came home at three o'clock this morn.

Tuesday 26. Rainy morn. I feel dull this morn, having slept only three hours last night. I have been practicing this morn. Adelia Craigmiles, Mary Edwards, and Sallie Reeder here this afternoon. Callie Swan stayed all night with Rhoda.

Wednesday 27. Very muddy and cloudy. Lizzie Lea received a letter from Lt. Simmons saying that he was married to a lady from Lynchfield, Mass. I went with Tom McMillin to a party at Mr. Cate's, Rhoda and Gid Thompson, Lizzie with Mel Osment. I feel sad and miserable this eve. We started out there about dark. Rhoda and I helped wash today.

Thursday 28. Rainy day. A miserable, gloomy day. Adelia Craigmiles here this eve. I have been hemming Annie a pair of pantalettes this eve.

Friday 29. Rainy day and cloudy day. Rhoda and I went to the choir at Dr. Thompson's tonight. I enjoyed it very well.

Saturday 30. Rainy day. I ironed all this morn, ground coffee this eve. I practiced "Ben-Bolt Var" tonight. Cousin John Lea here tonight.

Sunday 31. Rainy day. Mr. Kennedy here for tea. I went no where today. But spent a gloomy day at home.

1866

January 1866

Monday 1. Rained all New Years day. Rhoda and I helped wash today. Mr. Carter started to East Tennessee tonight.

Tuesday 2. Rainy and cloudy today. I wrote a letter to Mr. Crocker and Sallie Shields this morn. Several men here attending court. Miss Eva Miller, Sally Jennie commenced boarding here this eve.

Wednesday 3. I went down to see Elvira Lea [this] eve at Mr. Callaway's; enjoyed the evening very much.

Thursday 4. Cold day. Rhoda ironed all day today. I made me some linen collars.

Friday 5. Cold day. Mary Edwards, Adelia Craigmiles, and Tack Watkins here this eve. Adelia, Rhoda, Lizzie and I went in a hack to a party at the Ocoee House tonight. I enjoyed it only tolerably well. Mr. Carter home tonight.

Saturday 6. A pleasant but rather cold day. I have been sick this morn in consequence of going to the ball last eve. Sister, Mr. Carter, Johnnie, and Jimmie spent the day at old Mr. Carter's today. Rhoda went down to see Adelia this eve. Nannie Kennedy here this morn. I wrote to Cleo Watkins this morn and copied the minutes of the Society. I feel sad and lonely this eve. Would like to practice this eve but it too cold. Mr. DeLany quit boarding with us this morn. Life, what is it but one continued sorrow and gloom, [covered] over lightly with mirth and joy. Tack Watkins and Hugh Bell here this eve.

Sunday 7. Cold day. Cousin Joe Lea took tea here. Sister, Rhoda, and children went to church this morn. Rhoda, Miss Eva Miller, Lizzie, and I went to Methodist preaching at Presbyterian Church.

Monday 8. Cold--very cold. I sewed on Sisters plaid silk dress today.

Tuesday 9. Cold day. I sewed on Sisters dress. Cousin John Lea took dinner here; showed a letter he got from Cousin Joe Lea. The Mite Society[1] met here tonight; a great many here.

Wednesday 10. Pleasant day. I made starch this morn for the first time in my life. Mother and Sister went to Harles this eve. Mr. DeLany is boarding there.

Thursday 11. Pleasant day. Miss Lou Swan here this morn. I wrote off the minutes of the Society, and posted my journal this morn.

Friday 12. Rained late this eve. Cloudy all day. The choir met here tonight.

Saturday 13. Pretty all day. Rhoda and I called on Mrs. Harris, Mrs. Riddle, Mrs. Ewing and Miss Chamberlain this morn; also at the drugstore to see a stethoscope. Rhoda had her photograph taken this eve. Miss Boyd here this eve. Bob Smith took tea here. Rhoda and I spent the eve at Dr. Thompsons. We met with a Mr. Moss from New Orleans.

Sunday 14. Pretty day. Rhoda, Sister and I went to Presbyterian Church. Rhoda and I went tonight also.

Monday 15. Pretty day. Sewed all day for Sister. Sister commenced weaning little Rhoda this morn.

Tuesday 16. Pretty day. Rhoda, Sister and I went to the Mite Society at Mr. Carter's.

Wednesday 17. Pretty day. Sewed all day for Aunt Eliza. Sister, Rhoda, Miss Lou Swan, and Callie, Nannie Kennedy, and I spent the day there. Sallie Reeder and Mary Edwards stayed all night with us.

Thursday 18. Pretty day. I sewed some for Sister.

Friday 19. Warm this eve; we do not need any fire. Rhoda and I went to the choir at Dr. Thompsons. Nat Carson came home with Rhoda. Nannie Kennedy took tea here. Mrs. Harris, Mrs. Ewing, and Mrs. Riddle called this eve.

Saturday 20. Pretty day; rained this morn. Miss Eva Miller and Sister went round shopping and over to Mrs. DeLano's this eve. Cousin May Jarnagins piano was sent here this eve from Dr. Jordans.

---

[1] A women's church group based on the widows mite from the Bible.

Sunday 21. Cold day. Cousin John Lea dined here.

Monday 22. Weather moderated today. Moved Cousin May Jarnagin's piano in Mother's room this morn. Bell Cowan came here to board this morn. Adelia and Mrs. Thompson here today.

Tuesday 23. Pretty day. Sister commenced packing up to go to Cincinnati (Ohio). Dr. Carson and Nat called this eve.

Wednesday 24. Rainy day. Sister has given out going with Mr. Carter to Cincinnati. Will go in April.

Epilogue

About nine months after the war was over, Myra Inman made her last entry in her diary, her "old friend," her journal. Drastic changes had taken place in the Inman family, in Cleveland, and in Myra's world in general. Family members began to discuss the possibility of moving to a hotel, but John G. Carter would not hear of it. In late 1865 eight Northerners asked Mrs. Inman to board them. In mid December, E. S. Delany became a boarder in their home.

Edwin Stanton Delany, their temporary boarder, became a permanent resident and strong supporter of his adopted community. Born in Hopedale, Ohio, on 23 March 1833, he came to Cleveland in 1865 and lived here until his death fifty years later in 1915. He was a lawyer and a realtor. In 1874 he founded *Delany's Register* which promoted land sales in and around Cleveland. He also supported the unsuccessful effort to recharter the city of Cleveland in 1882. Delany was a member of the local drama group, the library association, and the local centennial committee for the Declaration of Independence.

Family members became concerned about Mrs. Inman's ability to support the family with the unpredictable income of a boarding house. The family faced a new fact of life. They had to do all of their work since they no longer had slaves. The full impact of the Emancipation Proclamation and the victorious presence of Federal troops brought a new way of life to Cleveland and the South. Problems were compounded; life was much more complex.

In Early October 1865 the Inman family hoped to purchase a house in Ringgold, Georgia. This idea was abandoned because the house was too expensive. Instead, they decided to buy the home of R.J. Farroe Callaway on Lea (now Broad) Street. Preparations were made to move in early November. On 8 November, the family spent their last night in the kitchen of their home of about a dozen years, which had been the location of many happy memories as well as sad. There had been some talk of leaving Tennessee and moving to Texas like many had done after the war but the purchase of their new house brought an end to that. Darthula, Mr. Carter, and their children lived with Mrs. Inman until the war was over. In 1867, they moved to a farm on the Hiwassee River at Charleston, Tennessee. He continued to help Mrs. Inman as he had always done.

Even though the war was over, the problems and death it brought were not. Myra, her family, friends, and the community had to go on. The heartache of burying friends, young and old, and the North and South fighting each other, greatly changed twenty-year-old Myra from the thirteen year old who began her diary.

The Inman family suffered another great loss in 1874 with the death of Darthula after giving birth. Two years later Mr. Carter and Myra were married. They moved to Chattanooga, Tennessee, and became the parents of three children: August Jarnagin Carter, born 11 August 1878; Peyton Lea Carter, born 8 January 1884; and Darthula Inman Carter, born 1 May 1887. Their last child was born when Myra was forty-two and John G. Carter was sixty-four. Myra preceded him in death on 7 December 1914. John G. Carter survived her until his death on 14 February 1915.

Myra Inman Carter and John Goodly Carter are buried in the Carter family plot at Fort Hill Cemetery. Ironically, the cemetery is located on the same hill that Federal troops camped on during the Civil War.

Appendix 1

Uncle Ned and Aunt Pheobe

Myra Inman's diary, which she kept from January 1, 1859 until January 24, 1866, contained first hand accounts of Uncle Ned and Aunt Phoebe including their deaths and how these deaths affected her. These two slaves were the Inman family's most reliable slaves. The couple performed their work well and were trusted more than the other slaves. They helped the Inmans hide food and valuables before the Yankees came to town to raid and steal. They were considered members of the family, with Phoebe serving as a mother figure and Ned as the jack-of-all trades. Ned was also a valuable member of the community and a key participant in the routine of daily life in the small town of Cleveland. Aunt Phoebe weighed about 169 pounds while Uncle Ned, a smaller person of medium height weighed 121 pounds. Conspicuous by his dress and manners, he was an institution in the community. Ned and Phoebe were members of the Southern Methodist Church. They sat in the gallery, which was customary. Ned's attire for Sunday church was a black scissor tail coat and a high silk hat brushed so shiny you could see yourself in it. Always aware of their duties, they warmed Sunday dinner for the Inman family when they got home after church. The food had been cooked on Saturday.

On a rainy Tuesday, 22 February 1864, Myra penned these words: "This eve, just after the last rays of our bright luminary gilded the western horizon, our old faithful servant, Aunt Phoebe, was suddenly called away from this wicked and tumultuous earth to inherit the blessings that are prepared for those who live and serve our Master. She went to milking in her usual health. I went up to the house and was sitting by the fire. I told her I was hungry. She made a fire and split up some pieces of bread and then stooped down and complained of swimming in her head. I looked at her and then resumed to reading *Rob-Roy*. She then arose and sat on a chair. She then said: 'Miss Mrya, do get me something.' I ran for Mother and I got the camphor. When I reached her, her hands were drawn, her features convulsed, and death was depicted in her distorted countenance. She then closed her eyes and after drawing a few long sighs as if bidding us a 'Long Farewell,' her soul had penioned its flight into vast eternity."

"Uncle Ned was in the woods at the time, came in, in a few minutes after she was dead. He takes her death very hard...I can never forget this night. Poor Aunt Phoebe, words cannot express the grief her death has caused us....From the time she was taken until she died, it did not exceed three minutes."

UNCLE NED

On a rainy Tuesday night, 12 December 1865, Myra recorded the death of Uncle Ned. She wrote these words: "A sad and gloomy eve to all of us. This afternoon at two o'clock another one of our old and faithful family servants, Uncle Ned, bid adieu to this terrestrial sphere and joined our friends in another world. When I reflect on past scenes and my mind reverts to memories of '*auld lang syne*' I feel sad, sad. Never, no never, will we see Uncle Ned's and Aunt Phoebe's cheerful faces again, spreading ease, comfort and happiness wherever they go. It seems as though two grand-parents had left us since they have been called away, for a parent would not have cared more for our comfort and pleasure than they did for 'Miss Annie and her children,' as they called us. It is growing late, and fain would I dwell on their virtues if I had the power to do them any good, but alas, the only duty left us is to be ready to join them in the spirit world when our hour comes, where there is no distinction in color or rank."

From 1 May 1854 until 1863 the *Cleveland Banner* was the main source for the history of the county seat of Bradley County. In addition to the many services which the paper provided, it furnished news for the joyous and the sad occasions of life. Marriage notices were included in a brief format. The names of the happy couple were featured in capital letters, while the names of other individuals were less prominently displayed—minister, place where married, and the date of the wedding.

Some death notices were also carried as news items, when they were interesting or unusual. The average death notice listed the name of the deceased, death date, cause of death, and age. One of the most generous obituary accounts was the demise of Uncle Ned in December 1865. His was a unique notice for that day and time, and one that would likely not be replicated. A look at Ned's life might give a reason for his special obitituary.

Ned was born a slave in South Carolina. Eventually, Mrs. Ann Inman acquired him from a family member. He moved with the family to Cleveland, Bradley County, Tennessee. His days as a slave ended in 1865. After the War Between the States was concluded, he was a free man. In addition he was one of the most honored and respected citizens of the community.

In 1852, Rosine Parmentier, a New Yorker, was en route to the Dutch Settlement in Polk County. She and her companion, Edward, stayed in the Railroad Inn in Cleveland, which was owned by the Inman family. She spent several days in town and wrote in her diary about her travels by the hack line to the utopian community in Polk County. The New Yorker was impressed with the community of Cleveland and some of its citizens. The one person in Cleveland, whom Miss Parmentier recorded in her journal, was none other than Uncle Ned. She penned these words: "The most polite Negro whom I have seen during our travels certainly is Ned, a servant belonging to Mrs. James W. Inman, the lady who kept the hotel. He always has hat in hand, bowing and smiling, ever ready to oblige."

"During the night rain fell in torrents. When old Ned came in to awaken us, Edward said, 'Well, Uncle Ned, what shall we do for a conveyance for the ladies?' Ned said: 'I was jus' thinkin' dat myself, sah, and I'll go hunt up one right away, sah.'" The travelers left for Dalton at 7 P.M., apparently in a proper conveyance.

Ben H. McClary, editor of Miss Parmentier's papers, indicated that "Ned was more than a servant to Mrs. Inman. He was a town ornament, alarm clock, welcome committee of one, and village jester." Ned was proud of these titles.

In connection with his work at the hotel, Ned met two trains daily, which chugged over the East Tennessee and Georgia Railroad, hoping to get customers for his mistress. This explains how Miss Parmentier met Ned for the first time.

A journalist who signed his article "H. B. Y." gave an account of the Cleveland Fair in 1858, at which Uncle Ned was to perform. He reported: "Old Uncle Ned was to perform in the ring on horseback—when a general rush was made by the men for the seats. But to their surprise, the heroic marshals succeeded in forcing many of them to give their seats to the ladies."

The journalist continued; "The Cleveland Brass Band was in attendance and gave Uncle Ned a blast from their bugles and the performance began. Uncle Ned, being dressed in a rather monkey costume, mounted a little gray horse, with cowhide in hand, galloped 'round bowing, whipping, cutting and slashing, and kicking up a terrible dust for some time. The managers then appointed a steward to pass 'round the hat to lift a collection which was promptly done."

After another fair, the correspondent for the *Athens Post* reported: "As some of you readers may not be acquainted with Uncle Ned, it may be necessary to give a sketch of his life. Uncle Ned, a gentleman of fast color, [very black] about 55 or 60 years of age; has resided in Cleveland since its infancy, and occupied almost all-prominent positions during said time. He now acts as city clock, or rather beats the reveille. Every morning when Ned blows his trumpet for an hour you can see people busily engaged in obeying the call. The fact is he is a great man, and is treated as such by the citizens generally."

Sam P. Ivins, editor of the *Athens Post* for 50 years, added his observations about Ned. He wrote: "We have known Uncle Ned for 10 years and we are free to say that we have always found him the same attentive, clever and urbane gentleman and richly meriting the respect and considerations he invariably received from his friends and acquaintances."

Robert McNelley (pronounced McAnelley), editor of the *Cleveland Banner*, was a Southerner of the old school and a strong supporter of the Confederacy after 1861. He was generally suspicious of the integrity and industry of blacks but displayed a different attitude toward Uncle Ned. When he learned of Uncle Ned's death, McNelley composed a lengthy obituary, which follows in its entirety.

"GONE.—Uncle Ned is no more.—He departed this life at the residence of Dr. Sam'l H. Jordan, on Tuesday evening last, after a very short illness, aged about 66 years. In making the announcement we must be allowed to say of the deceased, although he was a man of color, that few men have gone to the grave with a better record than 'Uncle Ned.' He was strictly honest and upright in all his transactions in this world, and had the confidence and respect of all who knew him. By his urbanity and general deportment he had won a reputation truly enviable. Although he is dead and gone he has left behind him the example worthy of emulation. 'Uncle Ned' was known by the little folks, middle aged and old, all of who venerated and respected him. When he left this world he left behind him no enemies to traduce his good name—all were his friends. During his short illness he received every attention from both white and black, to alleviate and solace his suffering, but medical skill and the nursing of kind friends could not stay the hand of death, and the spirit of the venerable old Negro was summoned to appear before the judgment bar.—His remains were followed to their last resting place by many friends, who consigned them to mother earth in a decent and praiseworthy manner. 'Uncle Ned' is gone, and the seasons will come and go, ere our community has the pleasure of meeting one possessed of all the virtues and ennobling traits of character which adorned his life. Peace to his ashes.'

John G. Carter, Myra's husband, as an octogenarian, was featured in a long article in the *Cleveland Journal and Banner* in 1912. The article included his remarks about Uncle Ned. Mr. Carter said: "Uncle Ned, one of the Inman slaves, was indispensable in the operation of the hotel. He was also one of the most universally respected colored men of his day. His sunny disposition and genuine courtesy made him a great favorite with all who frequented the hostelry." Carter recounted the following anecdote as an example of Ned's politeness: Henry Tibbs, a former Cleveland citizen, once met Uncle Ned when the latter was carrying a bucket of slop on his head. Mr. Tibbs knew the Negro would be unable to make a curtsey, so he thought he would embarrass him. He [Mr. Tibbs] bowed profusely to Uncle Ned thinking it would pain him that he could not bow in return. Imagine his surprise, when the Negro stopped, set the bucket on the ground, and made a sweeping bow to Mr. Tibbs." Mr. Carter continued his thoughts about Ned in the article. "Uncle Ned was very thrifty and at the time of his death had between $700 and $800 in tips saved up. He and his wife [Phoebe] now sleep at the city cemetery [Fort Hill], with their resting places marked by tombstones, paid for by the money saved by Uncle Ned while at the hotel."

Ned was buried in the family plot where Phoebe, who preceded him in 1864, is by his side. Her stone read: "Phoebe Inman—wife of Uncle Ned Inman, February 22, 1864, age 55 years." Ned's stone read: "Uncle Ned Inman, December 12, 1865, 65 years." Members of the Inman family have maintained the burial plot for the couple. Originally, the graves had a decorative chain. After the tombstones were badly eroded, the family replaced them with marble markers, which contain the names ands dates of the faithful couple. Her marker reads: "Aunt Phoebe Inman, at rest, February 22, 1864." His stone reads: "Uncle Ned Inman, at rest, December 12, 1865."

After the war was over Ned was employed by Dr. Samuel L. Jordan. The Inmans were not financially able to provide for or afford any servants of their own. On Sunday, 10 December 1865, Myra and Cleo Watkins of Ooltewah, went by Dr. Jordan's house to visit Uncle Ned. They found him very sick and not expected to live. On Tuesday afternoon, 12 December 1865, Uncle Ned died about two o'clock at the age of about 66. On Wednesday afternoon, Myra, with her sisters Mary Elizabeth and Rhoda, returned to Dr. Jordan's to see Uncle Ned and pay their respects. He was buried at 10:00 A.M. on Thursday, 14 December 1865 at Fort Hill Cemetery along side Aunt Phoebe. Since it was a very cold and windy day, Mr. John G. Carter and a host of friends went to the burial to pay the Carter and Inman families' respect.

Lea-Jarnagin-Inman-Carter Genealogy

LEA FAMILY
(Maternal Line)

JAMES LEA, Myra's great-great-grandfather, b. 1718, at Lea Hall in Cheshire, England, came to America in (1740?). He settled in Virginia before moving to Orange County, North Carolina, later named Caswell County. James Lea married Ann Tolbert and they were the parents of several children. James Lea died on 2 June 1788. One of their sons, MAJOR LEA, SR., born 26 November 1759, was Myra's great-grandfather. He married Elizabeth Herndon. They were the parents of several children. One of their sons:

MAJOR LEA, JR., Myra's grandfather, was b. 26 February 1775, in Orange County, North Carolina, d. 8 August 1821. He married RHODA JARNAGIN, Myra'a grandmother, on 5 November 1801. RHODA LEA, as she was called in the census, was born 26 January 1778, died 21 December 1852. In her latter years she lived with her daughter, Anna (Ann) Inman, Myra's mother, and is buried in Fort Hill Cemetery in Cleveland, Tennessee. Rhoda and Major Lea, Jr. were the parents of nine children, one of whom was Myra's mother. The others were Myra's aunts and uncles:

I. CASWELL LEA, b. 21 August 1802, d. 10 August 1874; m. Julia Carter; m. ELIZABETH BELL JOHNSON, b. 8 April 1813, d. 17 July 1876. This marriage took place on 23 September 1839. Caswell and Elizabeth are buried in Fort Hill Cemetery, Cleveland, Tennessee, near his sister, Anna Jarnagin Lea Inman. Myra and her family members made frequent trips to Uncle Caswell's farm and he and his family were often in their home. The nine children of these marriages were Myra's cousins:
By Julia Carter Lea:
1. JANE ANN LEA, m. William Davis; one child: Lea Davis
2. MARTHA LEA, m. William Riggs
3. By Elizabeth Bell Johnson Lea:
4. JOHN HOUSTON LEA, m. Lavena Seavy, four children, oldest: Laura
5. JOSEPH JOHNSON LEA, drowned in Tennessee River, 1875
6. JAMES PRYOR LEA, m. Mollie Earnest; nine children
7. GEORGE JOHNSON LEA, b. 11 November 1846, d. 30 July 1928; m. Mattie Briscoe

8. ELIZABETH BELL JOHNSON LEA (Bettie Bell), m. Thomas Boyd (4 children); m. William Neal Elrod
9. Caswell M. Lea, died in infancy; b. 3 February 1860, d. 14 June 1860
10. ELIZABETH LEA

II. ALFRED LEA, b. 15 February 1804, d. August 1874; m. Edith Amanda (possibly Miranda) Carter, 25 March 1834; their daughter: Esther Ann Lea, m. Mr.__ Lea; their children: Frances, Stephen; her second marriage, Mr.__ Burnett; their children: Joseph Houston, Willaim Crockett, Juliet, Darthula Tennessee, Elizabeth, Theresa, and Mary Virginia.

III. HERNDON HOUSTON LEA, b. 25 November 1805, d. 3 October 1853; m. Charity Allison (a widow) 1 December 1840; lived in Huntsville, Alabama; no children. Mary Elizabeth Inman (Myra's little sister) stayed with them for a time after the death of James Wilson Inman.

IV. PLEASANT JOHN GRAVES LEA, frequently called (P. J. G. Lea.), b. 6 November 1807; a doctor and merchant in Cleveland, Tennessee; m. Lucinda Callaway on 3 April 1838; m. FANNIE M. CLARK on 22 October 1859. Pleasant was killed on 12 September 1862 in Missouri by guerillas during the Civil War. He was a private citizen. Pleasant was the father of ten children, Myra's cousins:
By Lucinda Callaway
1. ALFRED LEA
2. THOMAS CALLAWAY LEA, two children by first wife: John H. (2 children); Frank (8 children); Thomas m. Edna Sevel (widow)
3. JOSEPH LEA
4. FRANK LEA
5. ELVIRA CALLAWAY LEA, m. Mr.__ Calfee (2 boys); m. Mr. Pierce
6. CAROLINE REBECCA LEA (Carrie), m. Robert T. Hayes (6 children)
7. ANNIE LEA, m. James L. Kirby, 17 September 1880, one child
8. MARY LEA
9. JOHN GRAVES LEA, m. Lottie Beard (5 children); m. Marie Lea (sister of Myra's cousin Luke Lea)
10.
By Fannie M. Clark
1. WATSON CLARK LEA

V. ANNA JARNAGIN LEA, (Ann), Myra's mother; b. 22 December 1809; d. 26 February 1882; (*see* JARNAGIN FAMILY); m. JAMES WILSON INMAN,

Myra's father, 1 April 1833; b. 1 March 1808, d. 25 March 1851;buried in Fort Hill Cemetery, Cleveland, Tennessee; (*see* INMAN FAMILY for their children.)

VI. WILLIAM PINCKNEY LEA, b. 17 May 1812, d. 2 (1?) April 1882 did not marry

VII. PRESTON JARNAGIN LEA, b. 24 (20?) November 1814, d. 1890; m. Mary H. Peck, March 25, 1834; their children and Myra's cousins: Sarah Adeline, m. William Shadrach Inman; Catherine, m. Mr.__, (twin girls); Alexander?, m.__ Campbell; Benjamin; Charity, m. Dr.__ Lincoln (two boys); Lucinda, m. Mr.__Ellis (5 children); Preston; William

VIII. ELIZABETH ADELINE LEA, b. 12 October 1817, d. 21 December 1895; did not marry, lived with her sister Anna Jarnagin Lea Inman; Myra called her "Aunt Eliza" as well as Aunt Elizabeth Adeline; buried in Fort Hill Cemetery, Cleveland, Tennessee

PRYOR NEWTON LEA, b.14 March 1820; m. Elizabeth Houston, his cousin, on 25
September 1847; their children and   Myra's cousins: May Wilson; Levi? m. Miss__ (3 children); Laura, m. Mr.__ Peel; Emma, m. Mr.__ (1 child); Preston, m. Miss__, their child: Luke

JARNAGIN FAMILY
(Maternal Line)

CHARLES WITT, b. about 1730; Myra's great-great grandfather, and his wife, Lavinia, lived in Halifax County, Virginia. Their daughter MARY WITT, b. 4 April 1753; married THOMAS JARNAGIN, b. 25 July 1746, d. 26 February 1802, Myra's great-grandfather. They were married in 1767 when Mary was fourteen. Their children, Myra's great aunts and uncles, were:
NOAH JARNAGIN, b. 9 June 1768
LAVENIA JARNAGIN, b. 2 October 1770
CHESLEY JARNAGIN, b. 21 November 1772
CHAROTY JARNAGIN, b. 26 April 1775

ANNA JARNAGIN and RHODA JARNAGIN, twins, were b. 26 January 1778. RHODA JARNAGIN, mother of Anna (Ann) and grandmother of Myra, d. 21 December 1852. She married MAJOR LEA, JR., Myra's grandfather on 5 November 1801. (*see* LEA FAMILY for their children).

PLEASANT JARNAGIN, b. 9 March 1794

INMAN FAMILY
(Paternal Line)

The Inman family was of English and Irish decent. According to family tradition, three of Abednego's four sons: Shadrack, Meshack and ABEDNEGO INMAN II, lived in North Carolina. They left there because of their stepmother. Meshack was killed by Indians, but Shadrack and Abednego II settled in upper East Tennessee. Myra's family line developed from ABEDNEGO INMAN II.

ABEDNEGO INMAN II, b. 1 July 1752, d. 2 February 1831; Myra's great-grandfather, married Mary Richie (Ritchy?). Their oldest son, WILLIAM HARDIN INMAN, b. Sept. 28, 1779, Myra's grandfather, married Eleanor Wilson. William Hardin died 18 January 1817 when a tree fell on him. William and Eleanor were the parents of six children in addition to James Wilson Inman, Myra's father. These are the brothers and sisters of James Wilson and Myra's aunts and uncles. Myra mentions two cousins, SAM C. INMAN and SAM M. INMAN who, are possibly, the sons of Benjamin and Joseph.

MARY RICHIE INMAN, b. 1799
ELIZABETH H. INMAN, b. 1802
BENJAMIN R. INMAN, b. 1805
JAMES WILSON INMAN, b. 1 March 1808, d. 25 March 1851
HANNAH H. INMAN, b. 1810
JANE TAYLOR INMAN, b. 1813
JOSEPH H. INMAN, b. 1816

William and Eleanor's fourth child, JAMES WILSON INMAN, b. 1 March 1808, d. 25 March 1851, Myra's father, married ANNA JARNAGIN LEA, Myra's mother on 1 (26?) April 1833. JAMES and ANNA were the parents of eight children, only four (daughters) lived to maturity. One daughter and two sons died in infancy and one son died at the age of seven.

JAMES and ANNA'S children, Myra's brothers and sisters, were:

I. DARTHULA ADELINE INMAN (Sister), b. 17 February 1834, d. 29 March 1874; m. JOHN GOODLY CARTER, 13 March (3 January?) 1853. John Goodly Carter was b. 14 April 1823 and d. 14 February 1915. Darthula and John are buried in the Carter family plot in Fort Hill Cemetery along with other family members. Their six children:

1. ANNA ELIZABETH CARTER, "Annie," b. 29 April 1855, d. 22 March 1907; m. W. Frank Hutchinson

2. JAMES INMAN CARTER, "Jimmie," b. 11 January1858, d. 18 February 1947; m. Samuella Childress, 27 December 1881 (5 children)

3. JOHN BOWIE CARTER, "Johnnie," b. 1 December 1861, d. 31 October 1910; m. Elizabeth Weems

4. RHODA INMAN CARTER, b. 18 February 1864, d. 24 April 1875

5. MAY CARTER, (Mae), b. May 3, 1871, d. 16 August 1938; m. William Albert

6. HUGH LEA CARTER, b. 9 March 1874, d. 12 June 1874; Darthula died the same day Hugh Lea was born

II. Myra Adelaide Inman, (Sister Myra), b./d. Infancy, 29 July 1835

III. Caswell Lea Inman, (first Caswell), b./d. Infancy, d. 6 August1839

IV. Caswell Lea Inman, (second Caswell,) b./d. Infancy, d. 8 June 1842

V. RHODA ANN INMAN, b. 30 January 1843 (1842?) d. 5 November 1888; m. Capt. John Cabel Morgan whose first marriage was to Margaret Shadden, John Goodly Carter's niece. John Morgan and Rhoda Ann had four children; one of which is ADELIA INMAN MORGAN, b. 23 February 1873, d. 21 December 1895, who transcribed Myra's diary and added notes given by her by her aunt, Mary Elizabeth Inman, Myra's sister.

VI. **MYRA ADELAIDE INMAN**, (author of the diary), **b. March 13, 1845, d. 7 December 1914**; m. JOHN GOODLY CARTER, Oct. 25, 1876, two years after Darthula died; Myra is buried beside John and Darthula in the Carter family plot in Fort Hill Cemetery, Cleveland, Tennessee; Myra and John's three children:

1. AUGUST INMAN CARTER, b. 11 August 1878, d. 7 December 1949, m. Edna Blance Crossland; m. Marie Surguine, b. 3 November 1878, d. 1 November 1962

2. PEYTON LEA CARTER, b. 8 January1884; m. Elizabeth Rowell (3 children)

3. DARTHULA INMAN CARTER (Della) b. 1 May 1887, d. 1906; m. Oscar Q. McLain

VII. MARY ELIZABETH INMAN, (Mary E.) and sometimes (Lizzie), b.1 April 1845; d. 28 January 1936; m. Edwin R. Hayes (1 child)

VIII. HOUSTON LEA INMAN, b. 27 June 1850; d. 23 September 1857; lived a short seven years.

CARTER FAMILY

PASCHAL CARTER, b. 3 March 1792, d. 10 June 1878, and his wife ELIZABETH DERRETT CARTER, b. 7 July 1787, d. 21 November 1869, moved from Danville, Virginia to Dandridge, Tennessee before coming to Cleveland. Their trip lasted about thirty days. In her diary Myra usually referred to him as "Old Mr. Carter." Paschal and Elizabeth were both born in Pittsylvania County, Virginia, and were buried in Fort Hill Cemetery, Cleveland, Tennessee, next to the Carter family plot. Paschal and Elizabeth had at six children:

SERENA JANE CARTER, b. 7 February 1813, d. 18 March 1895; m._____ Shadden; their daughter, Margaret (Mag) Shadden, m. Capt. John C. Morgan who later m. Rhoda Ann Inman, Myra's sister. Myra, out of respect, called Serena Jane Carter Shadden "Aunt Rennie Shadden," since she was John Carter's sister.

PRESLEY CARTER, b. 9 February 1815, d. in Virginia (about 2 years old)

ONEY (ANNIE), b. 12 May 1817, d. 31 July 1881

FONTEROY A. CARTER, b. 15 December 1859; killed by Rebel soldiers 23 September 1863

JOHN GOODLY CARTER, b. 14 April 1823, d. 14 February 1915; m. Darthula Inman, 30 March 1851; after her death, he m. Myra Inman. Myra called him "Mr. Carter." Since he traveled as a salesman, he, Darthula, and three children, lived with Mrs. Ann Inman until after the war. They moved to his 470 acre farm on the Hiwassee River near Charleston, Tennessee. After Darthula's death, he married Myra.

PEYTON THOMAS CARTER, b. 27 August 1826; Peyton passed through Cleveland as a Confederate prisoner on 25 December 1864, and was never heard again.

Index

Atlanta; later, m. John Houston
Lea; moved to Texas, 1877;
baby, Anna Laura), 11, 16, 20,
57, 61, 64, 66, 94, 96, 99, 102,
228
Seavey, Willard "Will" (brother of
Lavena), Lieutenant, CSA, died
at Bull Run, 108
secession, 100
secessionists, 107
settlers (sold supplies to the
military), boarders, 262
7th Alabama Rifles, Harrington,
Florida, *see* Isbell, Captain
Dennis; Jones, Henry L
17th Mississippi Regiment, 143
Sevier, Mary, 11, 24, 57, 72, 74, 76,
82, 88, 152, 172, 185
Seward, William H. (1801-1872),
xxvi; Lincoln's Secretary of
State, 121; stabbed, 306; *see
also* Lincoln, Abraham,
President
Sexton, Mrs. ___, 174, 175
Shadden, Mr. ___, 182
Shadden, Mr. Billy (cousin of
Margaret), 70;
Shadden, Mrs. Billy, 770
Shadden, George, came from
Dandridge, 165, 169, 175, 179
Shadden, Margaret "Mag"
(daughter of Serena Jane; m.
Joseph Harle after the war), 7,
16, 20, 30, 34, 45, 51, 54, 58, 60,
64, 69, 70, 74, 88, 91, 97, 136,
146 155, 156, 170, 183
Shadden, Mrs. Serena Jane "Aunt
Rennie", (m. John Cabel
Morgan, who later m. Rhoda
Ann Inman) 3, 7, 10, 15, 19, 25,
41, 51, 55, 64, 67, 132, 139, 144,
150, 156, 163

Shadden, Steel, 179
Sharp, John, 49, 115
Sharpe, Mr. Alex, 40, 79, 90
Shenandoah Valley, 107
Sherman, Major General William T.
(1820-1921), USA, 206; camped
around Inman home, 206;
encamped in Cleveland, 248;
thought to be falling back,
Atlanta, 291; fighting forty days,
271; marching on General
Johnston troops, 262; officers
came in, 248
Shields, Betsy (cousin), 284, 317
Shields, Mr. C. J. (merchant), 27,
32, 50; *see also* Cleveland Map
Shields, Mrs. C. J., 9, 11, 13, 53
Shields, Mr. Caswell "Cass,"
Company A, 2nd (Ashby's)
Cavalry, CSA; 10, 65; banished
to the North, 284; returned
from the North, 285; spent the
night with Inmans, 171, 174;
took tea, 174
Shields, Eliza, 9, 14, 38
Shields, Hester "Hettie," 42
Shields, Mrs. Joseph, had baby boy,
27; son died, 44
Shields, Martha, (later, m. a
Howell), 64
Shields, Sallie, 5, 16, 18, 21, 30, 57,
79, 87, 90, 92, 97, 98, 102, 275,
335; Myra's close friend, 82
Shields, William (cousin), 128, 251;
his son, 250
Shugart, Levi O., died, 31 October
1860, 73
Shugart, Mary Jane, 108, 118, 213
Siler, Bettie Jarrett, funeral, 92
Simmons, Mr.___ (merchant), 5, 7,
26